樋 口 大 輔

At long last, this is the year of the World
Cup.
When I started the series, my first editor
and I half-jokingly said to each other how
incredible it would be if we could keep it
going until the next World Cup. But who'd
have thought the day would actually come?
This is all thanks to your support.
Even though the series has been around
almost four years now, the manga is still far
from satisfactory. But please continue to
cheer me on. ♥
With a renewed frame of mind, I'll strive to
do my best... sort of.

- Daisuke Higuchi

Daisuke Higuchi's manga career began in 1992 when the
artist was honored with third prize in the 43rd Osamu
Tezuka Award. In that same year, Higuchi debuted as
creator of a romantic action story titled **Itaru**. In 1998,
Weekly Shonen Jump began serializing **Whistle!**
Higuchi's realistic soccer manga became an instant hit
with readers and eventually inspired an anime series,
debuting on Japanese TV in May of 2002.

WHISTLE!
VOL. 20: GO ON TOGETHER

The SHONEN JUMP Manga Edition

STORY AND ART BY
DAISUKE HIGUCHI

English Adaptation/Heidi Alayne
Translation/Naomi Kokubo
Touch-up Art & Lettering/Jim Keefe
Design/Matt Hinrichs
Editor/Jonathan Tarbox

Editor in Chief, Books/Alvin Lu
Editor in Chief, Magazines/Marc Weidenbaum
VP of Publishing Licensing/Rika Inouye
VP of Sales/Gonzalo Ferreyra
Sr. VP of Marketing/Liza Coppola
Publisher/Hyoe Narita

Printed in the U.S.A.

Published by VIZ Media, LLC
P.O. Box 77010
San Francisco, CA 94107

RLD'S
AR MANGA

jump.com

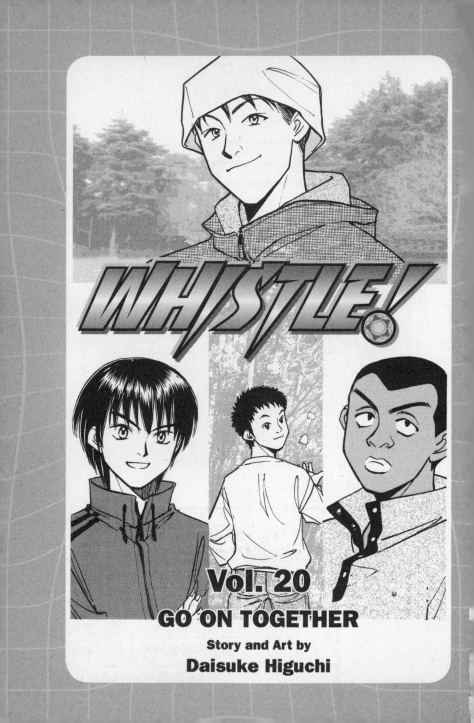

SHŌ KAZAMATSURI

● **JOSUI JUNIOR HIGH SOCCER TEAM FORWARD**

AKIRA SAIONJI

TSUBASA SHIINA

TATSUYA MIZUNO

● **JOSUI JUNIOR HIGH SOCCER TEAM MIDFIELDER**

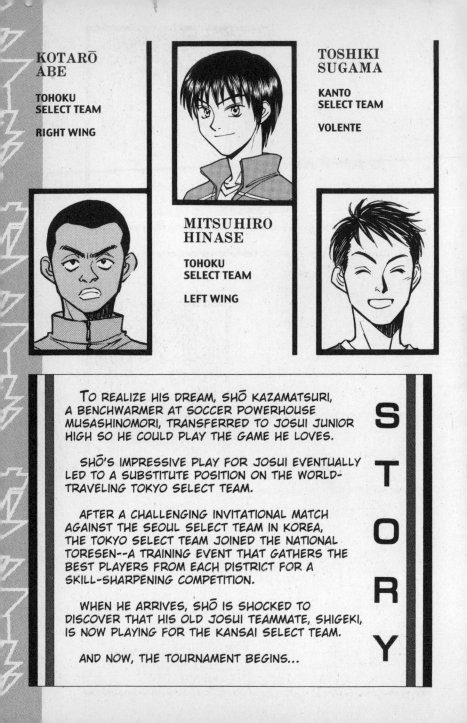

KOTARŌ ABE

TOHOKU SELECT TEAM

RIGHT WING

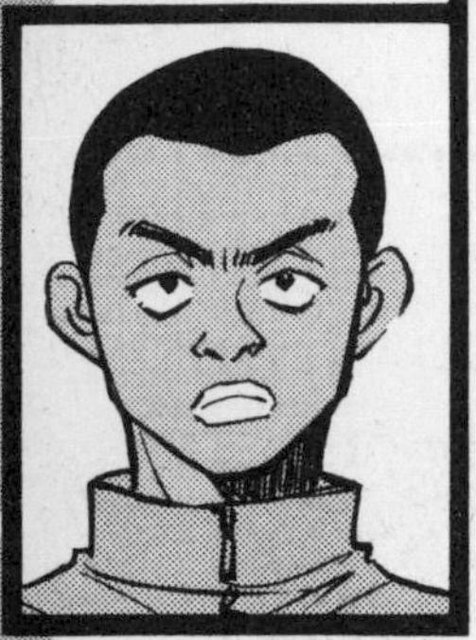

TOSHIKI SUGAMA

KANTO SELECT TEAM

VOLENTE

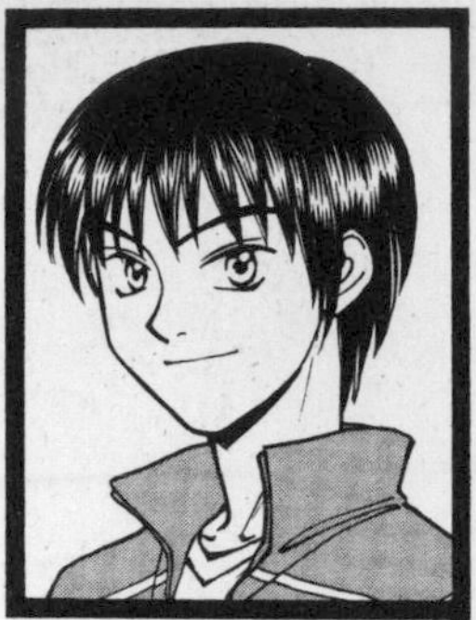

MITSUHIRO HINASE

TOHOKU SELECT TEAM

LEFT WING

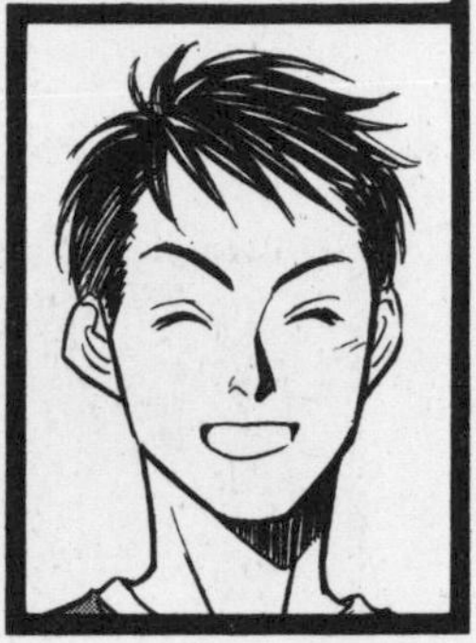

STORY

TO REALIZE HIS DREAM, SHŌ KAZAMATSURI, A BENCHWARMER AT SOCCER POWERHOUSE MUSASHINOMORI, TRANSFERRED TO JOSUI JUNIOR HIGH SO HE COULD PLAY THE GAME HE LOVES.

SHŌ'S IMPRESSIVE PLAY FOR JOSUI EVENTUALLY LED TO A SUBSTITUTE POSITION ON THE WORLD-TRAVELING TOKYO SELECT TEAM.

AFTER A CHALLENGING INVITATIONAL MATCH AGAINST THE SEOUL SELECT TEAM IN KOREA, THE TOKYO SELECT TEAM JOINED THE NATIONAL TORESEN--A TRAINING EVENT THAT GATHERS THE BEST PLAYERS FROM EACH DISTRICT FOR A SKILL-SHARPENING COMPETITION.

WHEN HE ARRIVES, SHŌ IS SHOCKED TO DISCOVER THAT HIS OLD JOSUI TEAMMATE, SHIGEKI, IS NOW PLAYING FOR THE KANSAI SELECT TEAM.

AND NOW, THE TOURNAMENT BEGINS...

WHISTLE!

**Vol. 20
GO ON
TOGETHER**

STAGE.173 King-Size Rival

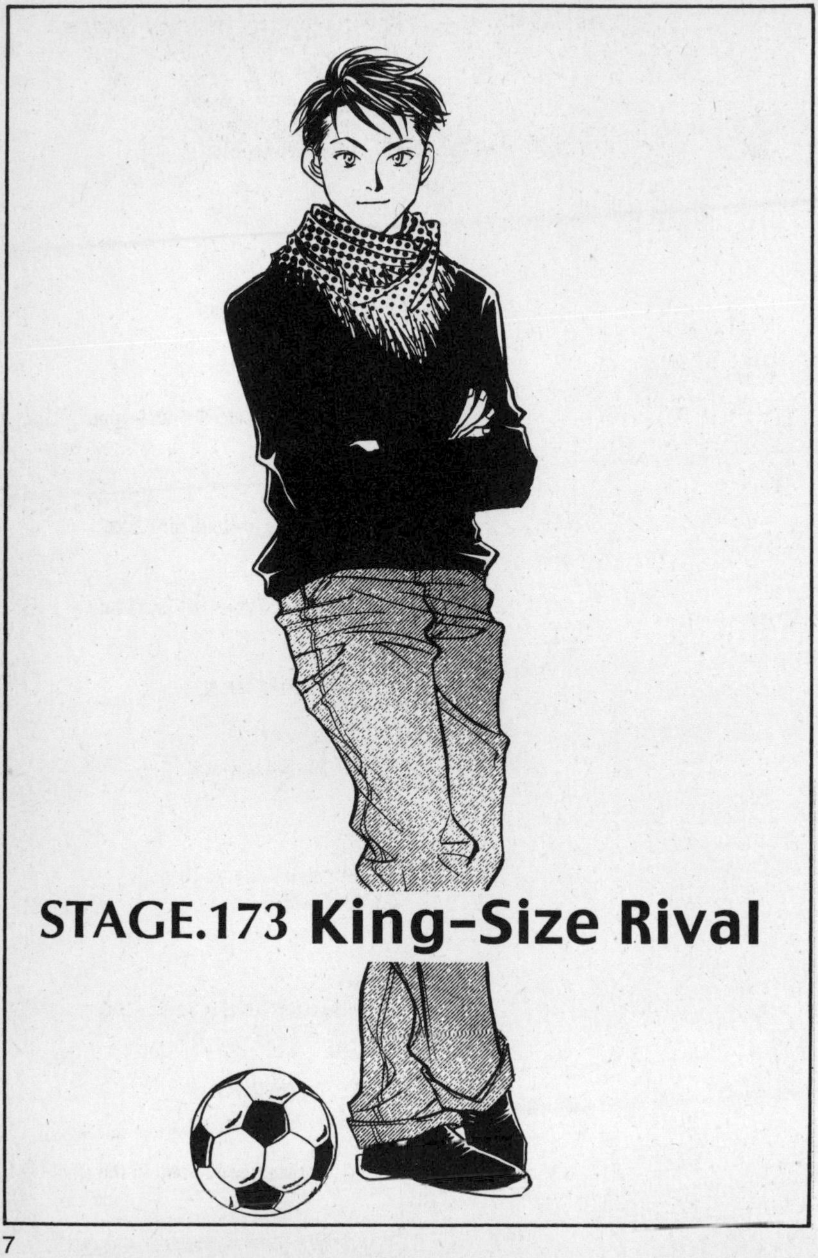

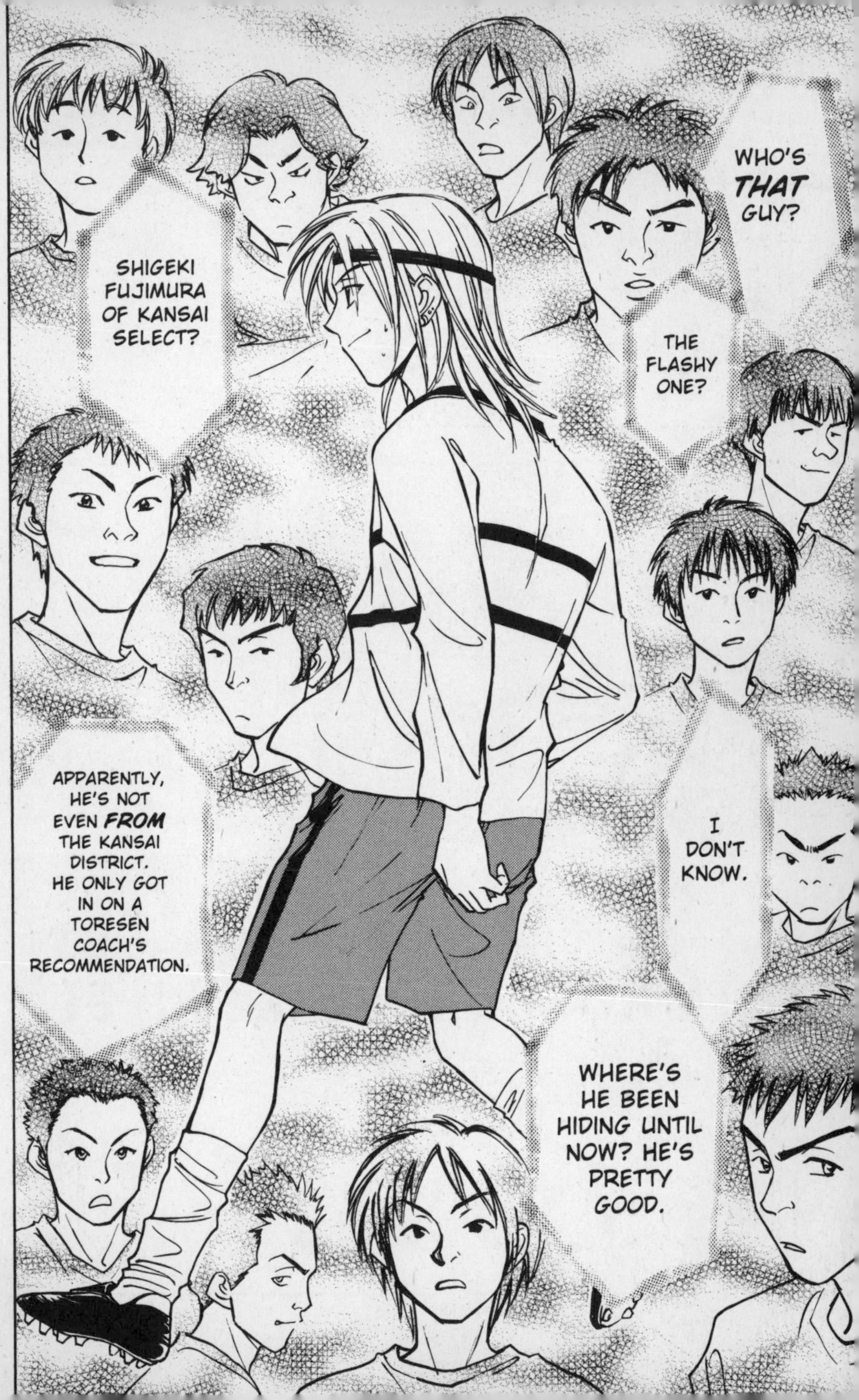
WHO'S *THAT* GUY?
SHIGEKI FUJIMURA OF KANSAI SELECT?
THE FLASHY ONE?
I DON'T KNOW.
APPARENTLY, HE'S NOT EVEN *FROM* THE KANSAI DISTRICT. HE ONLY GOT IN ON A TORESEN COACH'S RECOMMENDATION.
WHERE'S HE BEEN HIDING UNTIL NOW? HE'S PRETTY GOOD.

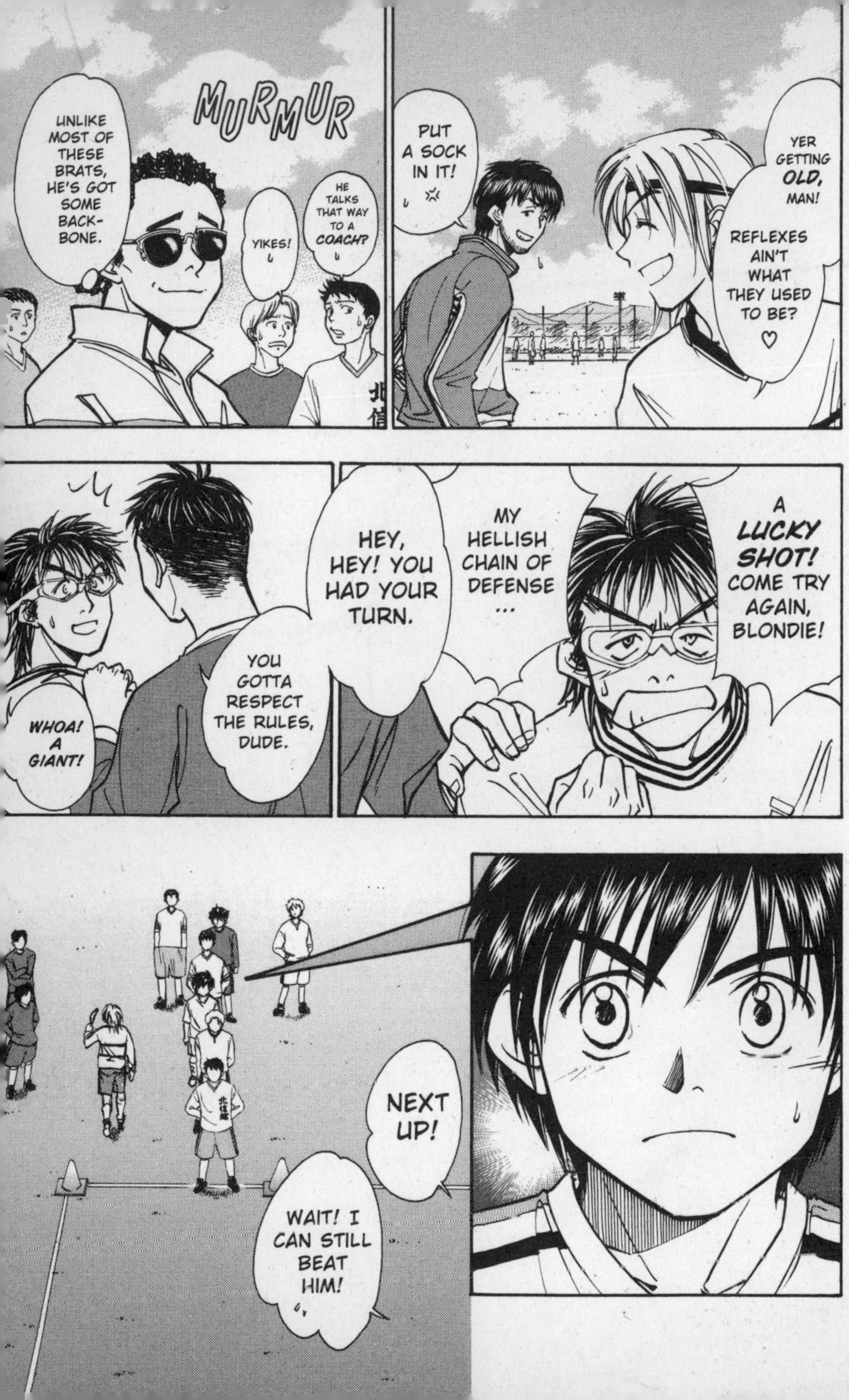
YER GETTING OLD, MAN!
REFLEXES AIN'T WHAT THEY USED TO BE? ♡
PUT A SOCK IN IT!
MURMUR
UNLIKE MOST OF THESE BRATS, HE'S GOT SOME BACK-BONE.
HE TALKS THAT WAY TO A COACH?
YIKES!
A LUCKY SHOT! COME TRY AGAIN, BLONDIE!
MY HELLISH CHAIN OF DEFENSE ...
HEY, HEY! YOU HAD YOUR TURN.
YOU GOTTA RESPECT THE RULES, DUDE.
WHOA! A GIANT!
NEXT UP!
WAIT! I CAN STILL BEAT HIM!

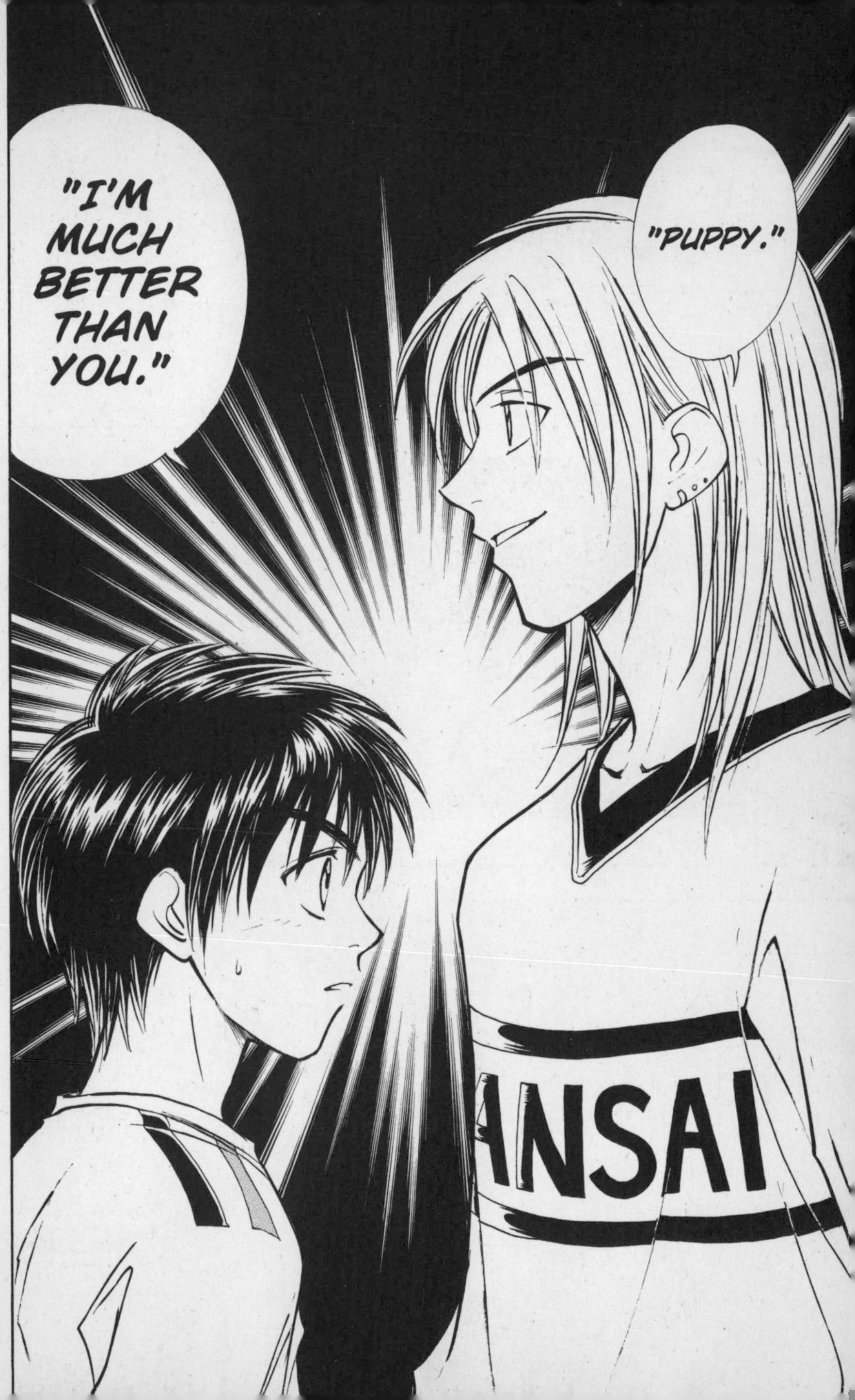
"PUPPY."
"I'M MUCH BETTER THAN YOU."
ANSAI

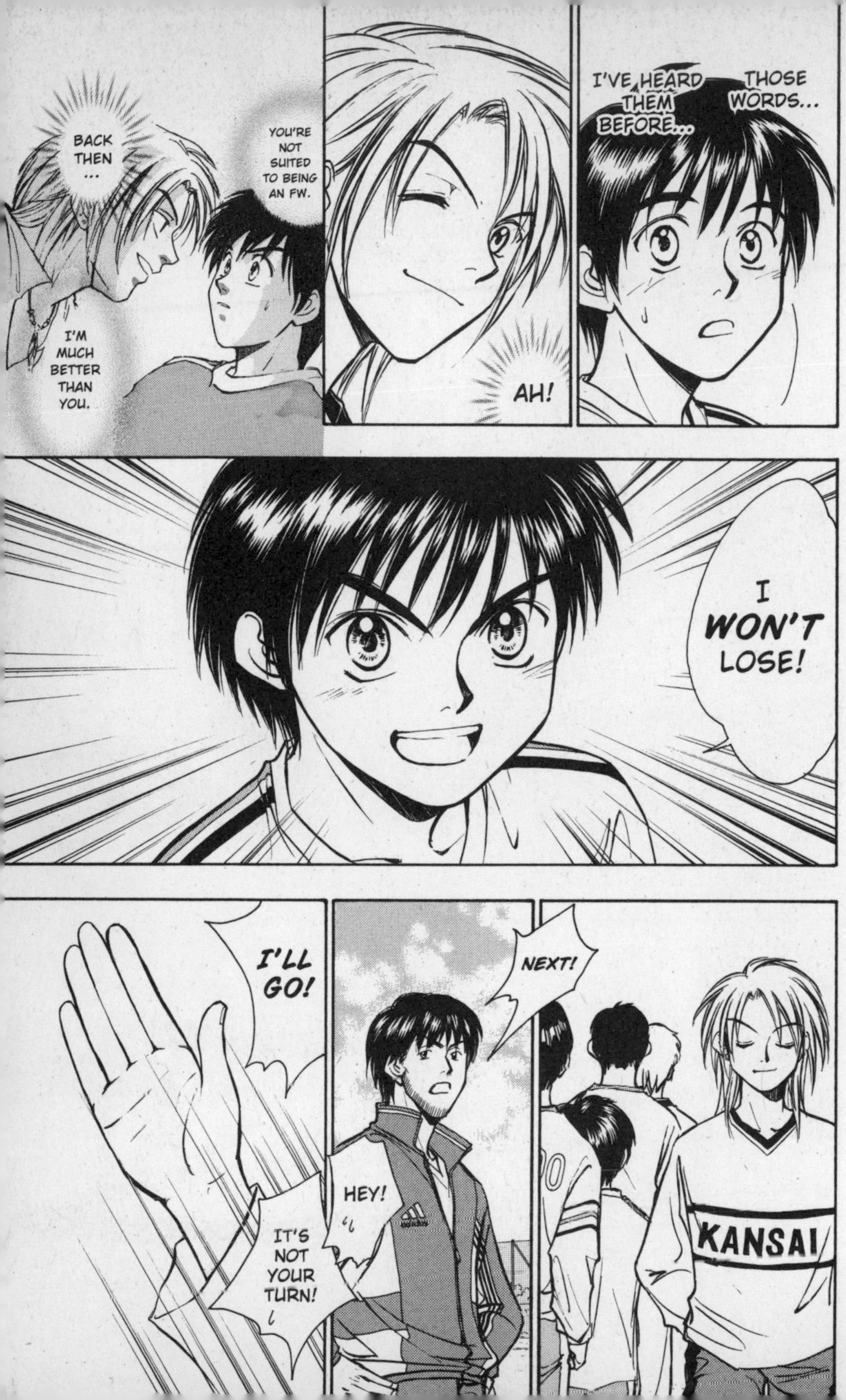
THOSE WORDS...
I'VE HEARD THEM BEFORE...
AH!
BACK THEN ...
YOU'RE NOT SUITED TO BEING AN FW.
I'M MUCH BETTER THAN YOU.
I WON'T LOSE!
NEXT!
KANSAI
I'LL GO!
HEY!
IT'S NOT YOUR TURN!

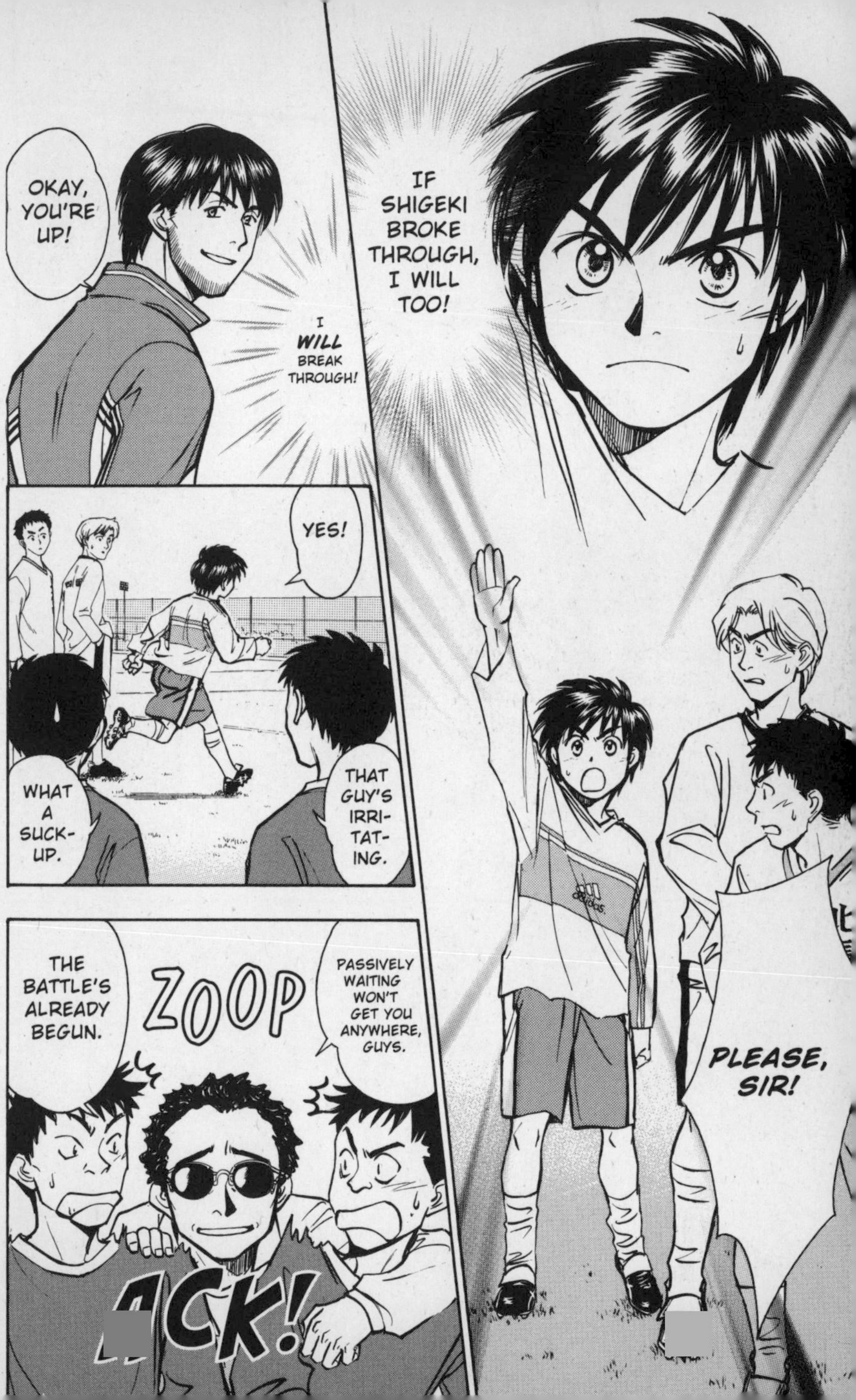
IF SHIGEKI BROKE THROUGH, I WILL TOO!
PLEASE, SIR!
OKAY, YOU'RE UP!
I ***WILL*** BREAK THROUGH!
YES!
THAT GUY'S IRRI-TAT-ING.
WHAT A SUCK-UP.
PASSIVELY WAITING WON'T GET YOU ANYWHERE, GUYS.
ZOOP
THE BATTLE'S ALREADY BEGUN.
ACK!

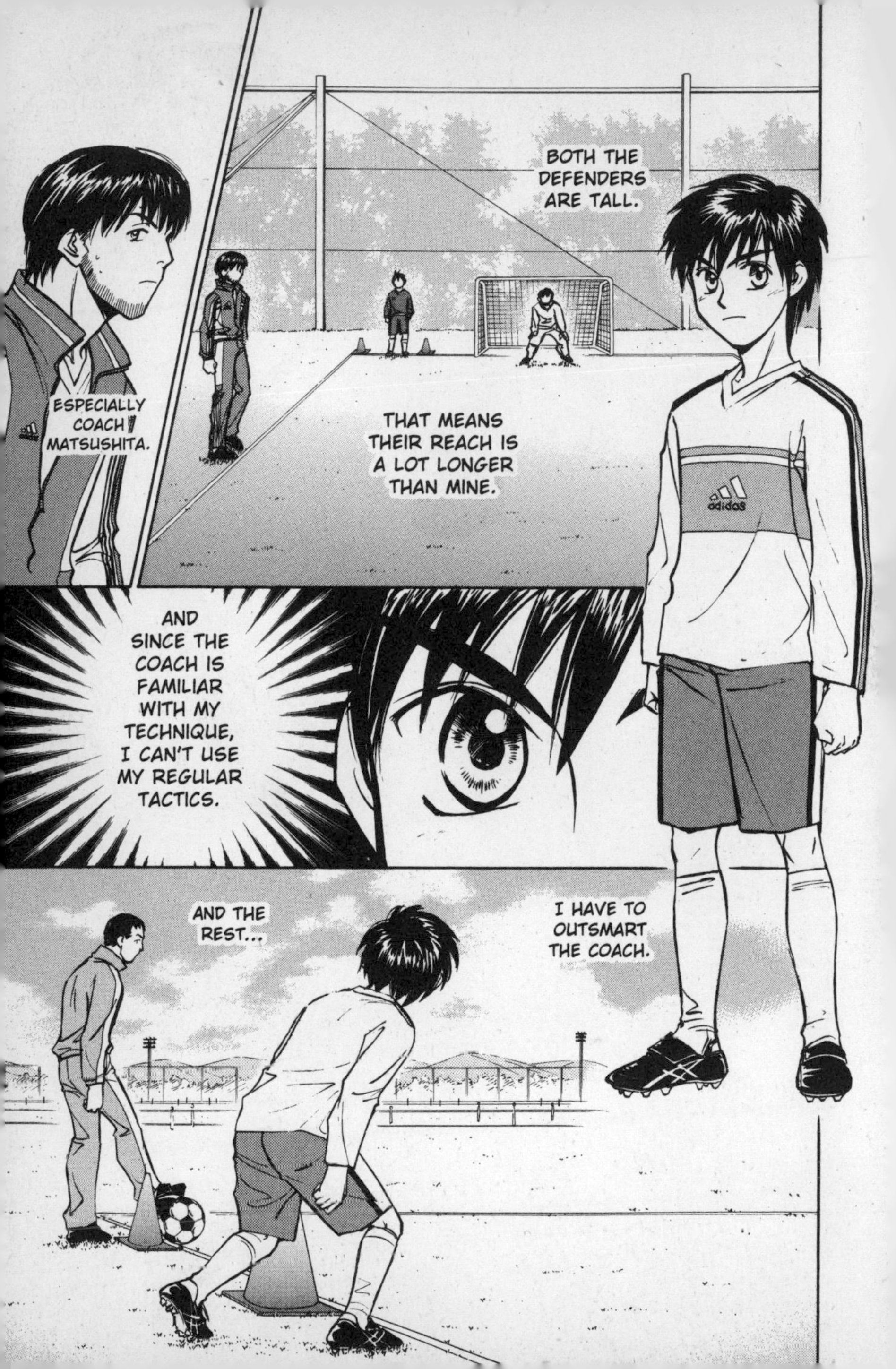
BOTH THE DEFENDERS ARE TALL.
THAT MEANS THEIR REACH IS A LOT LONGER THAN MINE.
ESPECIALLY COACH MATSUSHITA.
AND SINCE THE COACH IS FAMILIAR WITH MY TECHNIQUE, I CAN'T USE MY REGULAR TACTICS.
I HAVE TO OUTSMART THE COACH.
AND THE REST...

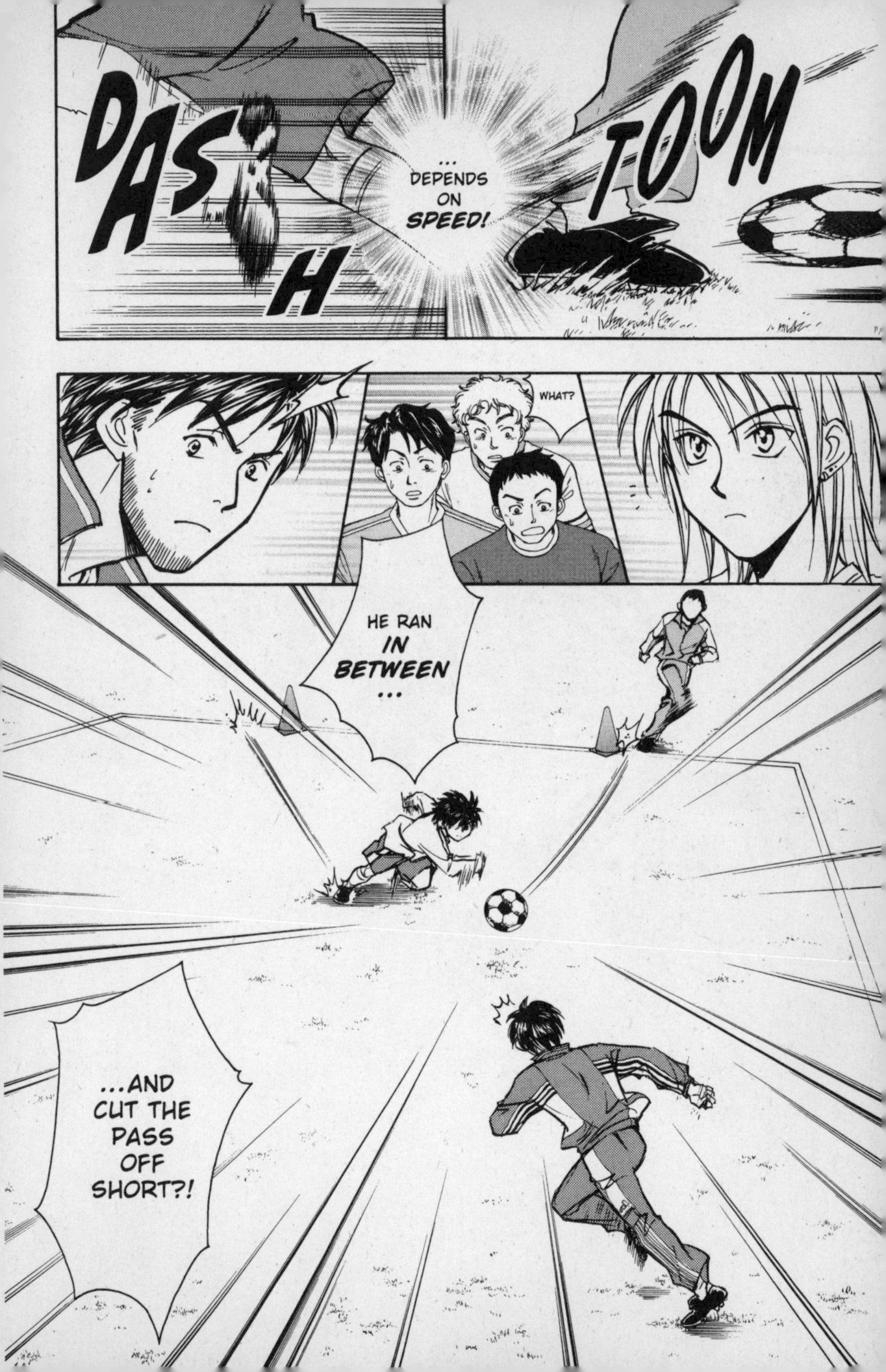
TOOM
... DEPENDS ON SPEED!
DASH
WHAT?
HE RAN IN BETWEEN ...
...AND CUT THE PASS OFF SHORT?!

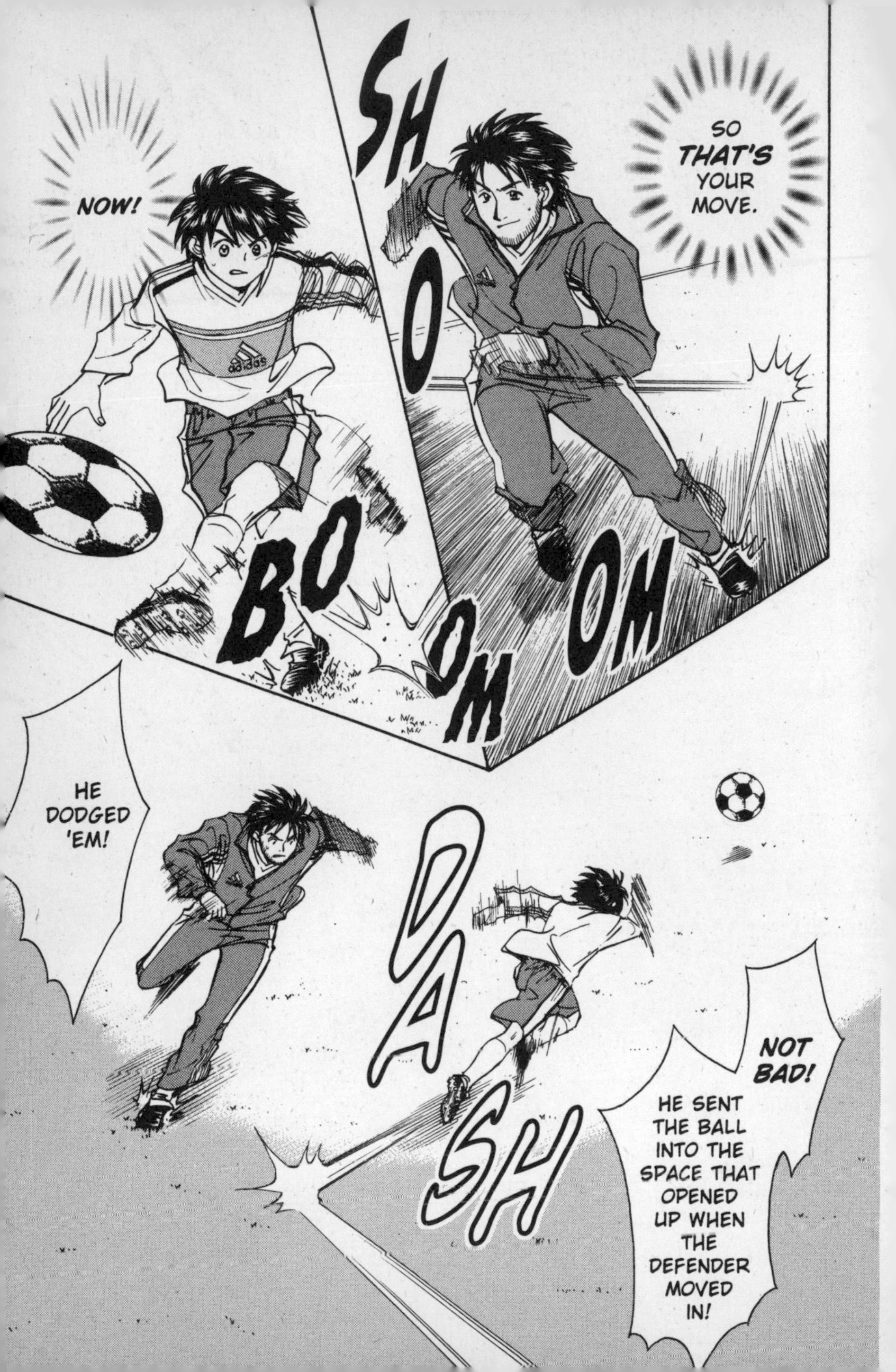
SHOOM
SO THAT'S YOUR MOVE.
NOW!
BOOM
NOT BAD!
HE SENT THE BALL INTO THE SPACE THAT OPENED UP WHEN THE DEFENDER MOVED IN!
DASH
HE DODGED 'EM!

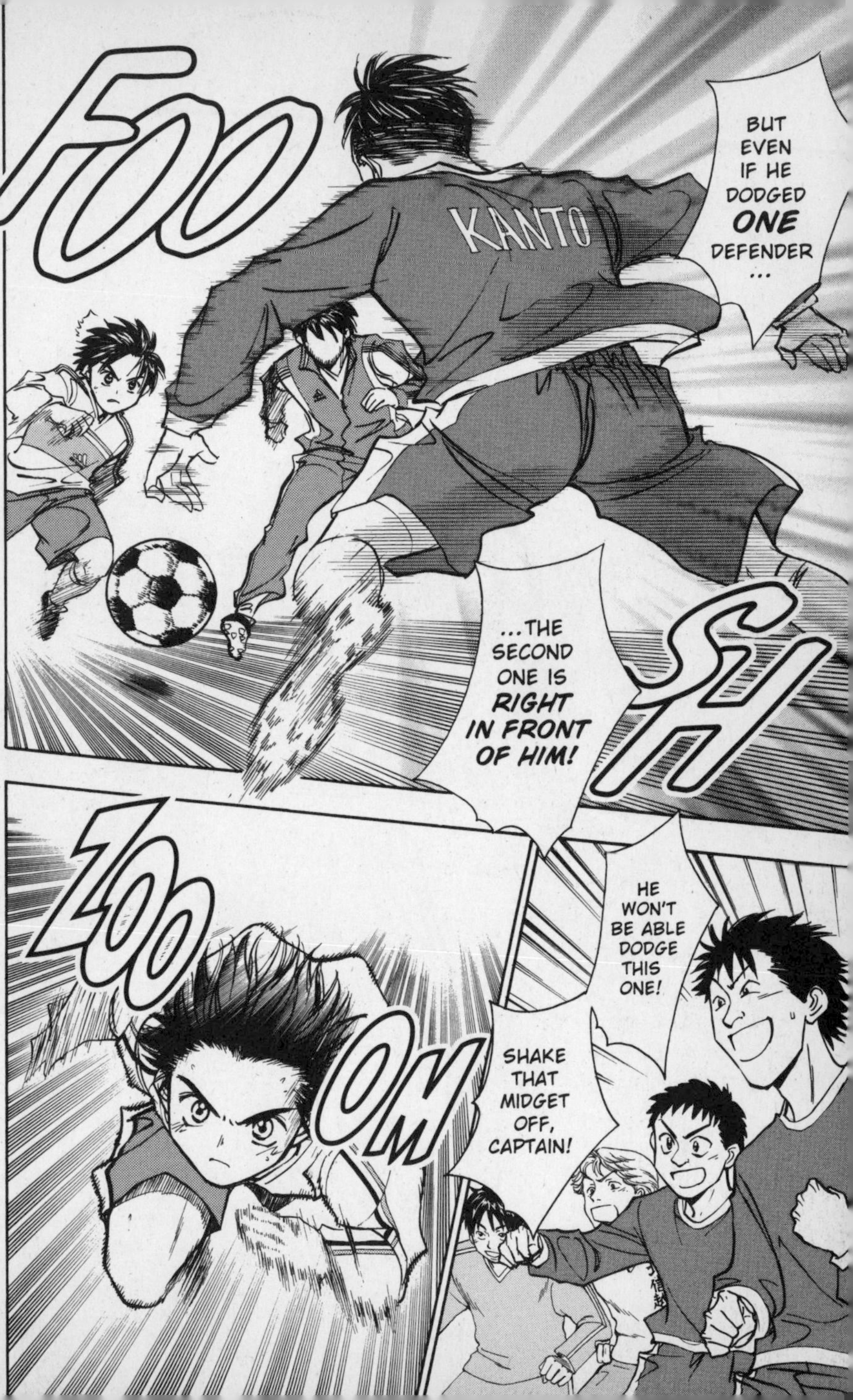
BUT EVEN IF HE DODGED ONE DEFENDER...
KANTO
FOO
...THE SECOND ONE IS RIGHT IN FRONT OF HIM!
SH
HE WON'T BE ABLE DODGE THIS ONE!
SHAKE THAT MIDGET OFF, CAPTAIN!
ZOO
OM

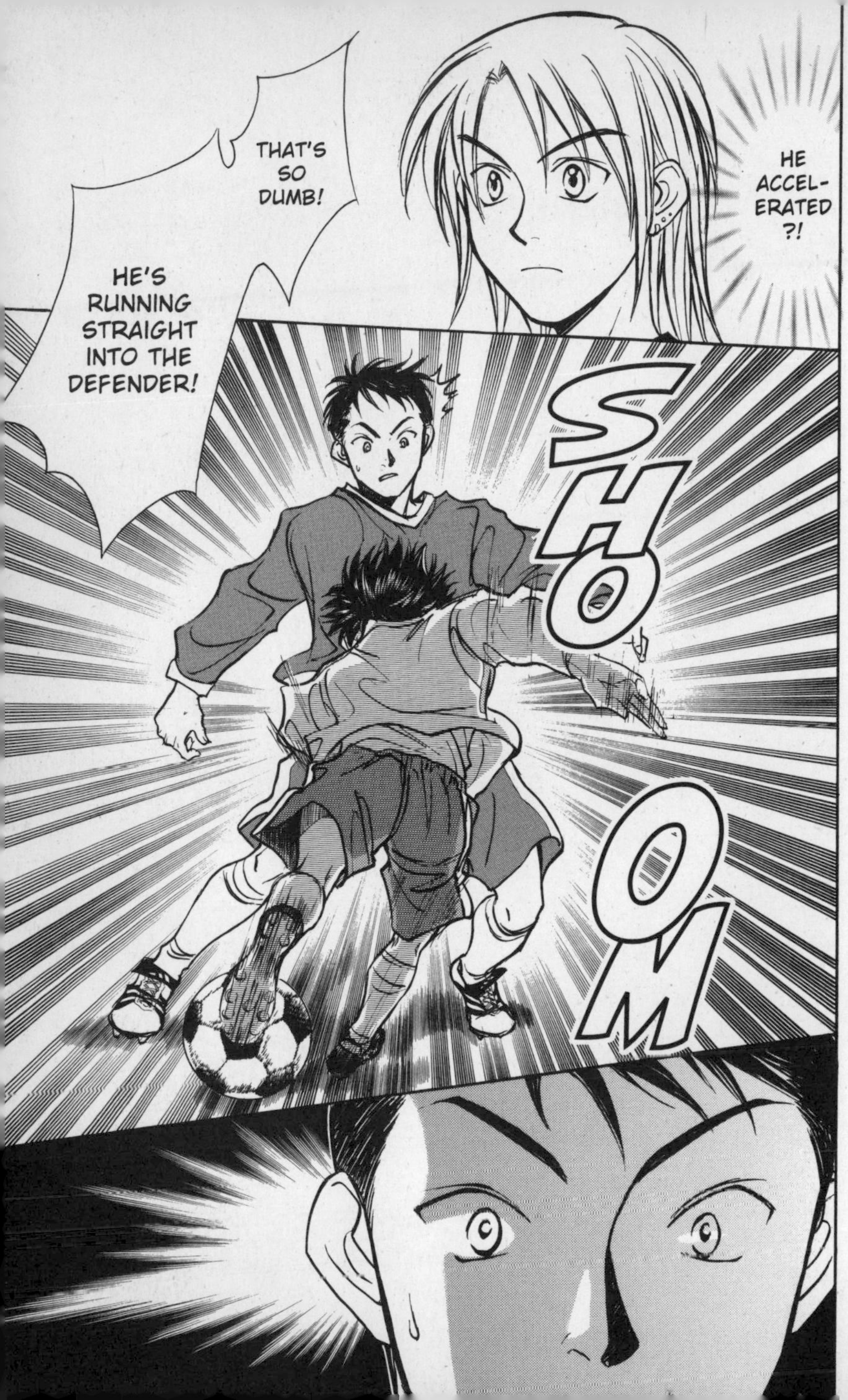
HE ACCEL-ERATED ?!
THAT'S SO DUMB!
HE'S RUNNING STRAIGHT INTO THE DEFENDER!
SHOOM

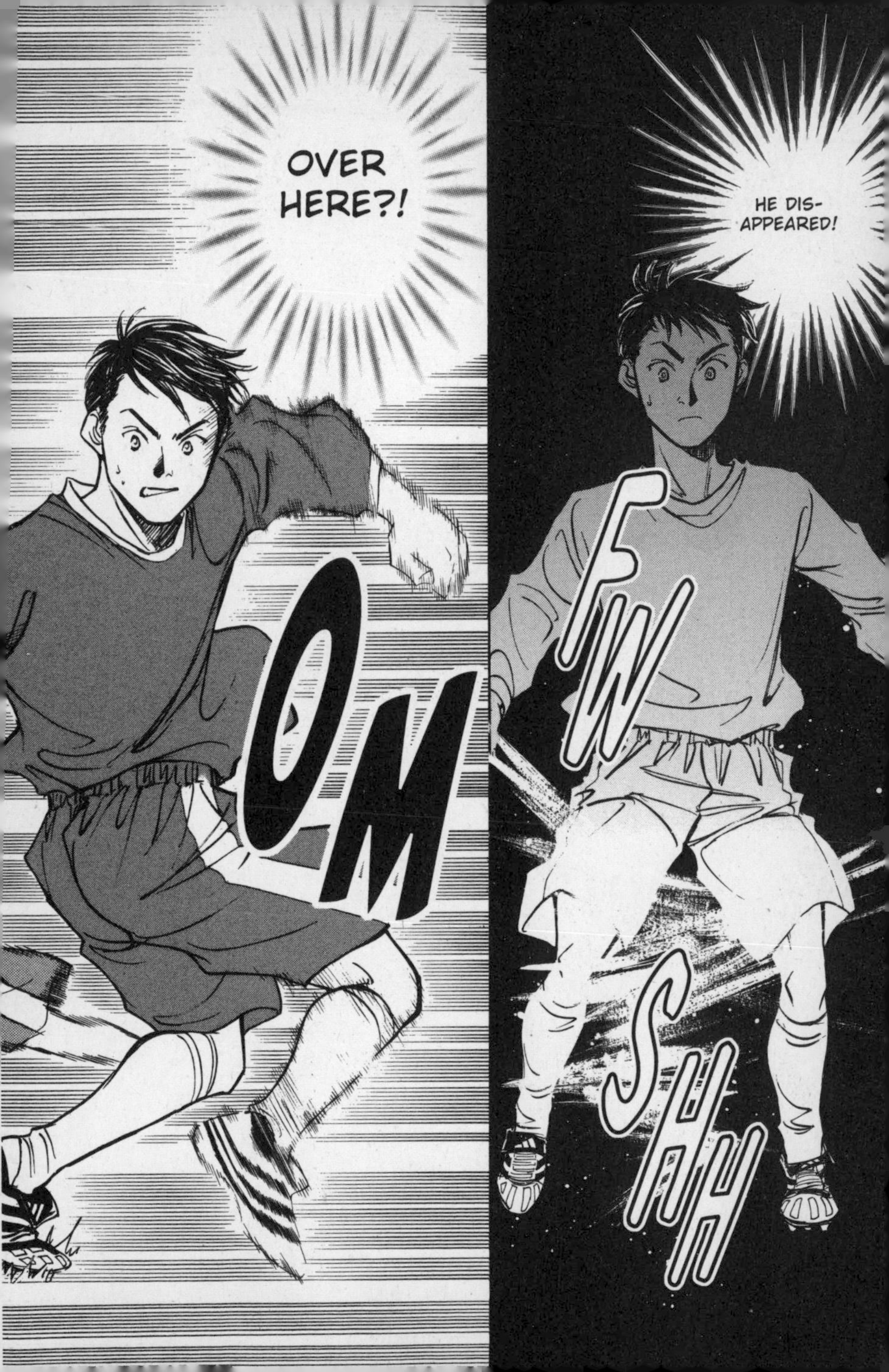
HE DIS-
APPEARED!
FWSHH
OVER
HERE?!
OM

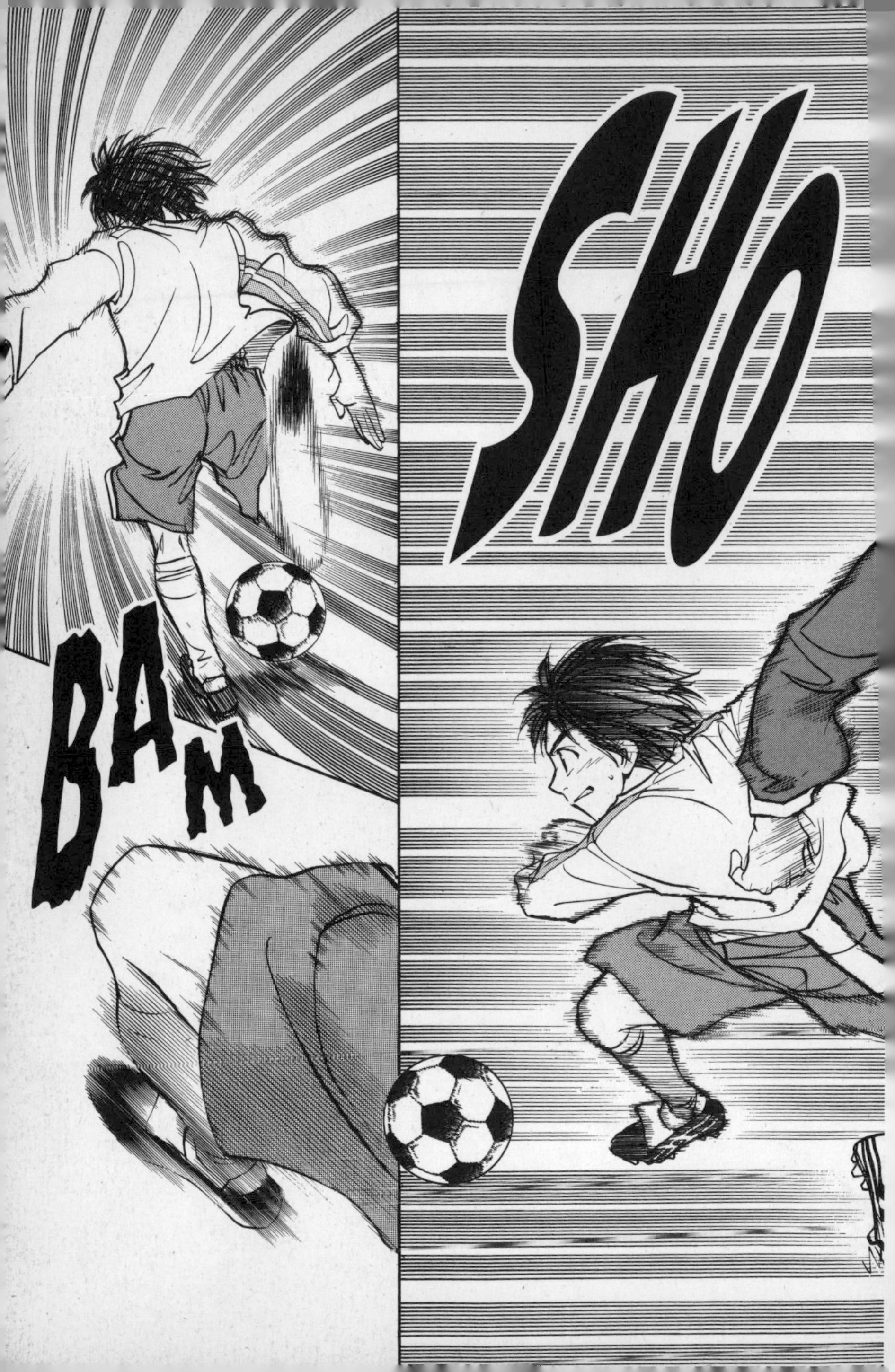
SHO
BAM

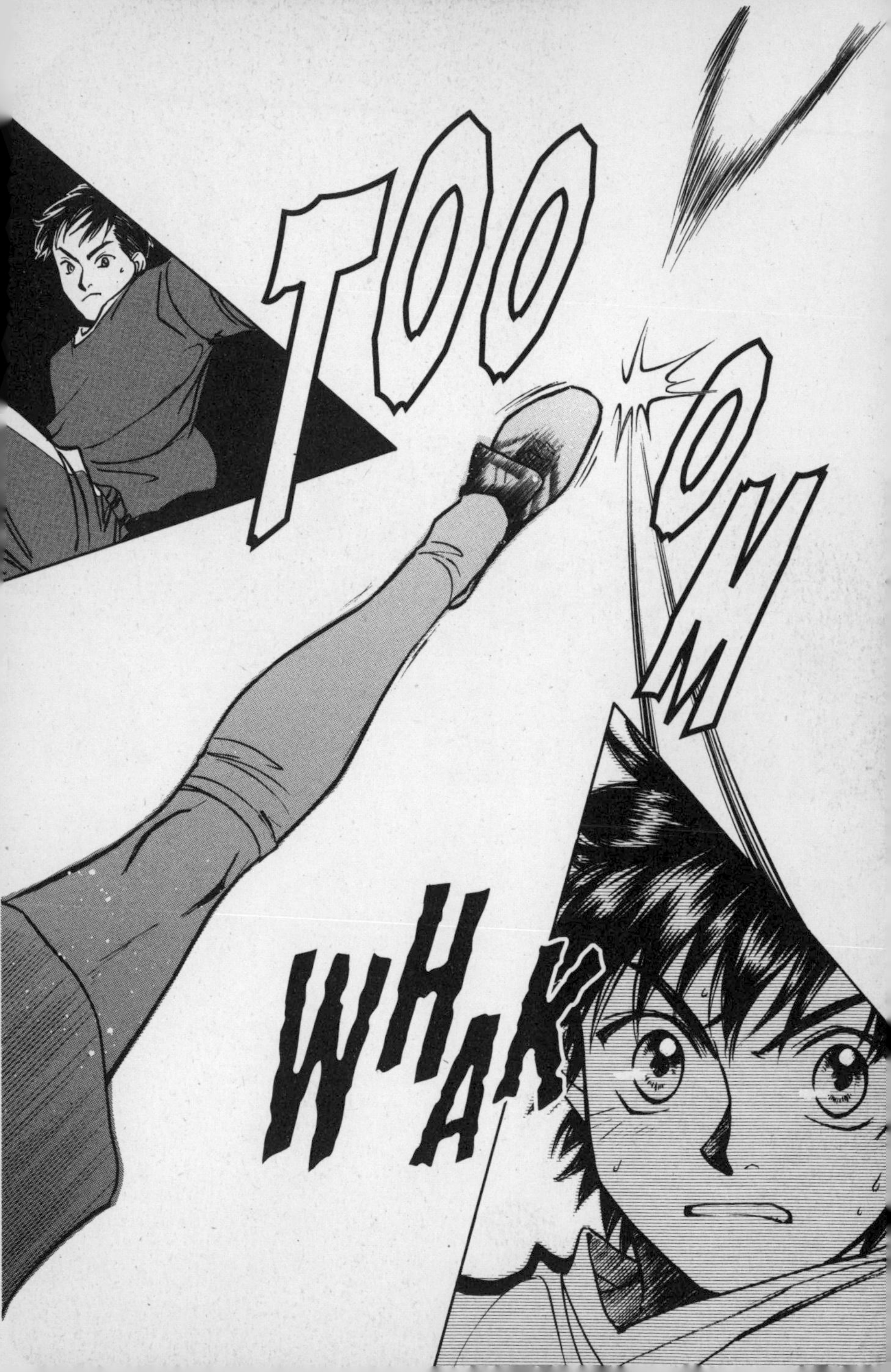
TOOOOM
WHAK

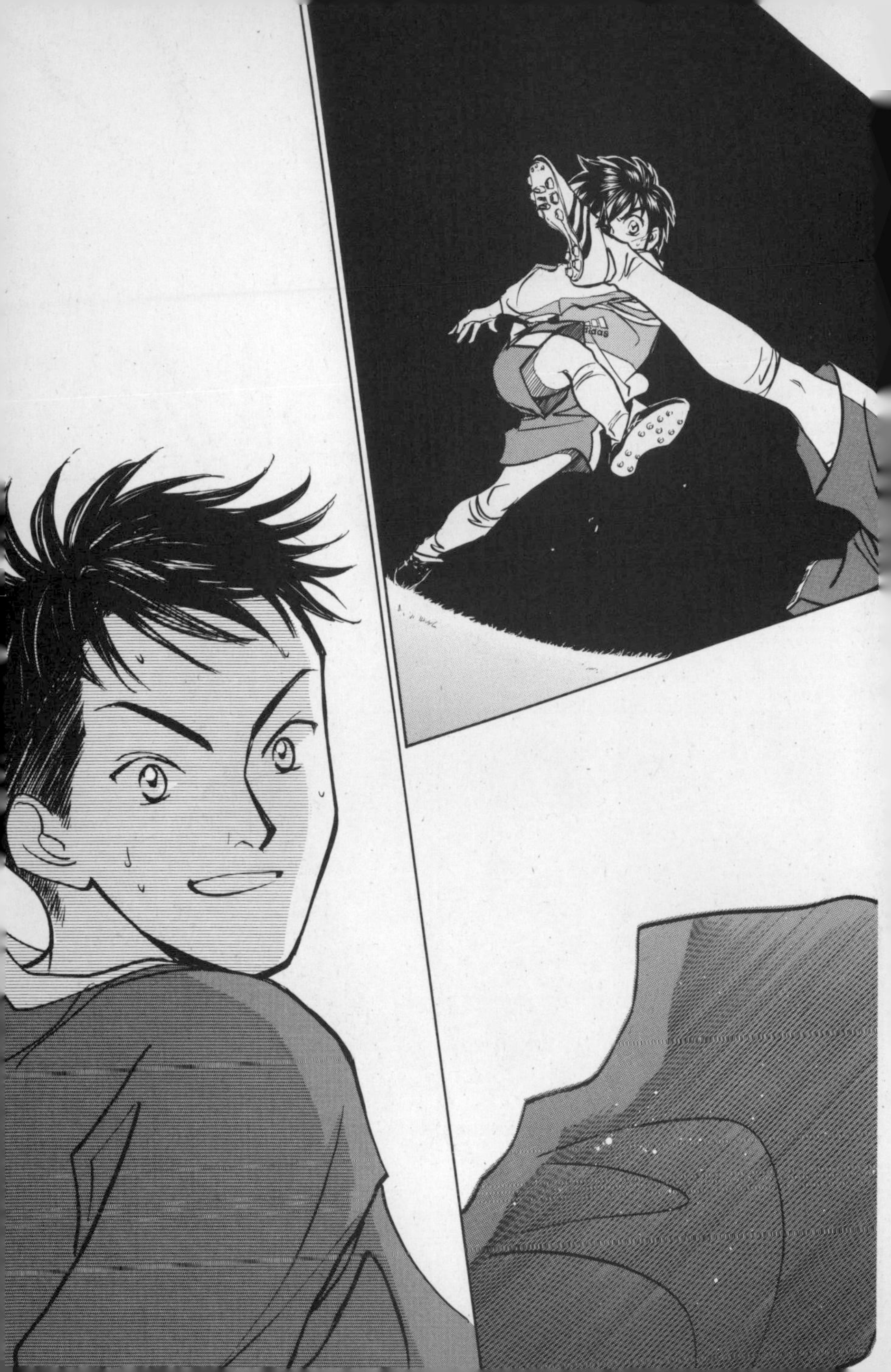

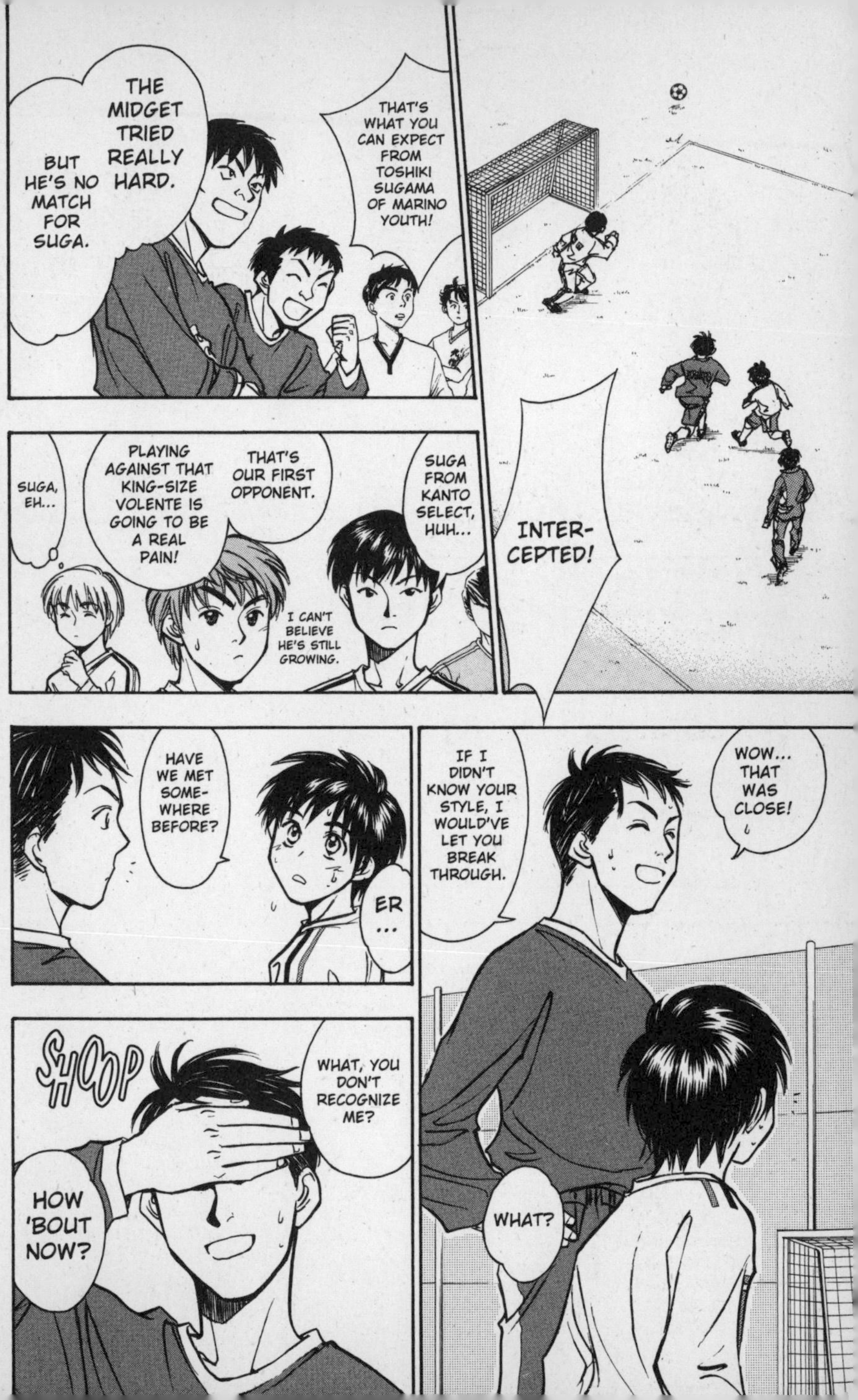
INTER-CEPTED!
THAT'S WHAT YOU CAN EXPECT FROM TOSHIKI SUGAMA OF MARINO YOUTH!
THE MIDGET TRIED REALLY HARD.
BUT HE'S NO MATCH FOR SUGA.
SUGA FROM KANTO SELECT, HUH...
I CAN'T BELIEVE HE'S STILL GROWING.
THAT'S OUR FIRST OPPONENT.
PLAYING AGAINST THAT KING-SIZE VOLENTE IS GOING TO BE A REAL PAIN!
SUGA, EH...
WOW... THAT WAS CLOSE!
IF I DIDN'T KNOW YOUR STYLE, I WOULD'VE LET YOU BREAK THROUGH.
WHAT?
HAVE WE MET SOME-WHERE BEFORE?
ER...
WHAT, YOU DON'T RECOGNIZE ME?
SHOOP
HOW 'BOUT NOW?

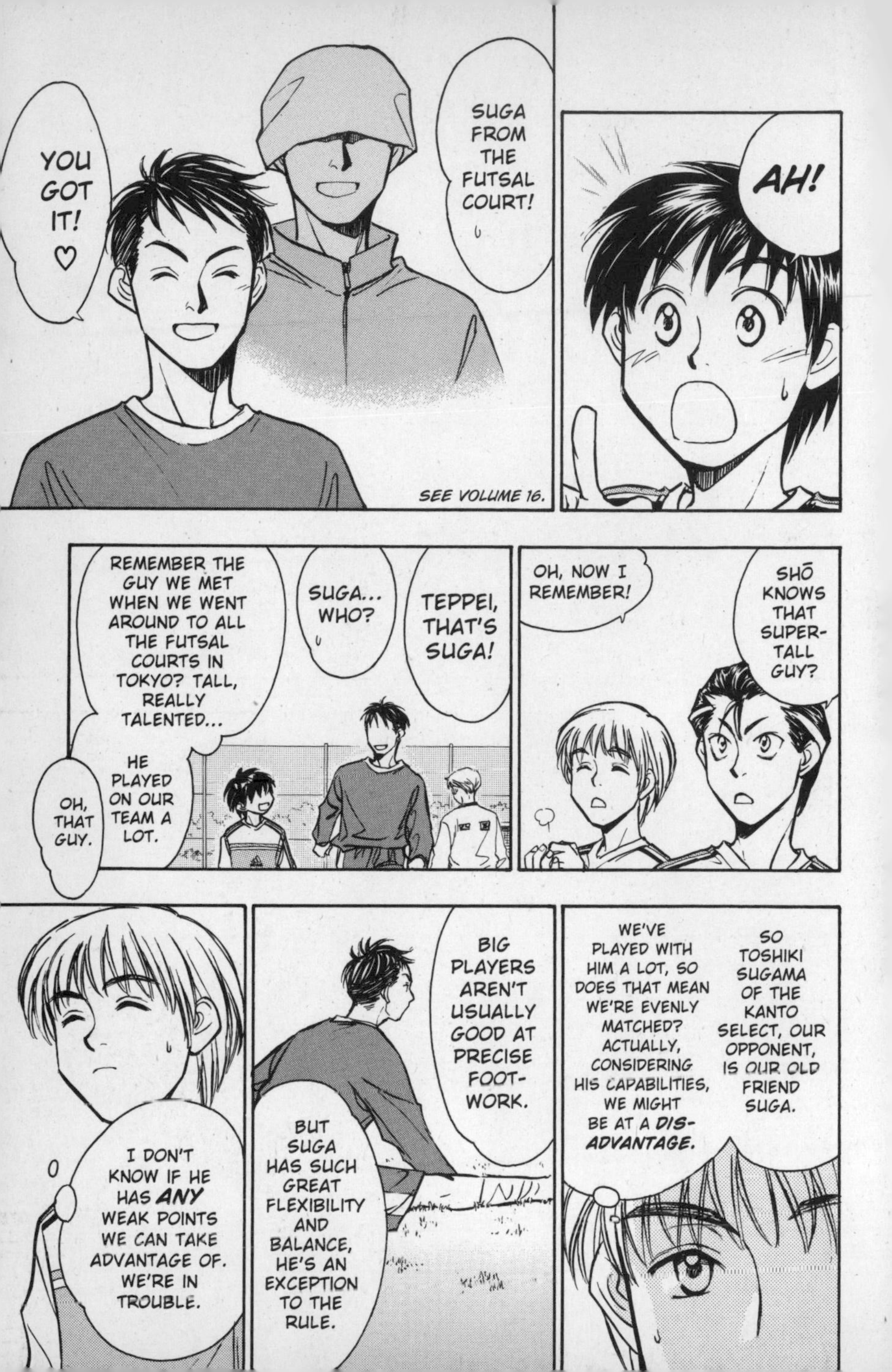
AH!
SUGA FROM THE FUTSAL COURT!
YOU GOT IT! ♥
SEE VOLUME 16.
SHŌ KNOWS THAT SUPER-TALL GUY?
OH, NOW I REMEMBER!
TEPPEI, THAT'S SUGA!
SUGA... WHO?
REMEMBER THE GUY WE MET WHEN WE WENT AROUND TO ALL THE FUTSAL COURTS IN TOKYO? TALL, REALLY TALENTED...
HE PLAYED ON OUR TEAM A LOT.
OH, THAT GUY.
SO TOSHIKI SUGAMA OF THE KANTO SELECT, OUR OPPONENT, IS OUR OLD FRIEND SUGA.
WE'VE PLAYED WITH HIM A LOT, SO DOES THAT MEAN WE'RE EVENLY MATCHED? ACTUALLY, CONSIDERING HIS CAPABILITIES, WE MIGHT BE AT A DIS-ADVANTAGE.
BIG PLAYERS AREN'T USUALLY GOOD AT PRECISE FOOT-WORK.
BUT SUGA HAS SUCH GREAT FLEXIBILITY AND BALANCE, HE'S AN EXCEPTION TO THE RULE.
I DON'T KNOW IF HE HAS ANY WEAK POINTS WE CAN TAKE ADVANTAGE OF. WE'RE IN TROUBLE.

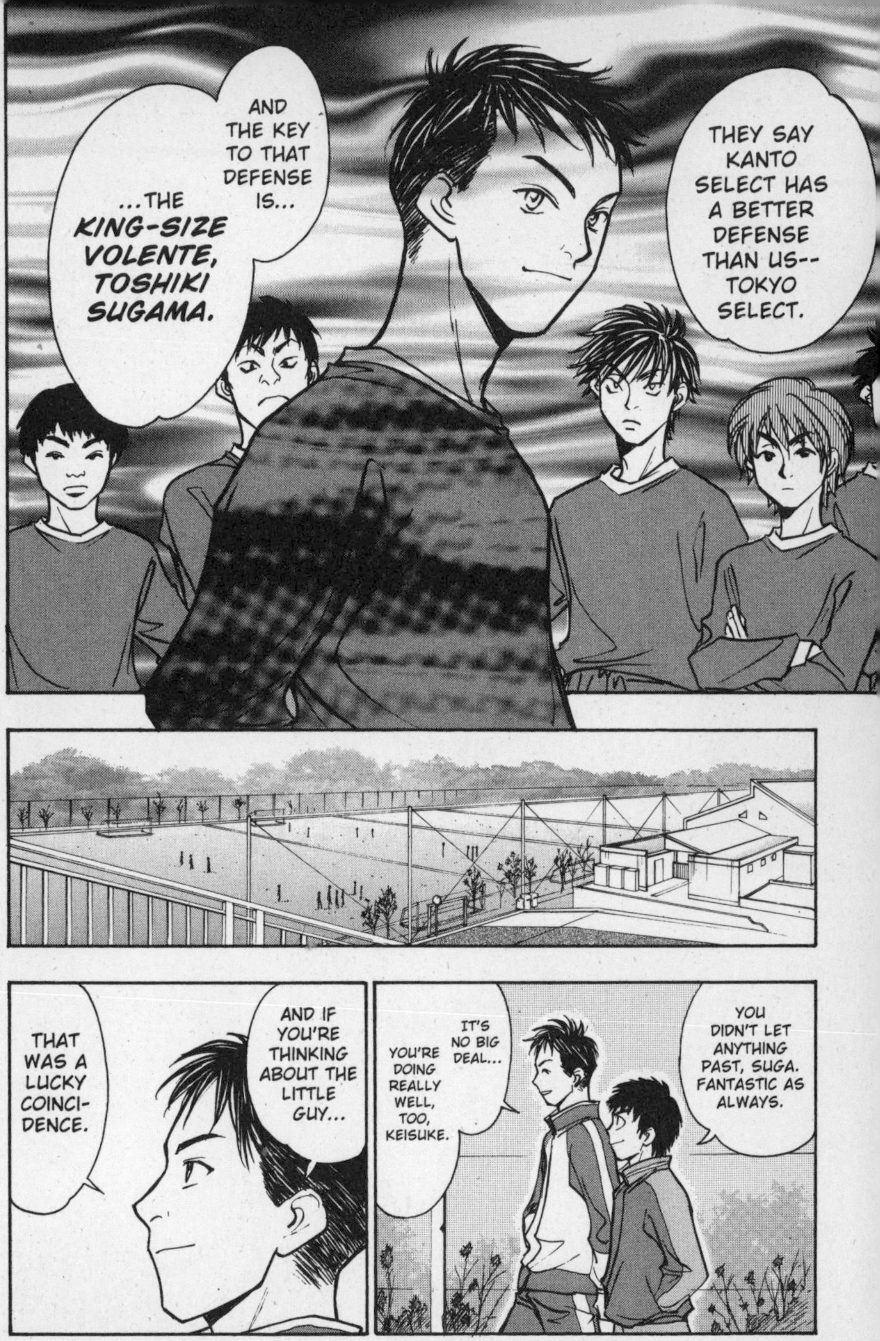
THEY SAY KANTO SELECT HAS A BETTER DEFENSE THAN US-- TOKYO SELECT.
AND THE KEY TO THAT DEFENSE IS...
...THE *KING-SIZE VOLENTE, TOSHIKI SUGAMA.*
YOU DIDN'T LET ANYTHING PAST, SUGA. FANTASTIC AS ALWAYS.
IT'S NO BIG DEAL...
YOU'RE DOING REALLY WELL, TOO, KEISUKE.
AND IF YOU'RE THINKING ABOUT THE LITTLE GUY...
THAT WAS A LUCKY COINCI-DENCE.

READ THIS WAY

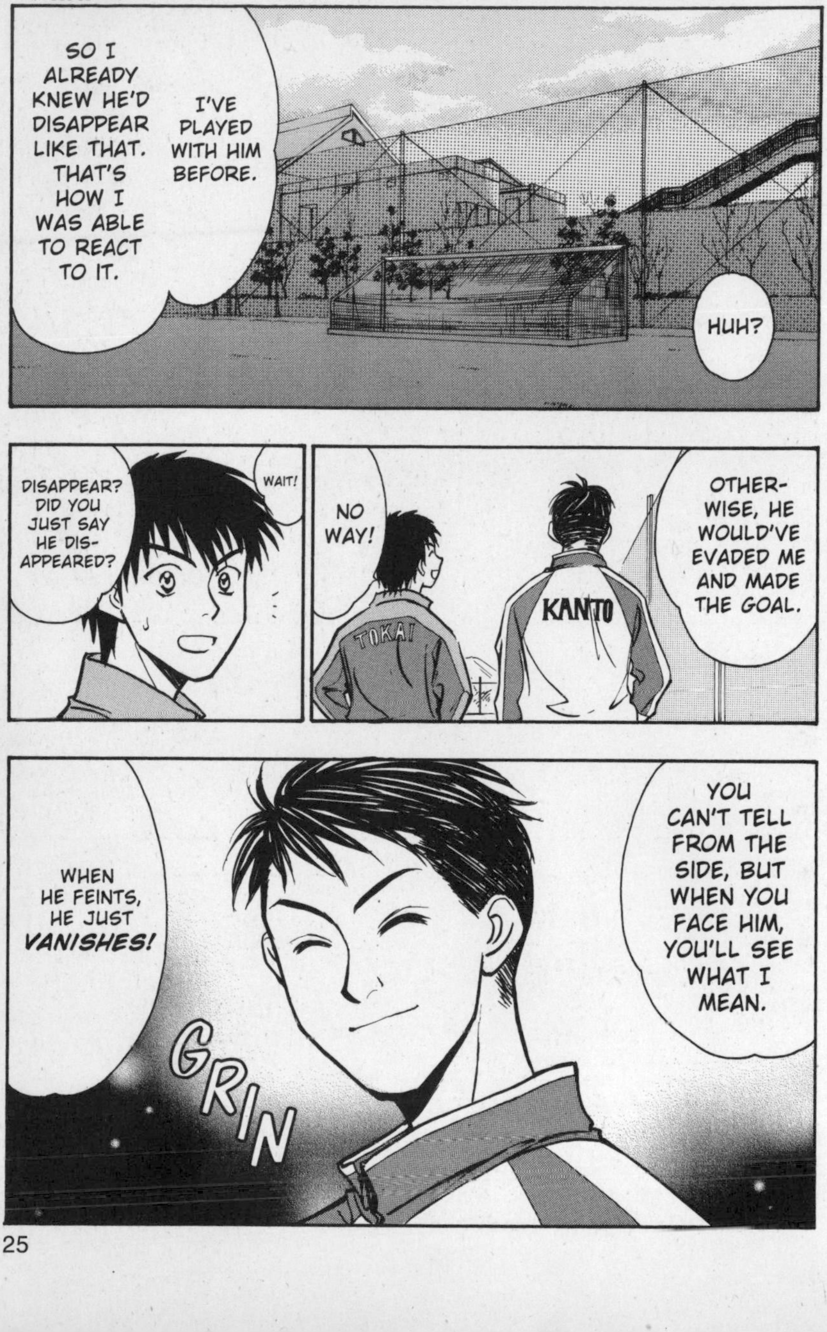
I'VE PLAYED WITH HIM BEFORE.
SO I ALREADY KNEW HE'D DISAPPEAR LIKE THAT. THAT'S HOW I WAS ABLE TO REACT TO IT.
HUH?
OTHER-WISE, HE WOULD'VE EVADED ME AND MADE THE GOAL.
NO WAY!
KANTO
TOKAI
WAIT!
DISAPPEAR? DID YOU JUST SAY HE DIS-APPEARED?
YOU CAN'T TELL FROM THE SIDE, BUT WHEN YOU FACE HIM, YOU'LL SEE WHAT I MEAN.
WHEN HE FEINTS, HE JUST *VANISHES!*
GRIN

WHISTLE!

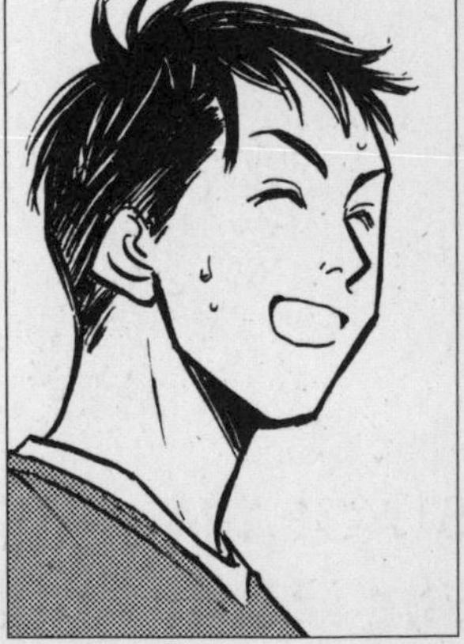

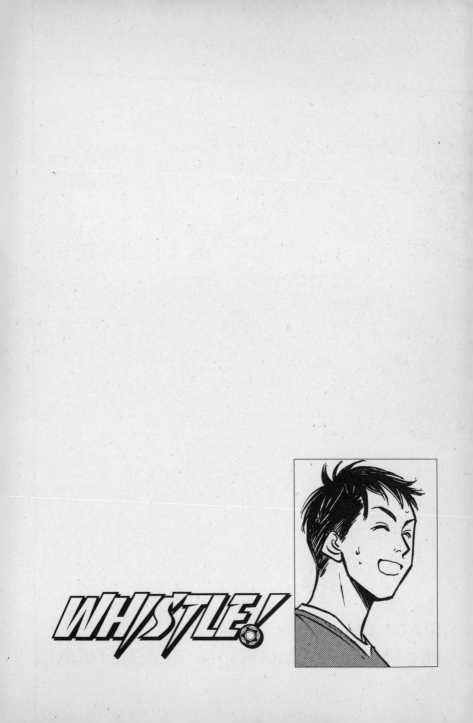

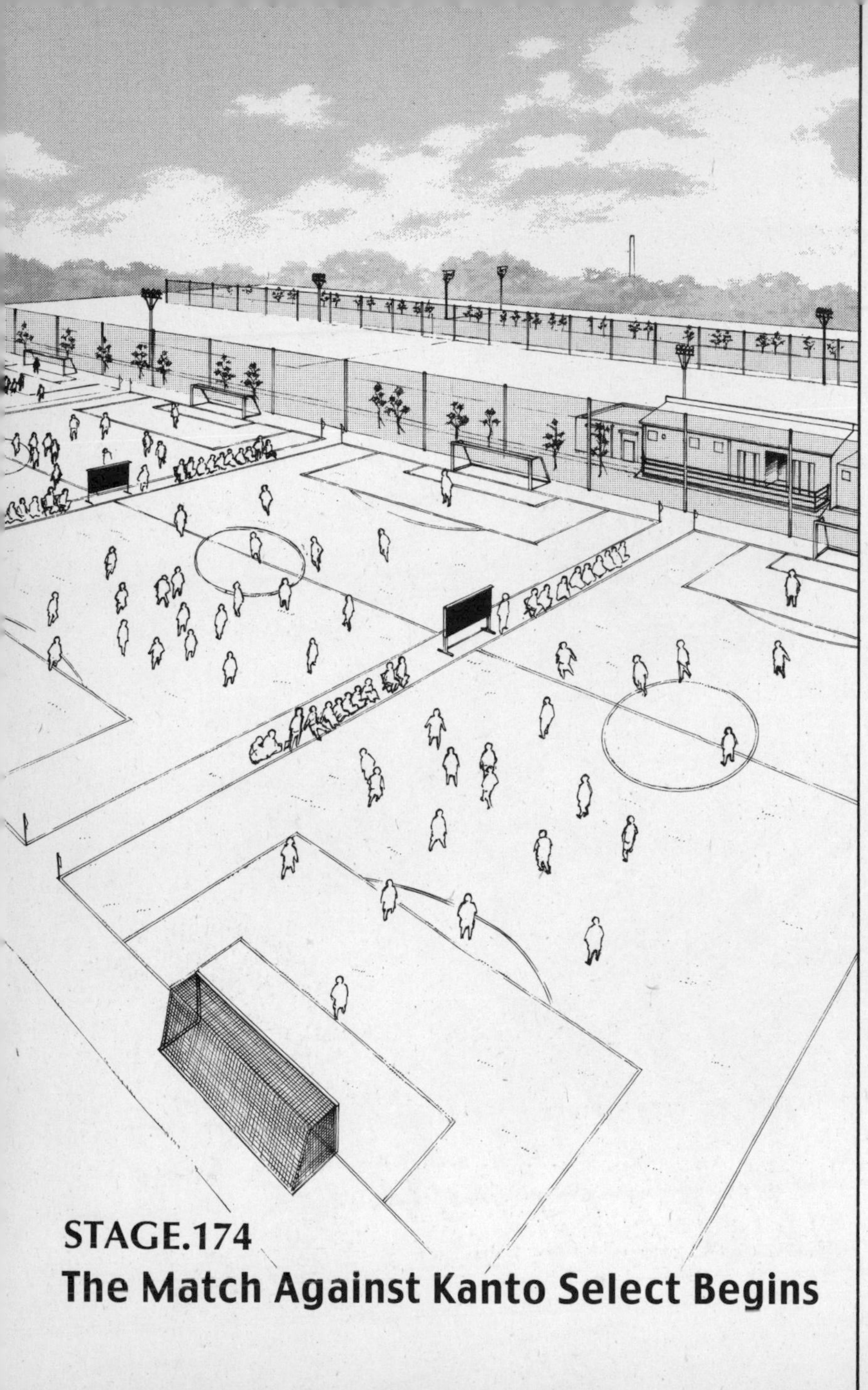

STAGE.174

The Match Against Kanto Select Begins

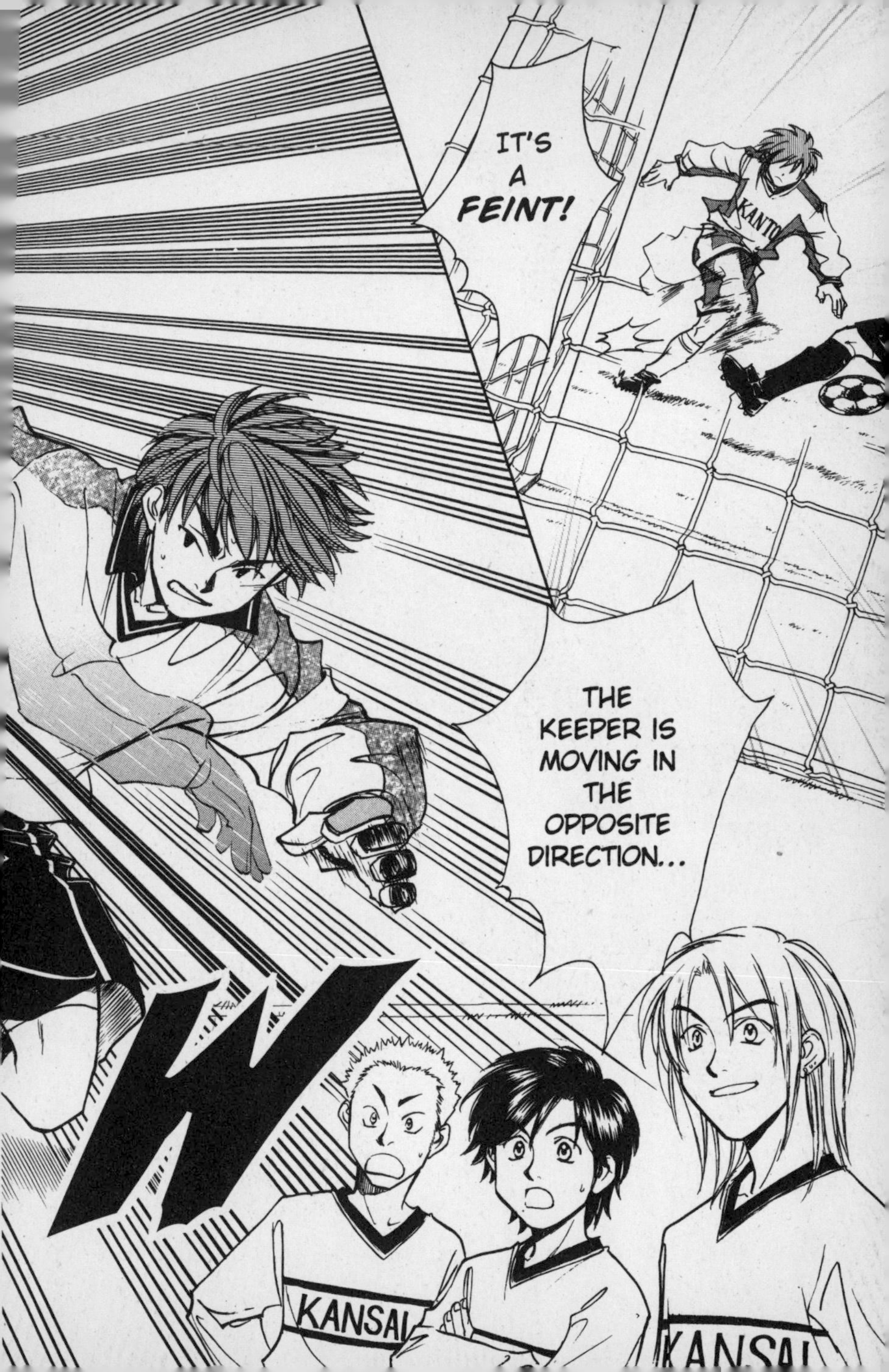
IT'S A FEINT!
KANTO
THE KEEPER IS MOVING IN THE OPPOSITE DIRECTION...
KANSAI
KANSAI

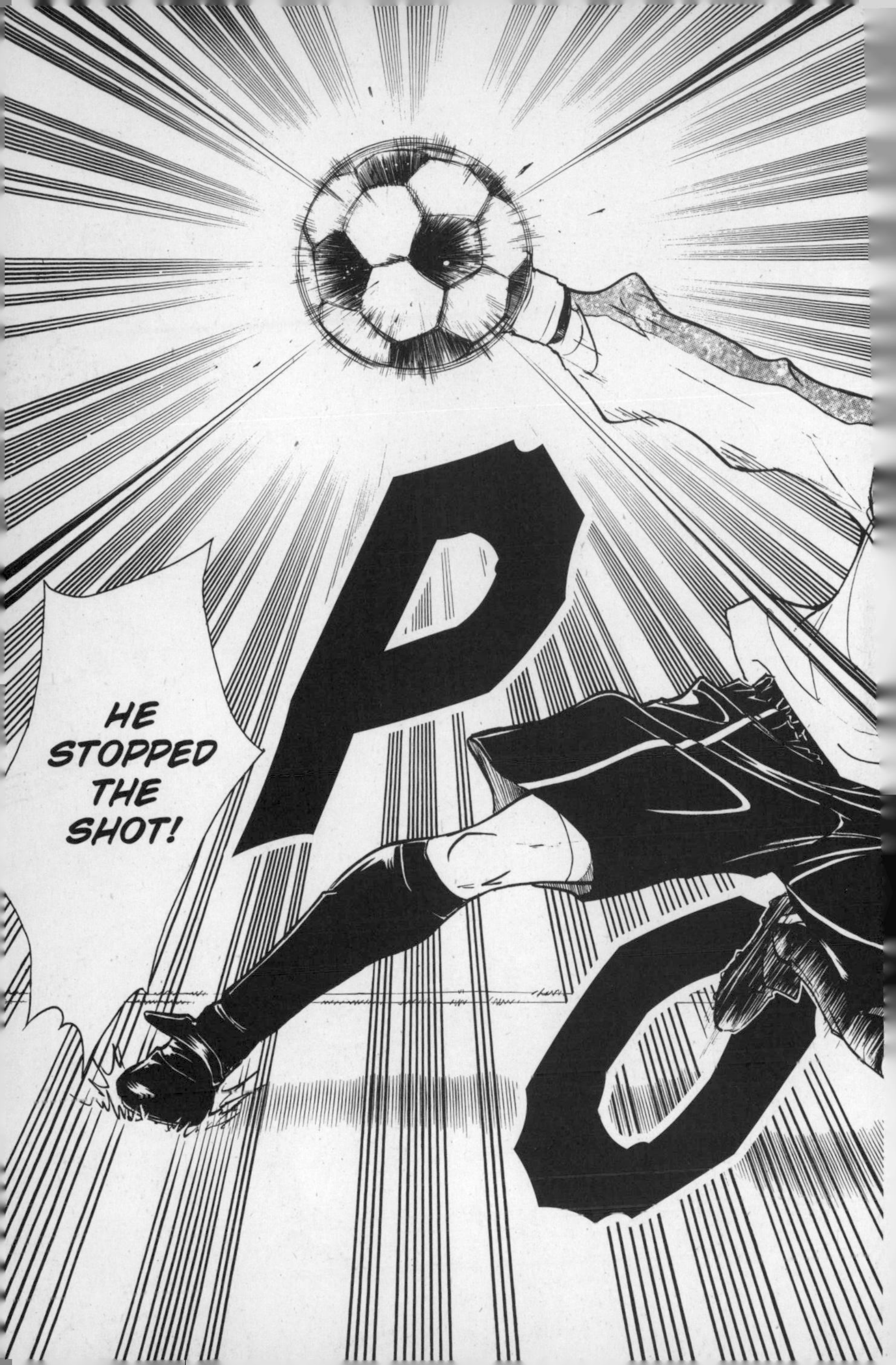
HE STOPPED THE SHOT!
PO

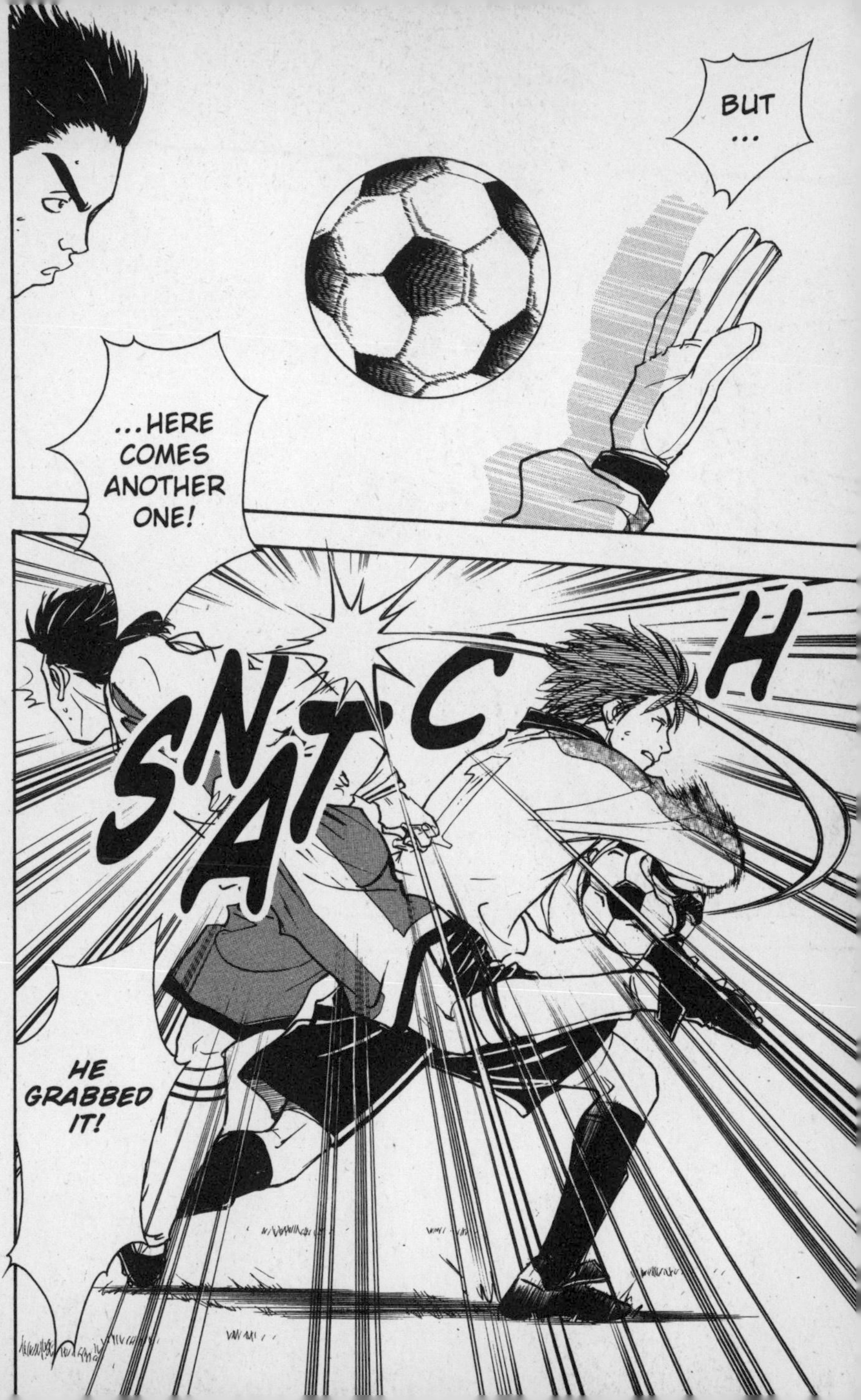
BUT...
...HERE COMES ANOTHER ONE!
SNATCH
HE GRABBED IT!

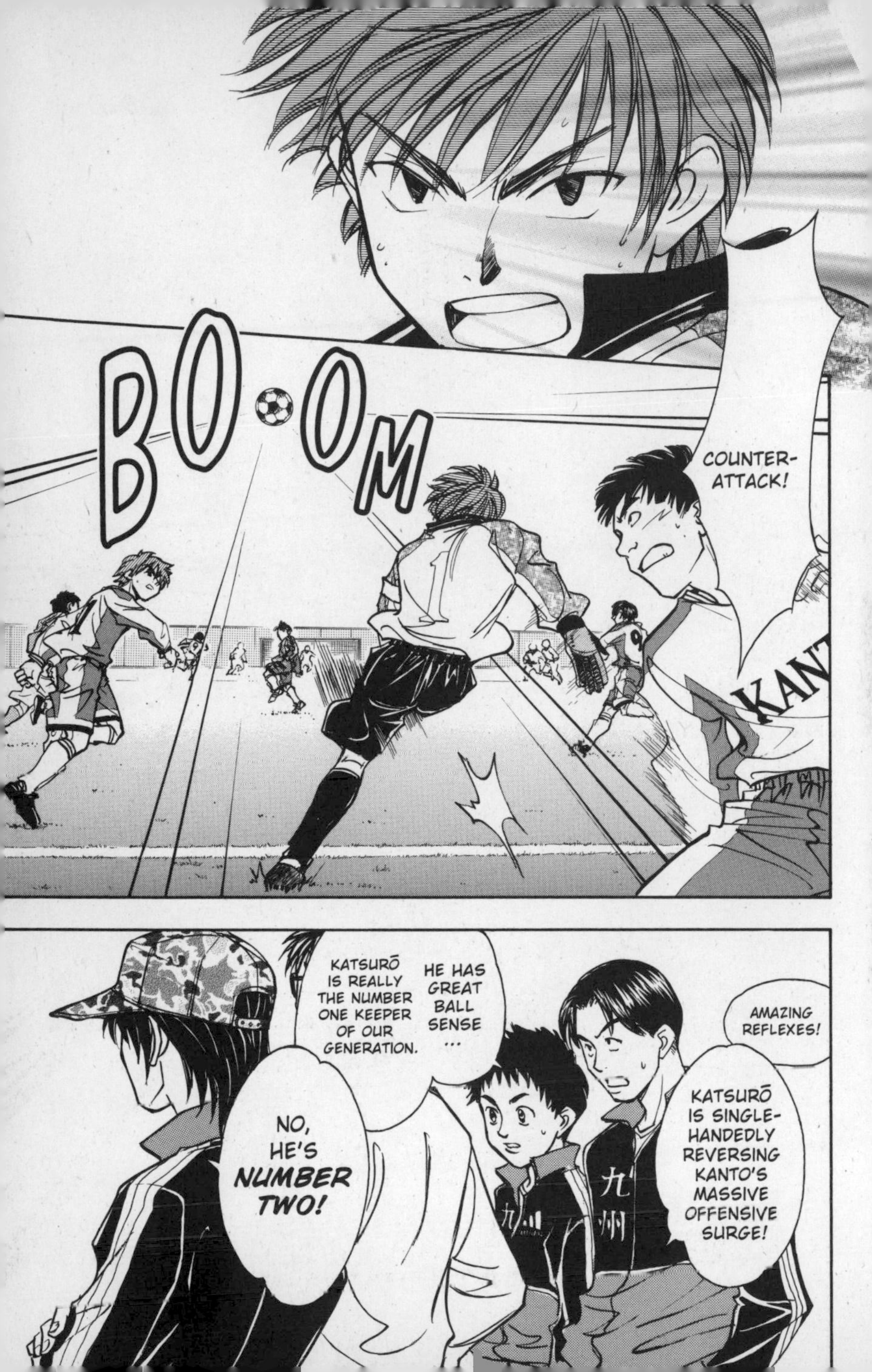
BO-OM
COUNTER-ATTACK!
AMAZING REFLEXES!
KATSURŌ IS SINGLE-HANDEDLY REVERSING KANTO'S MASSIVE OFFENSIVE SURGE!
HE HAS GREAT BALL SENSE...
KATSURŌ IS REALLY THE NUMBER ONE KEEPER OF OUR GENERATION.
NO, HE'S *NUMBER TWO!*

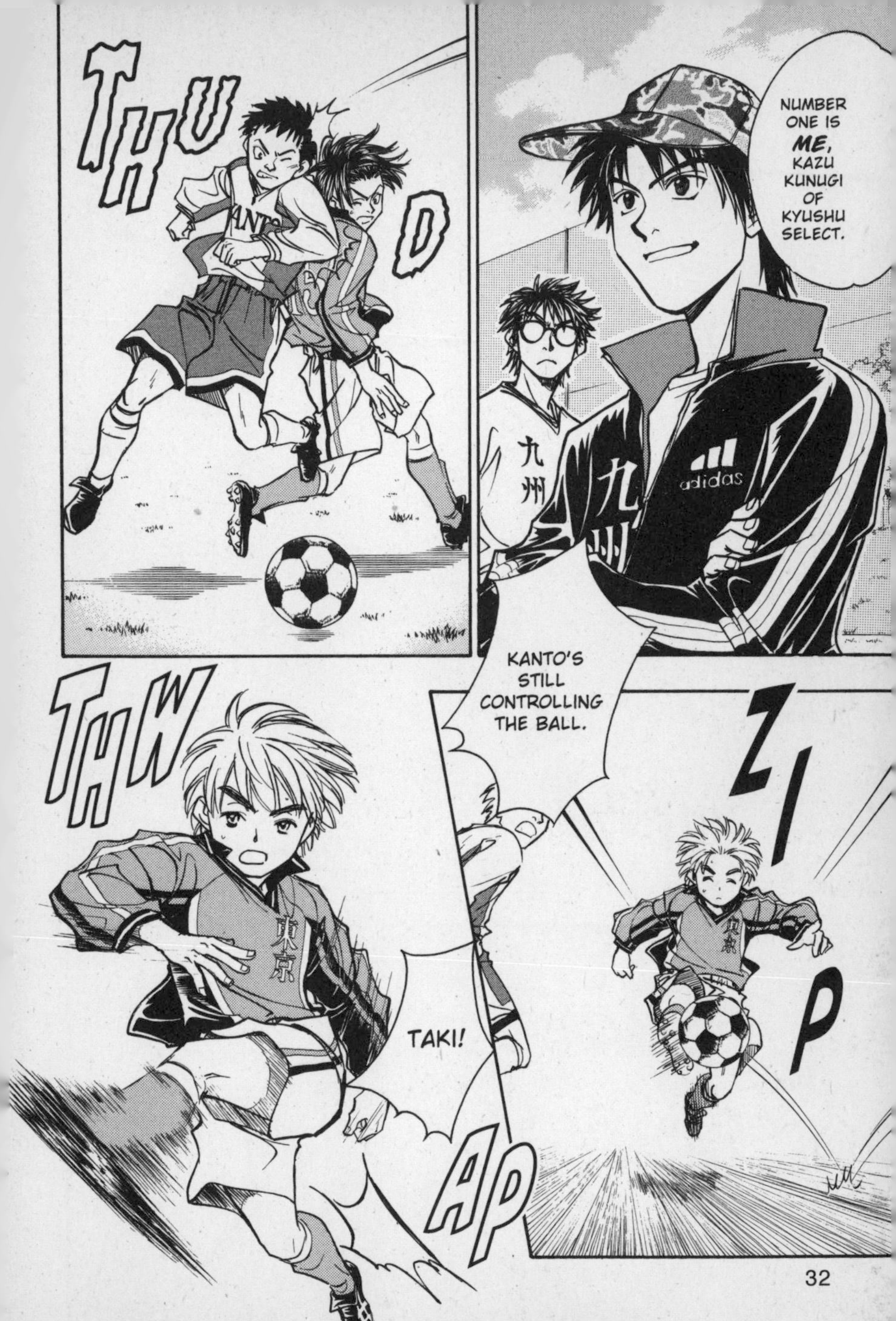
NUMBER ONE IS *ME*, KAZU KUNUGI OF KYUSHU SELECT.
THUD
KANTO'S STILL CONTROLLING THE BALL.
ZIP
THWAP
TAKI!

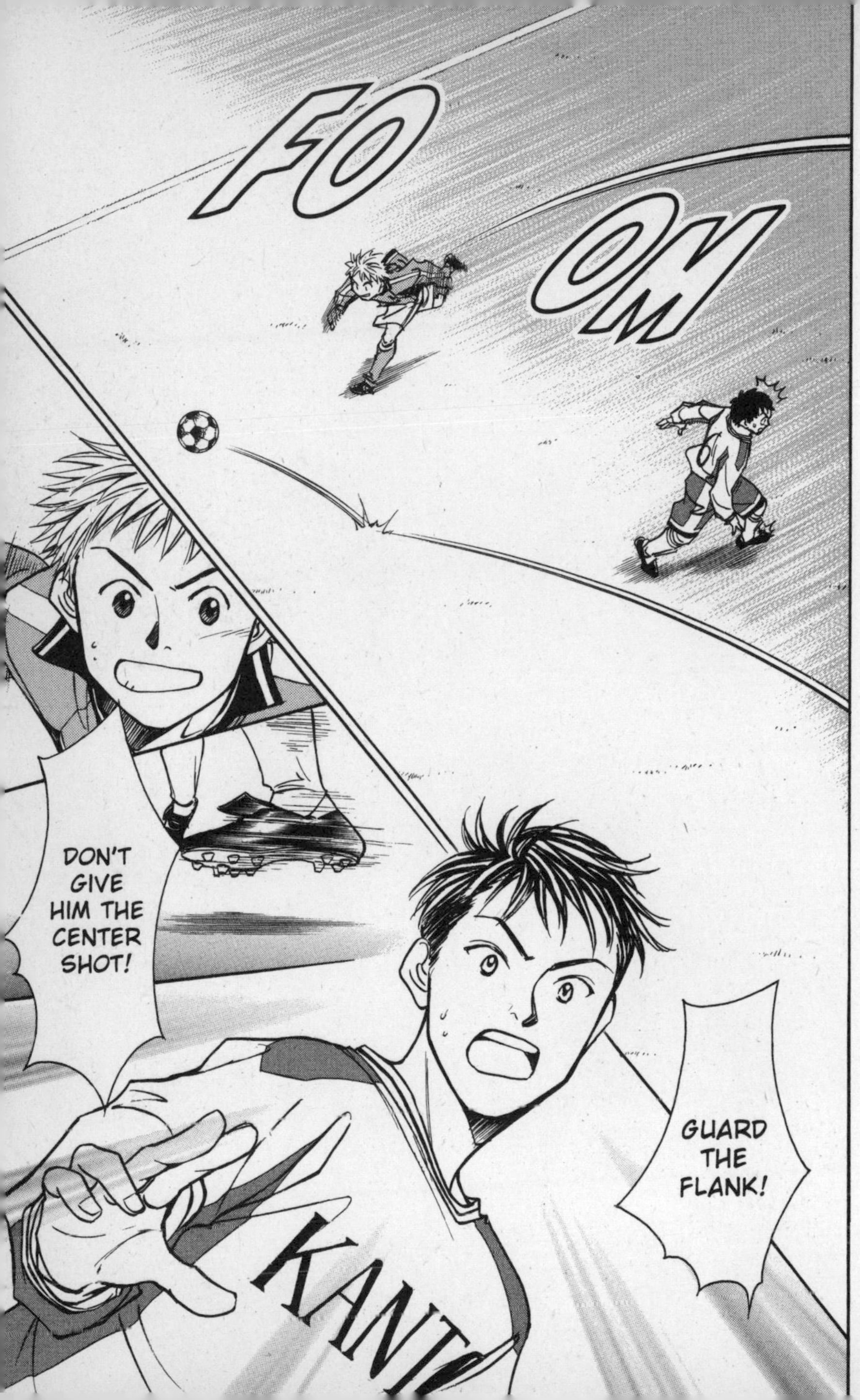
FOOOM
GUARD THE FLANK!
DON'T GIVE HIM THE CENTER SHOT!

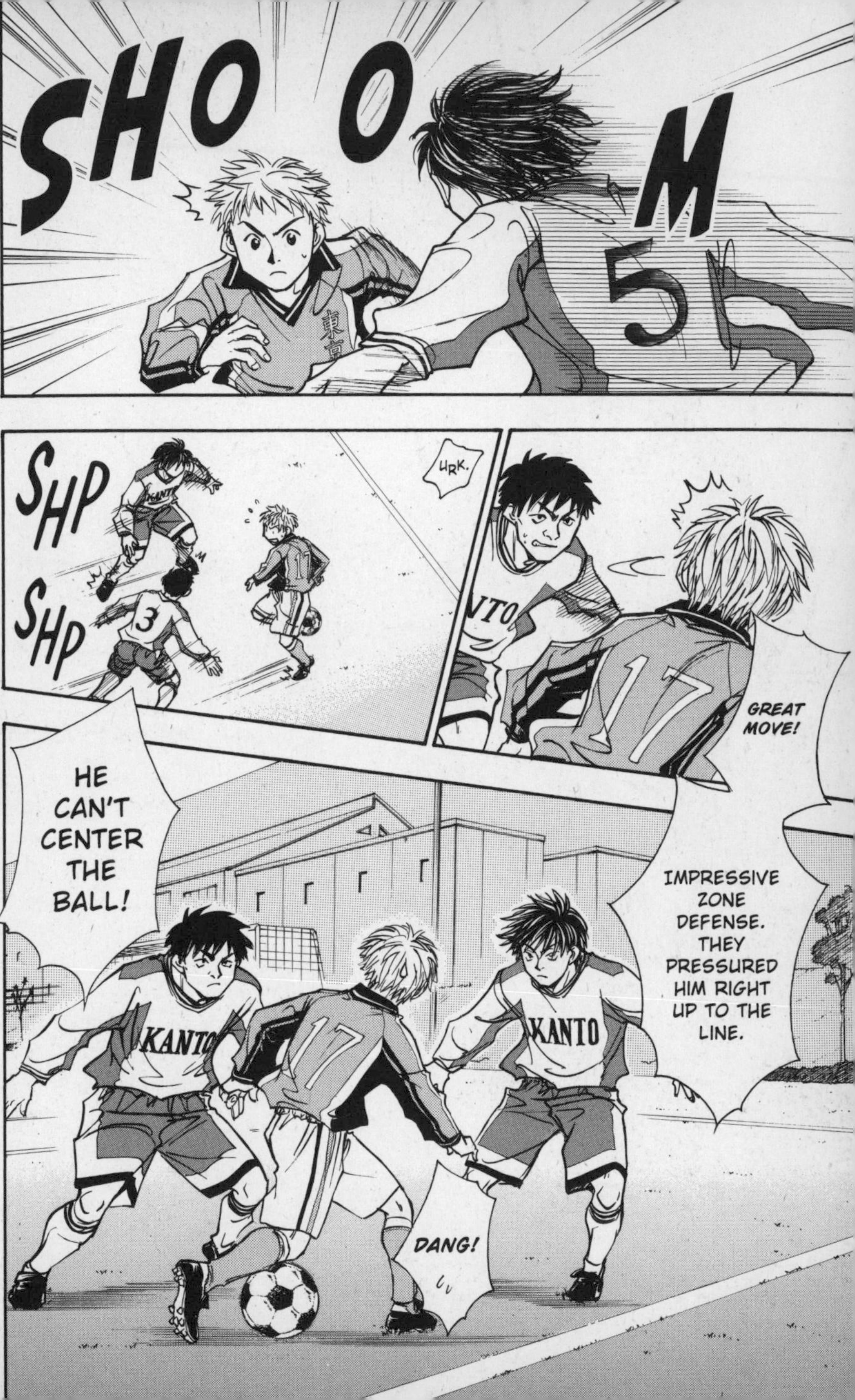
SHO O M
URK.
GREAT MOVE!
SHP
SHP
IMPRESSIVE ZONE DEFENSE. THEY PRESSURED HIM RIGHT UP TO THE LINE.
HE CAN'T CENTER THE BALL!
DANG!

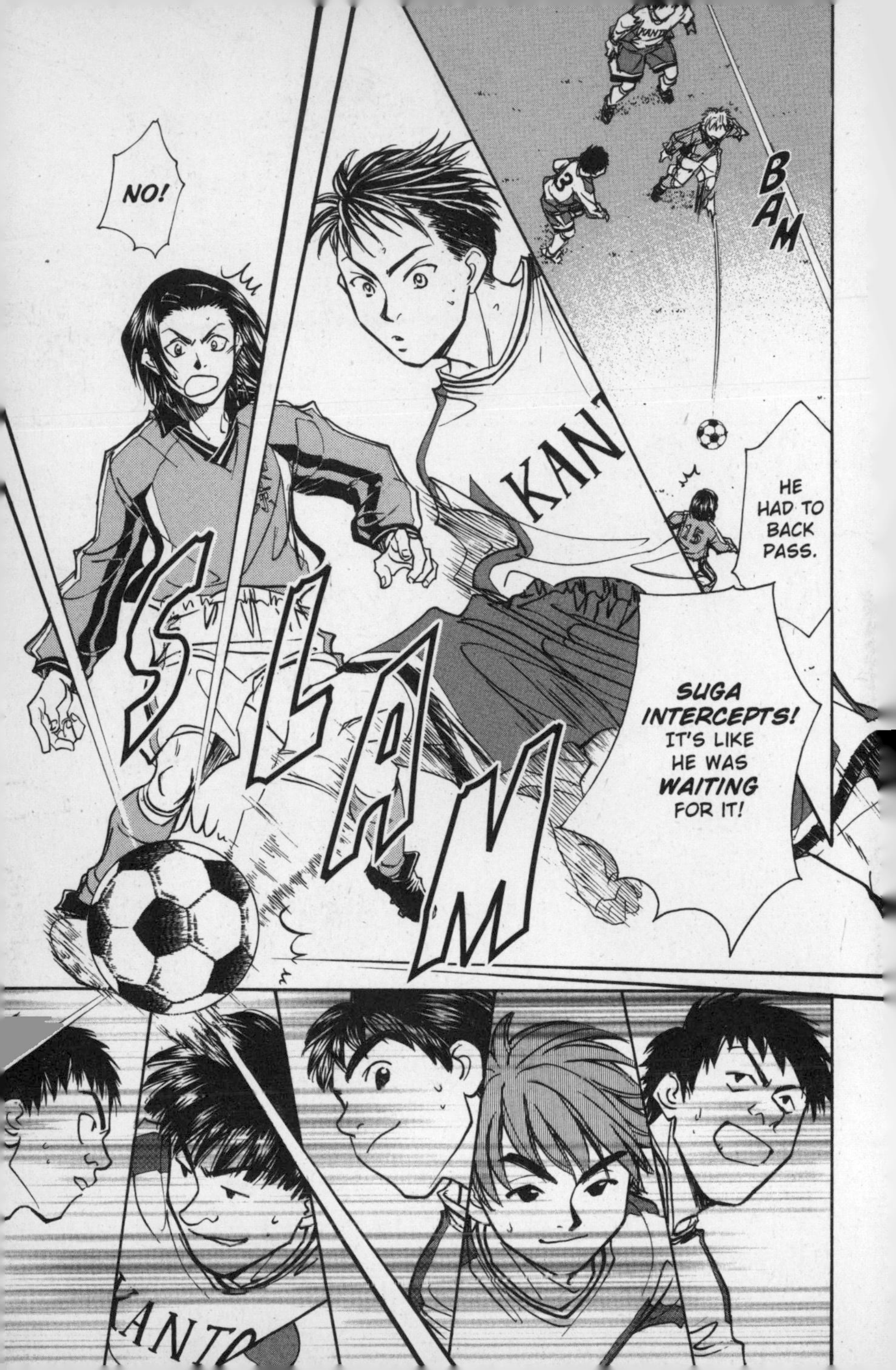
BAM
HE HAD TO BACK PASS.
SUGA INTERCEPTS! IT'S LIKE HE WAS WAITING FOR IT!
SLAM
NO!

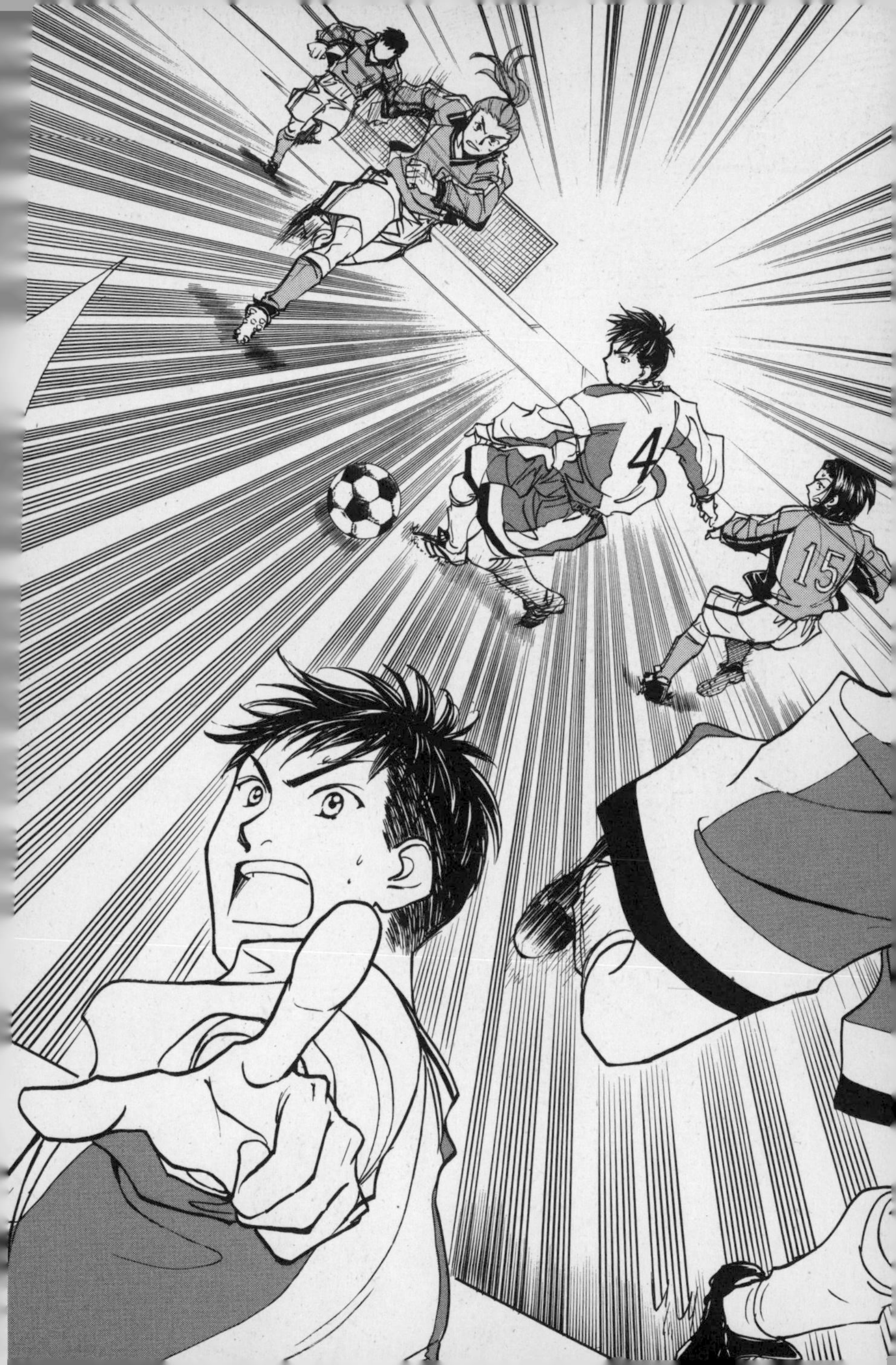

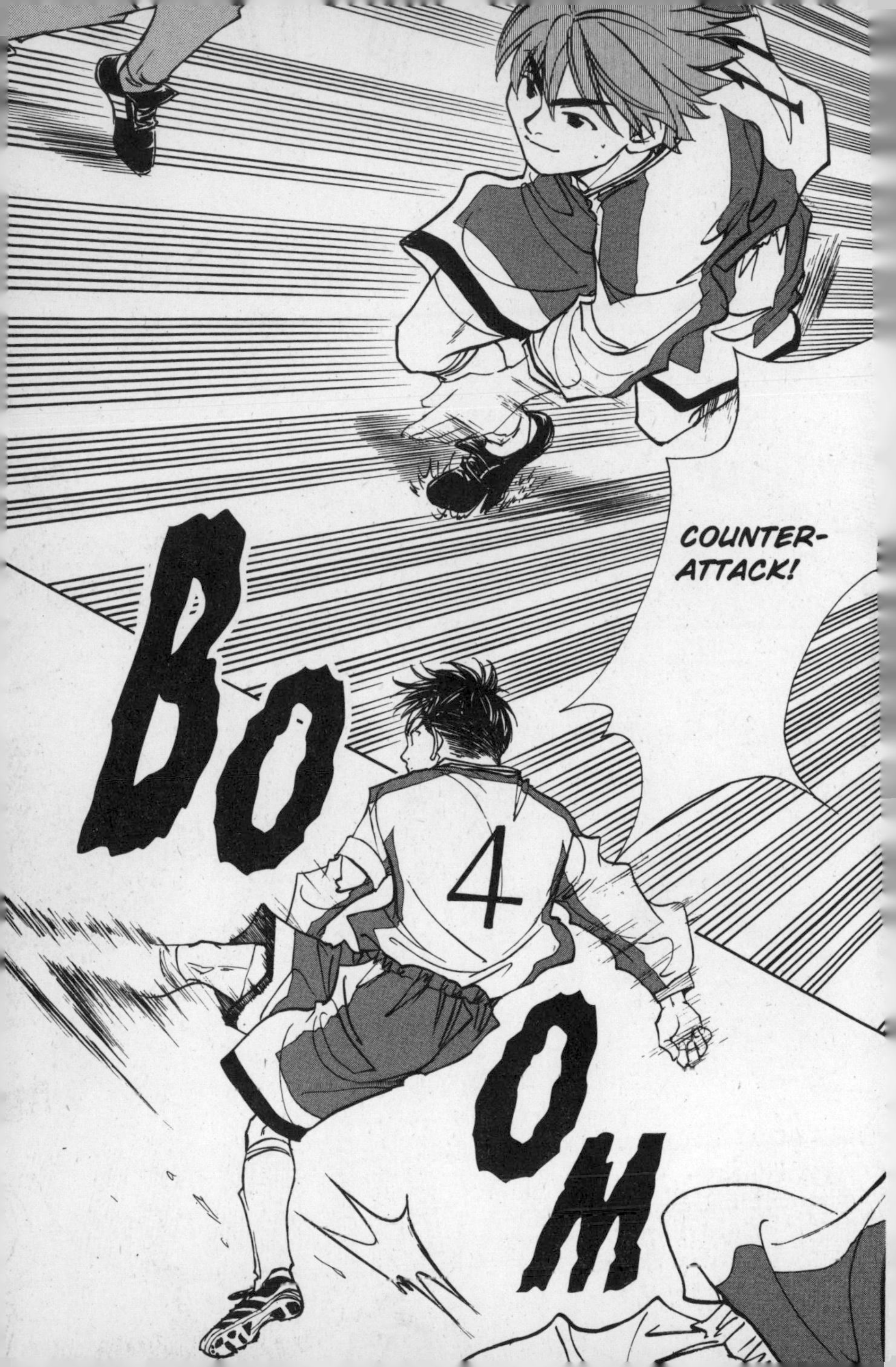
COUNTER-ATTACK!
BOOM

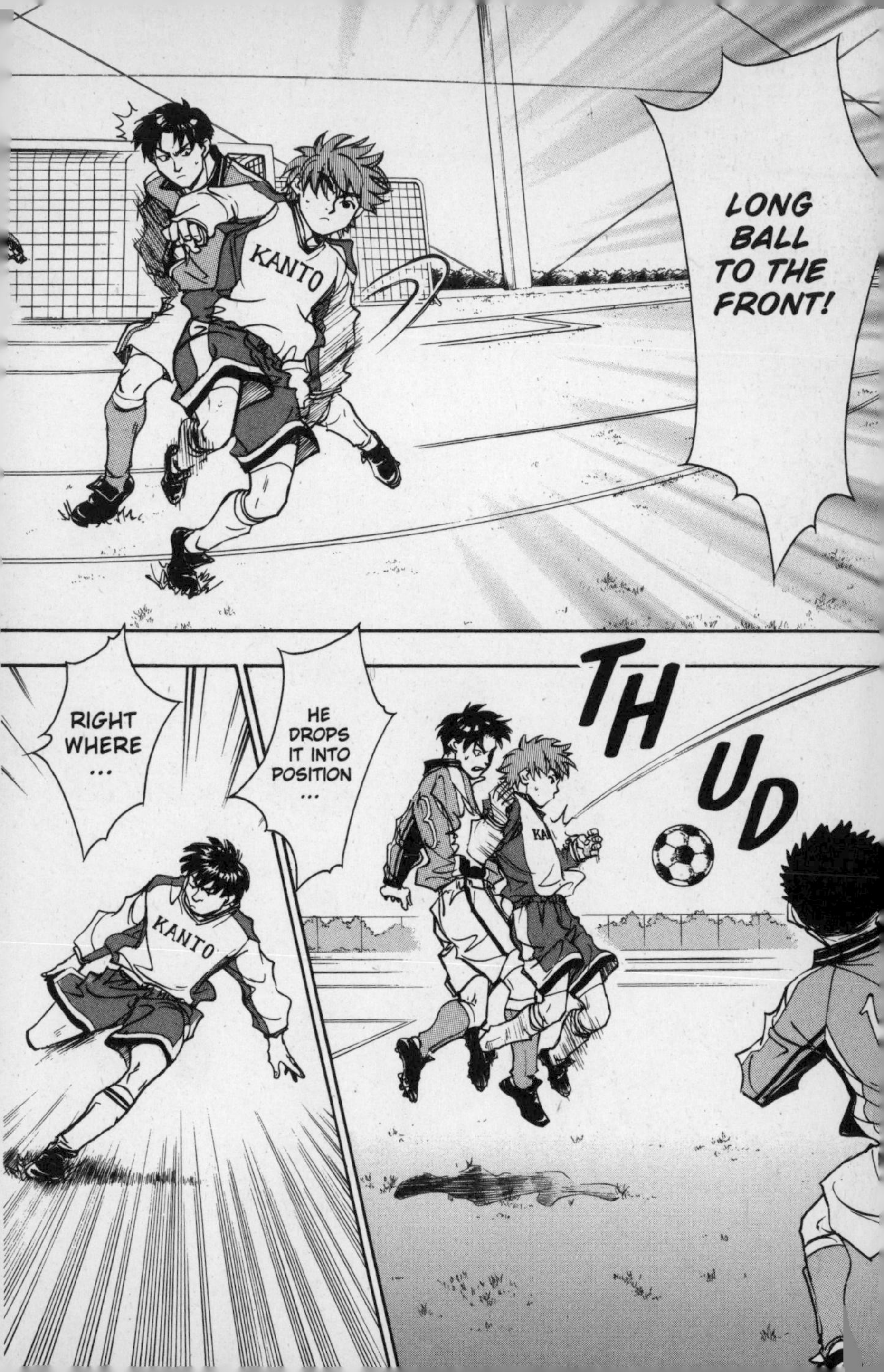
LONG BALL TO THE FRONT!
KANTO
THUD
KANTO
HE DROPS IT INTO POSITION ...
RIGHT WHERE ...
KANTO

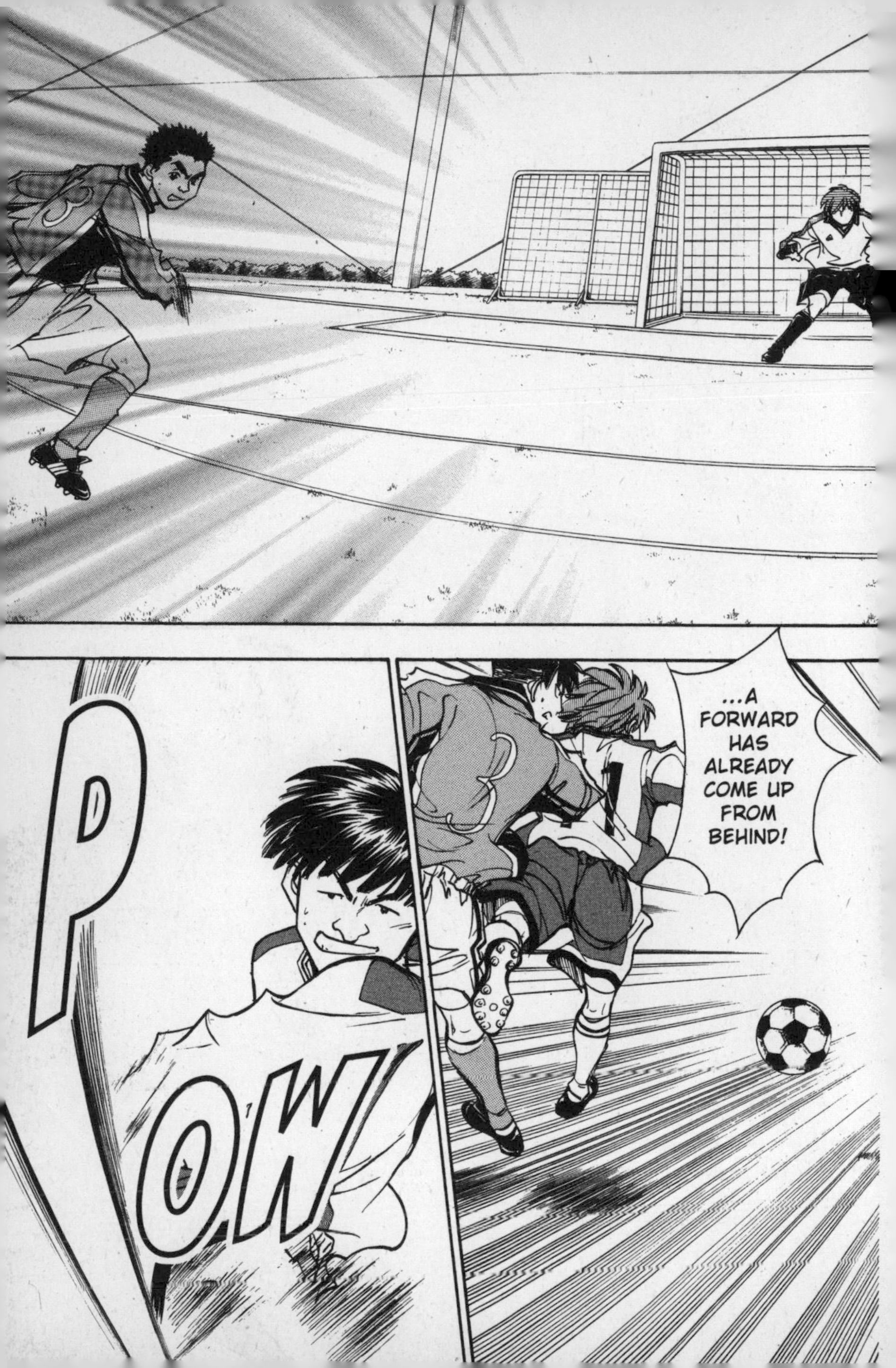
...A FORWARD HAS ALREADY COME UP FROM BEHIND!
POW

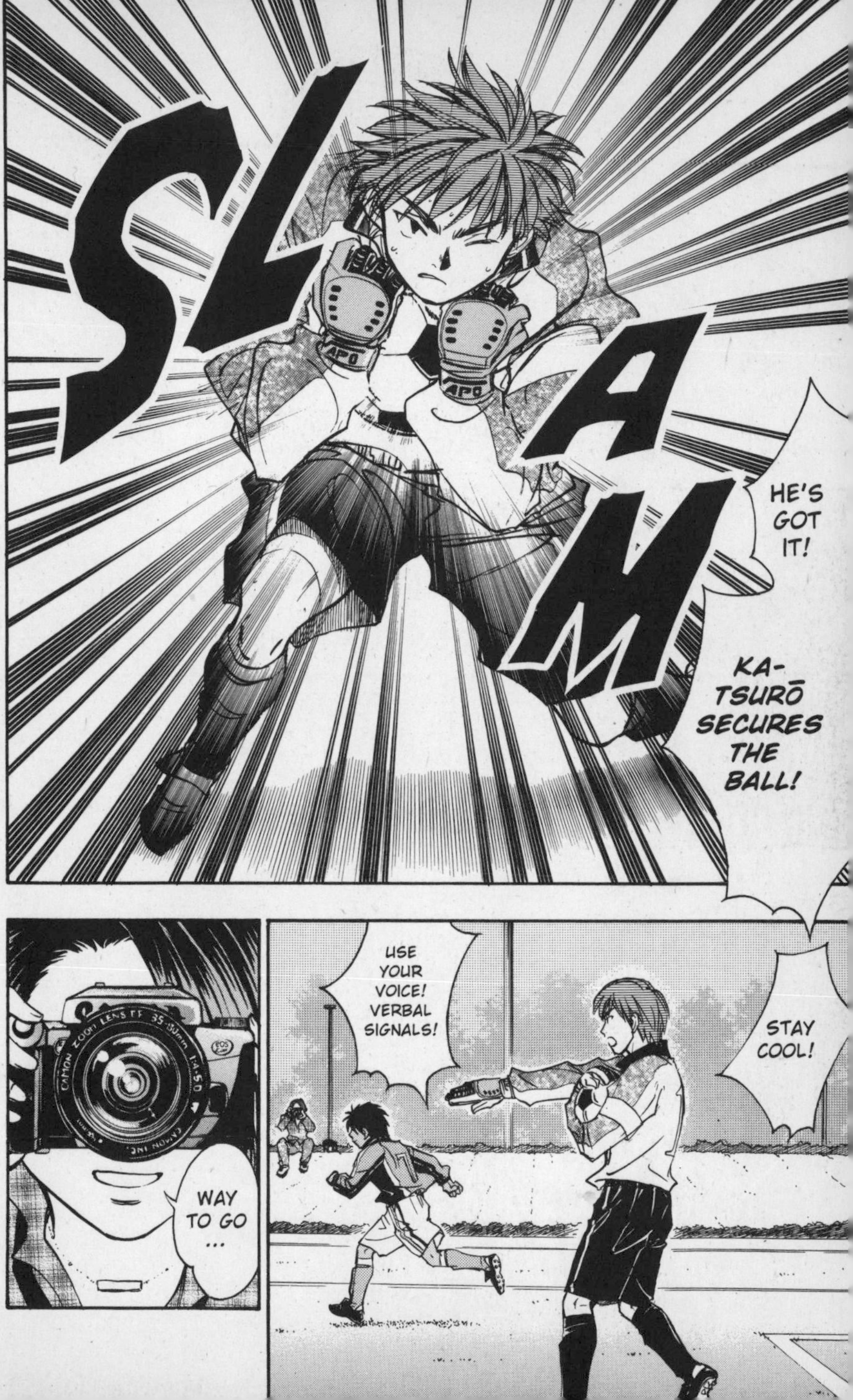
SLAM
HE'S GOT IT!
KA-TSURŌ SECURES THE BALL!
STAY COOL!
USE YOUR VOICE! VERBAL SIGNALS!
WAY TO GO ...

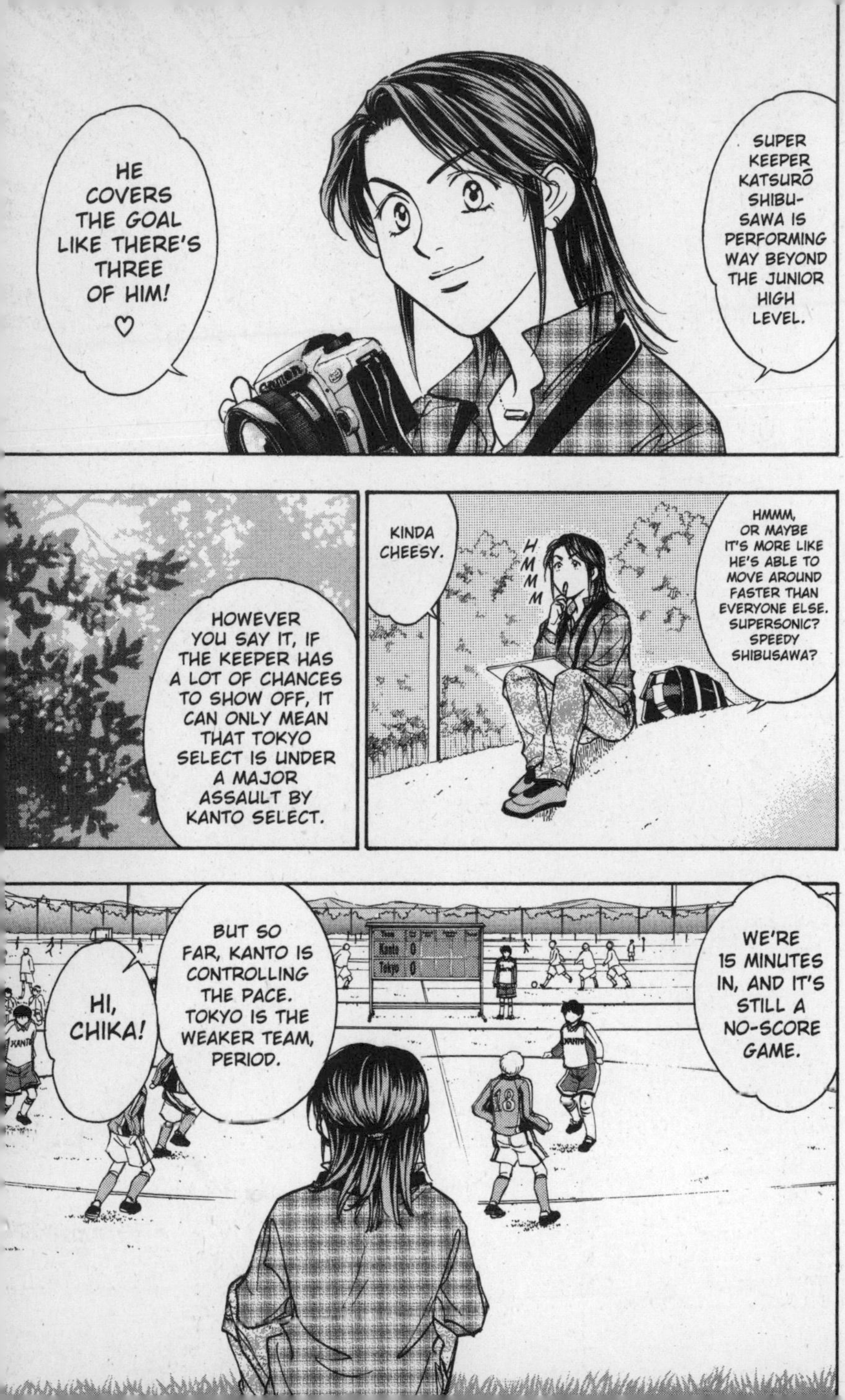
SUPER KEEPER KATSURŌ SHIBU-SAWA IS PERFORMING WAY BEYOND THE JUNIOR HIGH LEVEL.
HE COVERS THE GOAL LIKE THERE'S THREE OF HIM! ♡
HMMM, OR MAYBE IT'S MORE LIKE HE'S ABLE TO MOVE AROUND FASTER THAN EVERYONE ELSE. SUPERSONIC? SPEEDY SHIBUSAWA?
HMMM
KINDA CHEESY.
HOWEVER YOU SAY IT, IF THE KEEPER HAS A LOT OF CHANCES TO SHOW OFF, IT CAN ONLY MEAN THAT TOKYO SELECT IS UNDER A MAJOR ASSAULT BY KANTO SELECT.
WE'RE 15 MINUTES IN, AND IT'S STILL A NO-SCORE GAME.
BUT SO FAR, KANTO IS CONTROLLING THE PACE. TOKYO IS THE WEAKER TEAM, PERIOD.
HI, CHIKA!

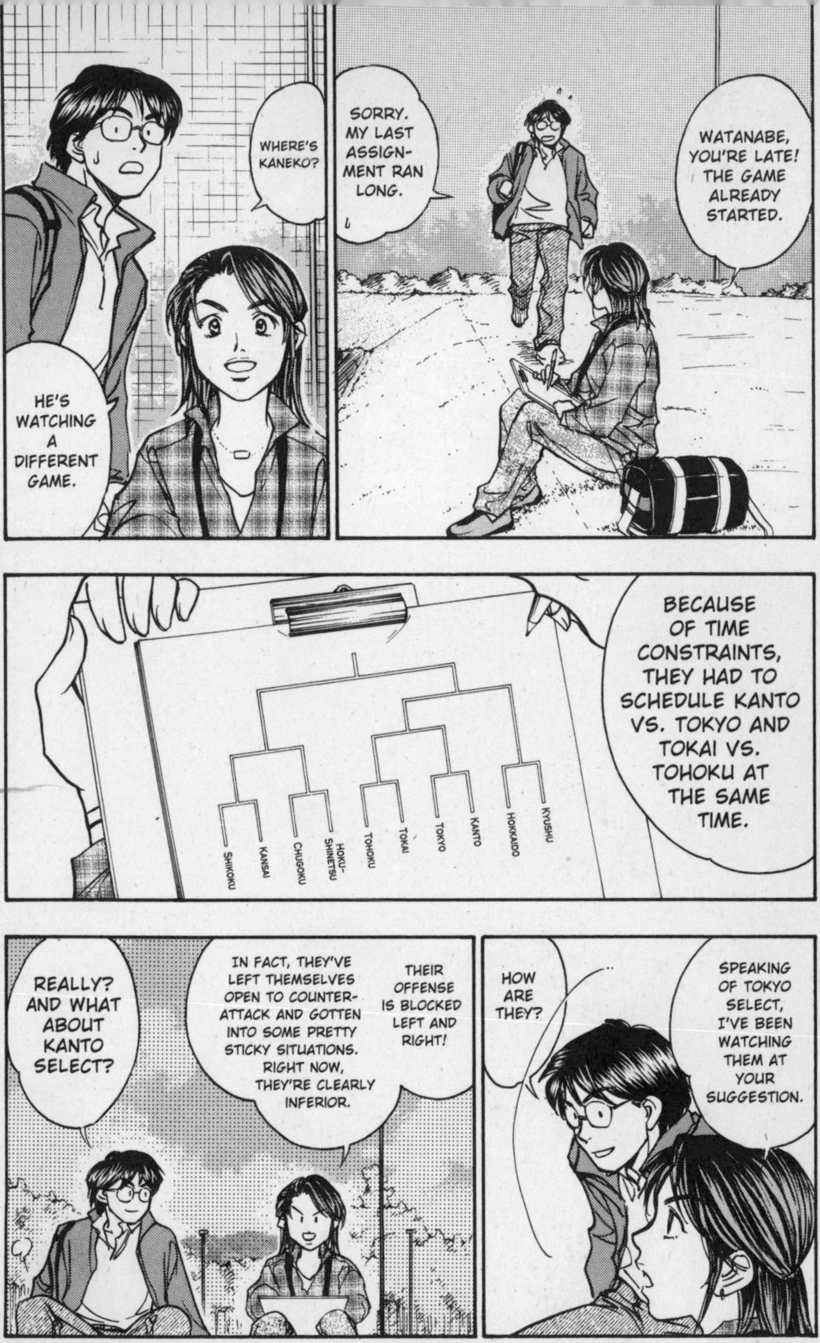
WATANABE, YOU'RE LATE! THE GAME ALREADY STARTED.
SORRY. MY LAST ASSIGNMENT RAN LONG.
WHERE'S KANEKO?
HE'S WATCHING A DIFFERENT GAME.
BECAUSE OF TIME CONSTRAINTS, THEY HAD TO SCHEDULE KANTO VS. TOKYO AND TOKAI VS. TOHOKU AT THE SAME TIME.
KYUSHU
HOKKAIDO
KANTO
TOKYO
TOKAI
TOHOKU
HOKU-SHINETSU
CHUGOKU
KANSAI
SHIKOKU
SPEAKING OF TOKYO SELECT, I'VE BEEN WATCHING THEM AT YOUR SUGGESTION.
...
HOW ARE THEY?
THEIR OFFENSE IS BLOCKED LEFT AND RIGHT!
IN FACT, THEY'VE LEFT THEMSELVES OPEN TO COUNTER-ATTACK AND GOTTEN INTO SOME PRETTY STICKY SITUATIONS. RIGHT NOW, THEY'RE CLEARLY INFERIOR.
REALLY? AND WHAT ABOUT KANTO SELECT?

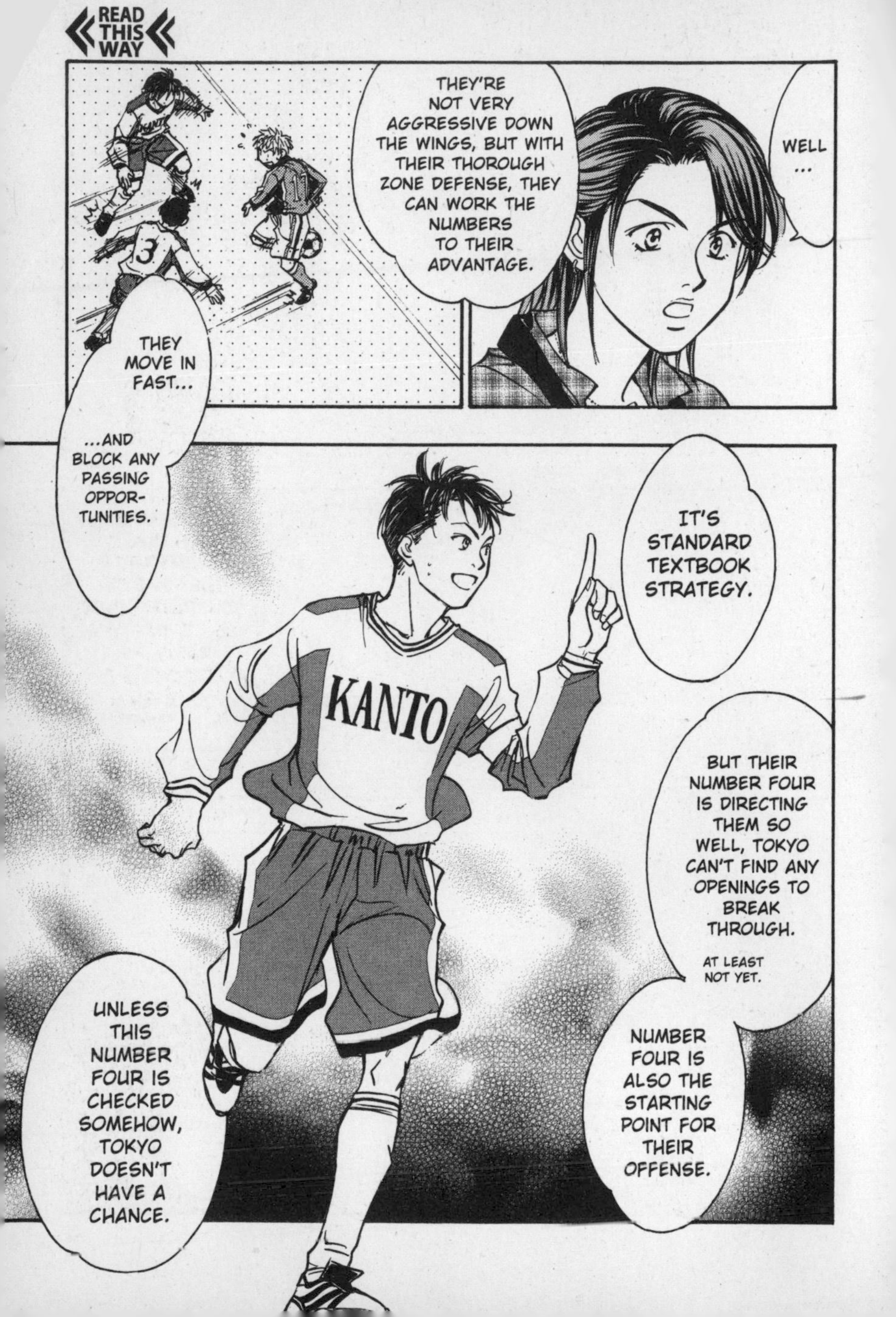
READ THIS WAY
WELL ...
THEY'RE NOT VERY AGGRESSIVE DOWN THE WINGS, BUT WITH THEIR THOROUGH ZONE DEFENSE, THEY CAN WORK THE NUMBERS TO THEIR ADVANTAGE.
THEY MOVE IN FAST...
...AND BLOCK ANY PASSING OPPOR-TUNITIES.
KANTO
IT'S STANDARD TEXTBOOK STRATEGY.
BUT THEIR NUMBER FOUR IS DIRECTING THEM SO WELL, TOKYO CAN'T FIND ANY OPENINGS TO BREAK THROUGH.
AT LEAST NOT YET.
NUMBER FOUR IS ALSO THE STARTING POINT FOR THEIR OFFENSE.
UNLESS THIS NUMBER FOUR IS CHECKED SOMEHOW, TOKYO DOESN'T HAVE A CHANCE.

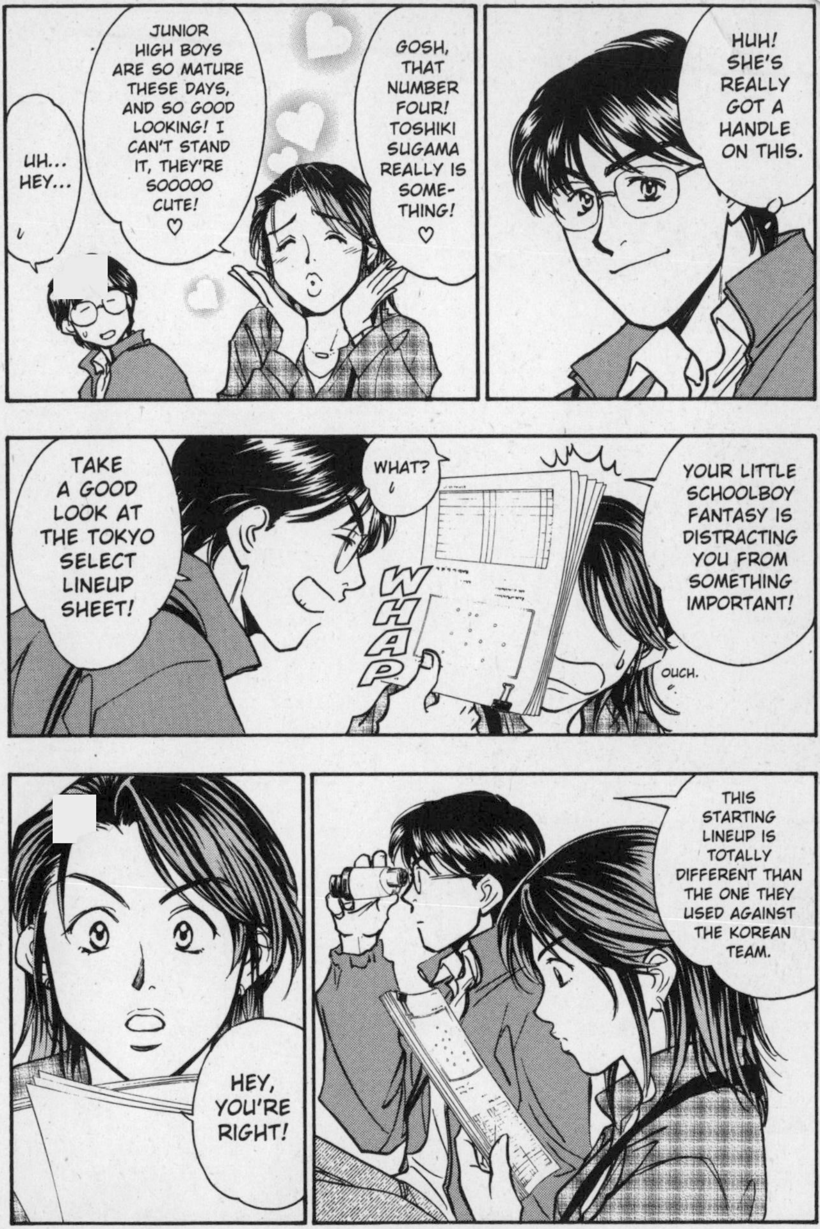
HUH! SHE'S REALLY GOT A HANDLE ON THIS.
GOSH, THAT NUMBER FOUR! TOSHIKI SUGAMA REALLY IS SOME-THING! ♡
JUNIOR HIGH BOYS ARE SO MATURE THESE DAYS, AND SO GOOD LOOKING! I CAN'T STAND IT, THEY'RE SOOOOO CUTE! ♡
UH... HEY...
YOUR LITTLE SCHOOLBOY FANTASY IS DISTRACTING YOU FROM SOMETHING IMPORTANT!
WHAT?
TAKE A GOOD LOOK AT THE TOKYO SELECT LINEUP SHEET!
WHAP
OUCH.
THIS STARTING LINEUP IS TOTALLY DIFFERENT THAN THE ONE THEY USED AGAINST THE KOREAN TEAM.
HEY, YOU'RE RIGHT!

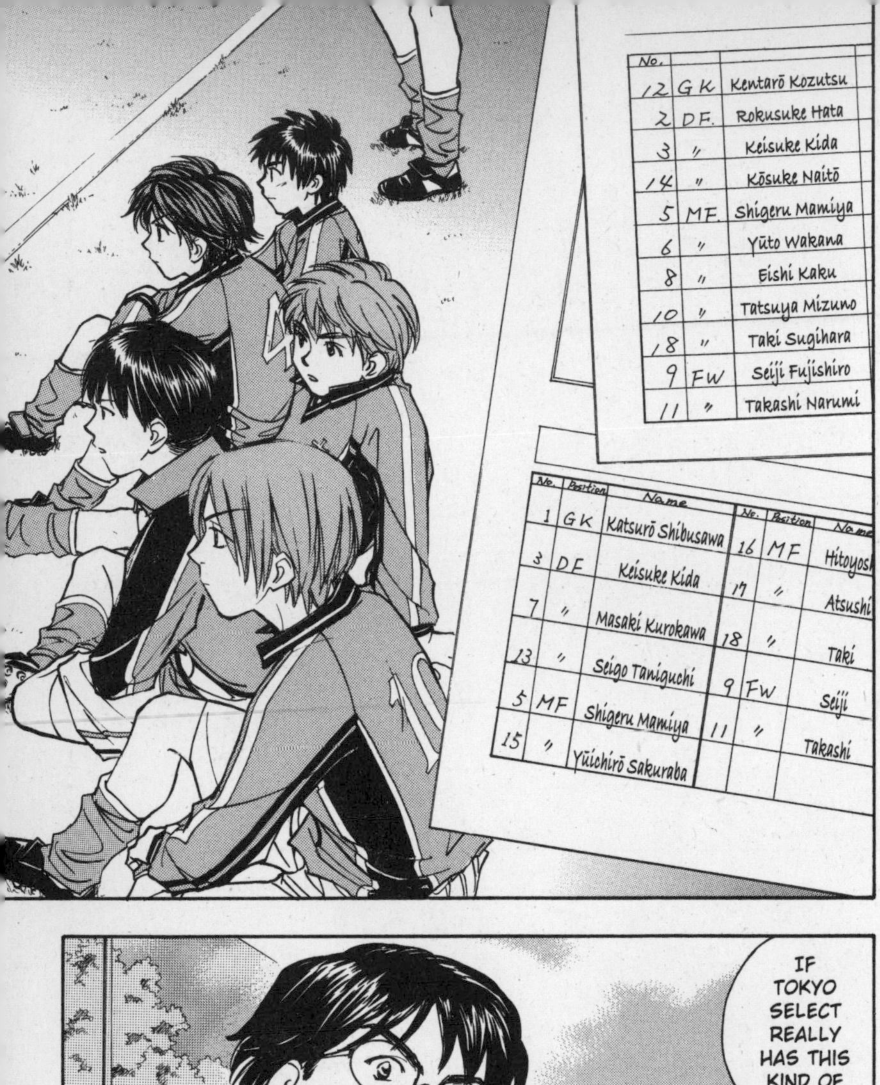
No.
12 GK Kentarō Kozutsu
2 DF. Rokusuke Hata
3 " Keisuke Kida
14 " Kōsuke Naitō
5 MF. Shigeru Mamiya
6 " Yūto Wakana
8 " Eishi Kaku
10 " Tatsuya Mizuno
18 " Taki Sugihara
9 FW Seiji Fujishiro
11 " Takashi Narumi
No. Position Name
1 GK Katsurō Shibusawa
3 DF Keisuke Kida
7 " Masaki Kurokawa
13 " Seigo Taniguchi
5 MF Shigeru Mamiya
15 " Yūichirō Sakuraba
No. Position Name
16 MF Hitoyosh
17 " Atsushi
18 " Taki
9 FW Seiji
11 " Takashi

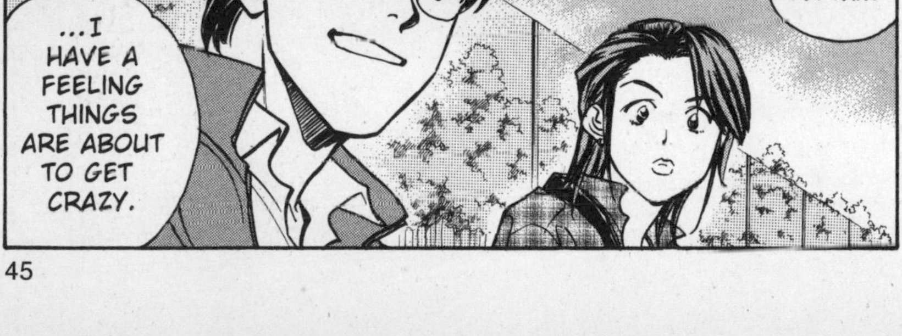
IF TOKYO SELECT REALLY HAS THIS KIND OF DEPTH...
...I HAVE A FEELING THINGS ARE ABOUT TO GET CRAZY.

WHISTLE!

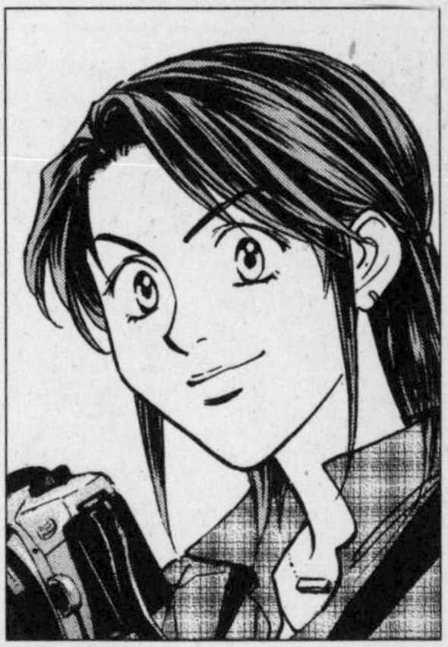

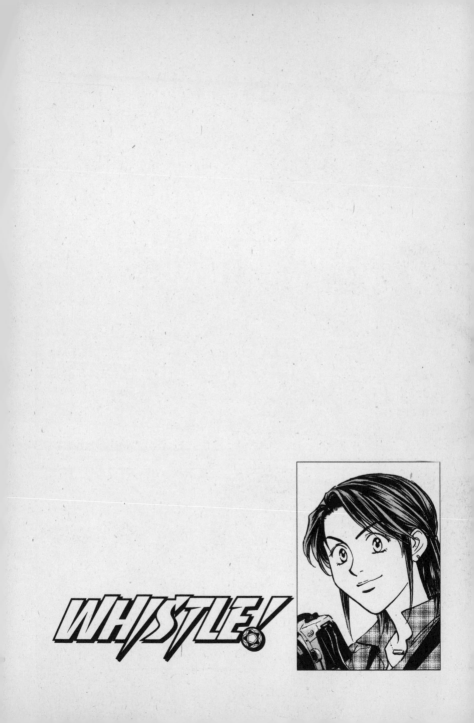

STAGE.175 The Secret Strategy to Conquer Kanto

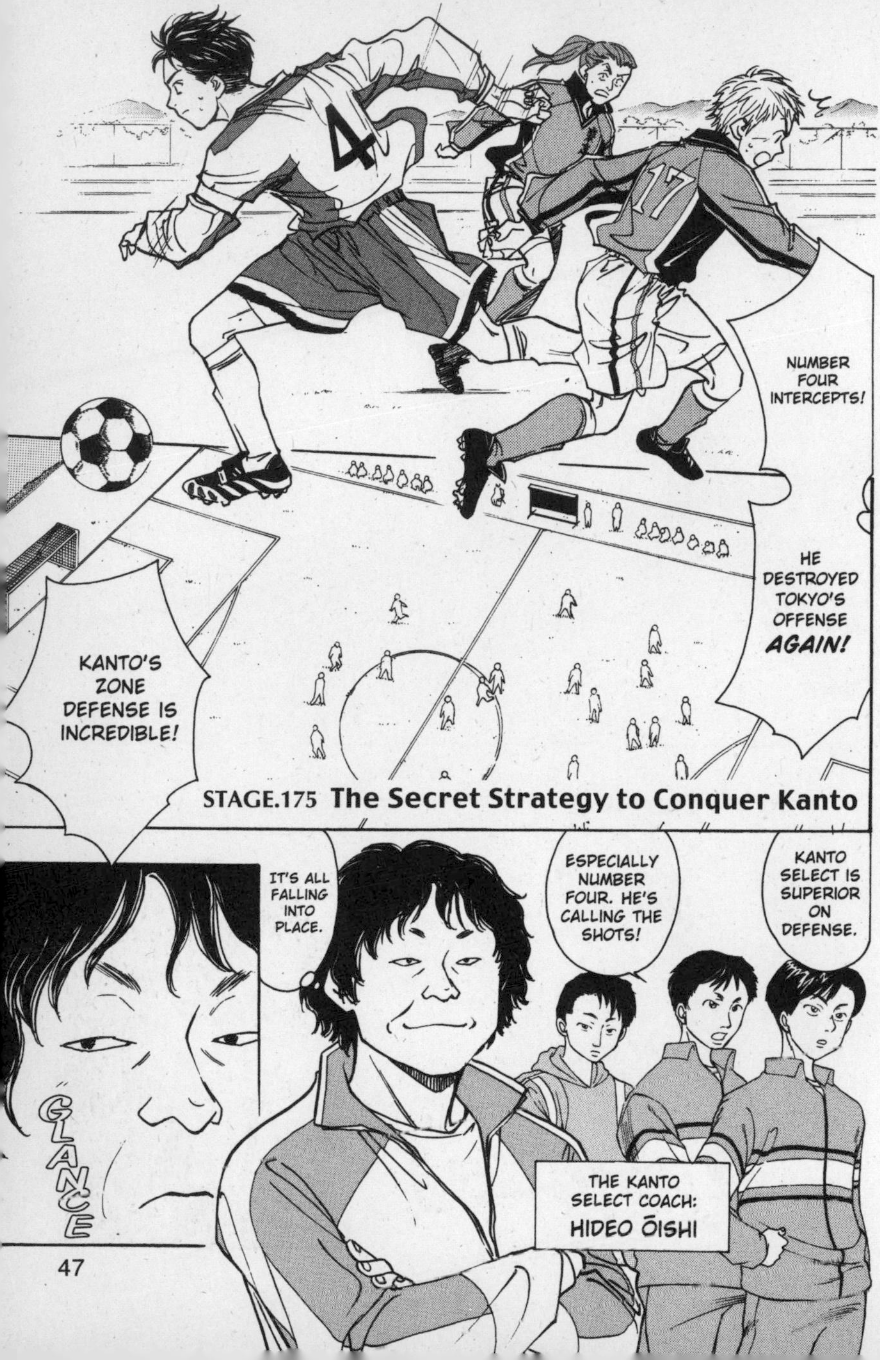

NUMBER FOUR INTERCEPTS!
HE DESTROYED TOKYO'S OFFENSE AGAIN!
KANTO'S ZONE DEFENSE IS INCREDIBLE!
STAGE.175 The Secret Strategy to Conquer Kanto
KANTO SELECT IS SUPERIOR ON DEFENSE.
ESPECIALLY NUMBER FOUR. HE'S CALLING THE SHOTS!
IT'S ALL FALLING INTO PLACE.
THE KANTO SELECT COACH: HIDEO ŌISHI
GLANCE

STAGE.175 The Secret Strategy to Conquer Kanto

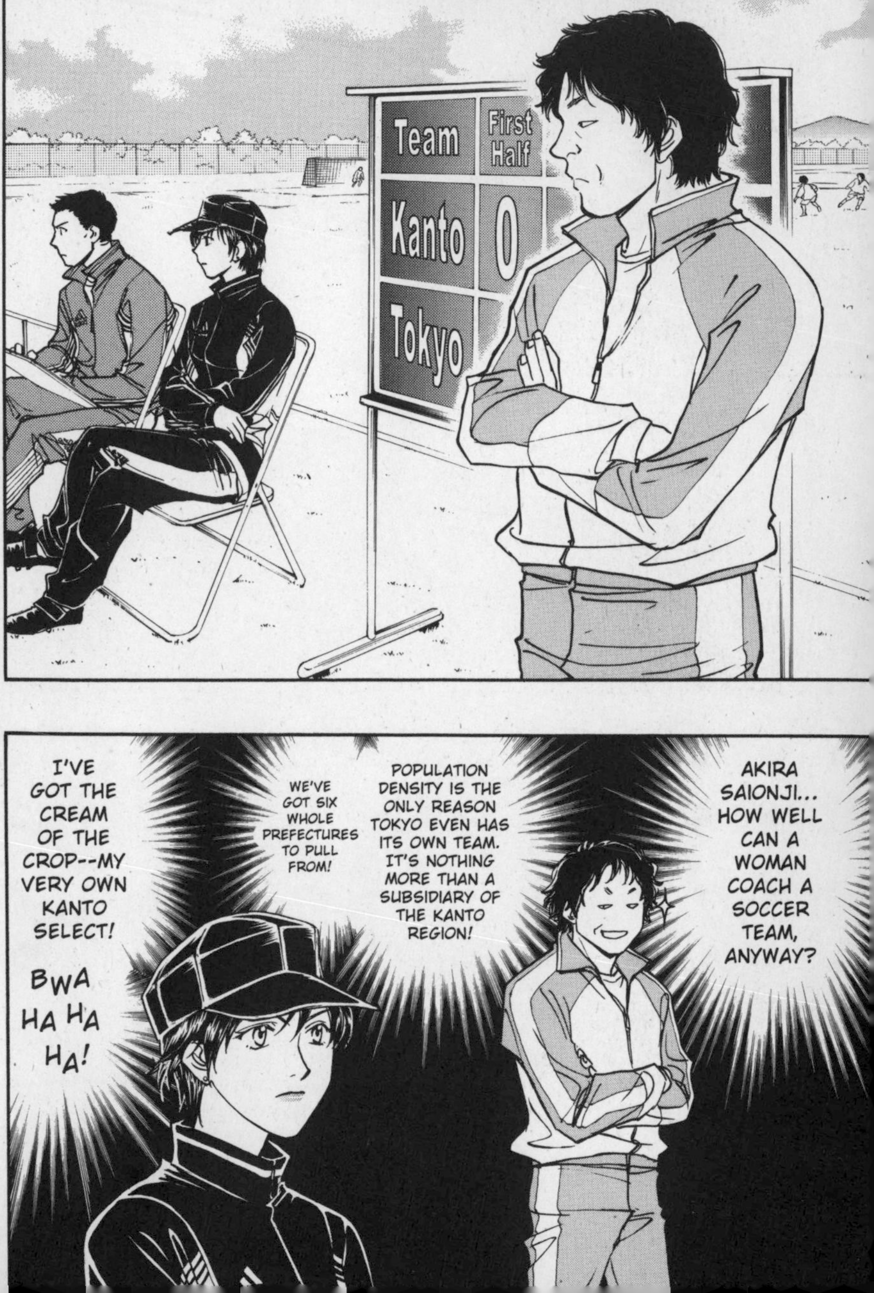
Team
First Half
Kanto
0
Tokyo
AKIRA SAIONJI... HOW WELL CAN A WOMAN COACH A SOCCER TEAM, ANYWAY?
POPULATION DENSITY IS THE ONLY REASON TOKYO EVEN HAS ITS OWN TEAM. IT'S NOTHING MORE THAN A SUBSIDIARY OF THE KANTO REGION!
WE'VE GOT SIX WHOLE PREFECTURES TO PULL FROM!
I'VE GOT THE CREAM OF THE CROP--MY VERY OWN KANTO SELECT!
BWA HA HA HA!

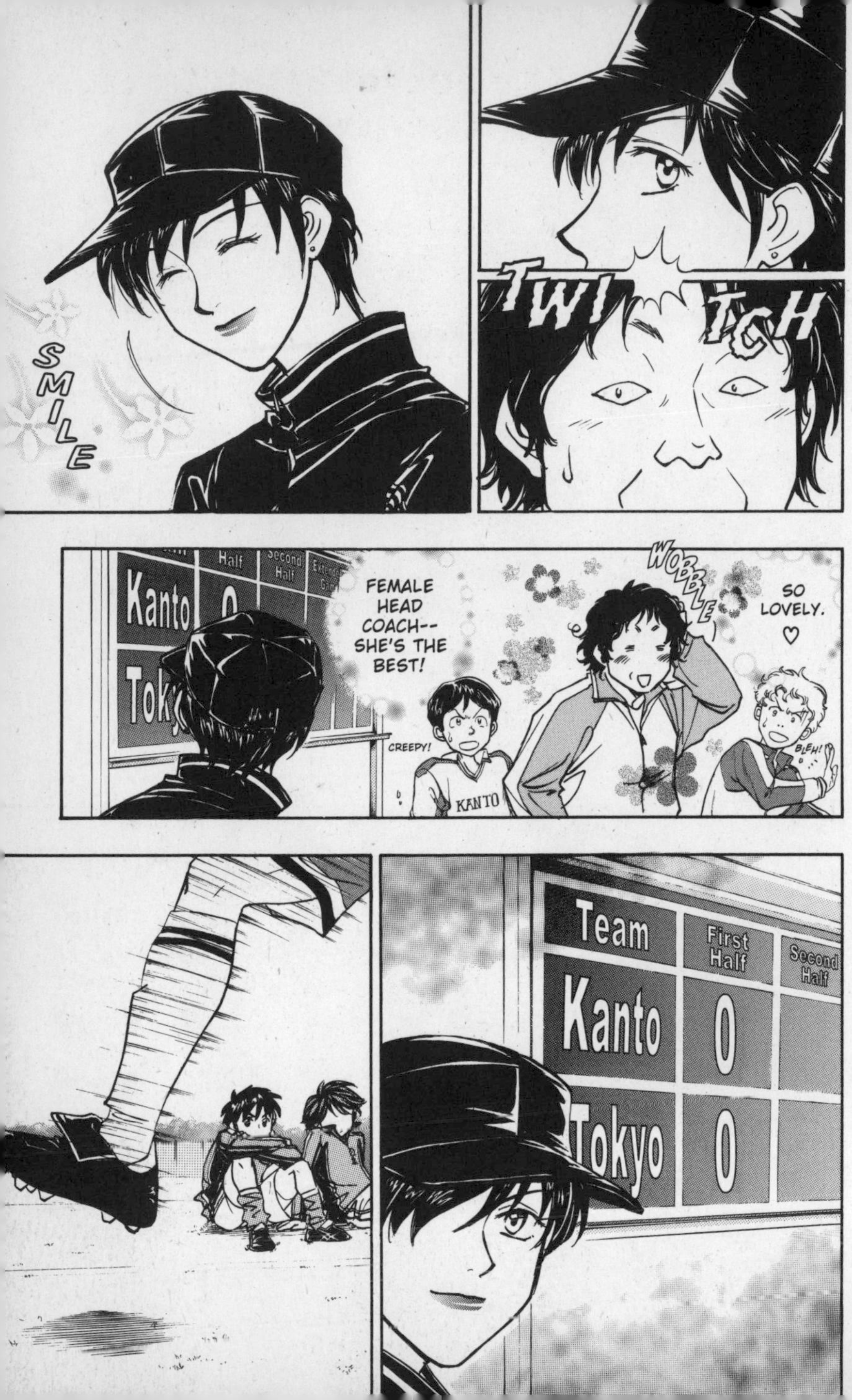
TWITCH
SMILE
SO LOVELY. ♡
BLEH!
WOBBLE
FEMALE HEAD COACH--SHE'S THE BEST!
CREEPY!
KANTO
Team
First Half
Second Half
Kanto
0
Tokyo
0

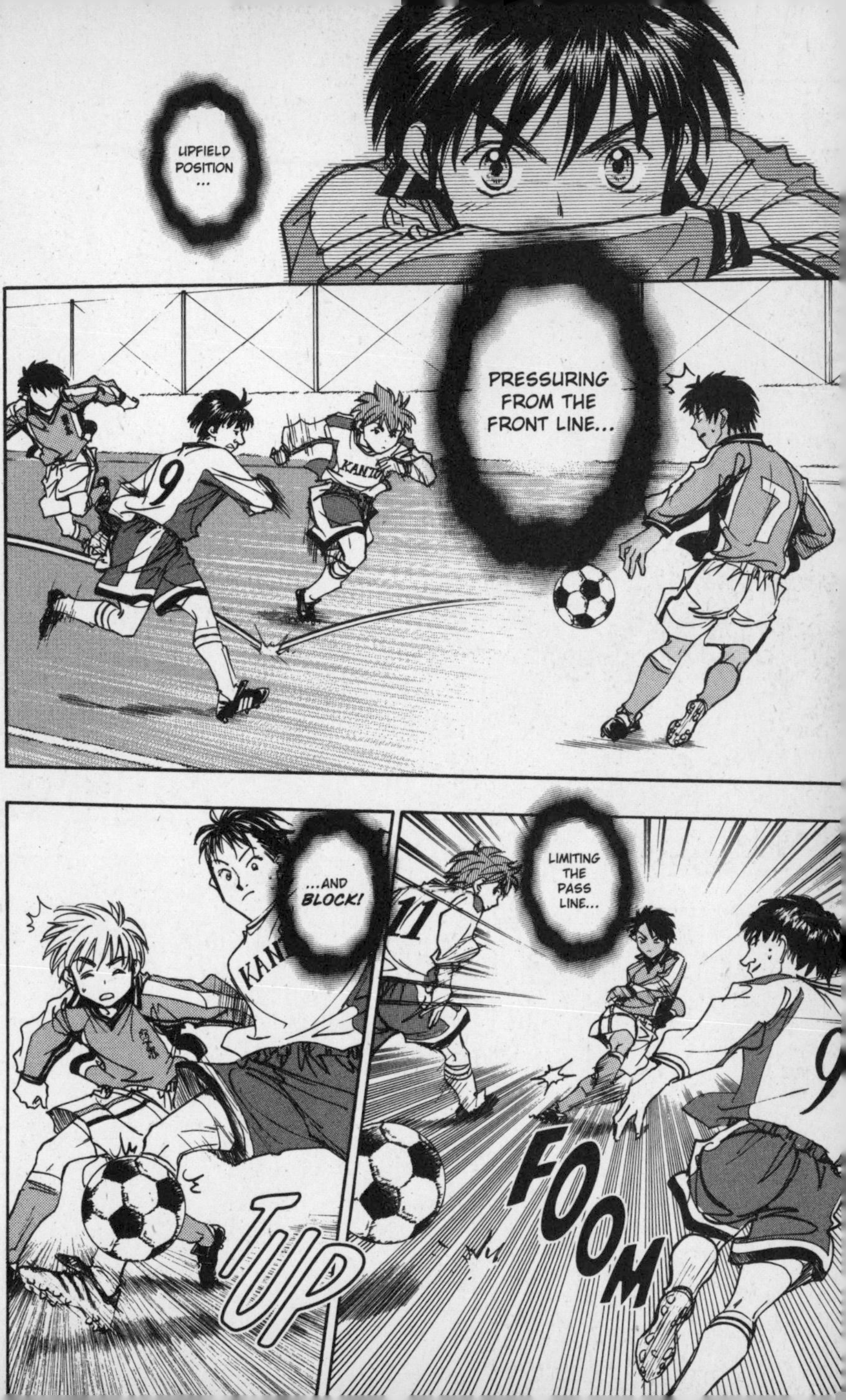
UPFIELD POSITION ...
PRESSURING FROM THE FRONT LINE...
LIMITING THE PASS LINE...
FOOM
...AND BLOCK!
TUP

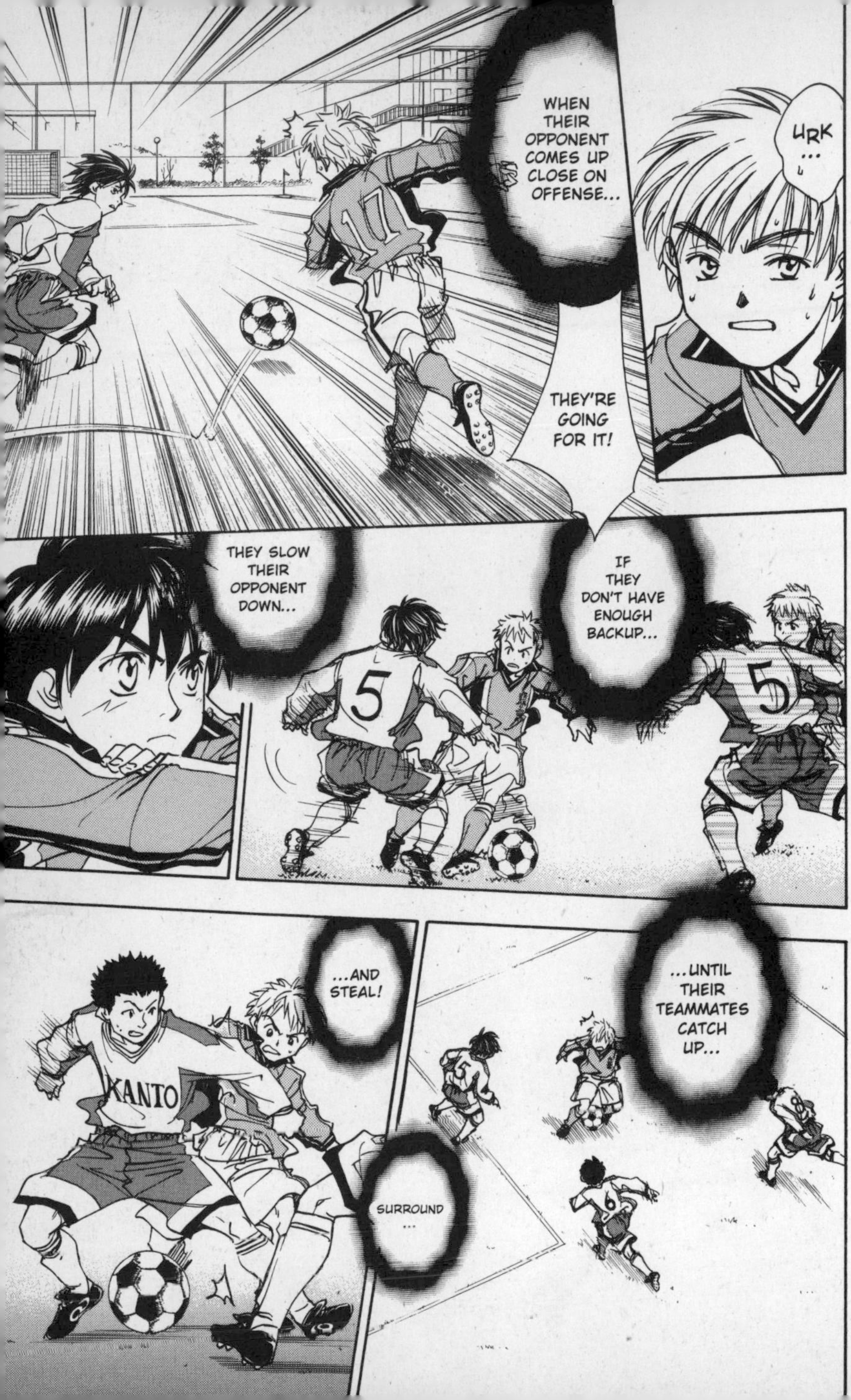
URK...
WHEN THEIR OPPONENT COMES UP CLOSE ON OFFENSE...
THEY'RE GOING FOR IT!
IF THEY DON'T HAVE ENOUGH BACKUP...
THEY SLOW THEIR OPPONENT DOWN...
...UNTIL THEIR TEAMMATES CATCH UP...
SURROUND...
...AND STEAL!
KANTO

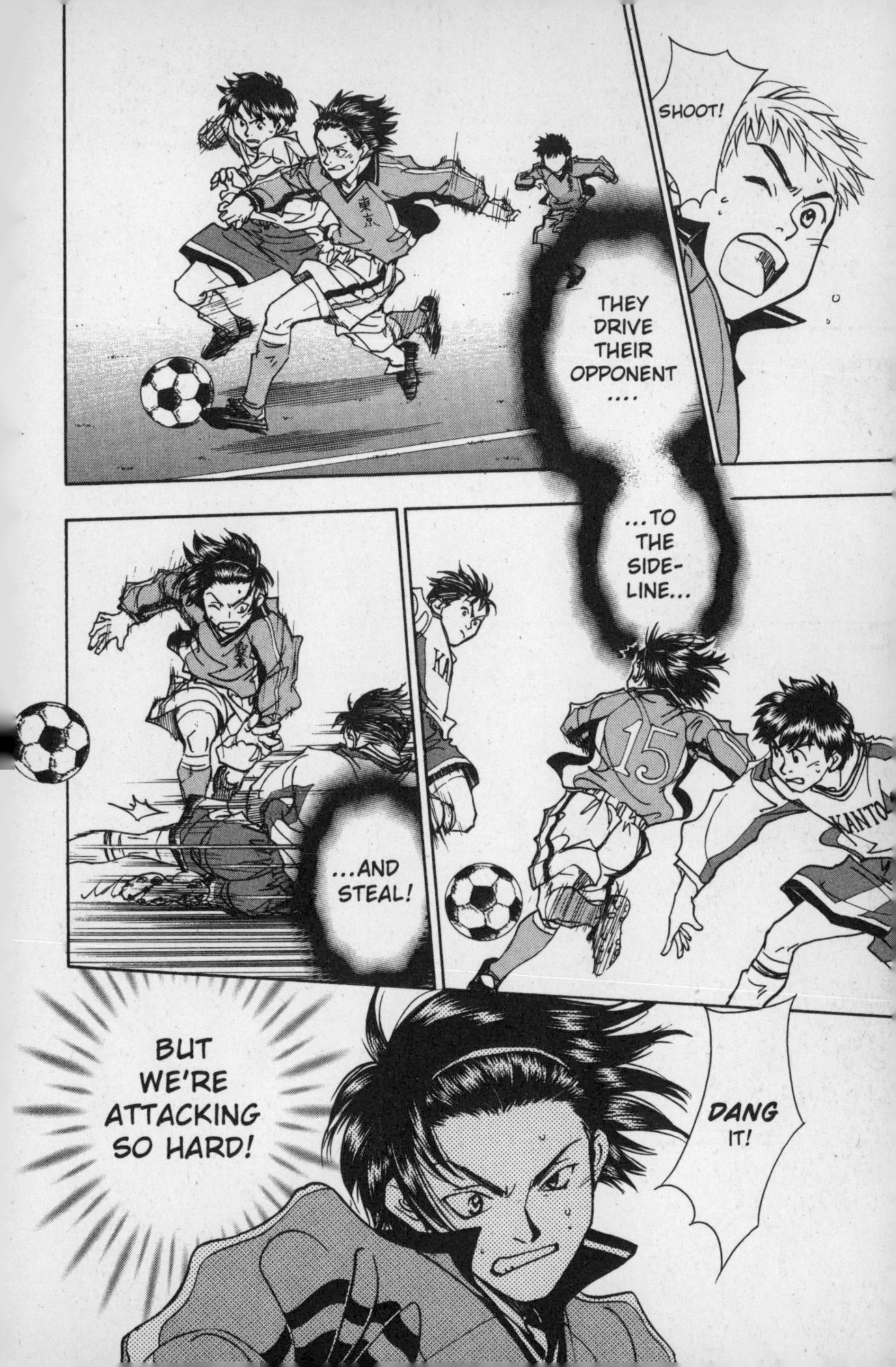
SHOOT!
THEY DRIVE THEIR OPPONENT ....
...TO THE SIDE-LINE...
...AND STEAL!
DANG IT!
BUT WE'RE ATTACKING SO HARD!

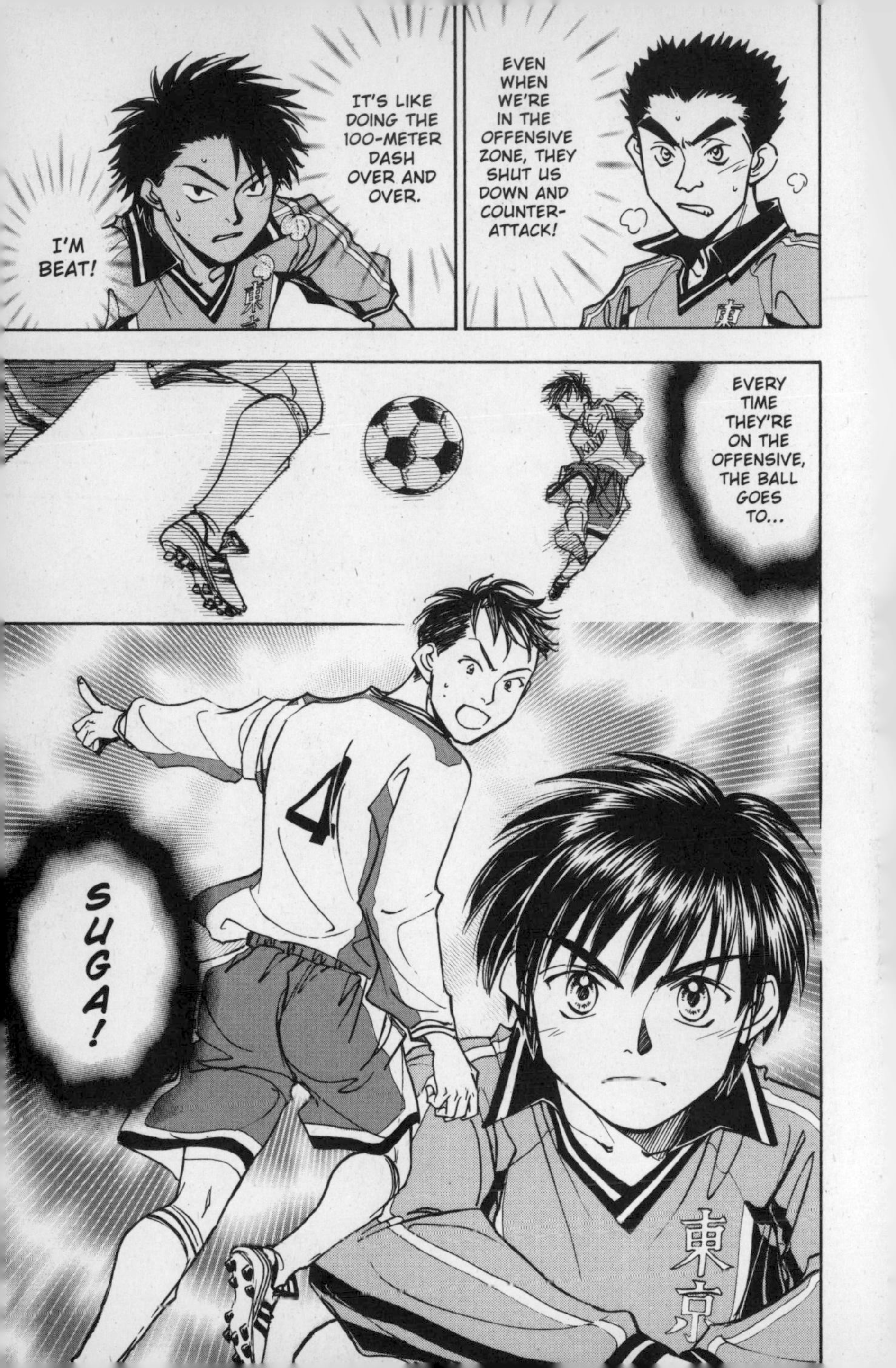
EVEN WHEN WE'RE IN THE OFFENSIVE ZONE, THEY SHUT US DOWN AND COUNTER-ATTACK!
IT'S LIKE DOING THE 100-METER DASH OVER AND OVER.
I'M BEAT!
EVERY TIME THEY'RE ON THE OFFENSIVE, THE BALL GOES TO...
SUGA!

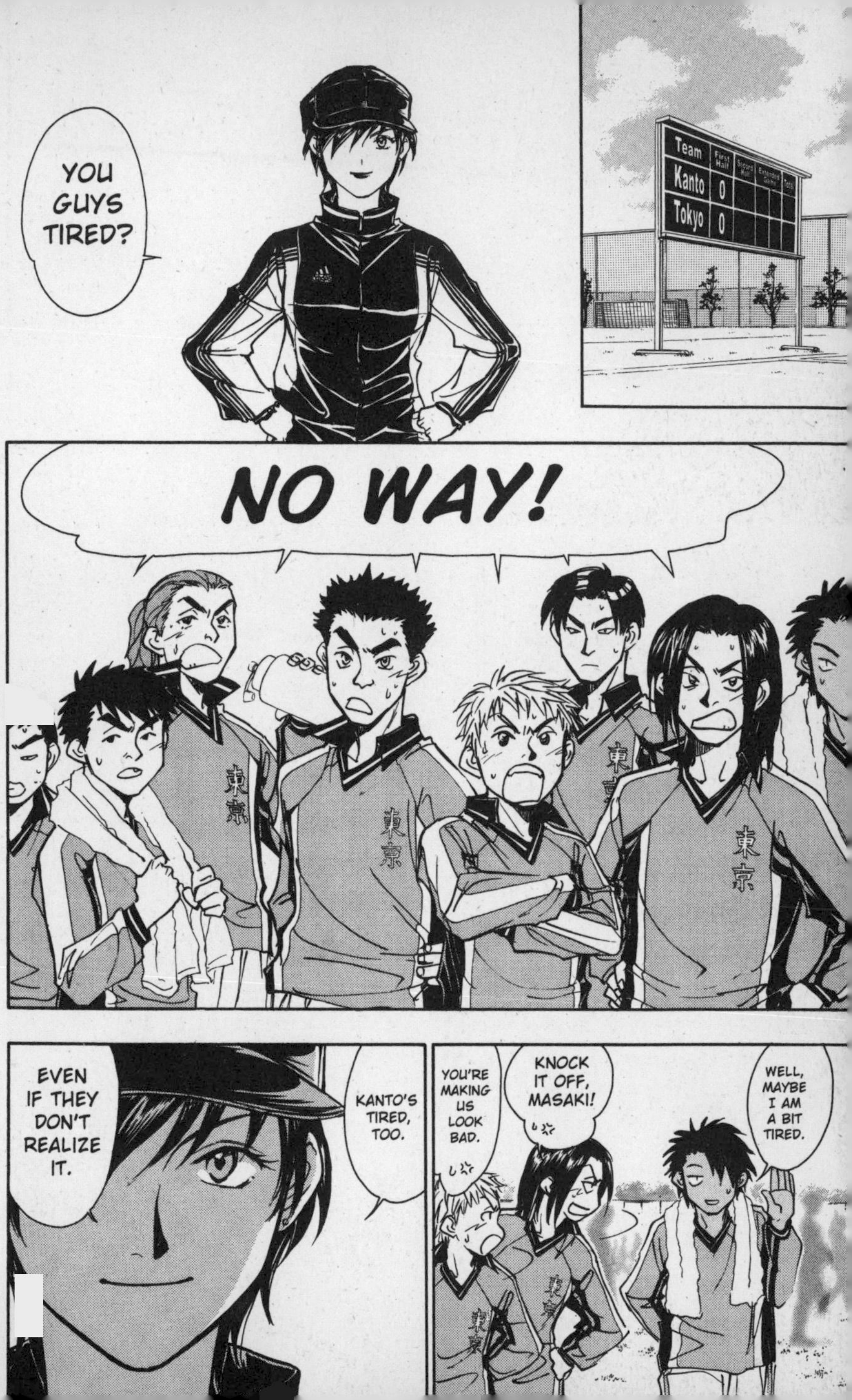

Team
First Half
Kanto 0
Tokyo 0
YOU GUYS TIRED?
NO WAY!
WELL, MAYBE I AM A BIT TIRED.
KNOCK IT OFF, MASAKI!
YOU'RE MAKING US LOOK BAD.
KANTO'S TIRED, TOO.
EVEN IF THEY DON'T REALIZE IT.

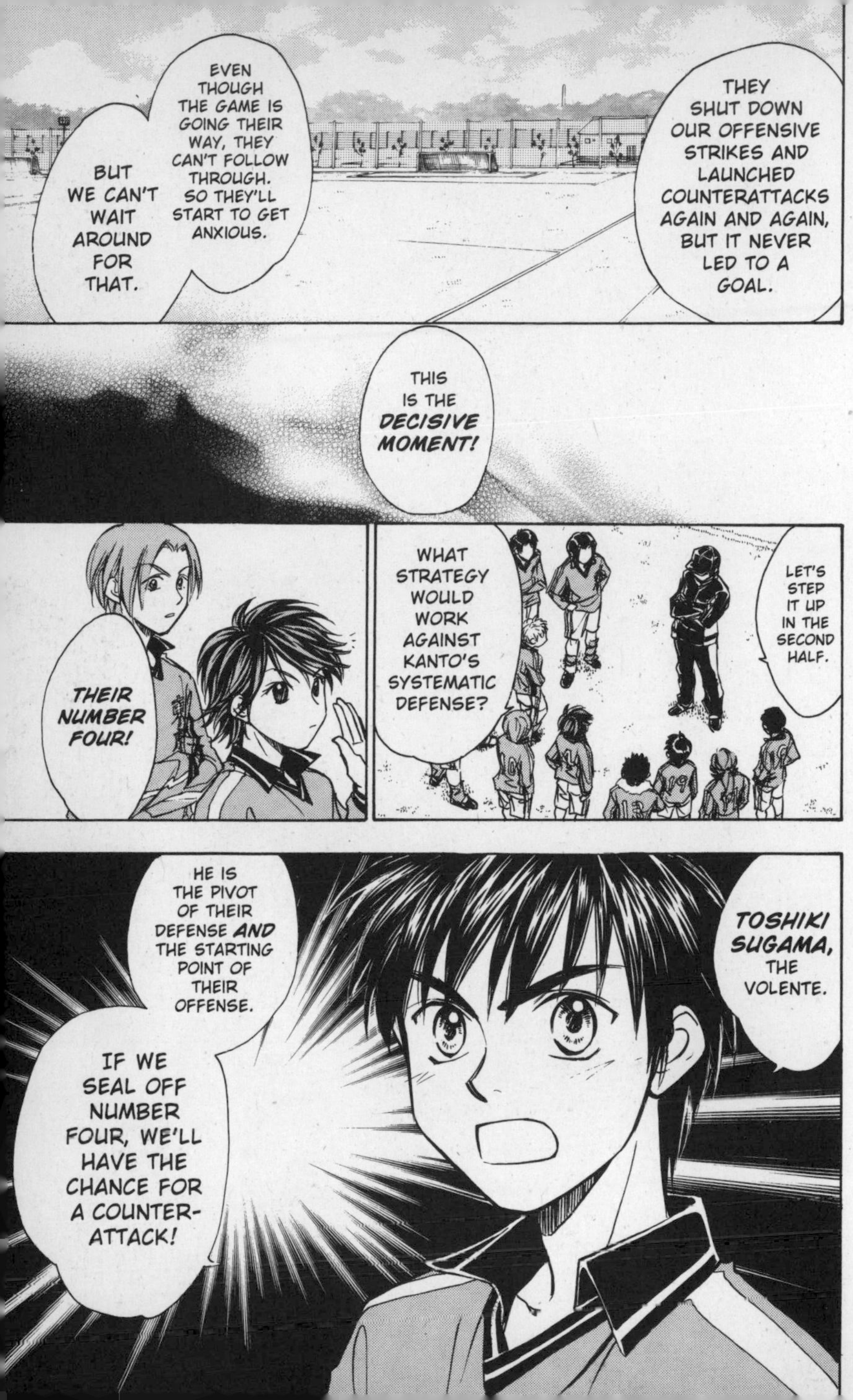
THEY SHUT DOWN OUR OFFENSIVE STRIKES AND LAUNCHED COUNTERATTACKS AGAIN AND AGAIN, BUT IT NEVER LED TO A GOAL.
EVEN THOUGH THE GAME IS GOING THEIR WAY, THEY CAN'T FOLLOW THROUGH. SO THEY'LL START TO GET ANXIOUS.
BUT WE CAN'T WAIT AROUND FOR THAT.
THIS IS THE *DECISIVE MOMENT!*
LET'S STEP IT UP IN THE SECOND HALF.
WHAT STRATEGY WOULD WORK AGAINST KANTO'S SYSTEMATIC DEFENSE?
THEIR NUMBER FOUR!
TOSHIKI SUGAMA, THE VOLENTE.
HE IS THE PIVOT OF THEIR DEFENSE *AND* THE STARTING POINT OF THEIR OFFENSE.
IF WE SEAL OFF NUMBER FOUR, WE'LL HAVE THE CHANCE FOR A COUNTER-ATTACK!

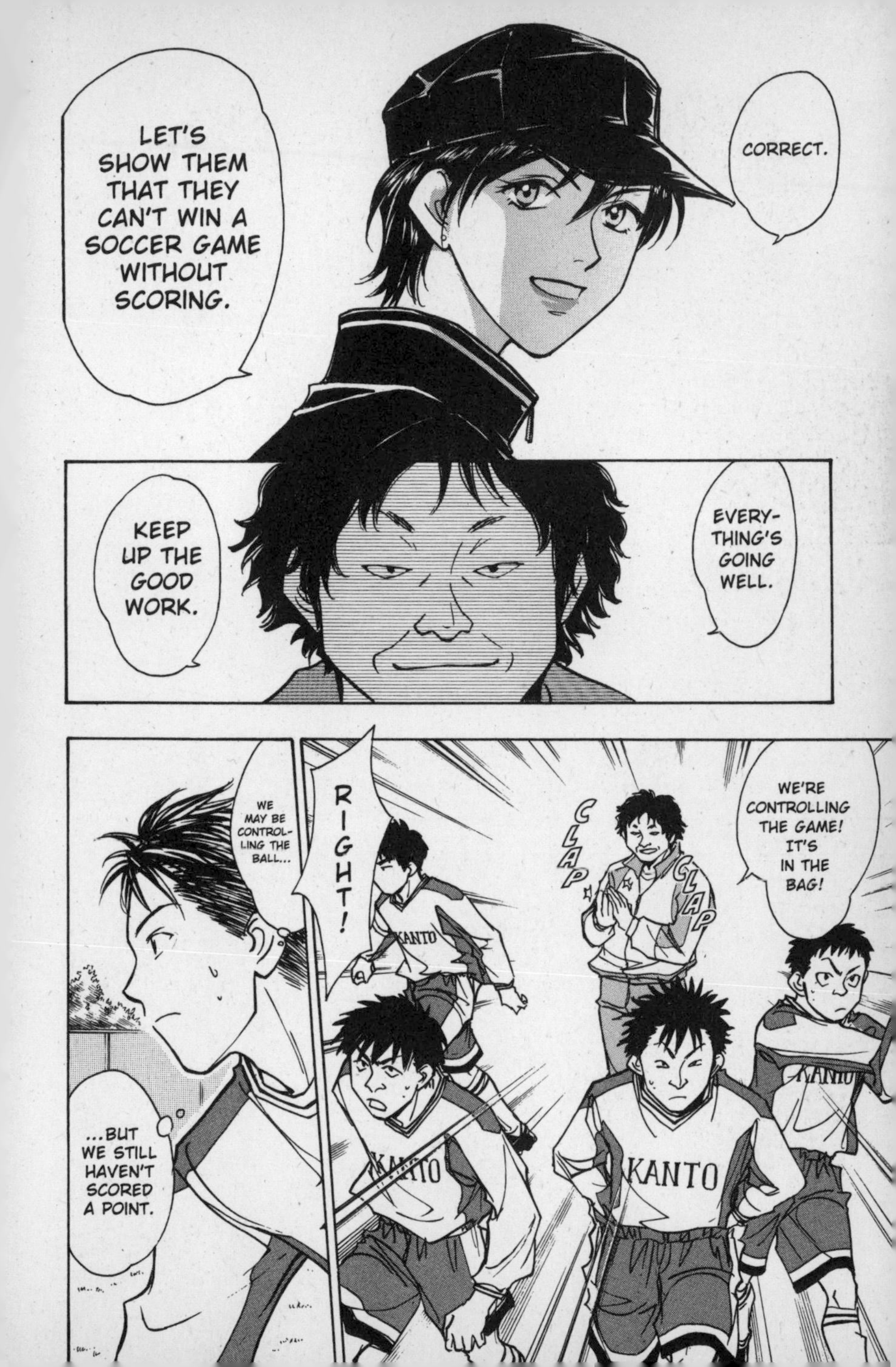
CORRECT.
LET'S SHOW THEM THAT THEY CAN'T WIN A SOCCER GAME WITHOUT SCORING.
EVERY-THING'S GOING WELL.
KEEP UP THE GOOD WORK.
WE'RE CONTROLLING THE GAME! IT'S IN THE BAG!
CLAP CLAP
RIGHT!
WE MAY BE CONTROL-LING THE BALL...
...BUT WE STILL HAVEN'T SCORED A POINT.

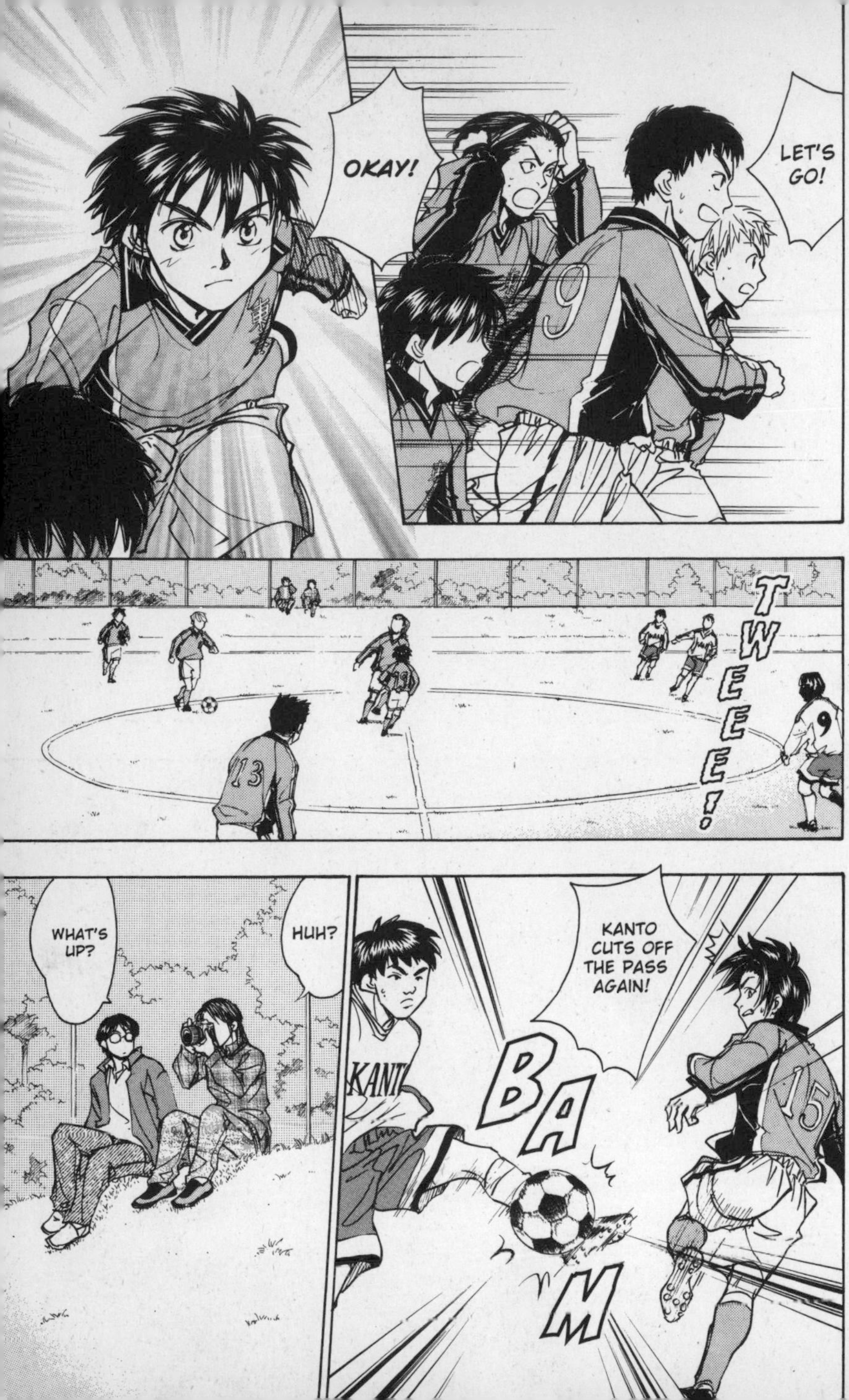
LET'S GO!
OKAY!
TWEEEE!
KANTO CUTS OFF THE PASS AGAIN!
BAM
KANTO
HUH?
WHAT'S UP?

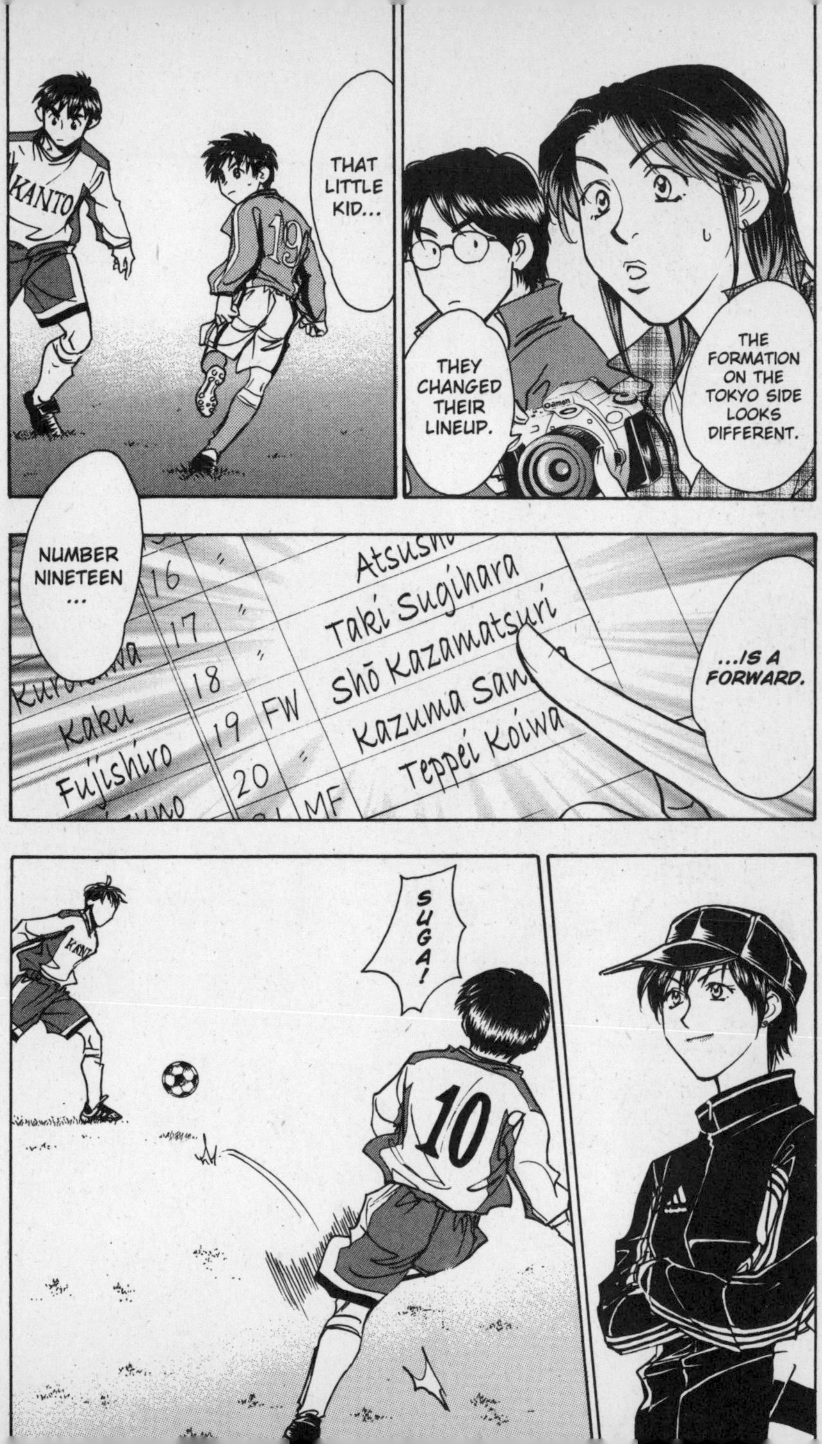
THE FORMATION ON THE TOKYO SIDE LOOKS DIFFERENT.
THEY CHANGED THEIR LINEUP.
THAT LITTLE KID...
NUMBER NINETEEN ...
16 Taki Sugihara
17 Shō Kazamatsuri
Kaku 18
Fujishiro 19 FW
20 Teppei Koiwa
...IS A FORWARD.
SUGA!

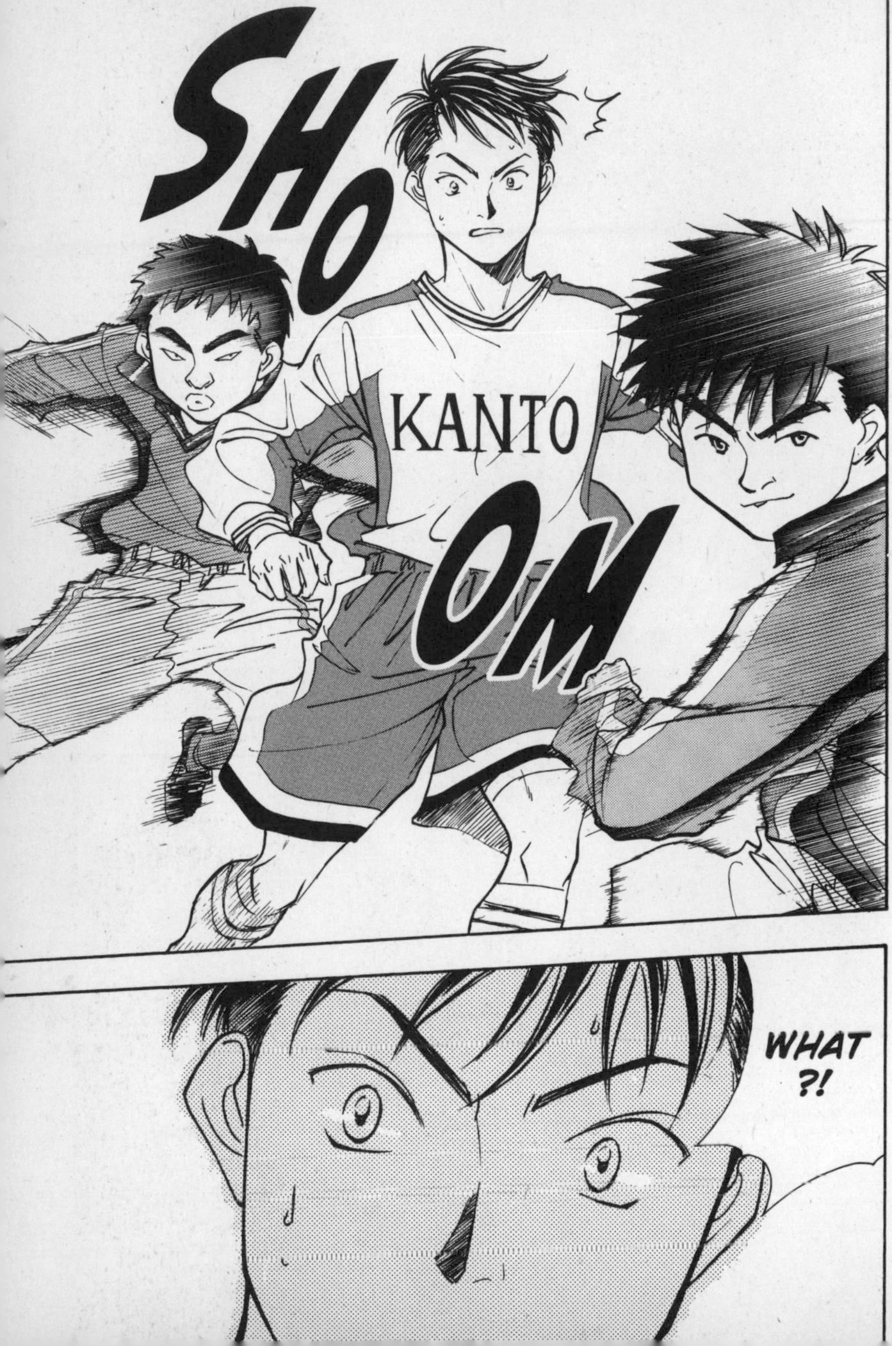
SHOOM
KANTO
WHAT ?!

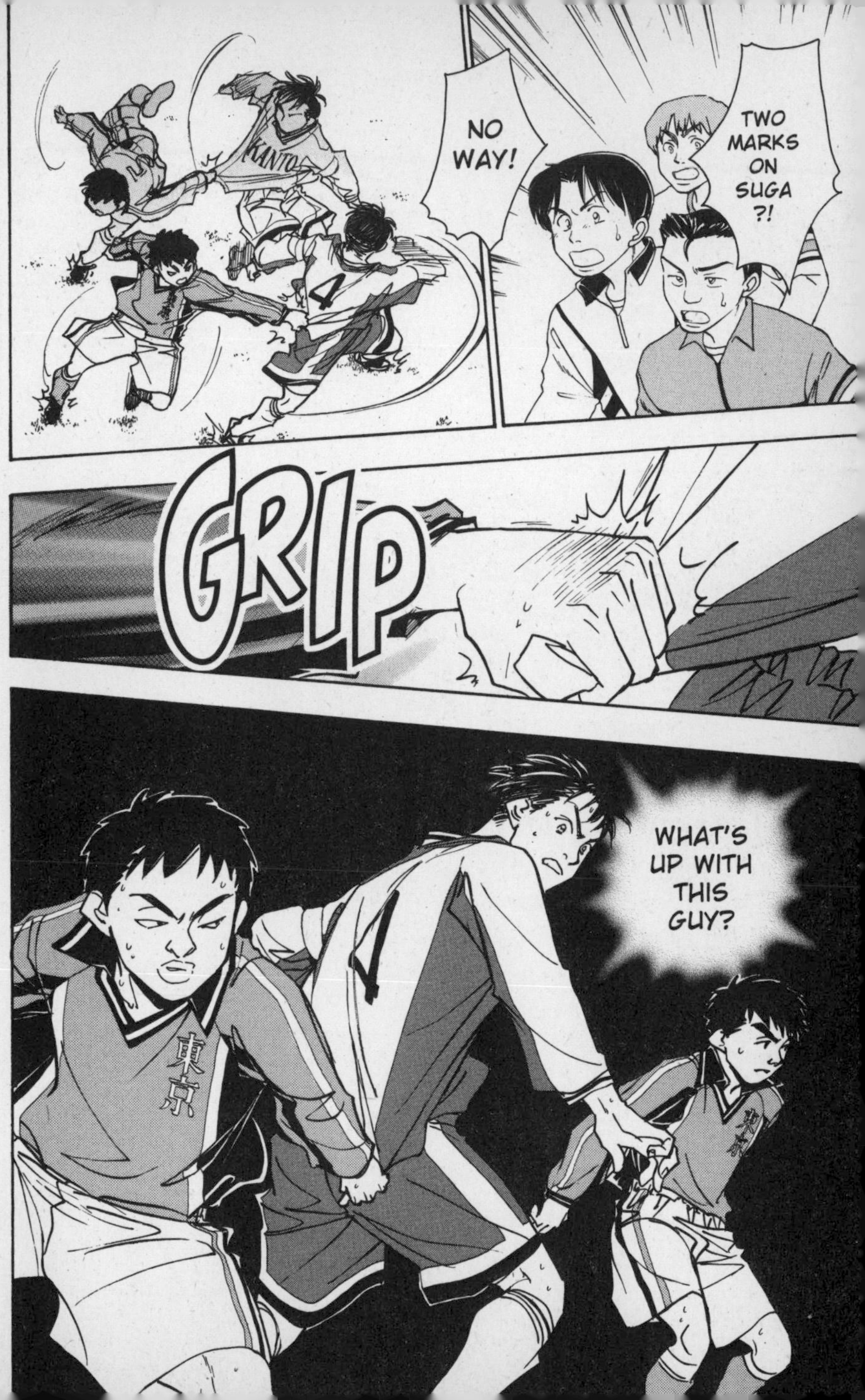
TWO MARKS ON SUGA ?!
NO WAY!
KANTO
GRIP
WHAT'S UP WITH THIS GUY?

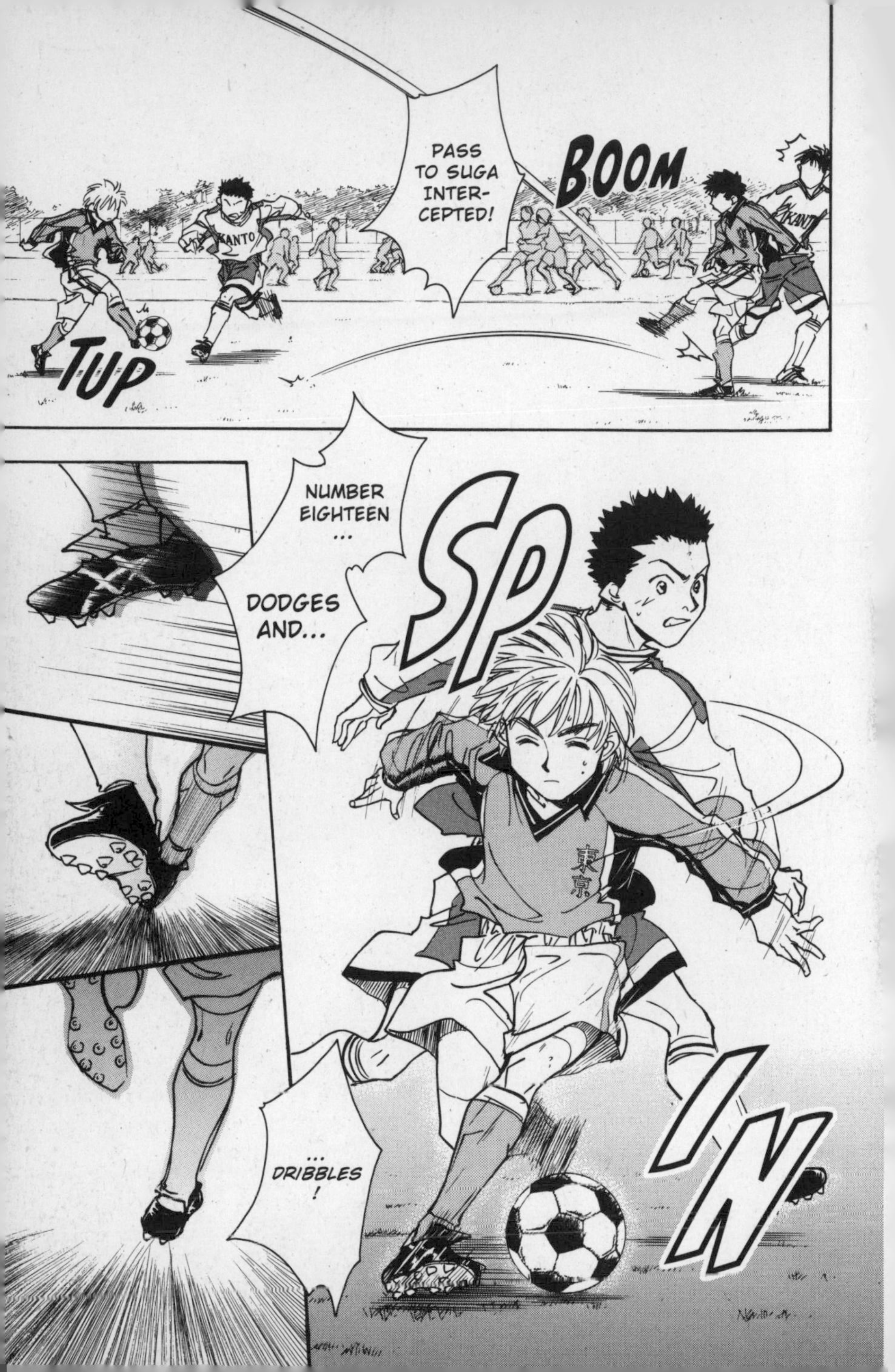
BOOM
PASS TO SUGA INTERCEPTED!
TUP
NUMBER EIGHTEEN ...
DODGES AND...
SP
... DRIBBLES !
IN

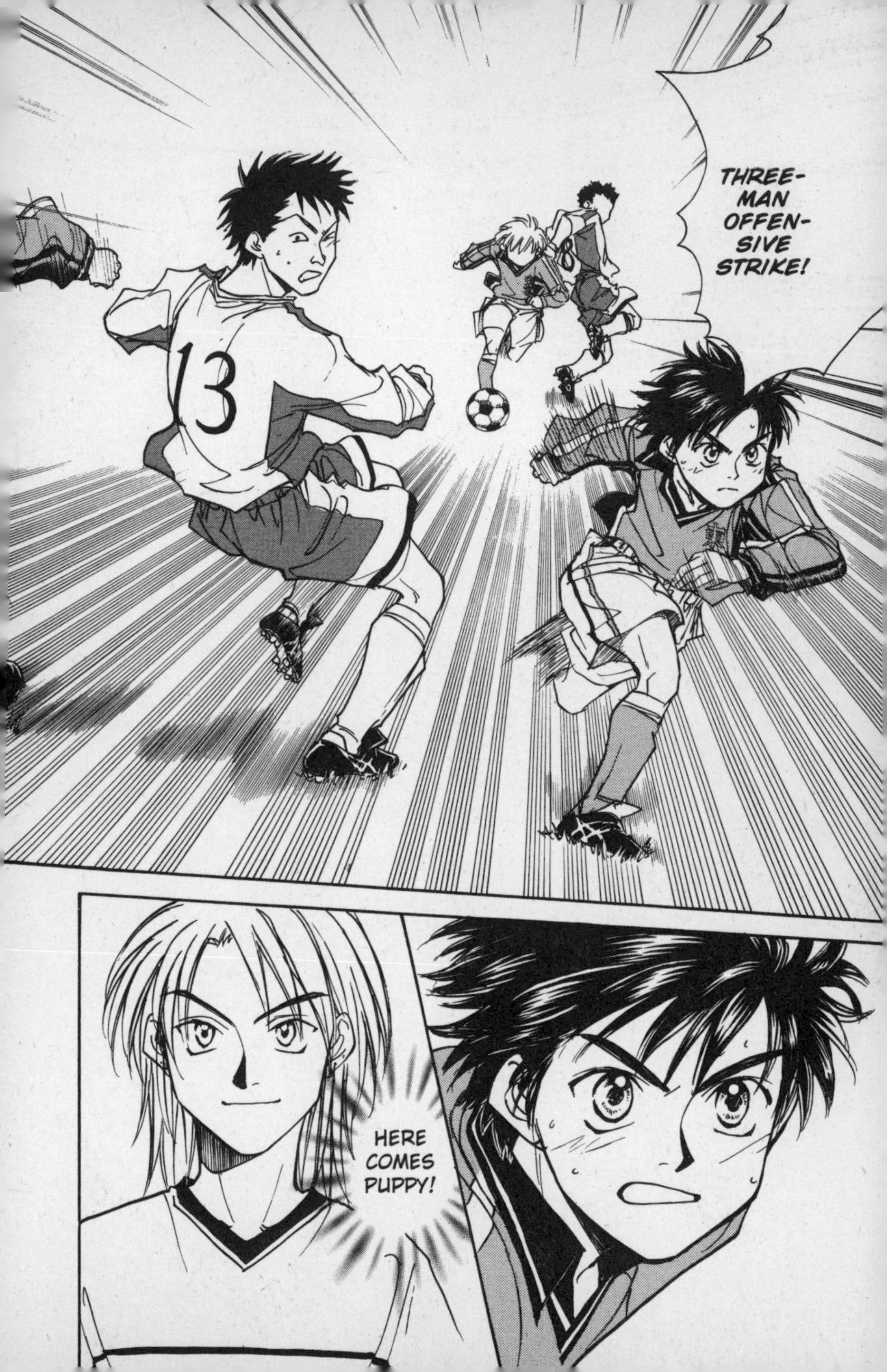
THREE-MAN OFFENSIVE STRIKE!
HERE COMES PUPPY!

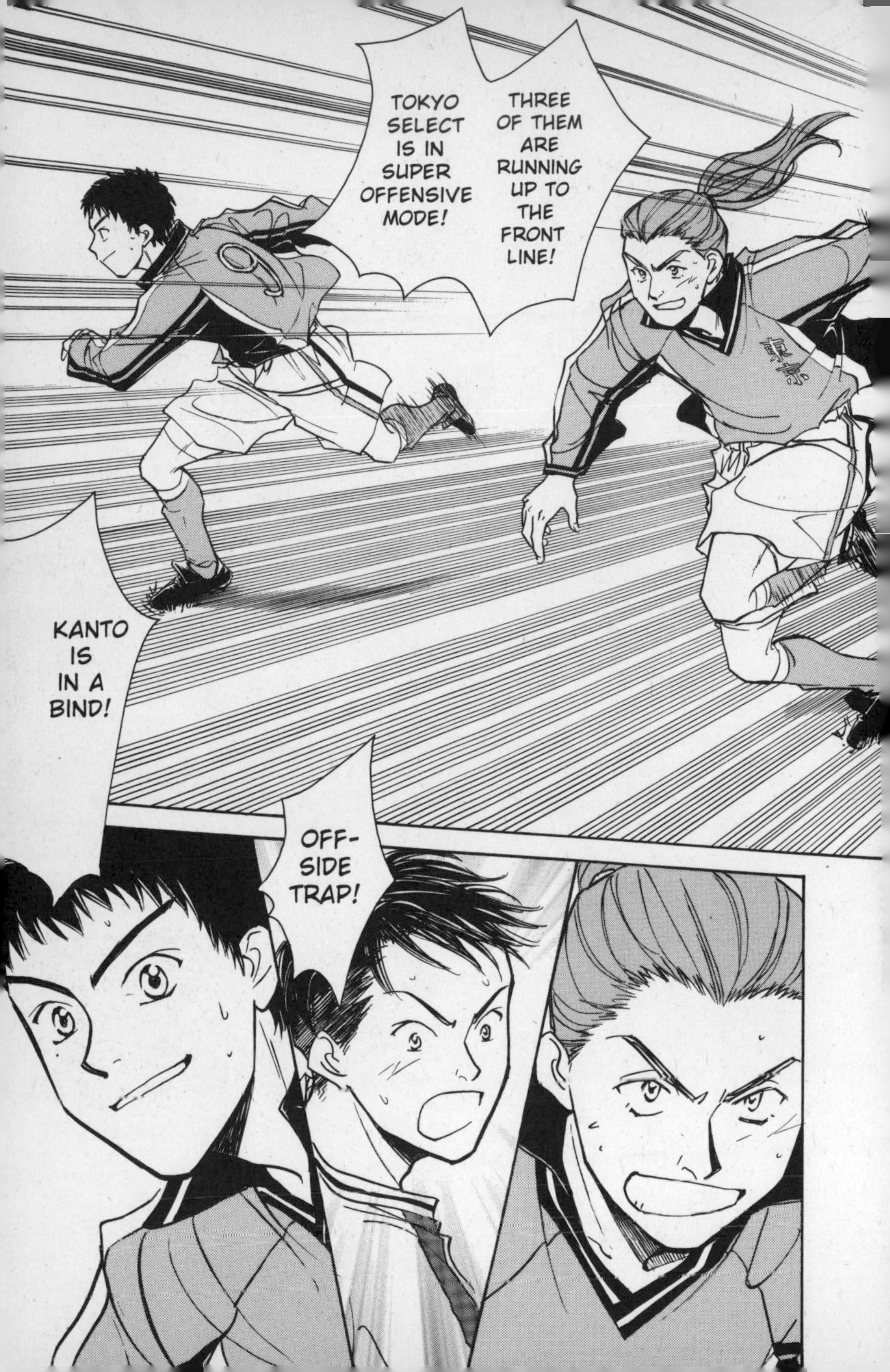
TOKYO SELECT IS IN SUPER OFFENSIVE MODE!
THREE OF THEM ARE RUNNING UP TO THE FRONT LINE!
KANTO IS IN A BIND!
OFF-SIDE TRAP!

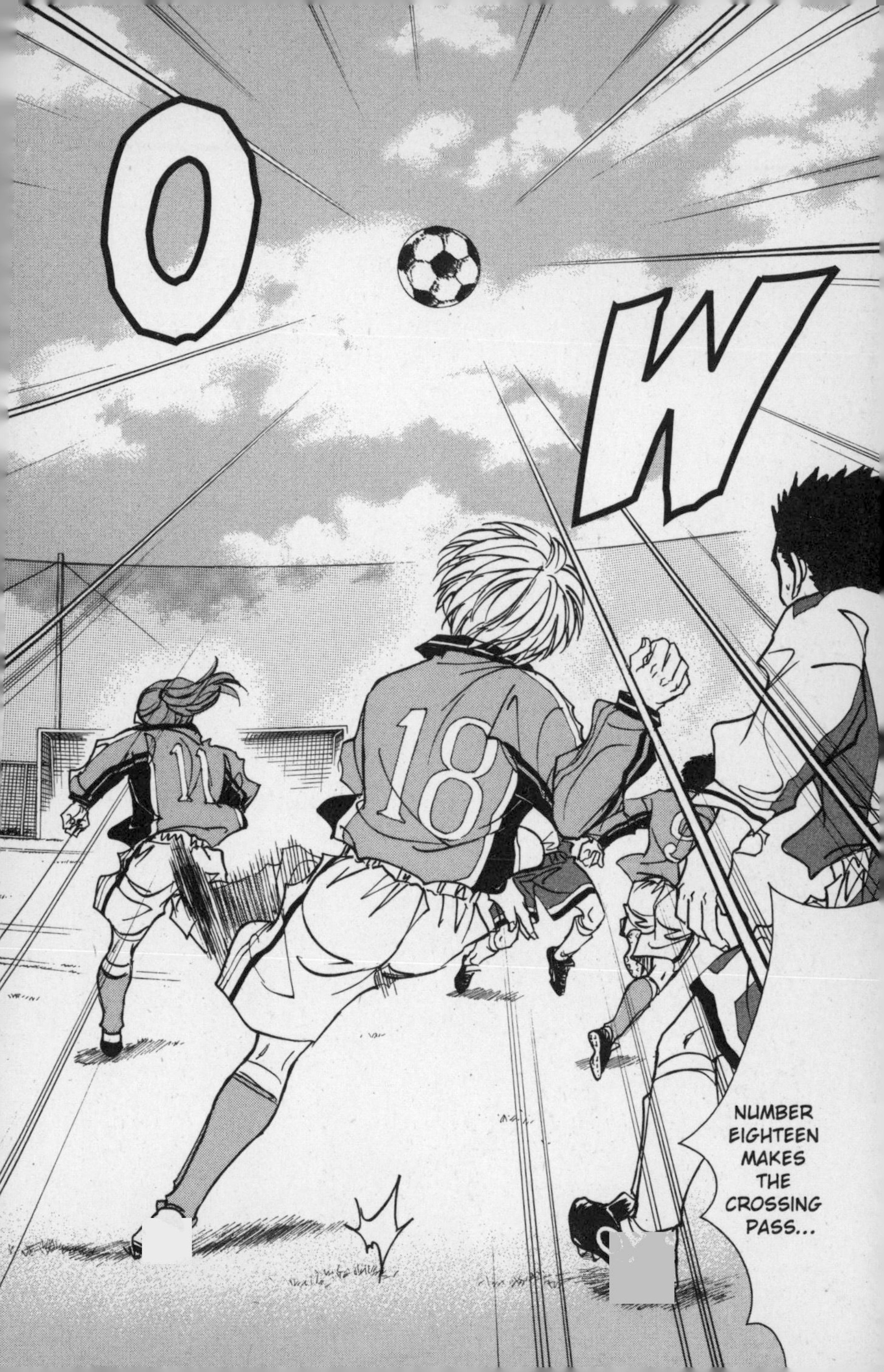
O
W
NUMBER EIGHTEEN MAKES THE CROSSING PASS...

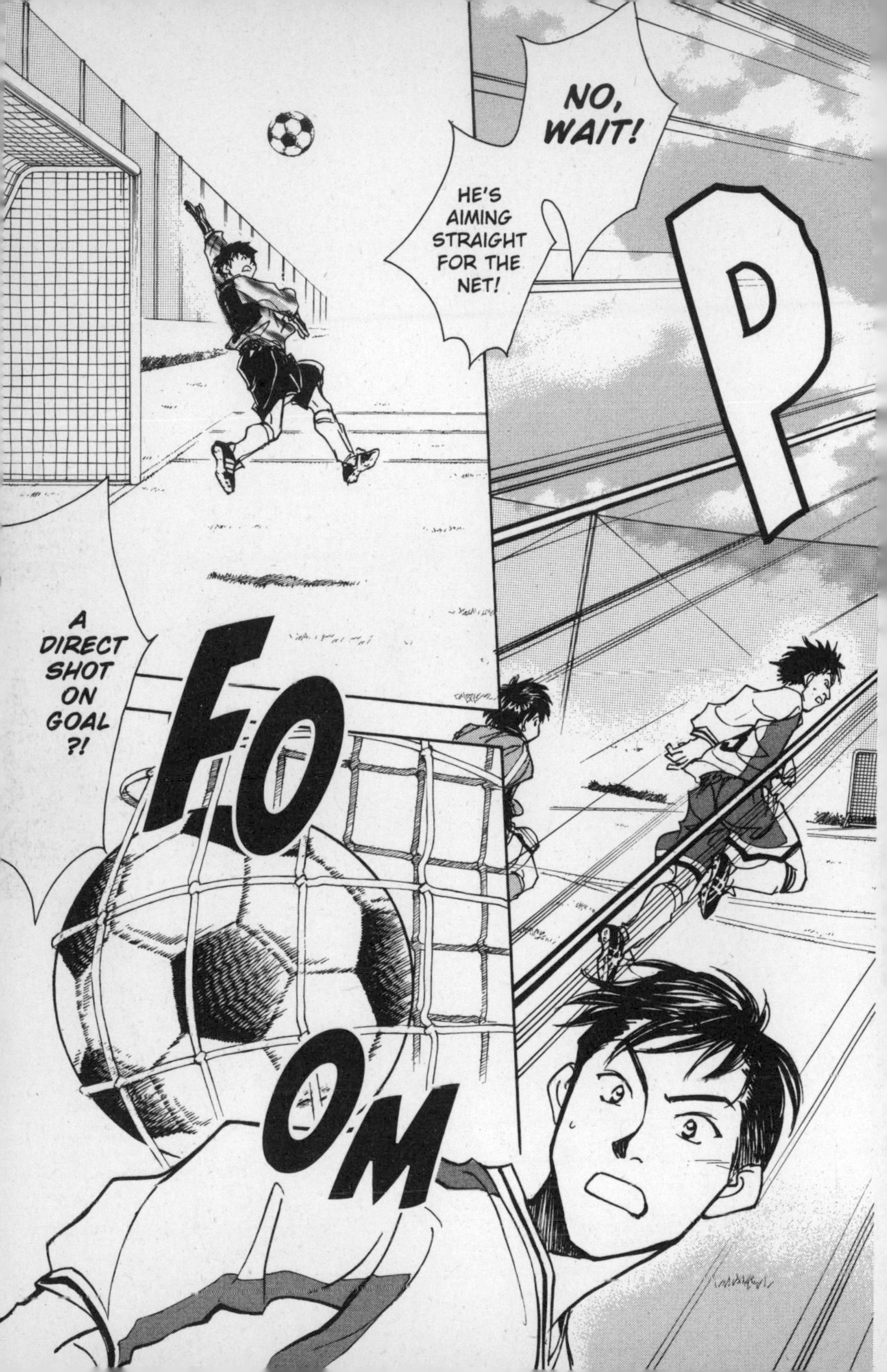
NO, WAIT!
HE'S AIMING STRAIGHT FOR THE NET!
P
A DIRECT SHOT ON GOAL ?!
FO
OM

WHISTLE!

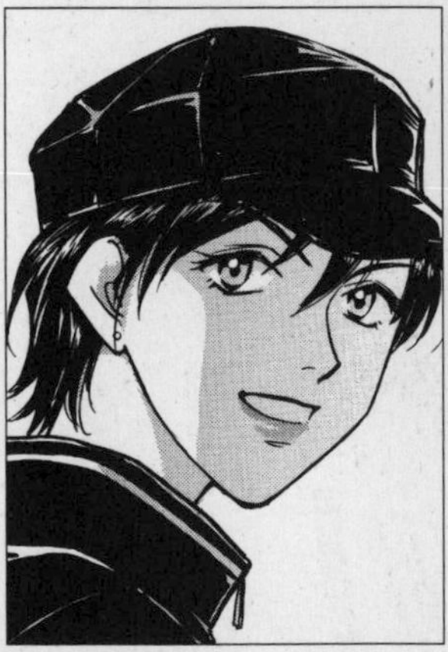

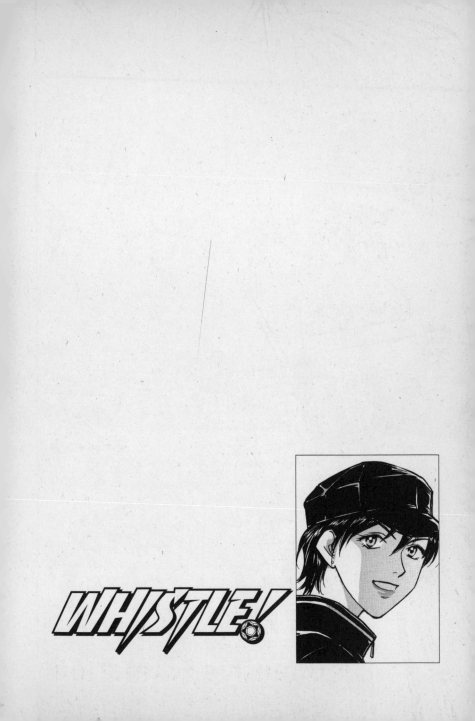

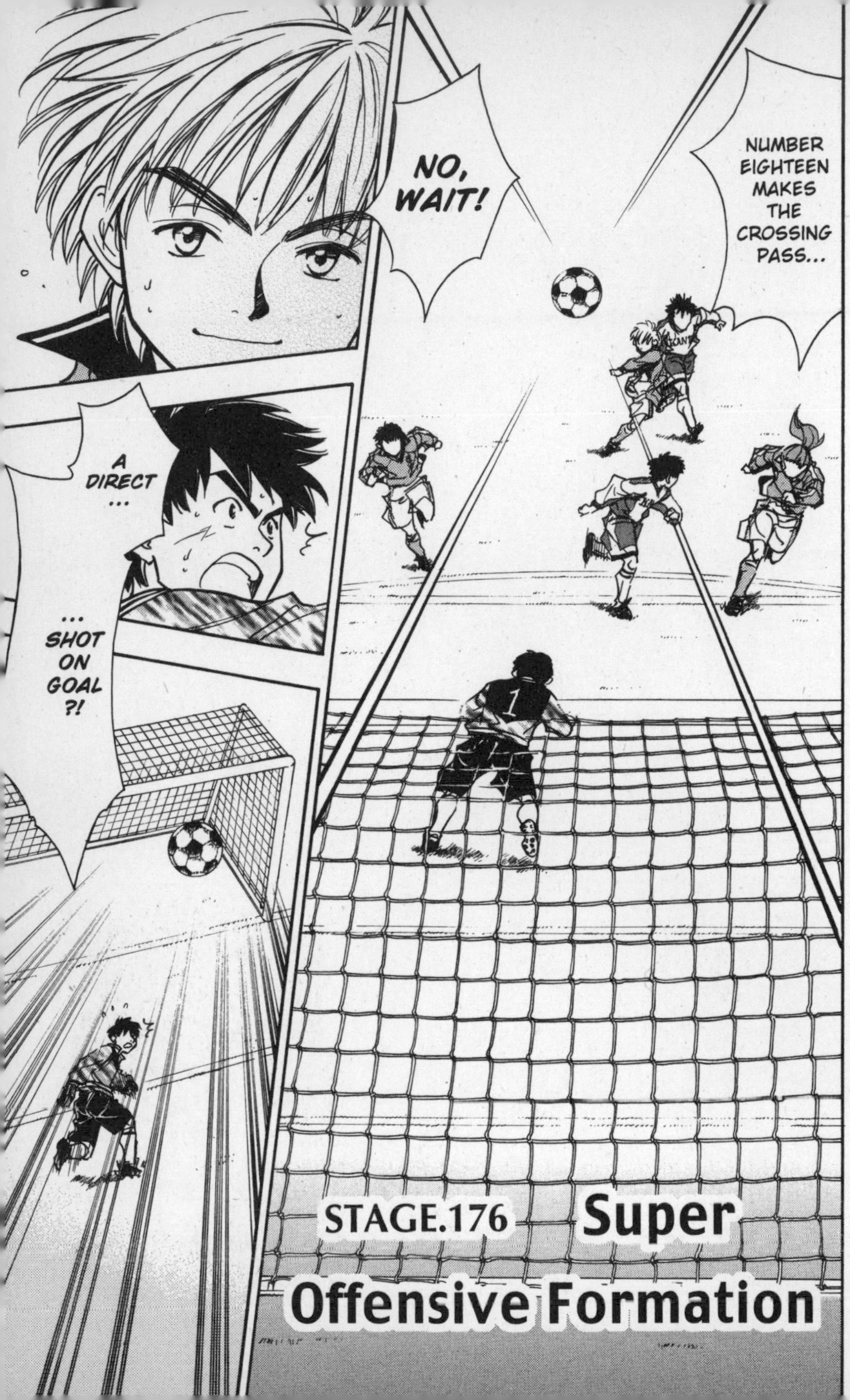
NUMBER EIGHTEEN MAKES THE CROSSING PASS...
NO, WAIT!
STAGE.176 Super Offensive Formation
A DIRECT ...
... SHOT ON GOAL ?!

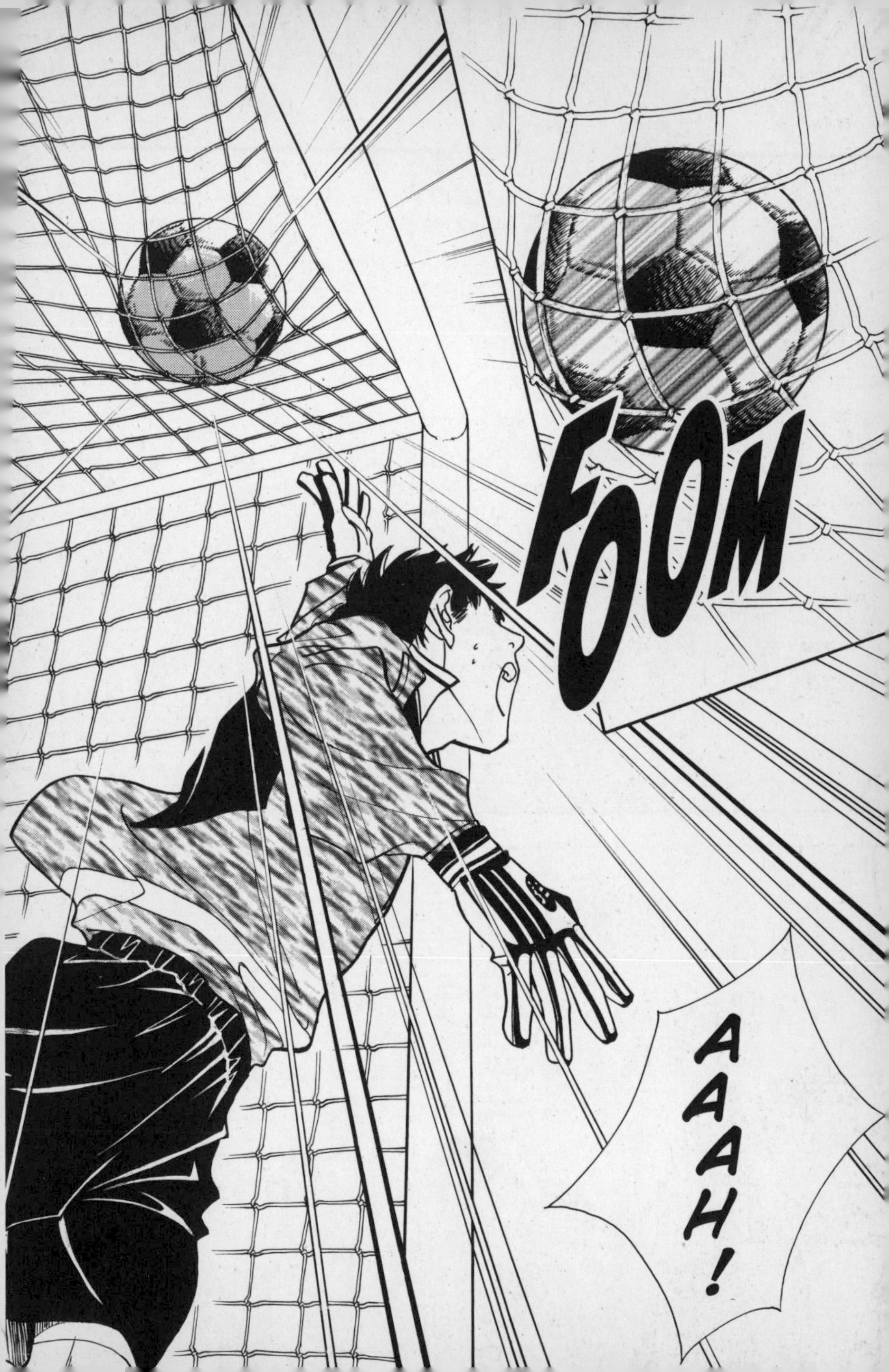
FOOM
AAAH!

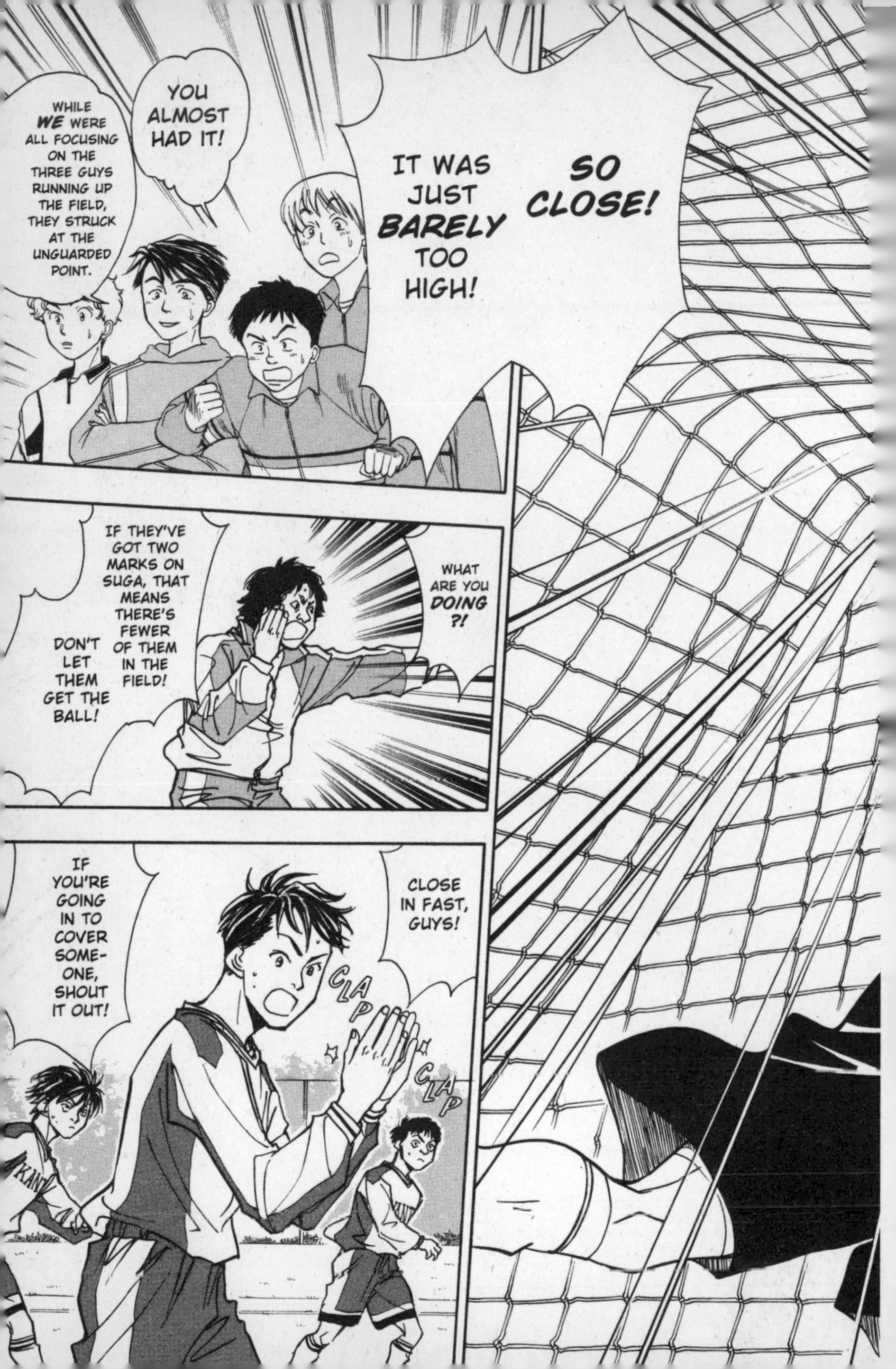

IT WAS JUST BARELY TOO HIGH!
SO CLOSE!
YOU ALMOST HAD IT!
WHILE WE WERE ALL FOCUSING ON THE THREE GUYS RUNNING UP THE FIELD, THEY STRUCK AT THE UNGUARDED POINT.
WHAT ARE YOU DOING?!
IF THEY'VE GOT TWO MARKS ON SUGA, THAT MEANS THERE'S FEWER OF THEM IN THE FIELD!
DON'T LET THEM GET THE BALL!
CLOSE IN FAST, GUYS!
CLAP
CLAP
IF YOU'RE GOING IN TO COVER SOME-ONE, SHOUT IT OUT!

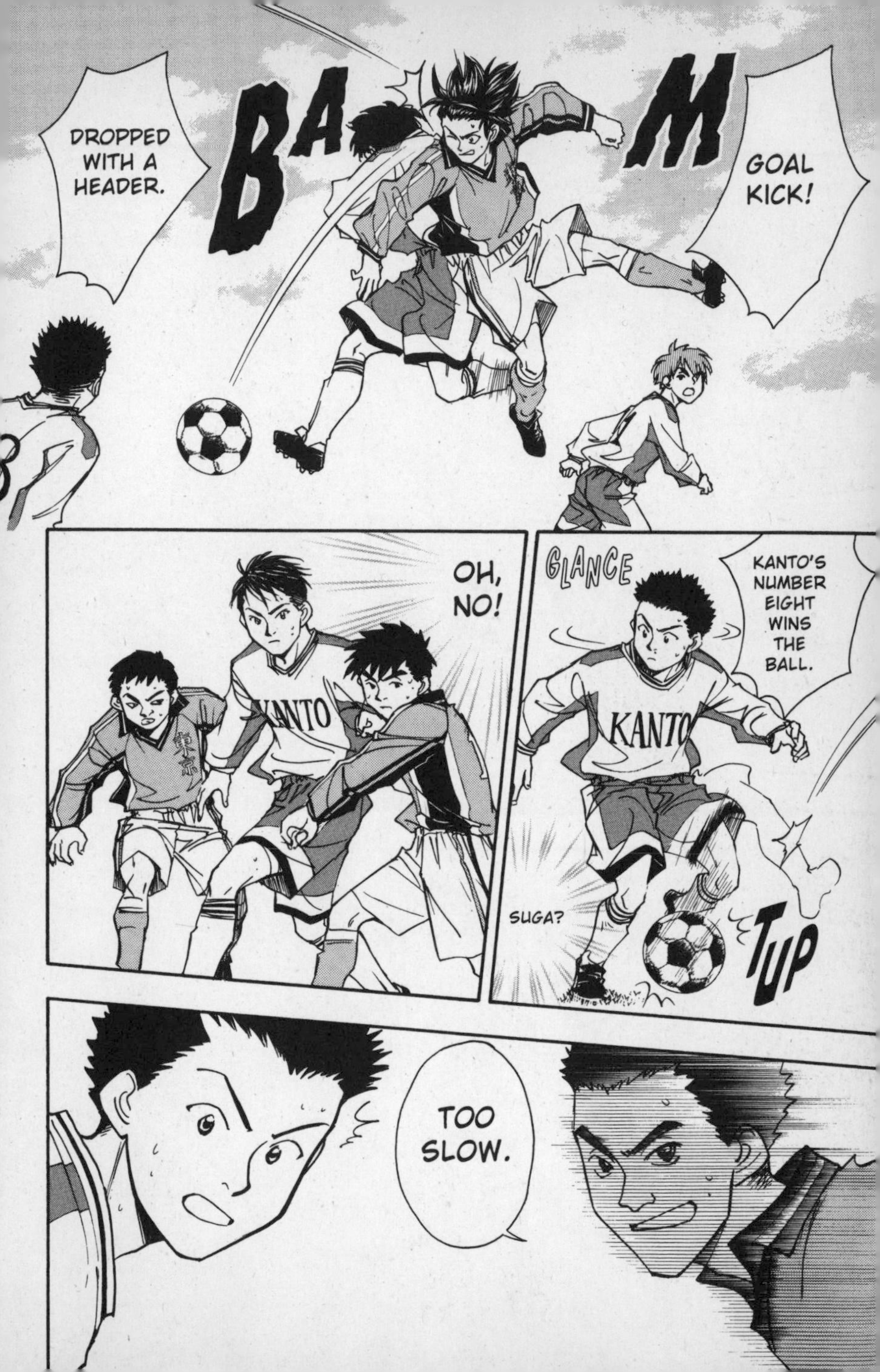
GOAL KICK!
BAM
DROPPED WITH A HEADER.
KANTO'S NUMBER EIGHT WINS THE BALL.
GLANCE
SUGA?
TUP
OH, NO!
TOO SLOW.

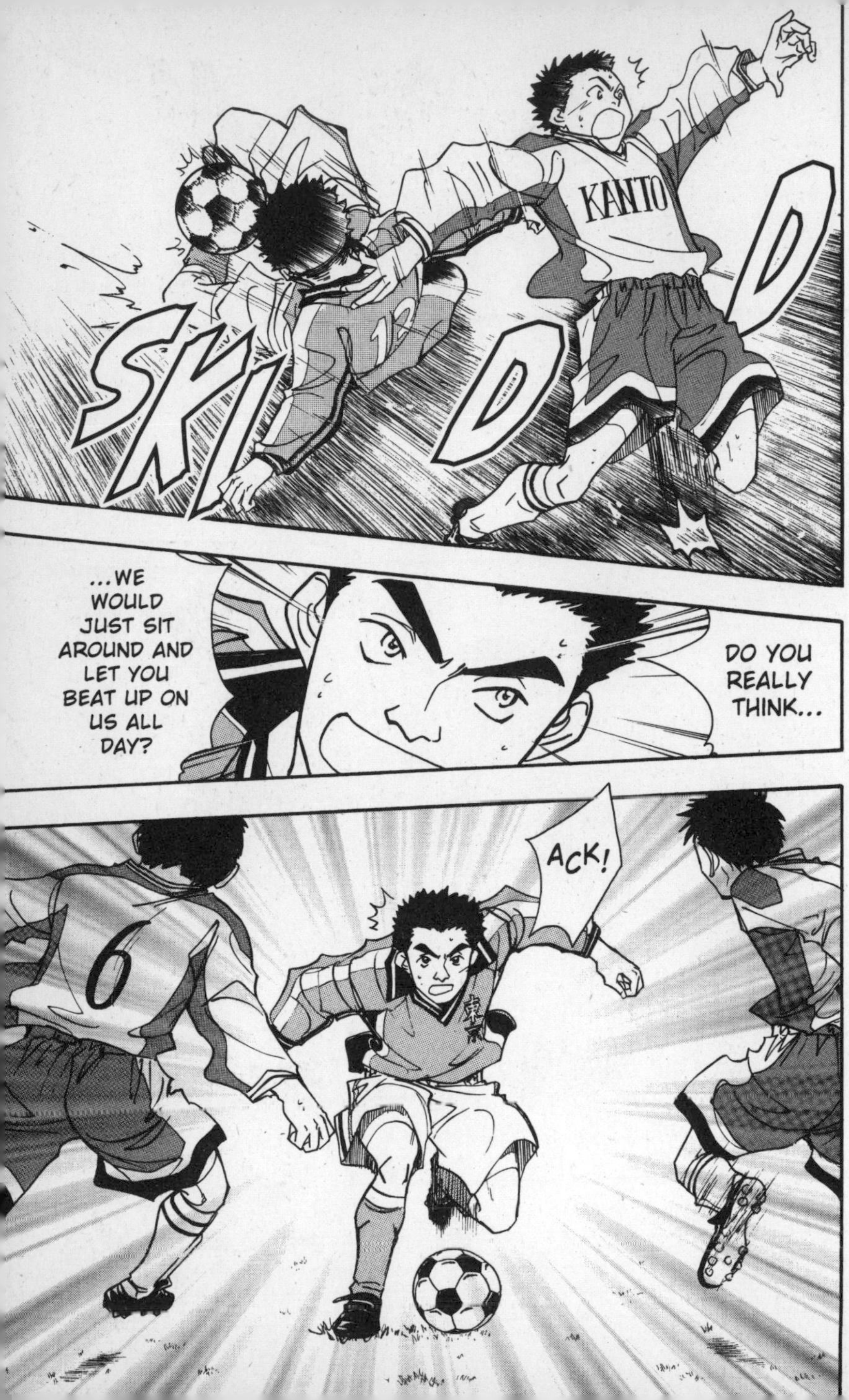
SKIDDD
DO YOU REALLY THINK...
...WE WOULD JUST SIT AROUND AND LET YOU BEAT UP ON US ALL DAY?
ACK!

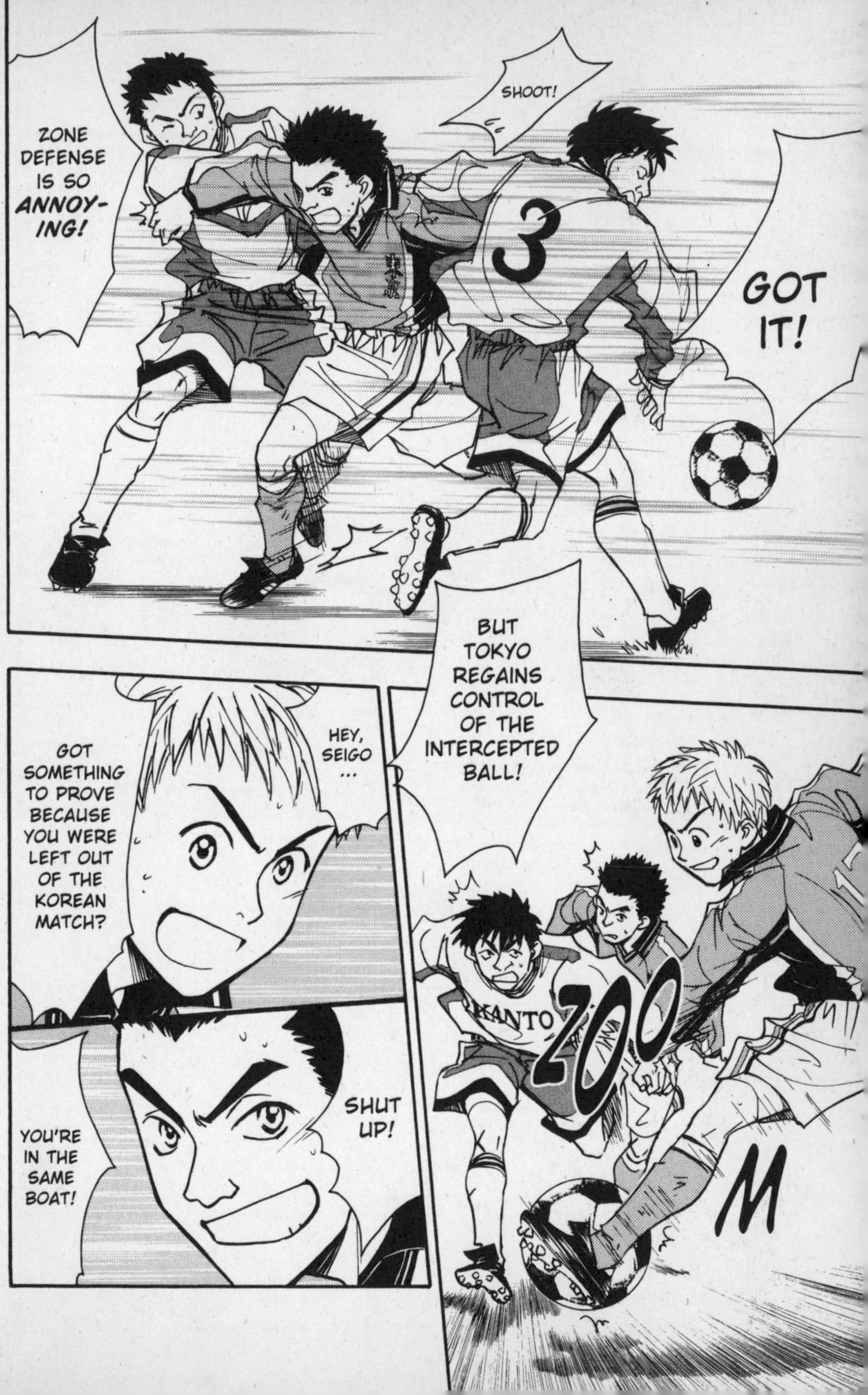
GOT IT!
SHOOT!
ZONE DEFENSE IS SO ANNOYING!
BUT TOKYO REGAINS CONTROL OF THE INTERCEPTED BALL!
ZOOM
KANTO
HEY, SEIGO ...
GOT SOMETHING TO PROVE BECAUSE YOU WERE LEFT OUT OF THE KOREAN MATCH?
SHUT UP!
YOU'RE IN THE SAME BOAT!

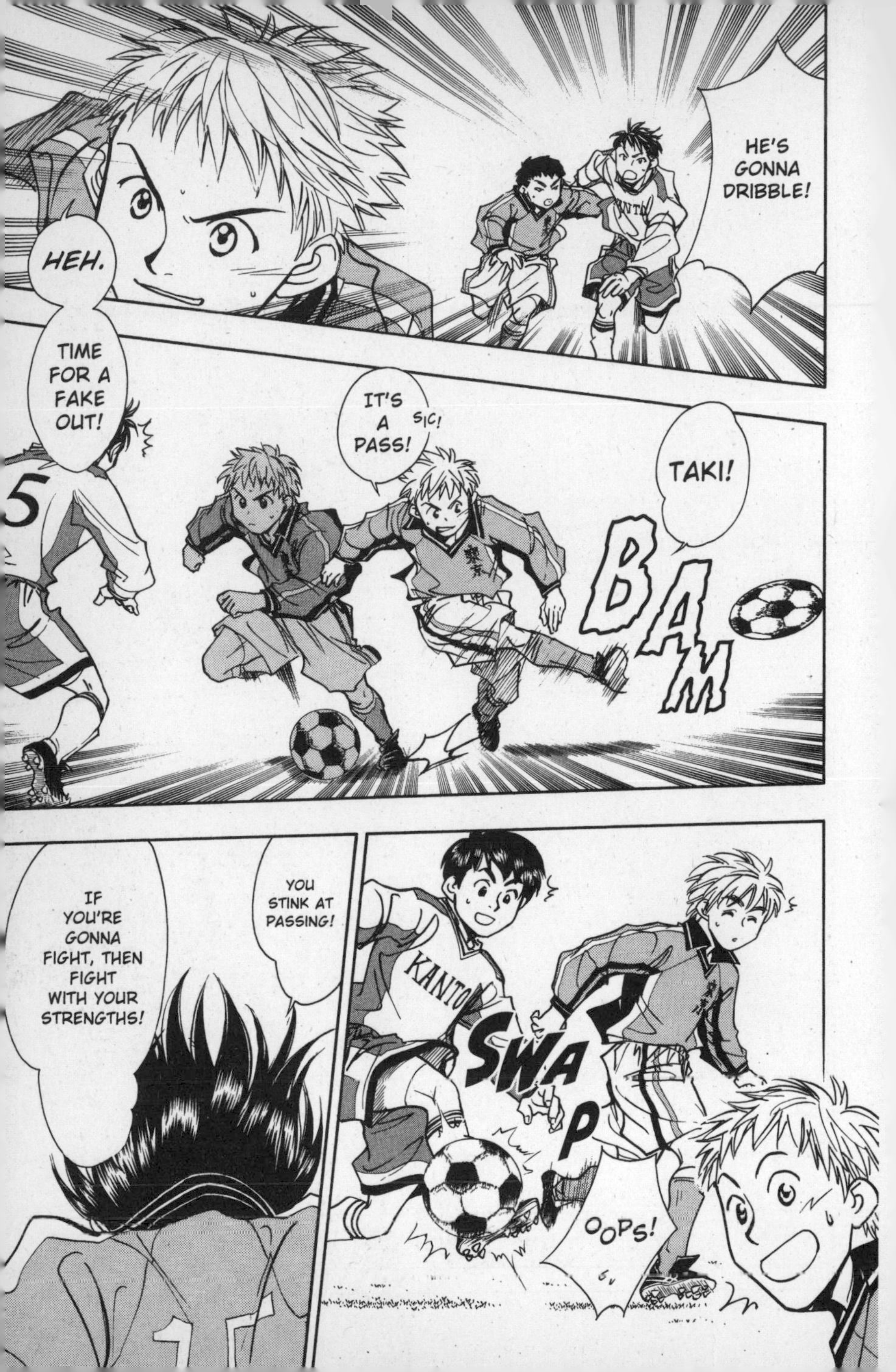
HE'S GONNA DRIBBLE!
HEH.
TIME FOR A FAKE OUT!
TAKI!
IT'S A PASS!
SIC!
BAM
SWAP
OOPS!
YOU STINK AT PASSING!
IF YOU'RE GONNA FIGHT, THEN FIGHT WITH YOUR STRENGTHS!

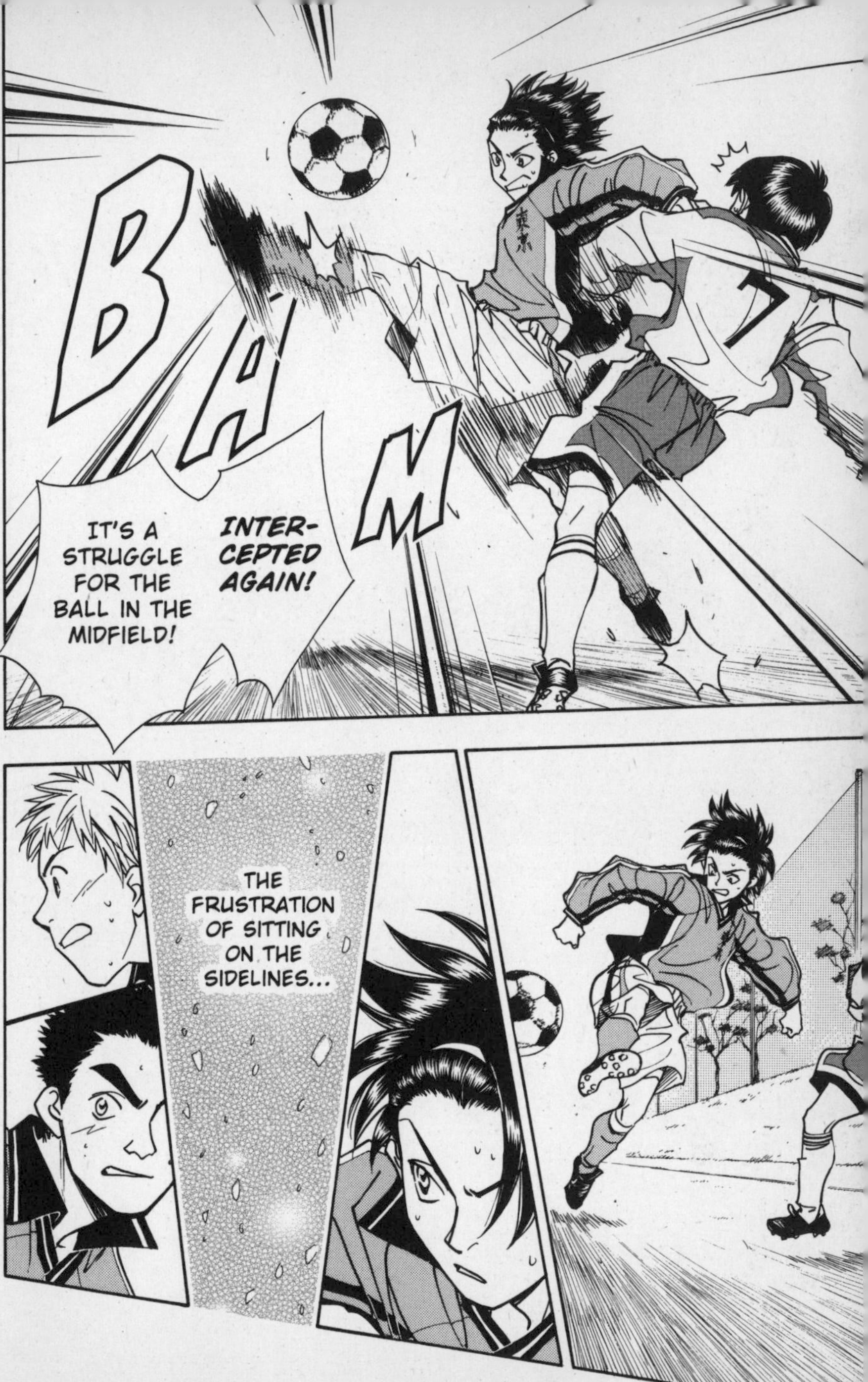
BAM
INTER-CEPTED AGAIN!
IT'S A STRUGGLE FOR THE BALL IN THE MIDFIELD!
THE FRUSTRATION OF SITTING ON THE SIDELINES...

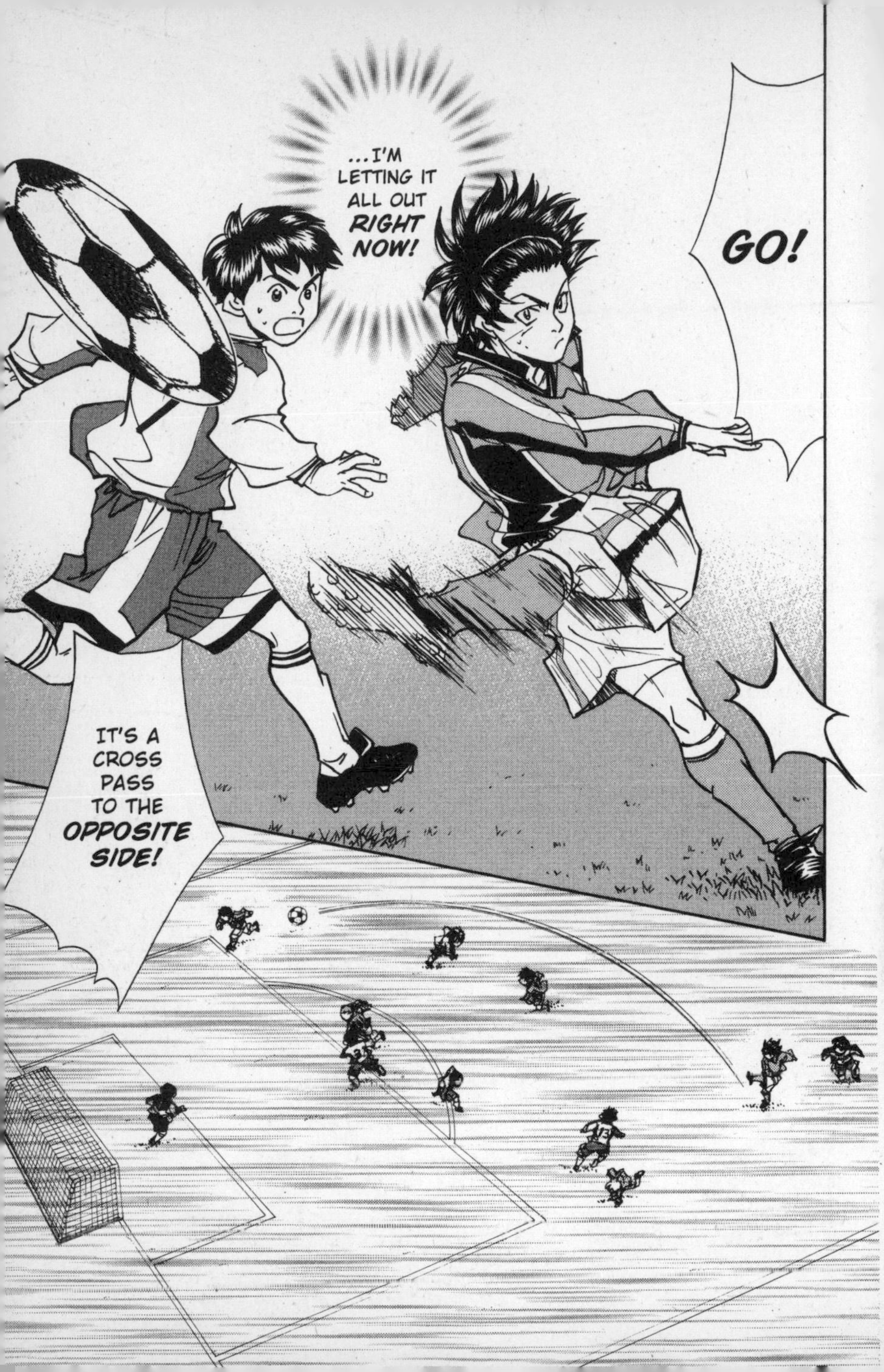
GO!
...I'M LETTING IT ALL OUT RIGHT NOW!
IT'S A CROSS PASS TO THE OPPOSITE SIDE!

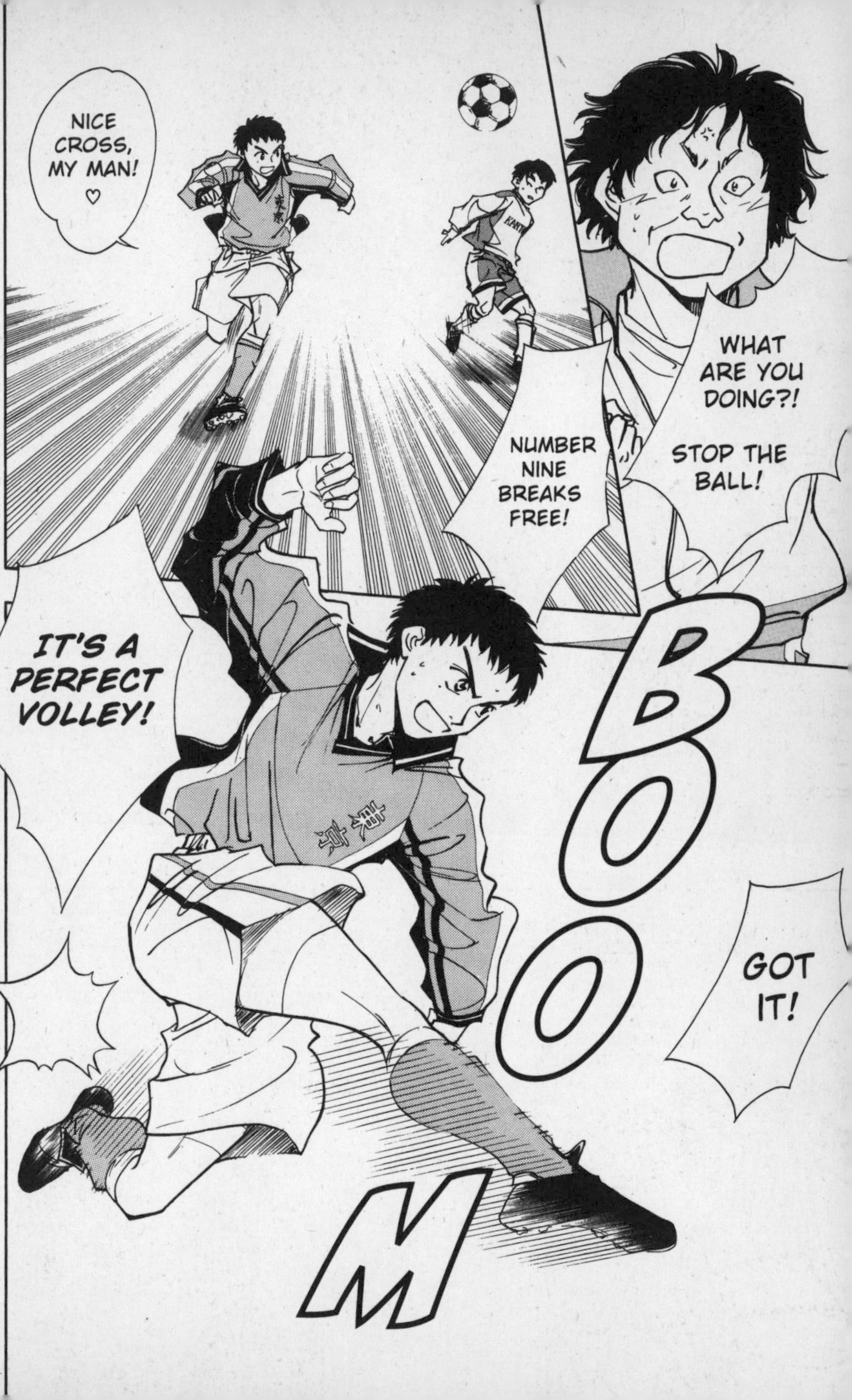
WHAT ARE YOU DOING?!
STOP THE BALL!
NUMBER NINE BREAKS FREE!
NICE CROSS, MY MAN! ♡
GOT IT!
BOOOM
IT'S A PERFECT VOLLEY!

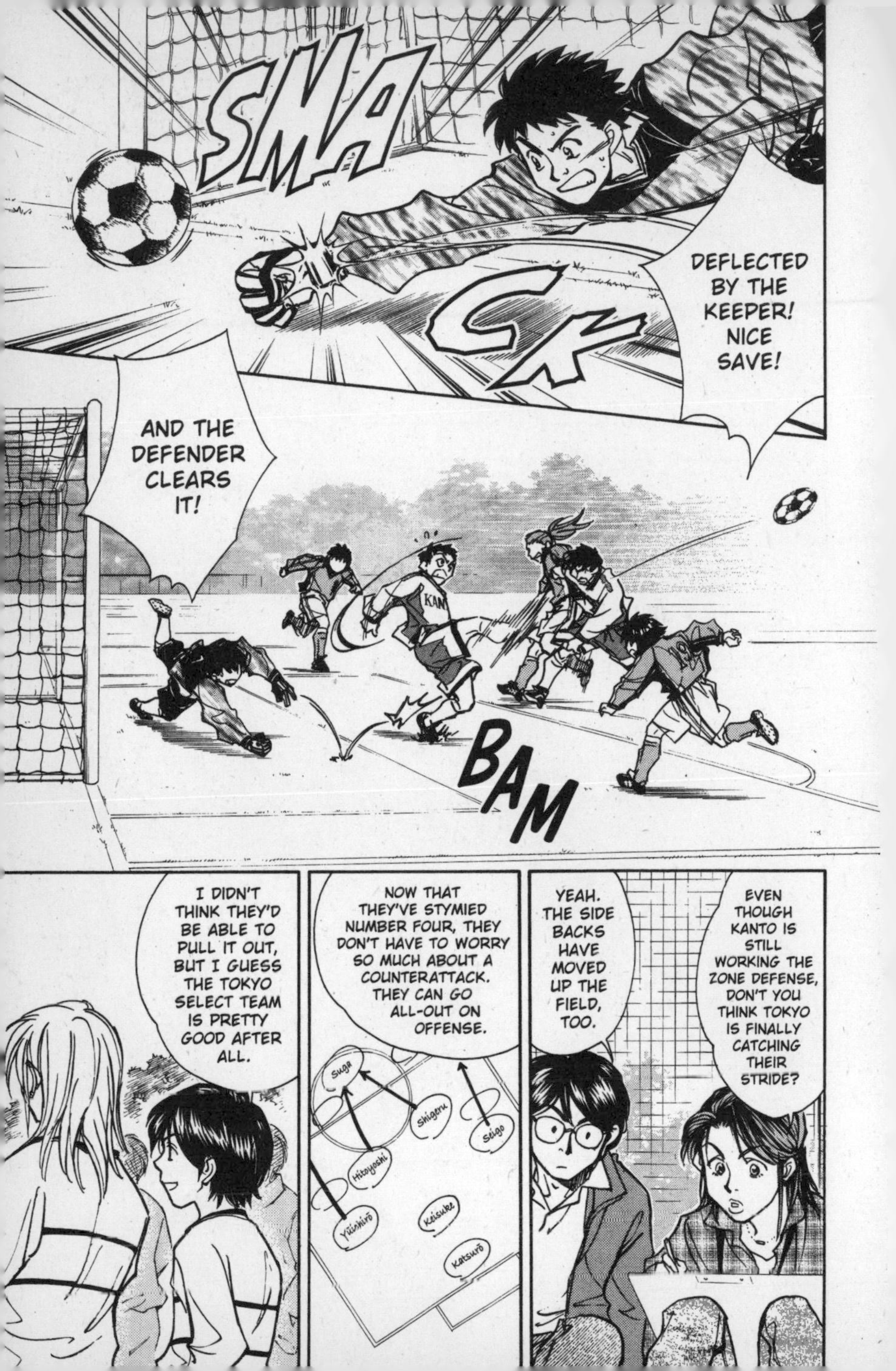

SMA
DEFLECTED BY THE KEEPER! NICE SAVE!
CK
AND THE DEFENDER CLEARS IT!
BAM
EVEN THOUGH KANTO IS STILL WORKING THE ZONE DEFENSE, DON'T YOU THINK TOKYO IS FINALLY CATCHING THEIR STRIDE?
YEAH. THE SIDE BACKS HAVE MOVED UP THE FIELD, TOO.
NOW THAT THEY'VE STYMIED NUMBER FOUR, THEY DON'T HAVE TO WORRY SO MUCH ABOUT A COUNTERATTACK. THEY CAN GO ALL-OUT ON OFFENSE.
Suga
Shigeru
Seigo
Hitoyoshi
Yūshirō
Keisuke
Katsurō
I DIDN'T THINK THEY'D BE ABLE TO PULL IT OUT, BUT I GUESS THE TOKYO SELECT TEAM IS PRETTY GOOD AFTER ALL.

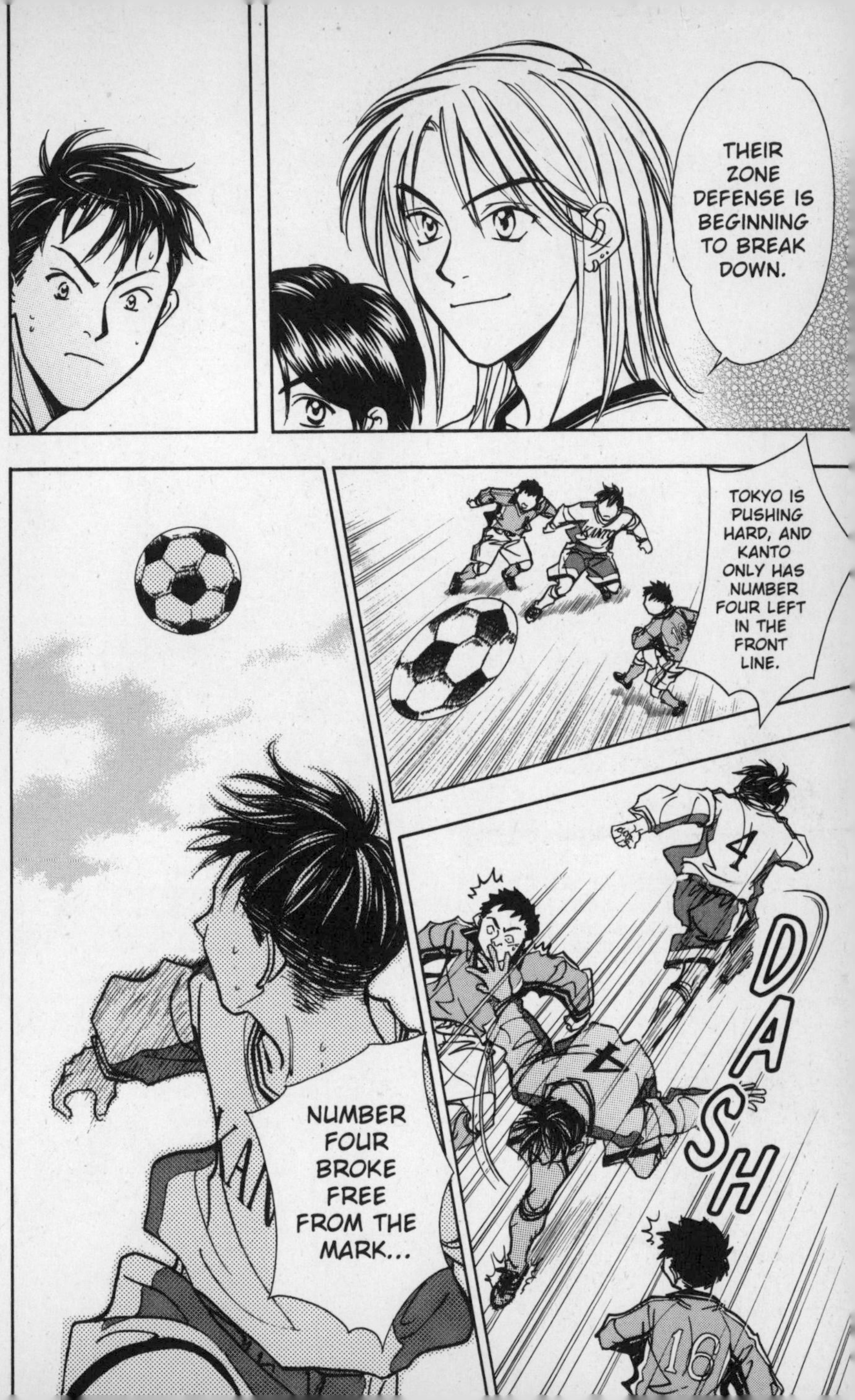
THEIR ZONE DEFENSE IS BEGINNING TO BREAK DOWN.
TOKYO IS PUSHING HARD, AND KANTO ONLY HAS NUMBER FOUR LEFT IN THE FRONT LINE.
DASH
NUMBER FOUR BROKE FREE FROM THE MARK...

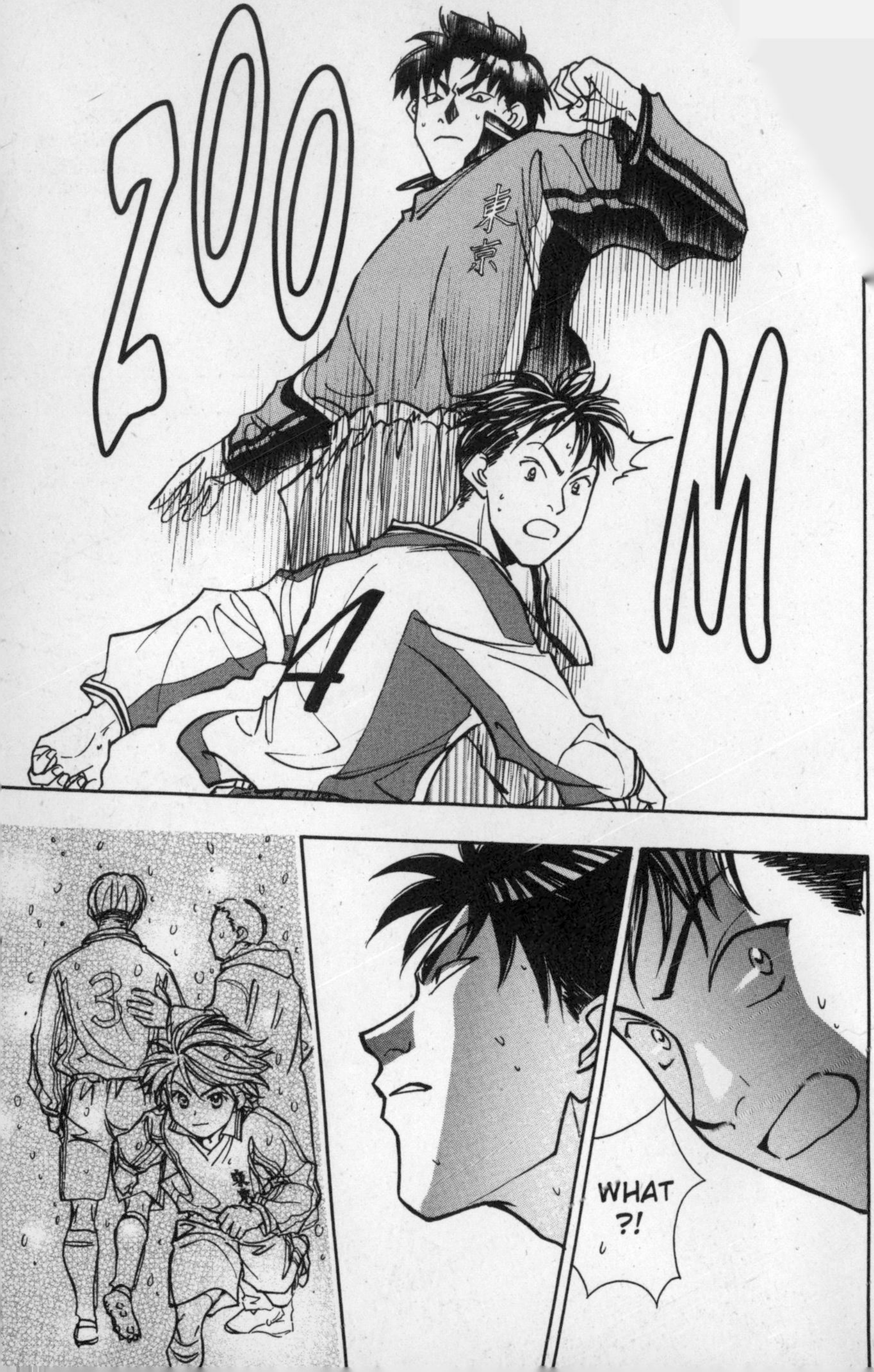
ZOOM
東京
WHAT ?!

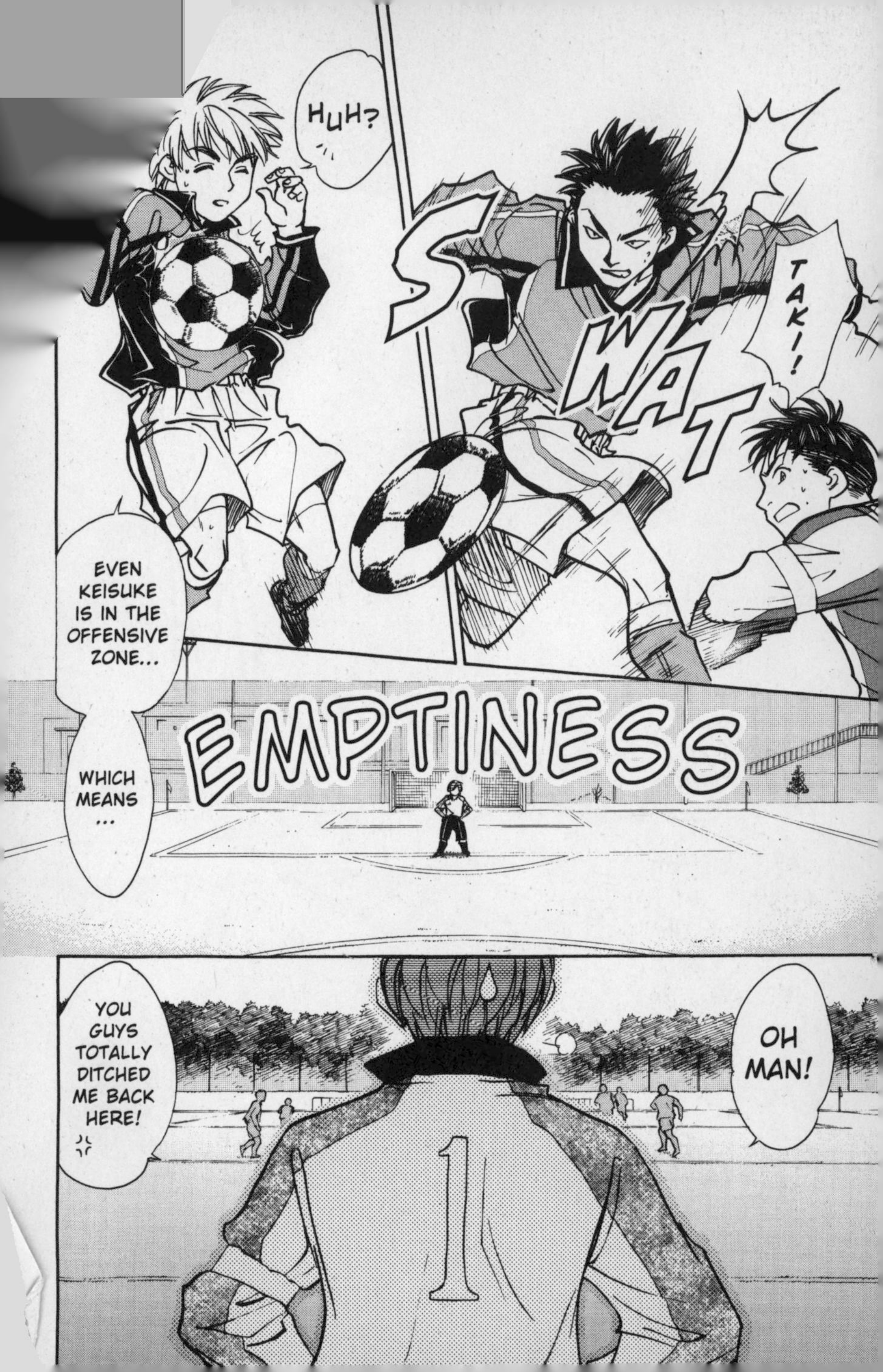
TAKI!
SWAT
HUH?
EVEN KEISUKE IS IN THE OFFENSIVE ZONE...
EMPTINESS
WHICH MEANS...
OH MAN!
YOU GUYS TOTALLY DITCHED ME BACK HERE!

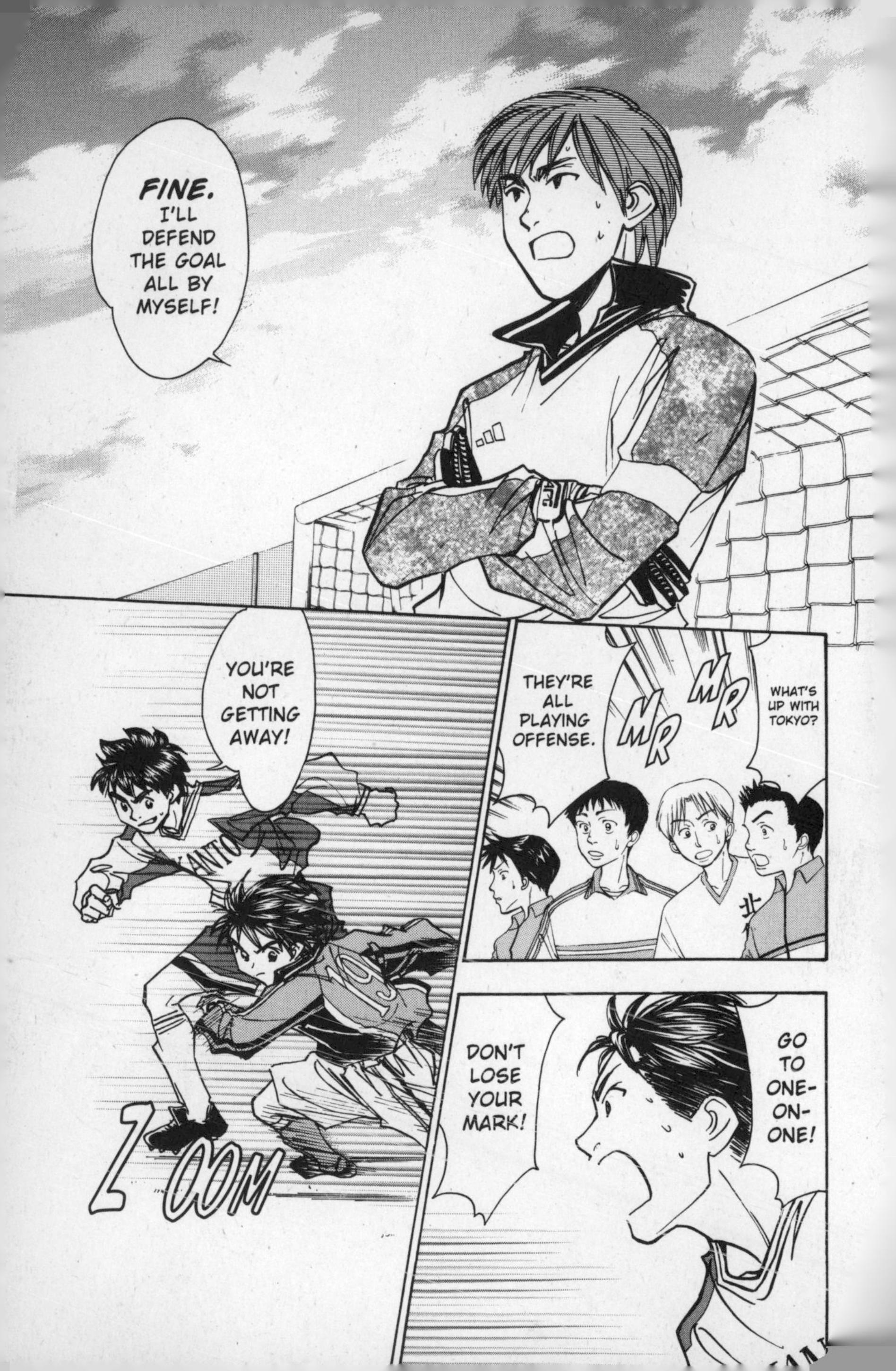
FINE. I'LL DEFEND THE GOAL ALL BY MYSELF!
WHAT'S UP WITH TOKYO?
MR MR
THEY'RE ALL PLAYING OFFENSE.
GO TO ONE-ON-ONE!
DON'T LOSE YOUR MARK!
YOU'RE NOT GETTING AWAY!
ZOOM

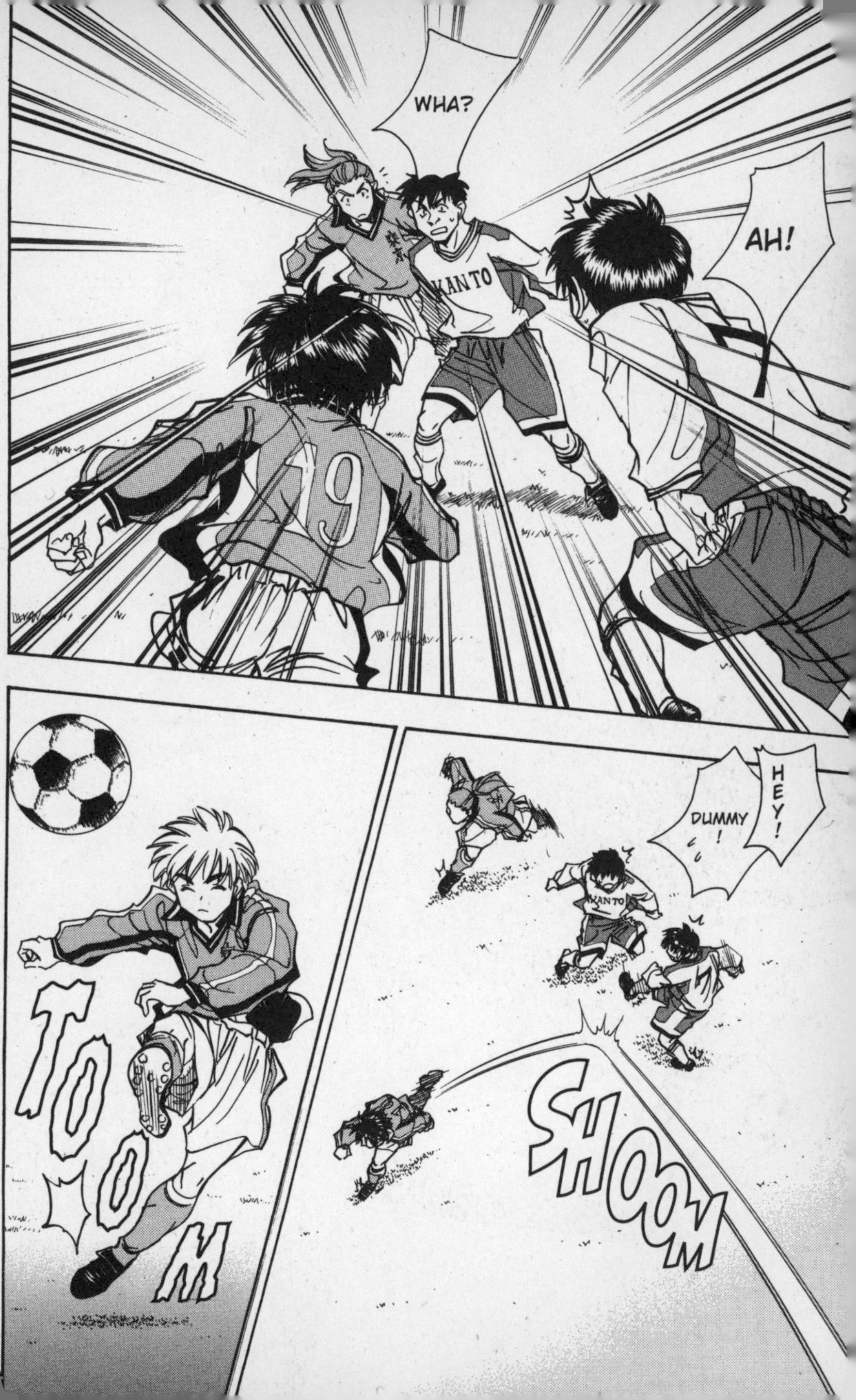
AH!
WHA?
HEY!
DUMMY!
SHOOM
TOOM

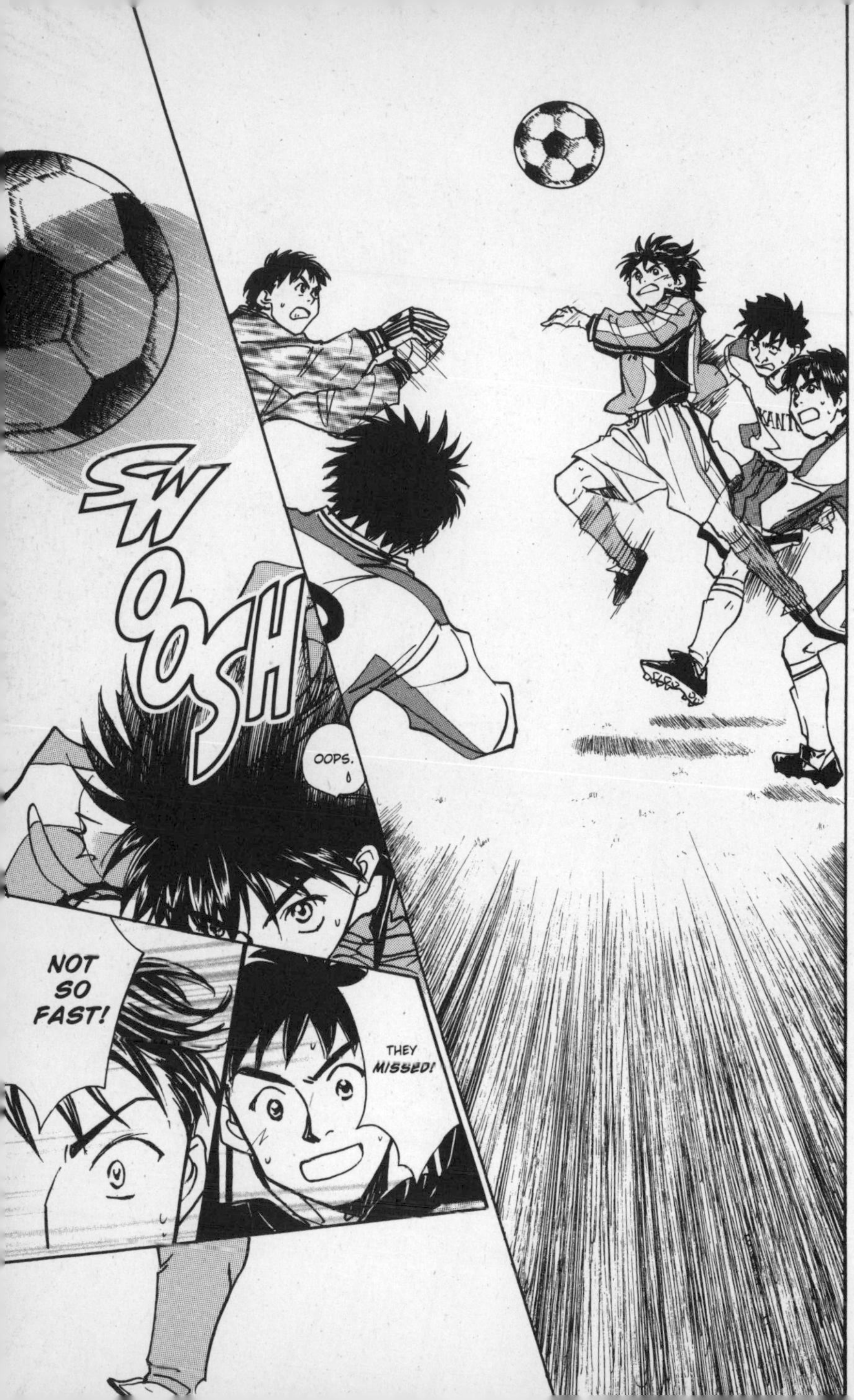
OOPS.
SWOOSH
THEY MISSED!
NOT SO FAST!

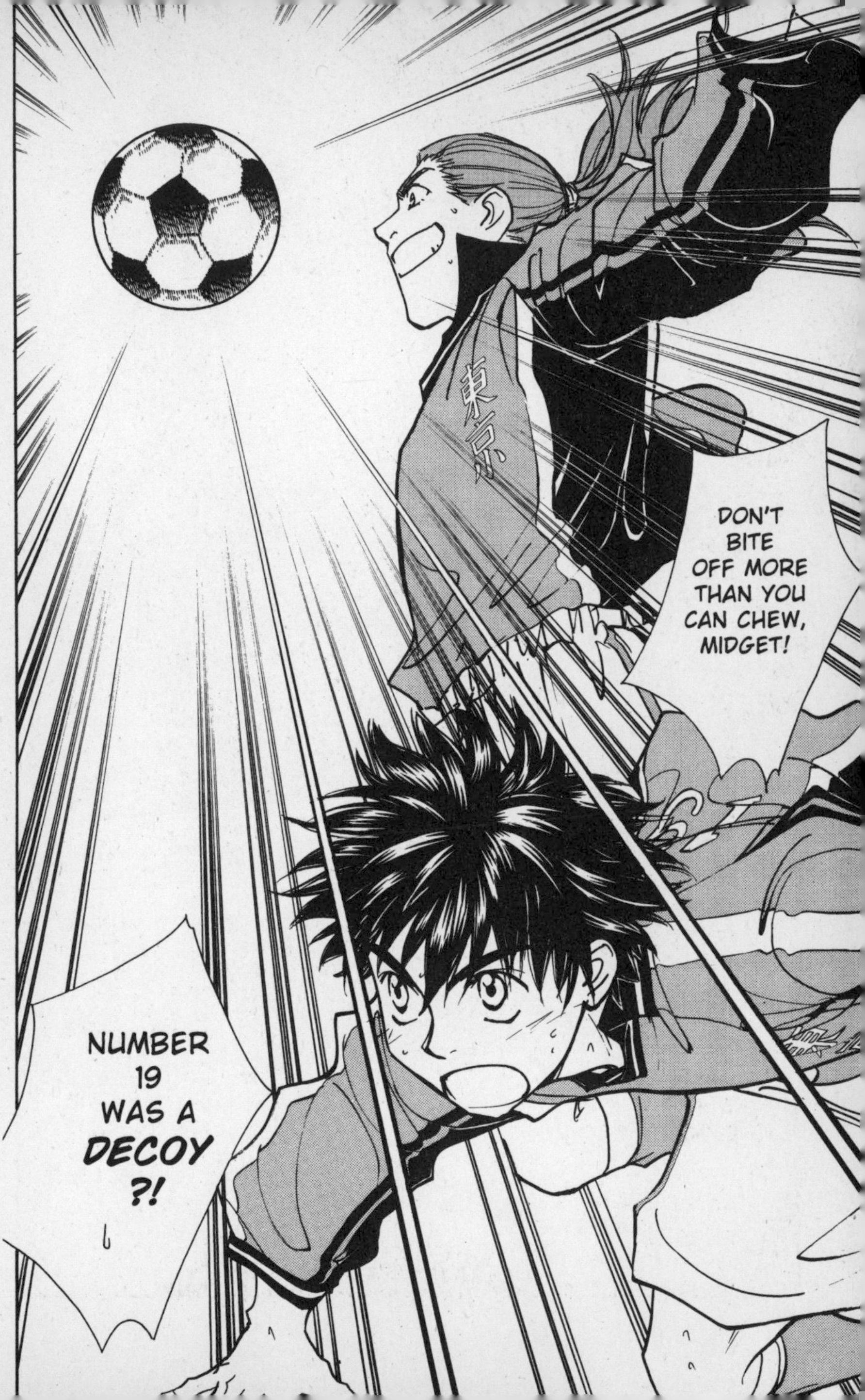
DON'T BITE OFF MORE THAN YOU CAN CHEW, MIDGET!
NUMBER 19 WAS A DECOY ?!

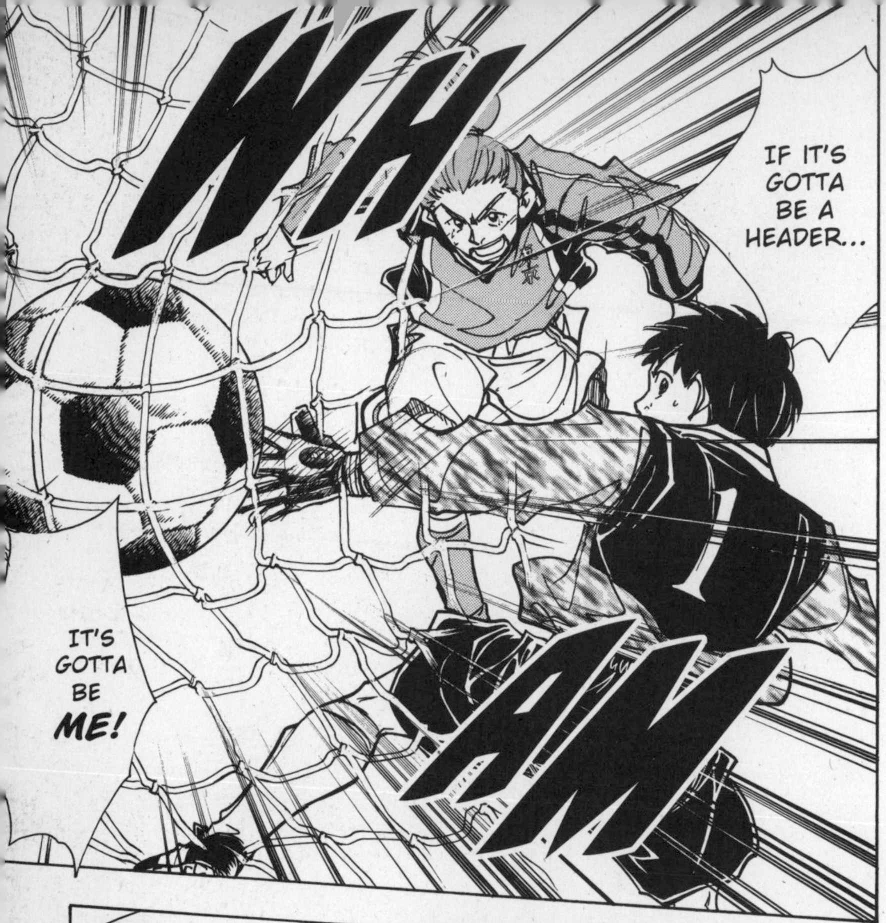
IF IT'S GOTTA BE A HEADER...
WH
AM
IT'S GOTTA BE ME!

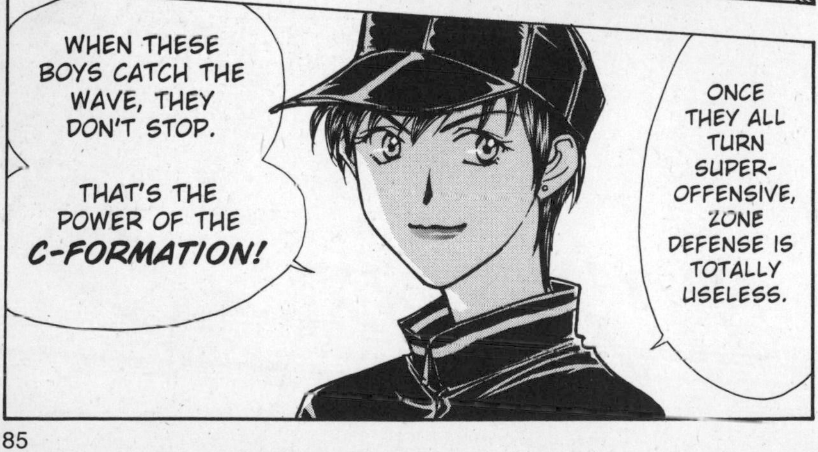
ONCE THEY ALL TURN SUPER-OFFENSIVE, ZONE DEFENSE IS TOTALLY USELESS.
WHEN THESE BOYS CATCH THE WAVE, THEY DON'T STOP.
THAT'S THE POWER OF THE C-FORMATION!

WHISTLE!

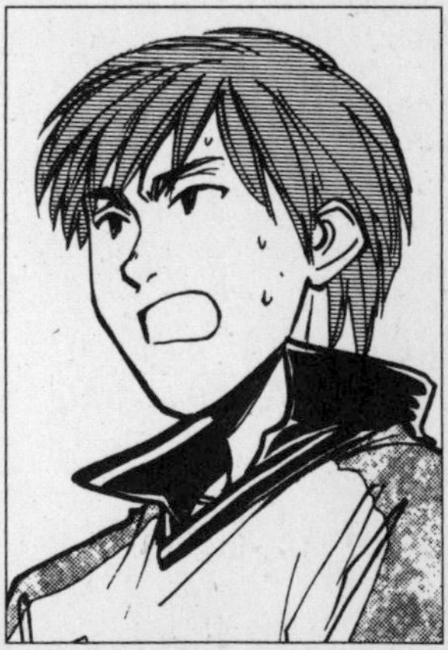

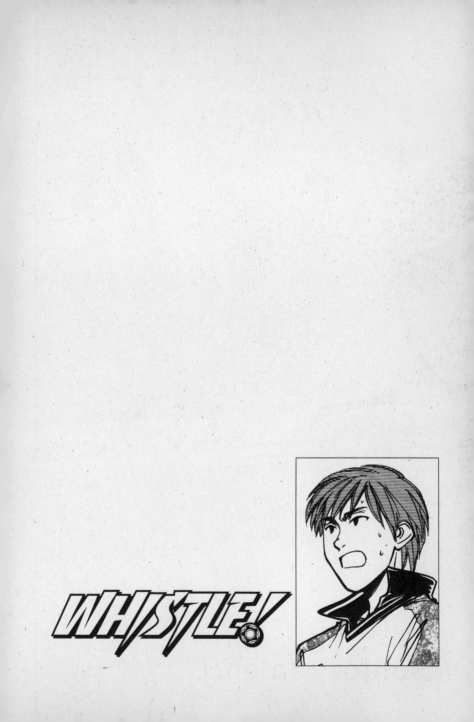

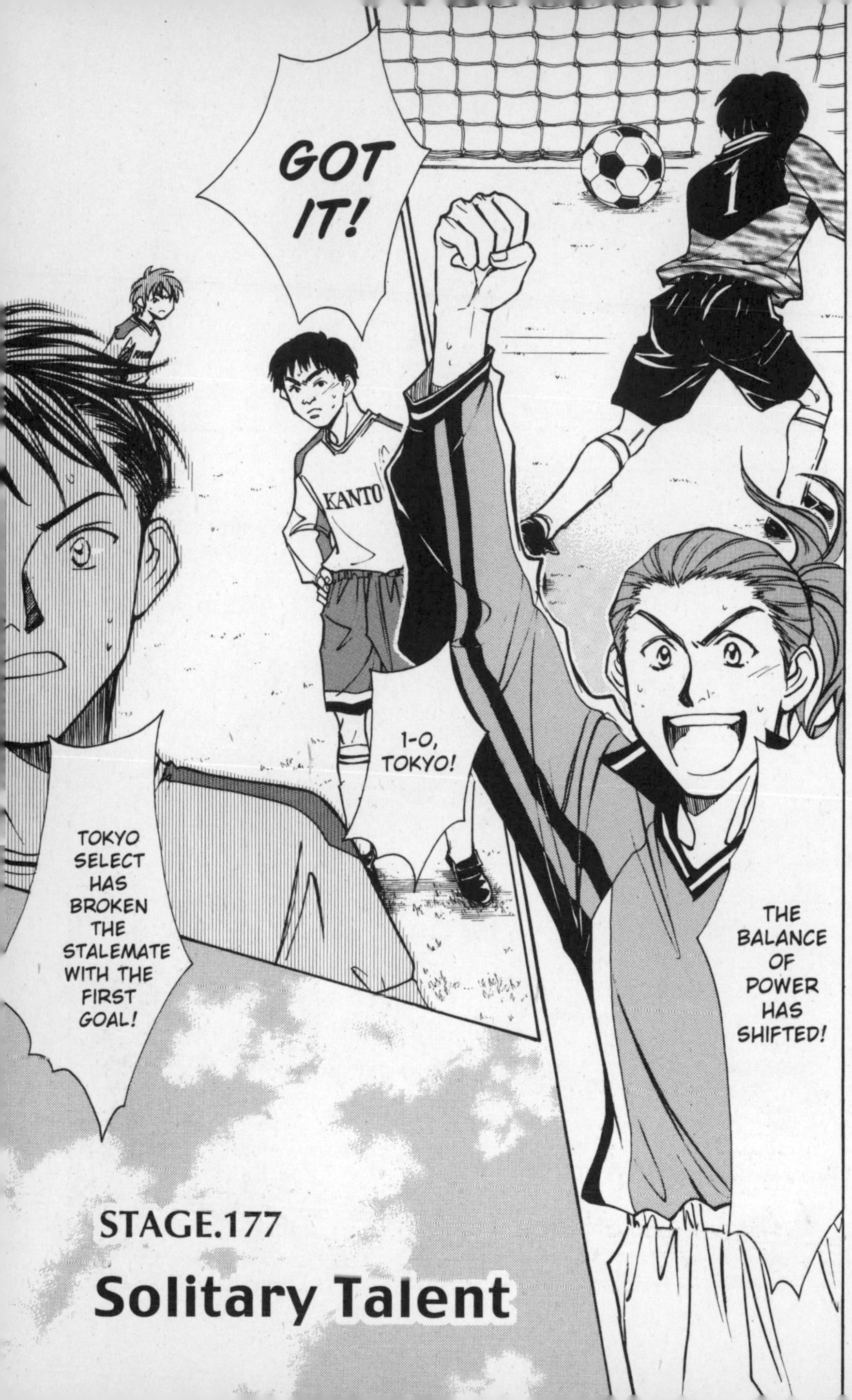
GOT IT!
1-0, TOKYO!
THE BALANCE OF POWER HAS SHIFTED!
TOKYO SELECT HAS BROKEN THE STALEMATE WITH THE FIRST GOAL!
KANTO

STAGE.177

Solitary Talent

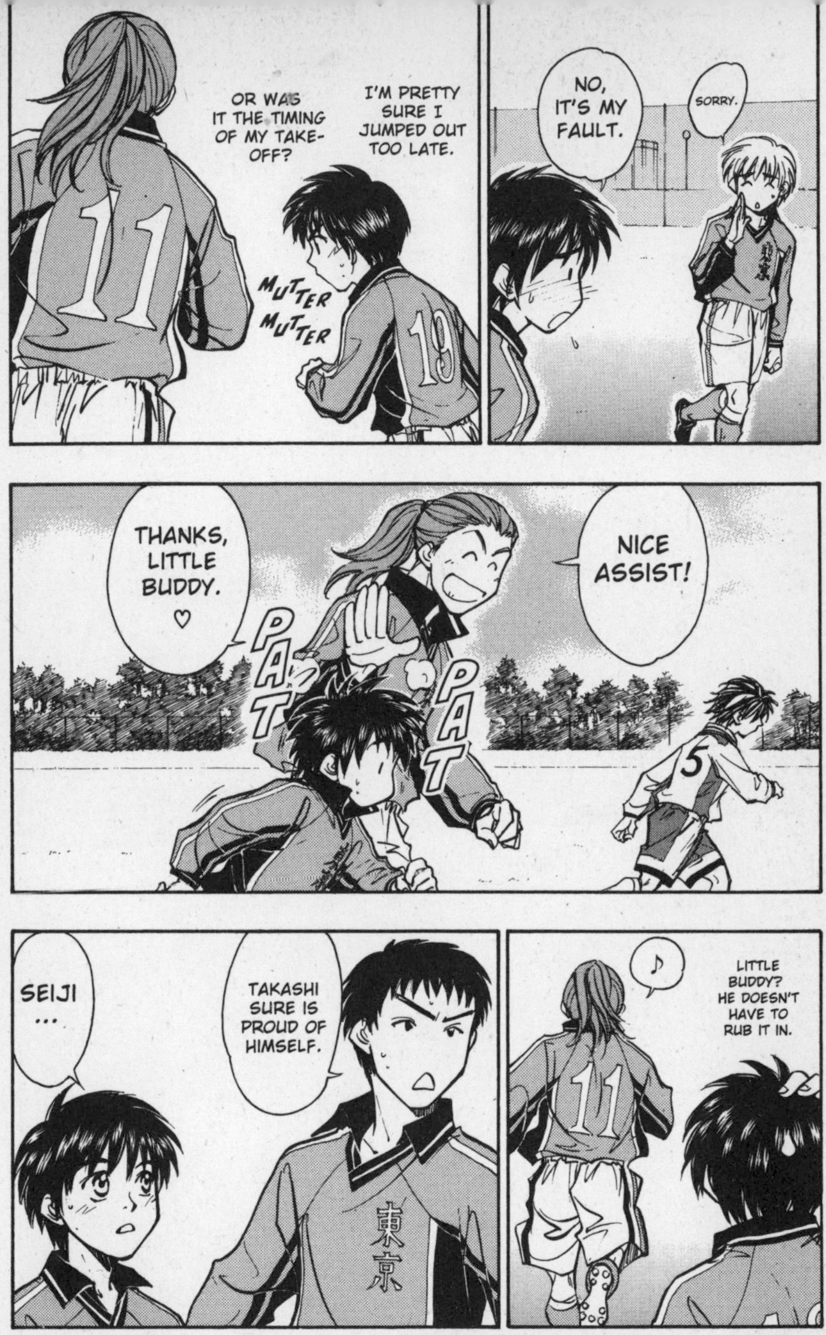

SORRY.
NO, IT'S MY FAULT.
I'M PRETTY SURE I JUMPED OUT TOO LATE.
OR WAS IT THE TIMING OF MY TAKE-OFF?
MUTTER MUTTER
NICE ASSIST!
PAT
THANKS, LITTLE BUDDY. ♡
PAT
LITTLE BUDDY? HE DOESN'T HAVE TO RUB IT IN.
♪
TAKASHI SURE IS PROUD OF HIMSELF.
SEIJI ...

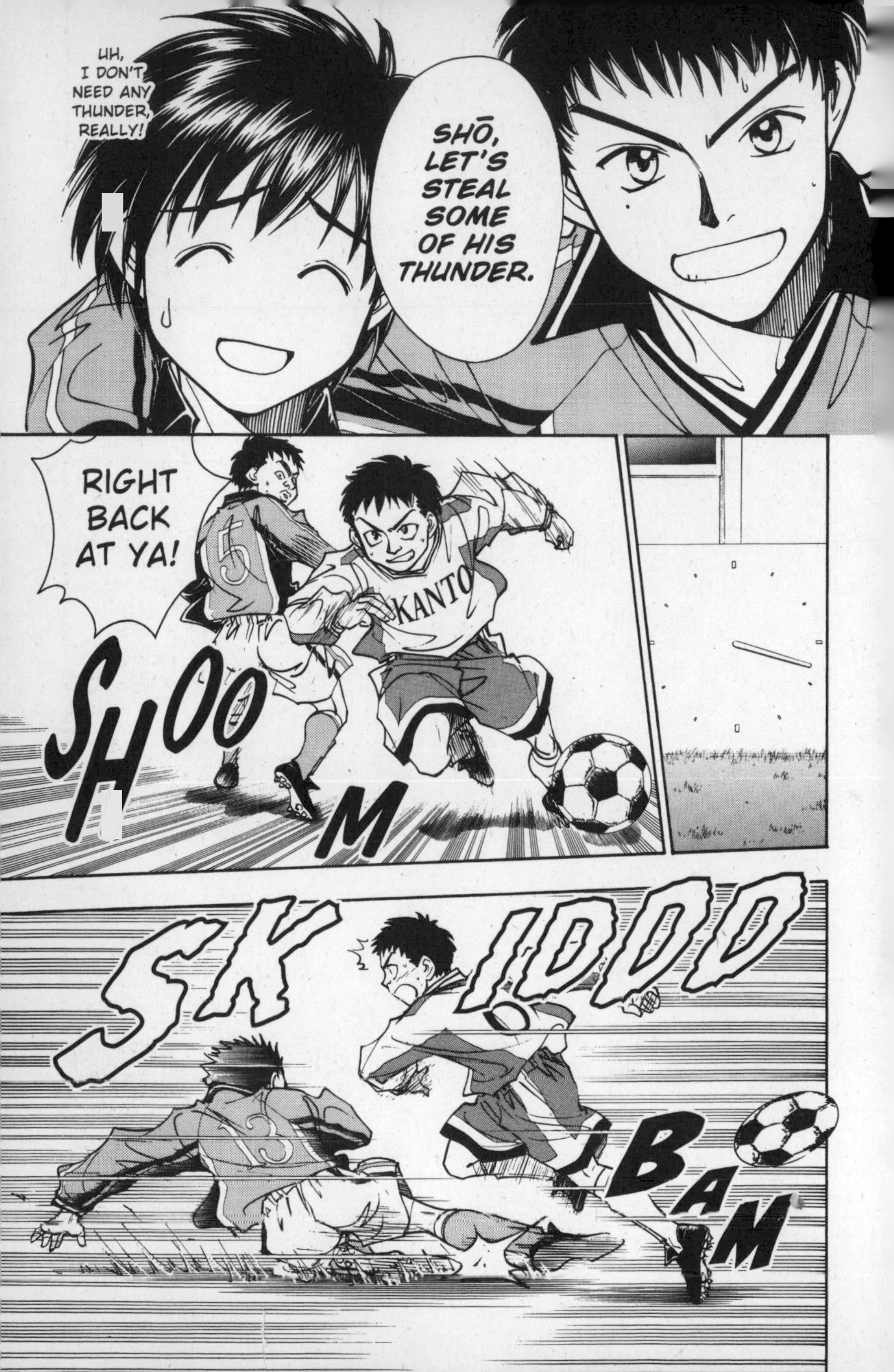
SHŌ, LET'S STEAL SOME OF HIS THUNDER.
UH, I DON'T NEED ANY THUNDER, REALLY!
RIGHT BACK AT YA!
SHOOOM
KANTO
SKIDOOO
BAM

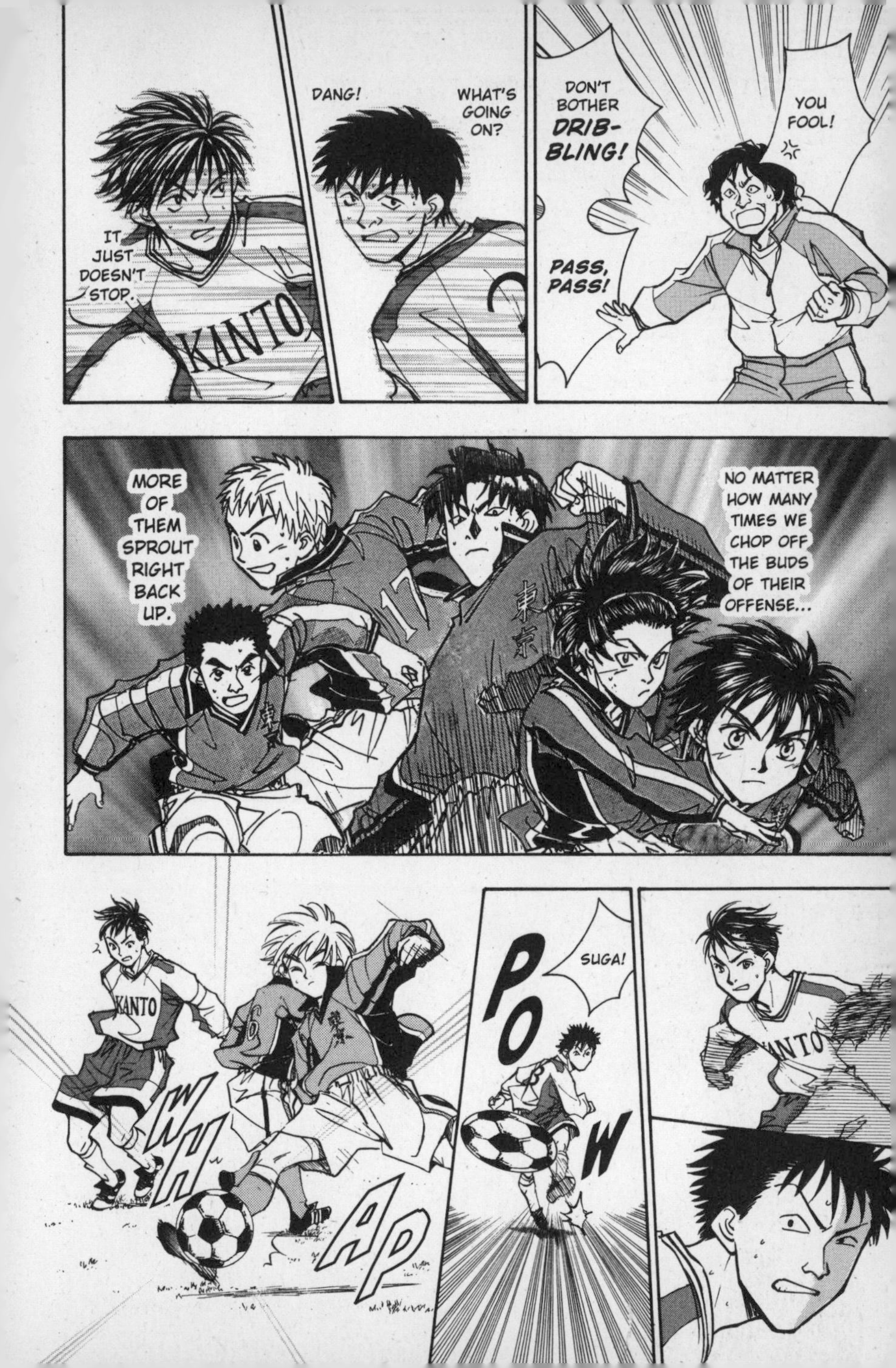
YOU FOOL!
DON'T BOTHER DRIBBLING!
PASS, PASS!
WHAT'S GOING ON?
DANG!
IT JUST DOESN'T STOP.
NO MATTER HOW MANY TIMES WE CHOP OFF THE BUDS OF THEIR OFFENSE...
MORE OF THEM SPROUT RIGHT BACK UP.
SUGA!
POW
WHAP

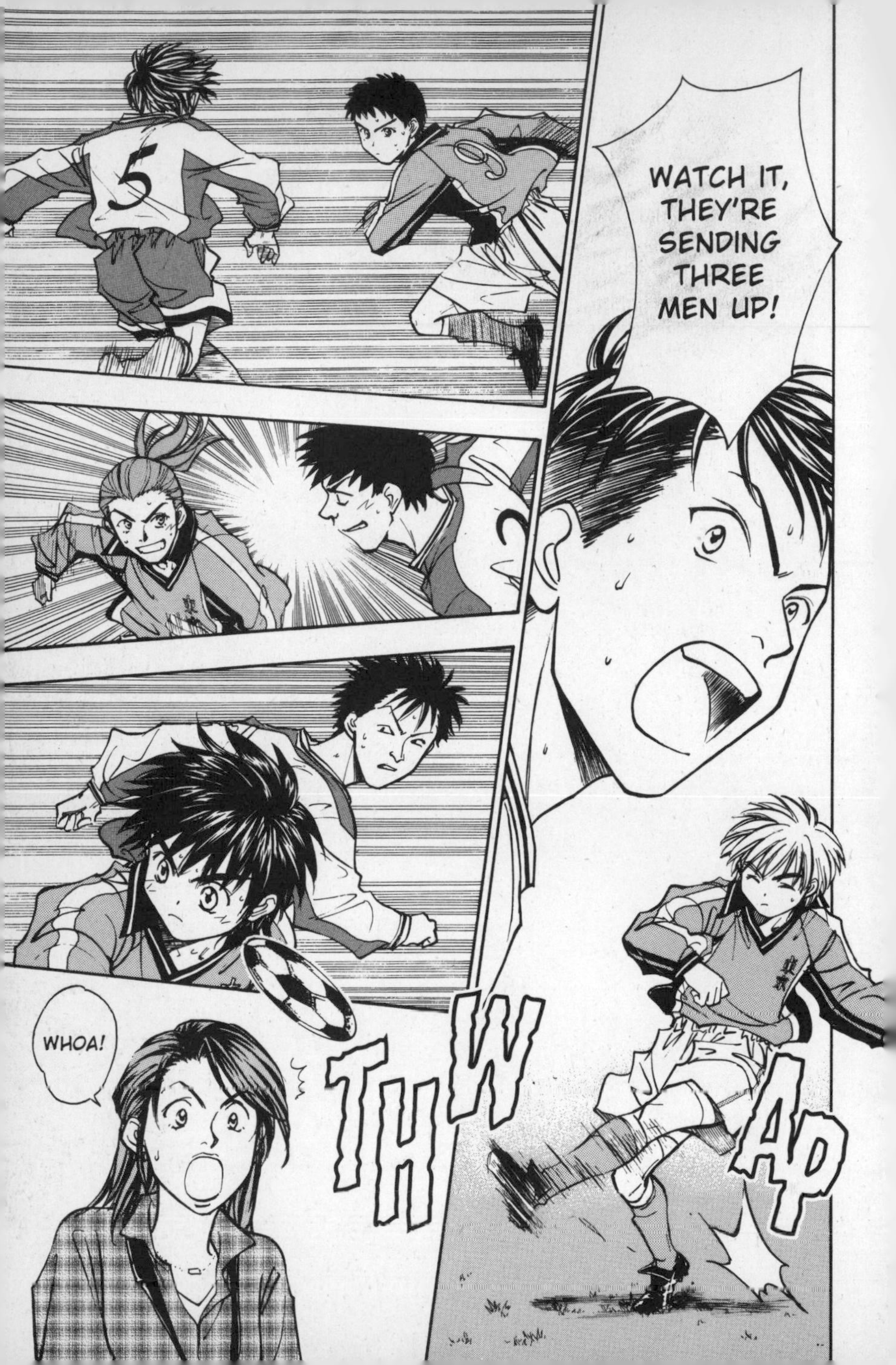
WATCH IT, THEY'RE SENDING THREE MEN UP!
THWAP
WHOA!

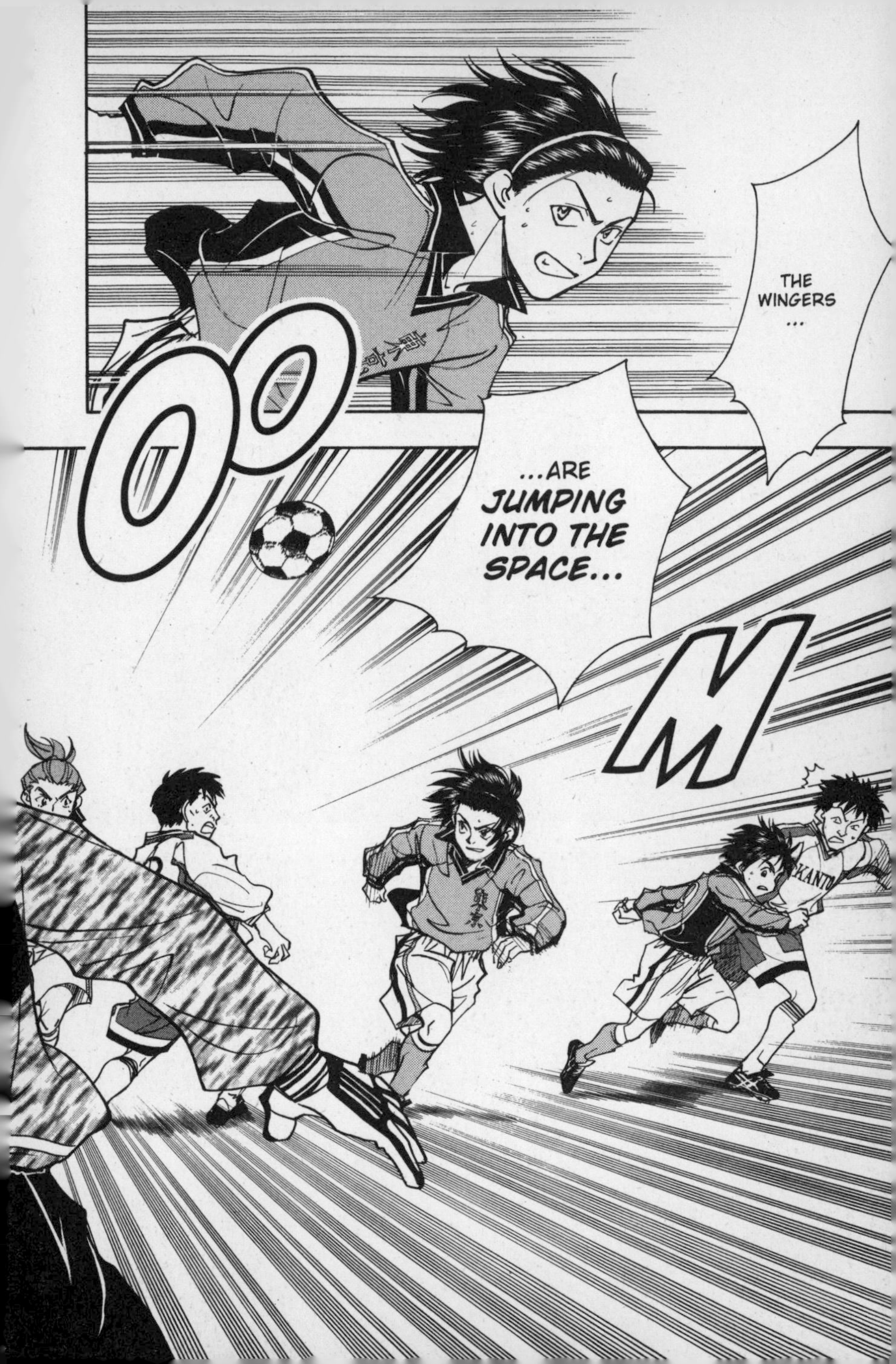
THE WINGERS ...
...ARE JUMPING INTO THE SPACE...
KANTO

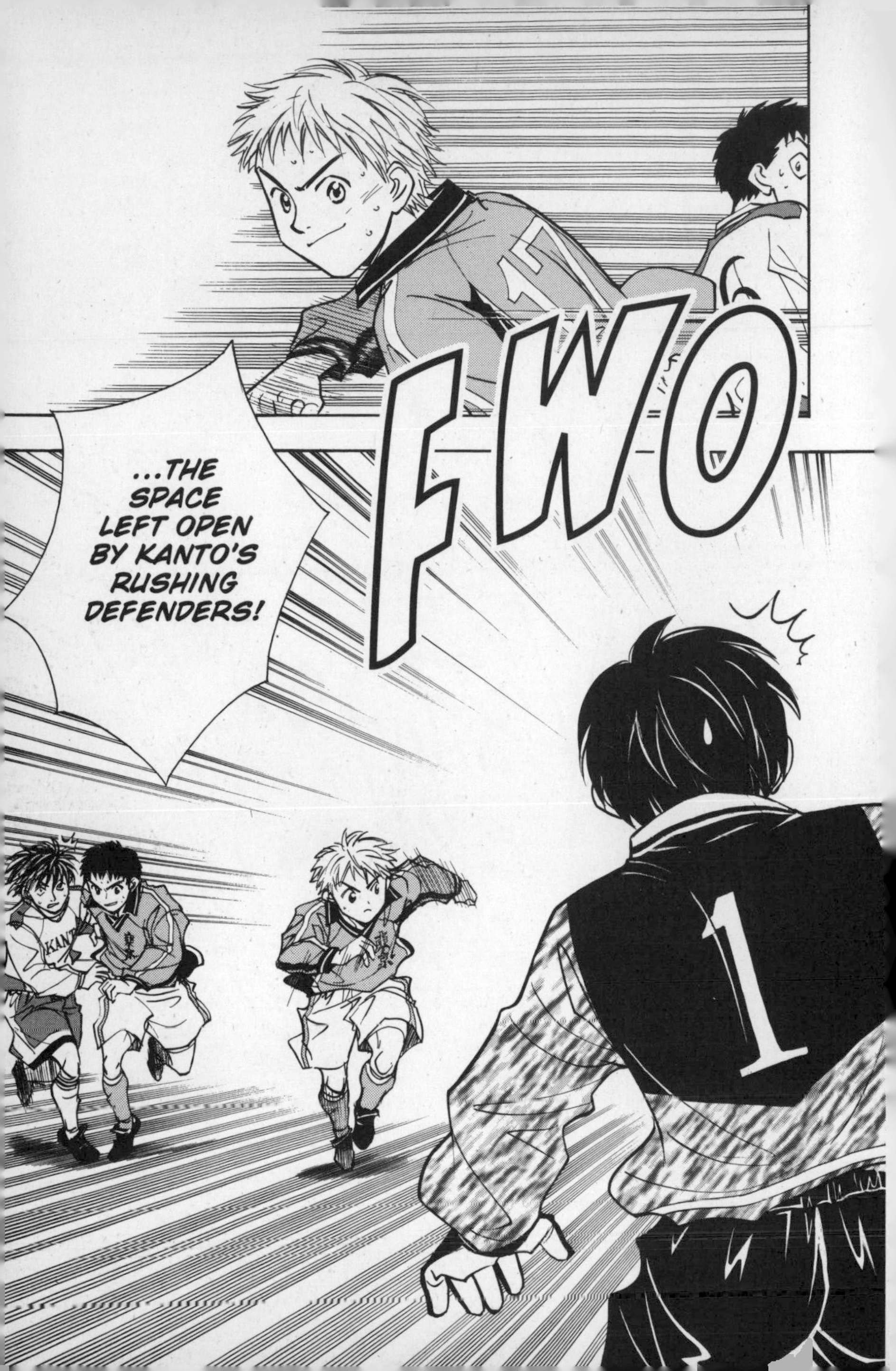

FWO
...THE SPACE LEFT OPEN BY KANTO'S RUSHING DEFENDERS!
1

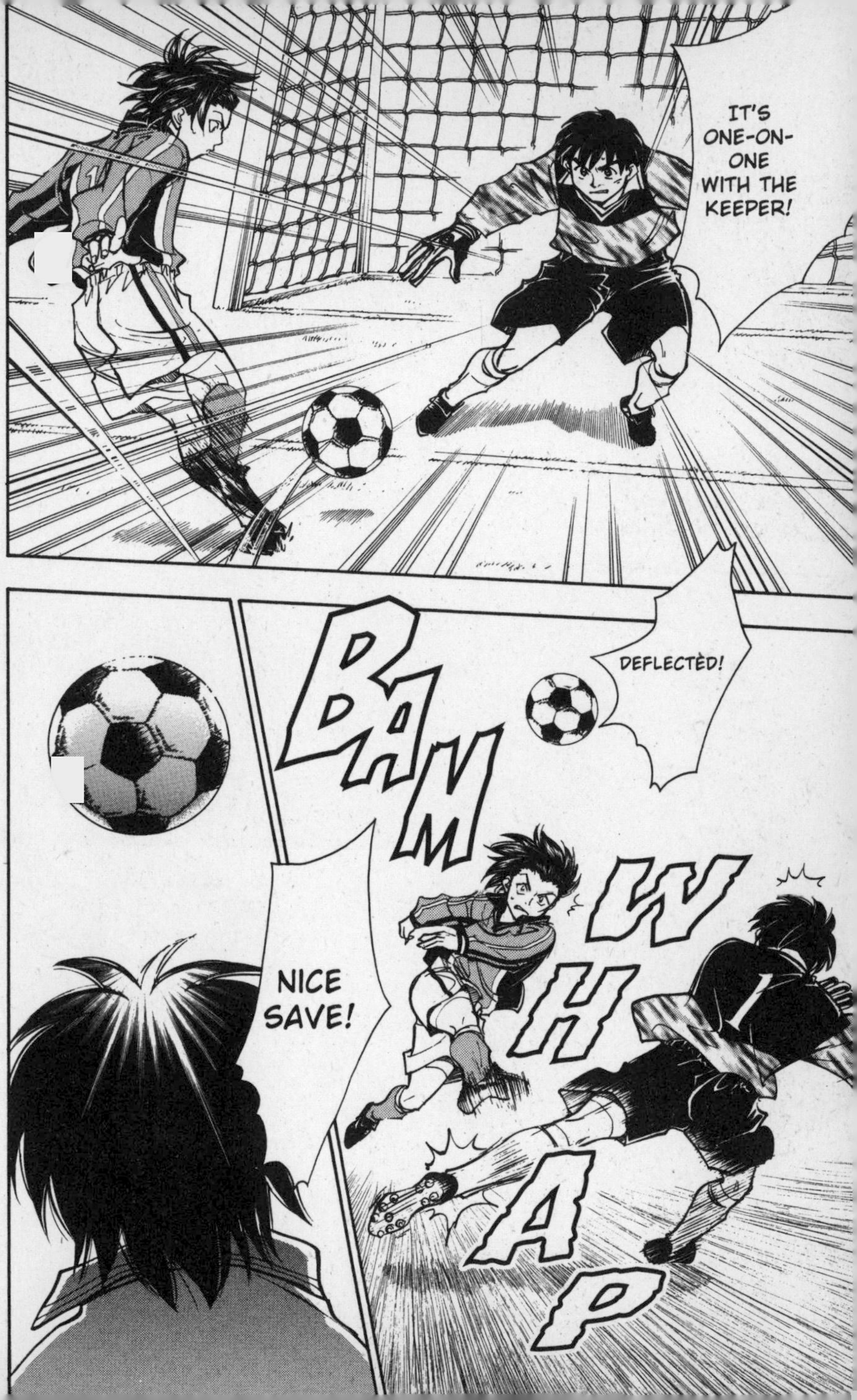
IT'S ONE-ON-ONE WITH THE KEEPER!
DEFLECTED!
BAM
WHAP
NICE SAVE!

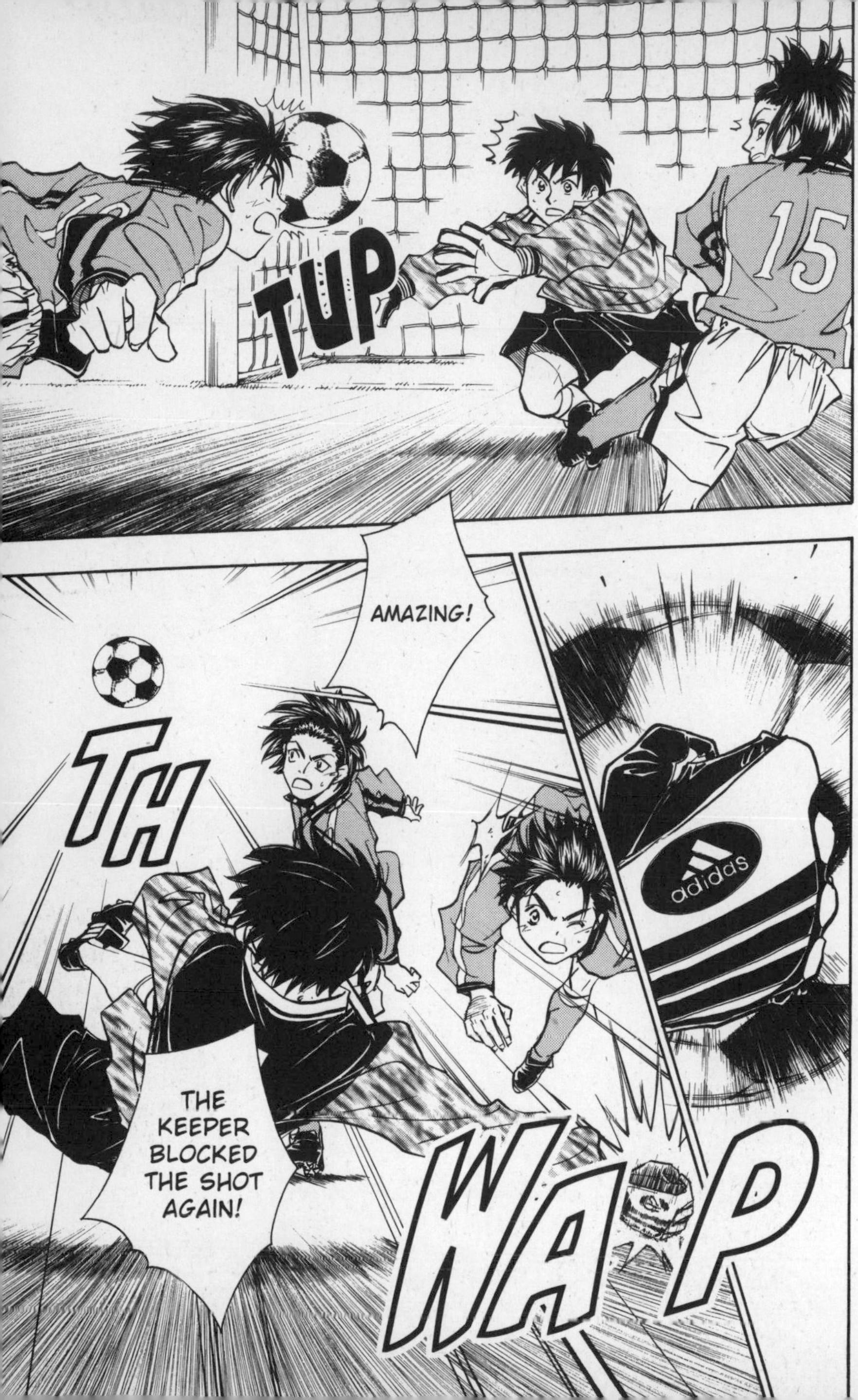
TUP
adidas
WHAP
AMAZING!
TH
THE KEEPER BLOCKED THE SHOT AGAIN!

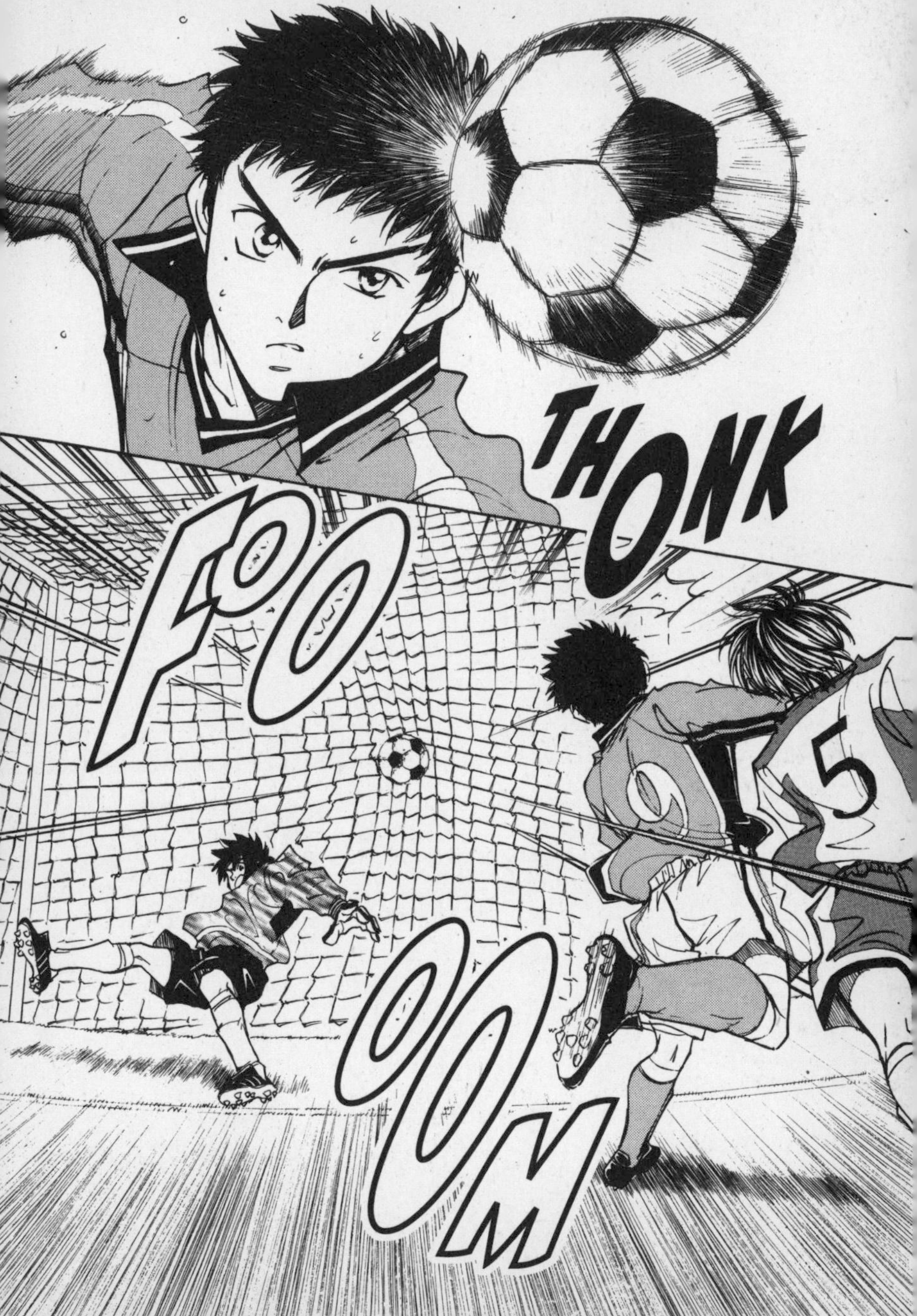
THONK
FOOOOOM

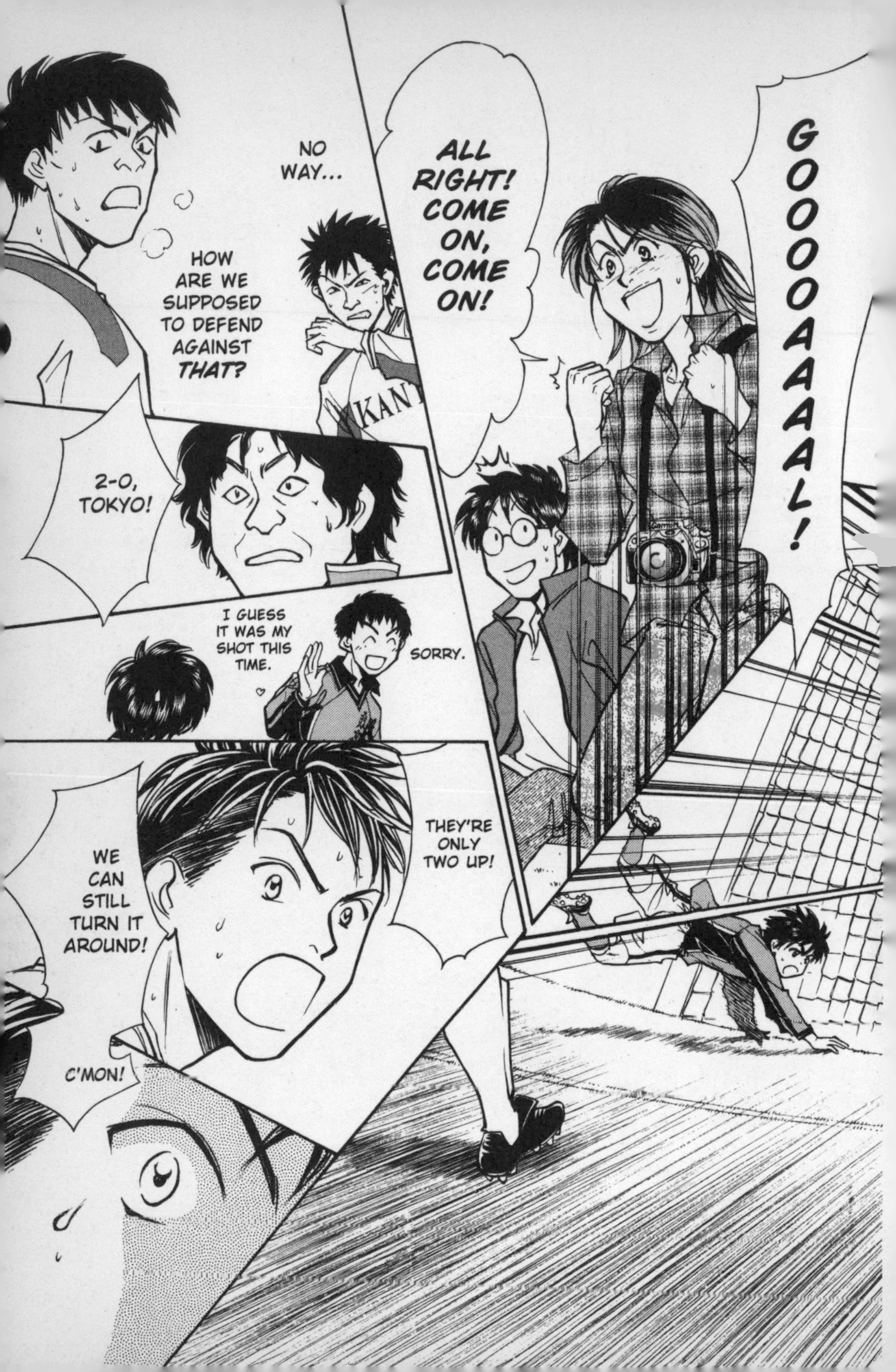
GOOOOAAAAAL!
ALL RIGHT! COME ON, COME ON!
NO WAY...
HOW ARE WE SUPPOSED TO DEFEND AGAINST *THAT?*
2-0, TOKYO!
SORRY.
I GUESS IT WAS MY SHOT THIS TIME.
THEY'RE ONLY TWO UP!
WE CAN STILL TURN IT AROUND!
C'MON!

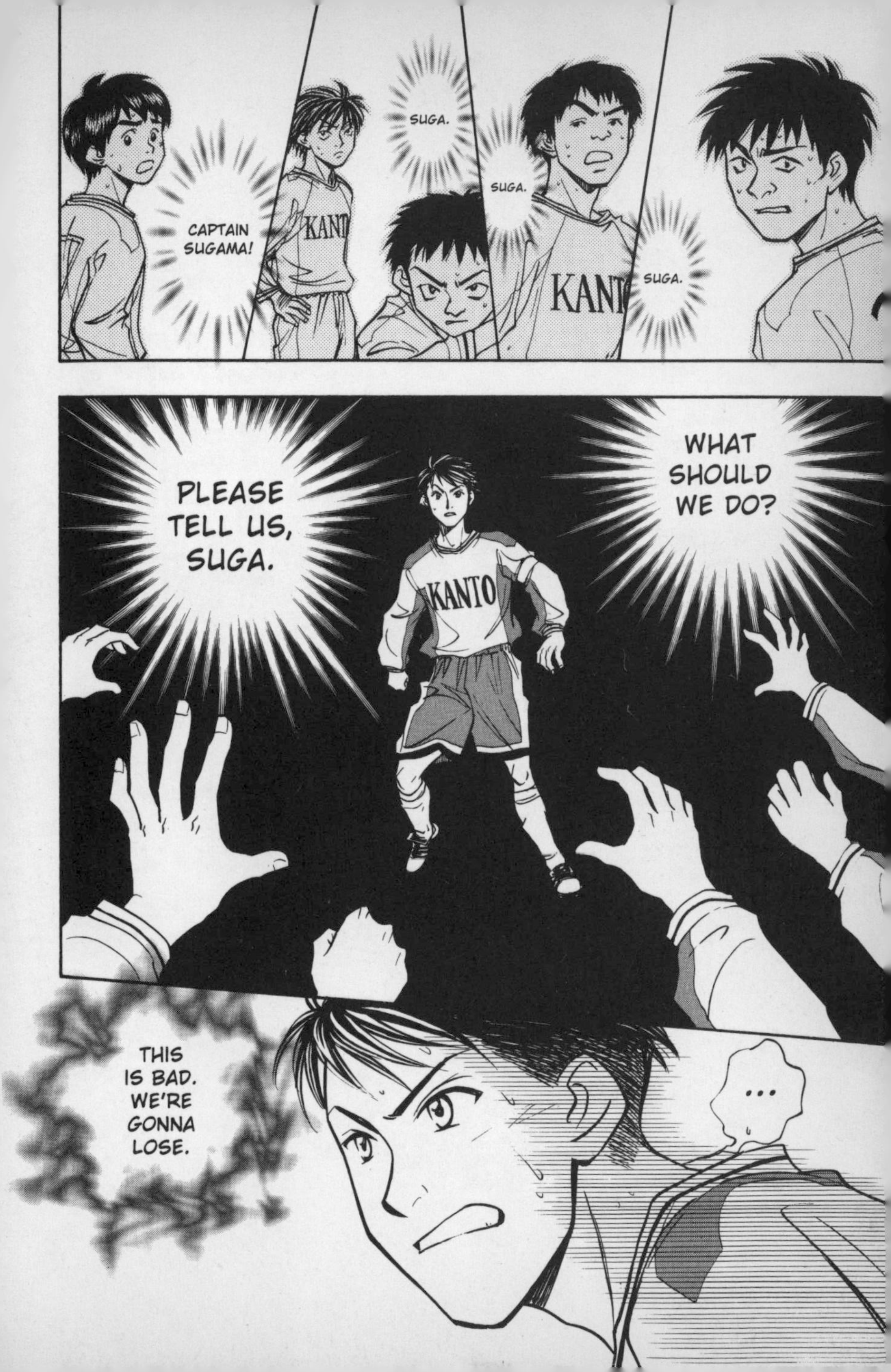
SUGA.
SUGA.
SUGA.
CAPTAIN SUGAMA!
KANTO
WHAT SHOULD WE DO?
PLEASE TELL US, SUGA.
...
THIS IS BAD. WE'RE GONNA LOSE.

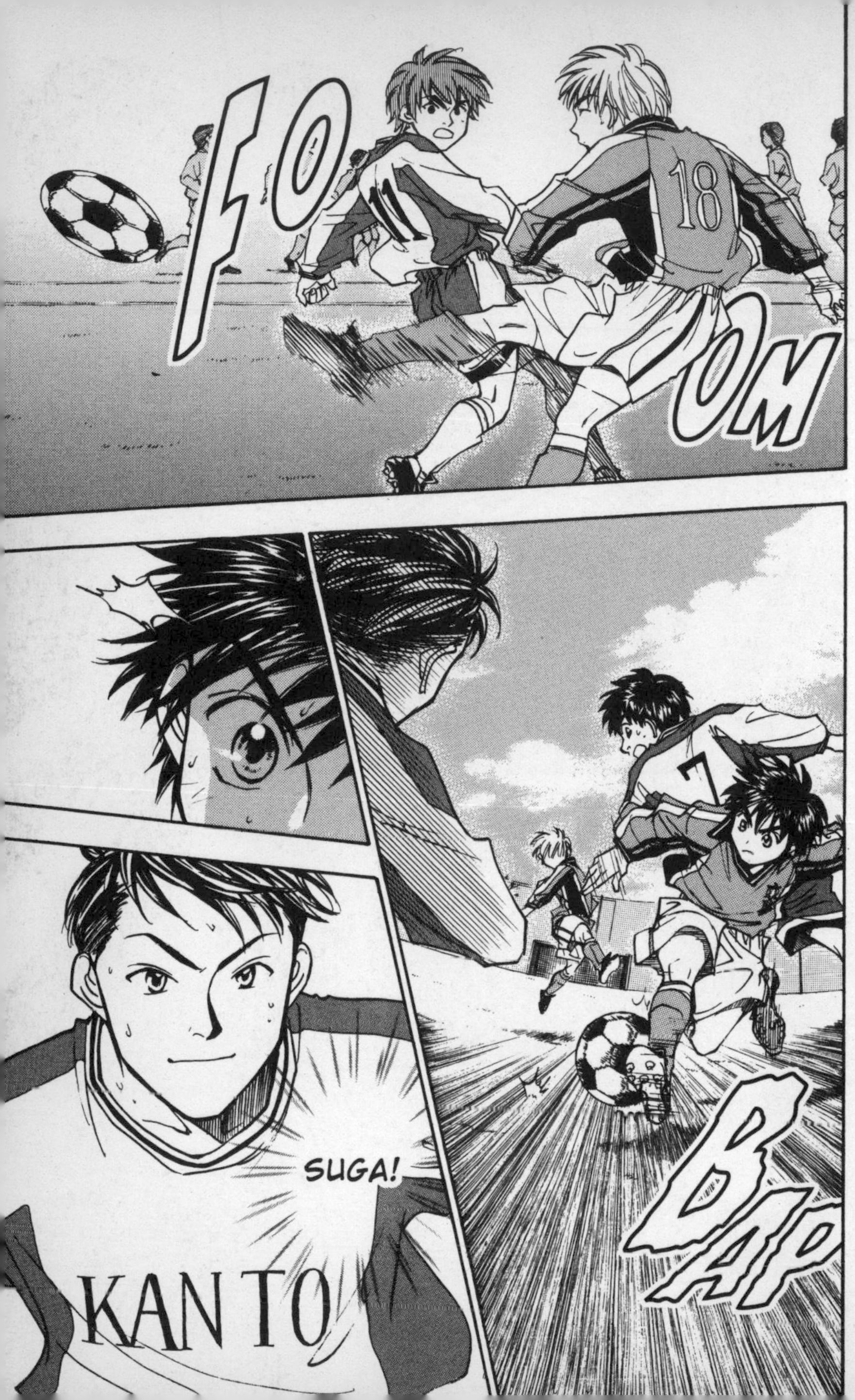
FOOM
BAP
SUGA!
KANTO

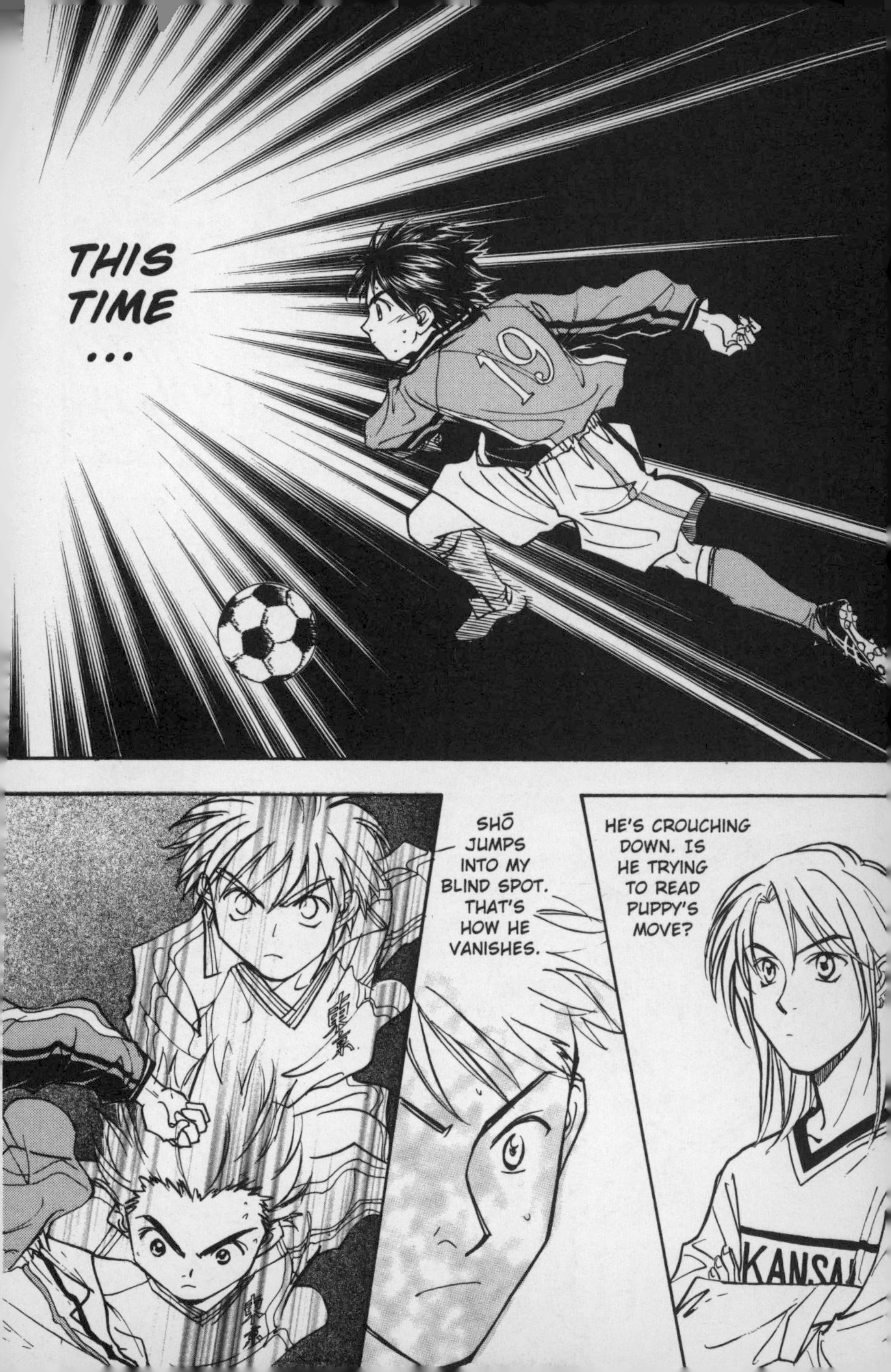
THIS TIME ...
HE'S CROUCHING DOWN. IS HE TRYING TO READ PUPPY'S MOVE?
SHŌ JUMPS INTO MY BLIND SPOT. THAT'S HOW HE VANISHES.
KANSAI

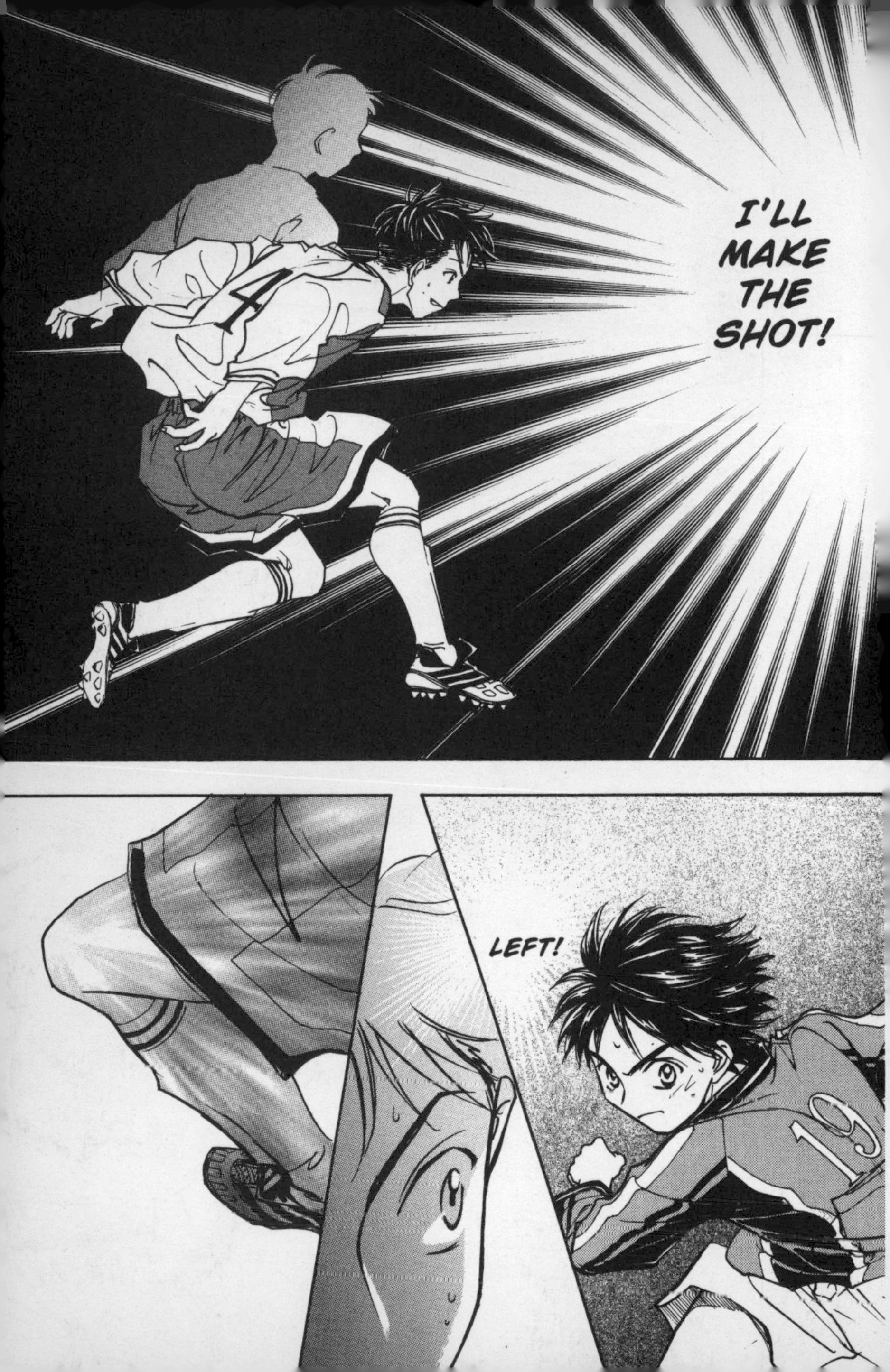
I'LL MAKE THE SHOT!
LEFT!

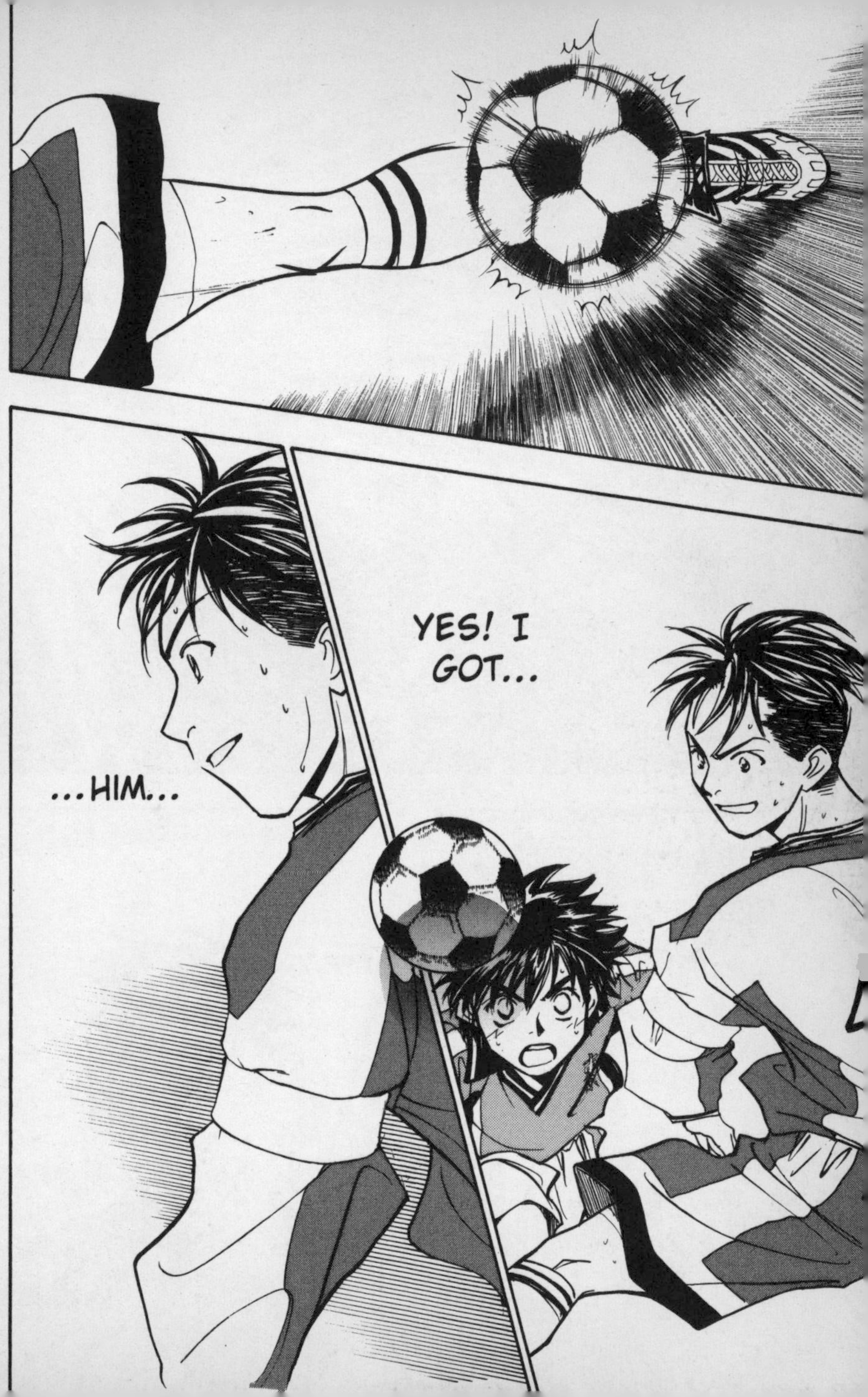
YES! I GOT...
...HIM...

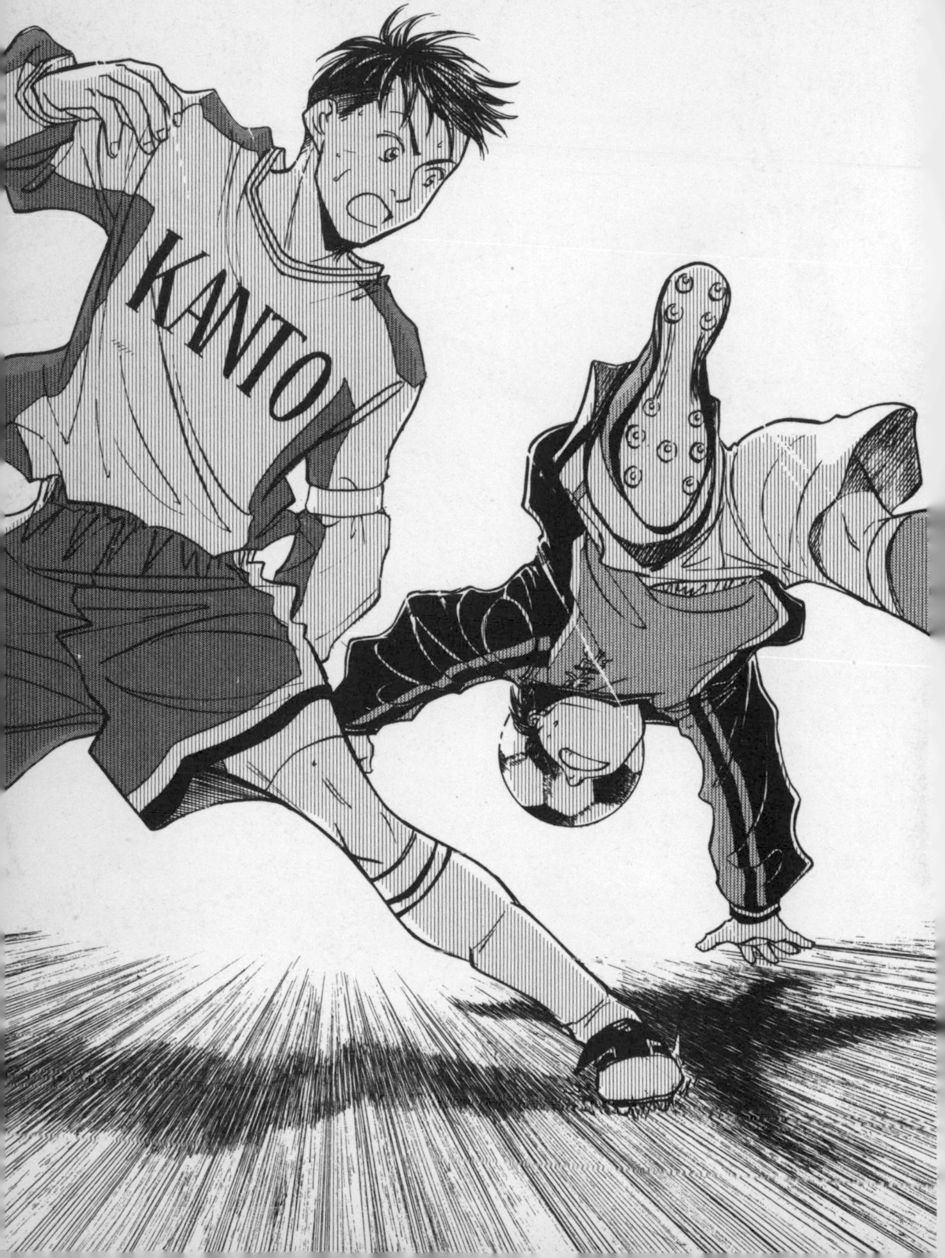
KANTO

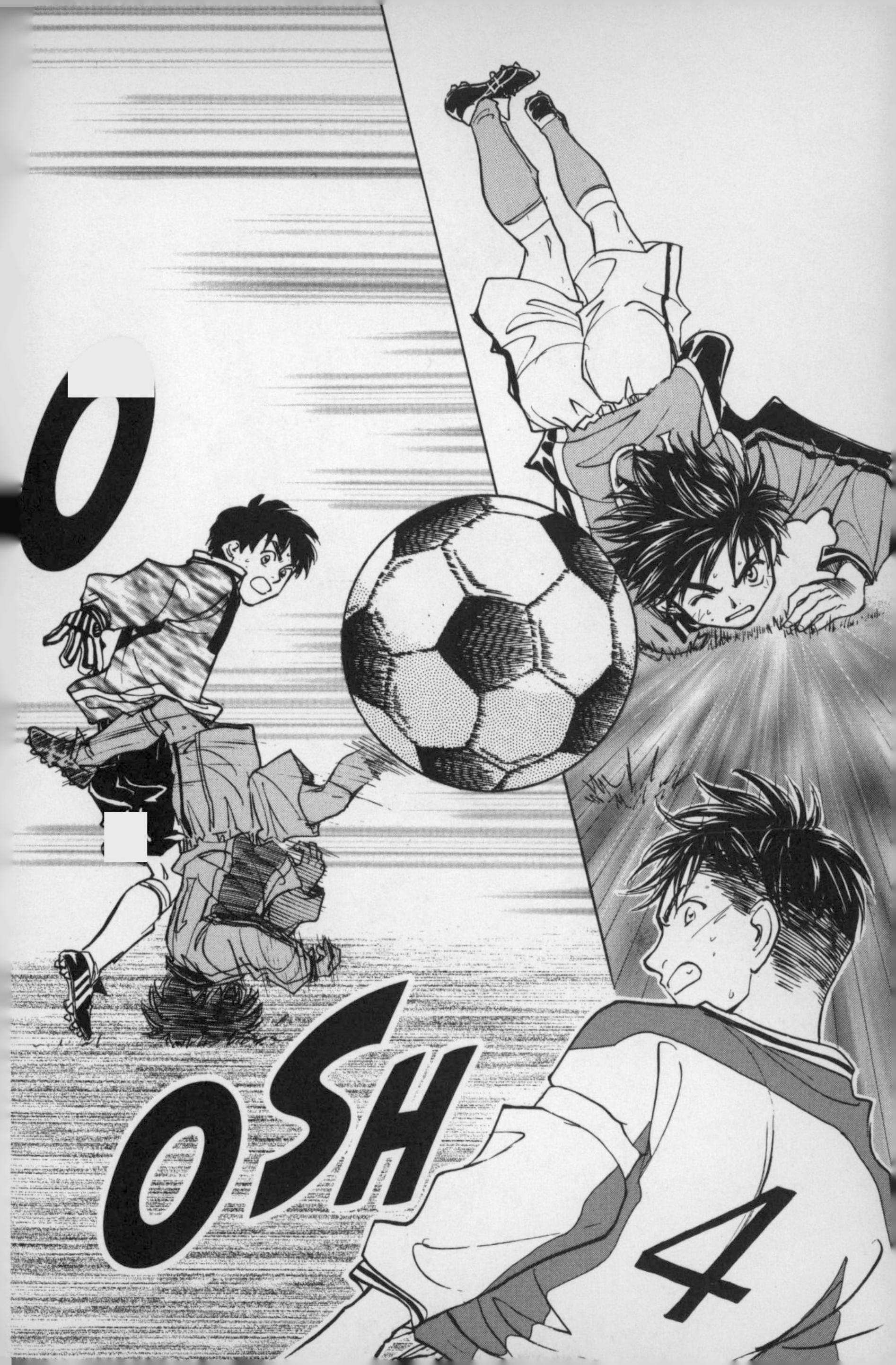
O
OSH

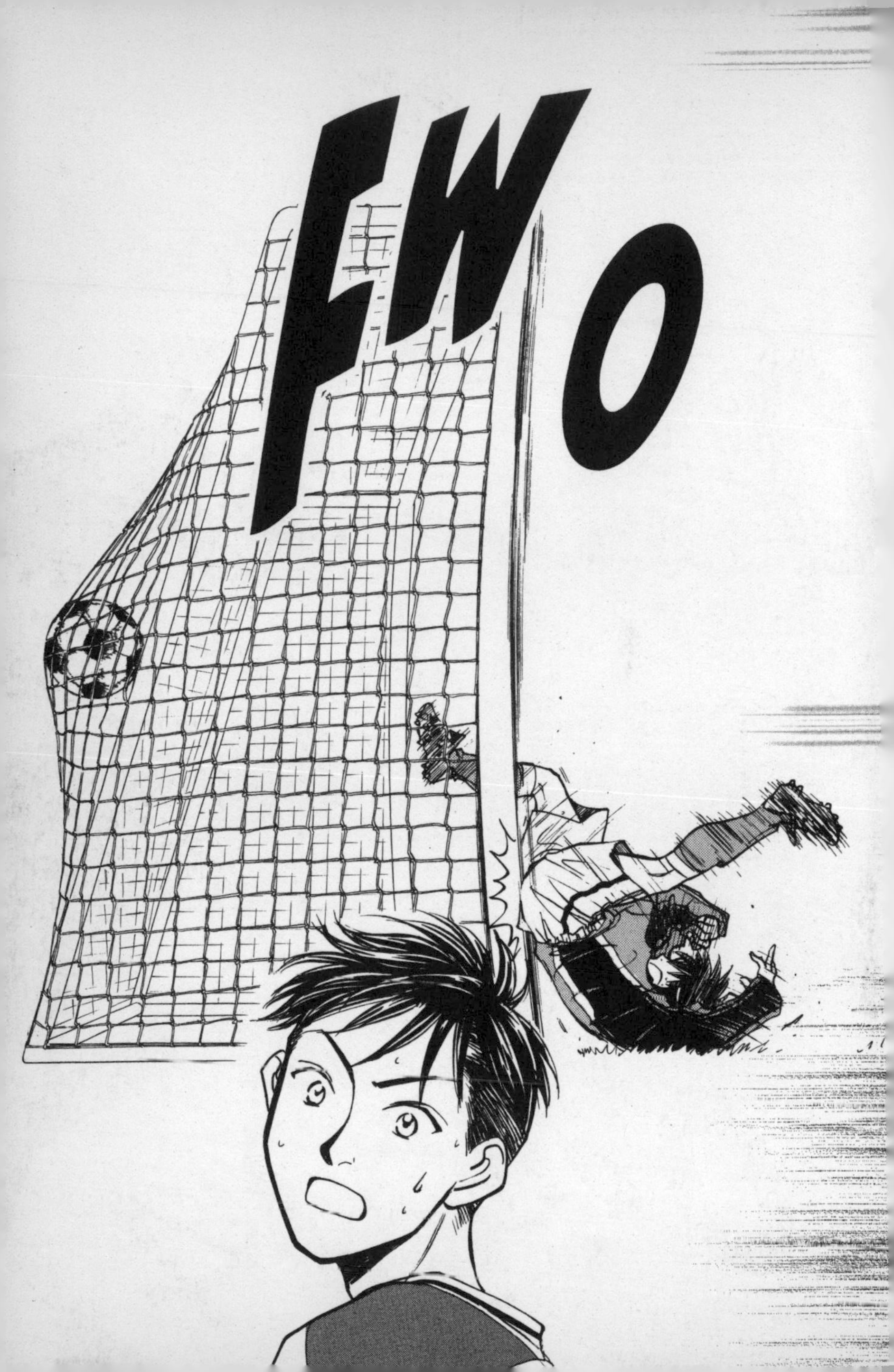
FWO

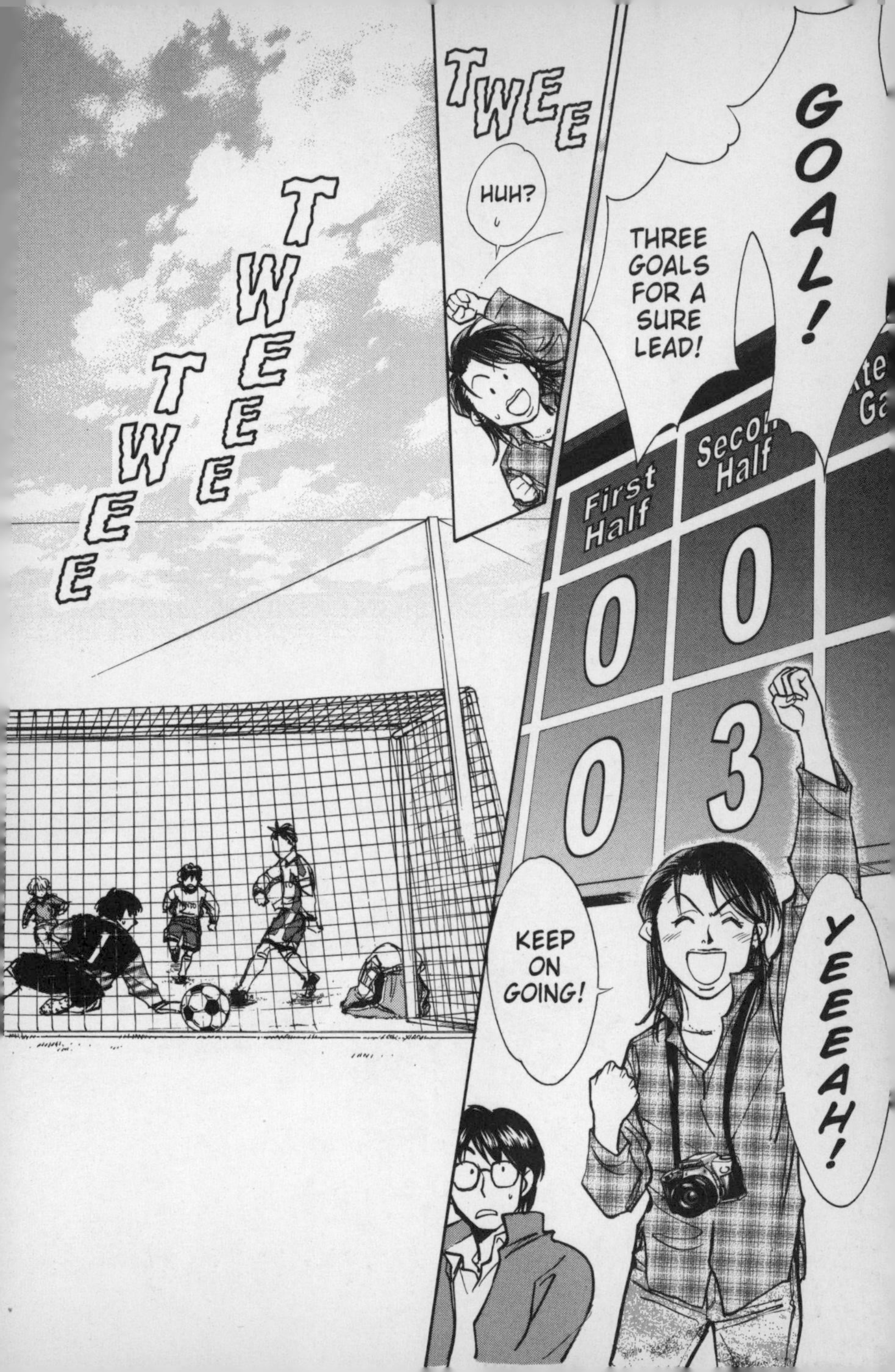
GOAL!
THREE GOALS FOR A SURE LEAD!
First Half
YEEEAH!
KEEP ON GOING!
TWEE
HUH?
TWEE TWEE TWEE

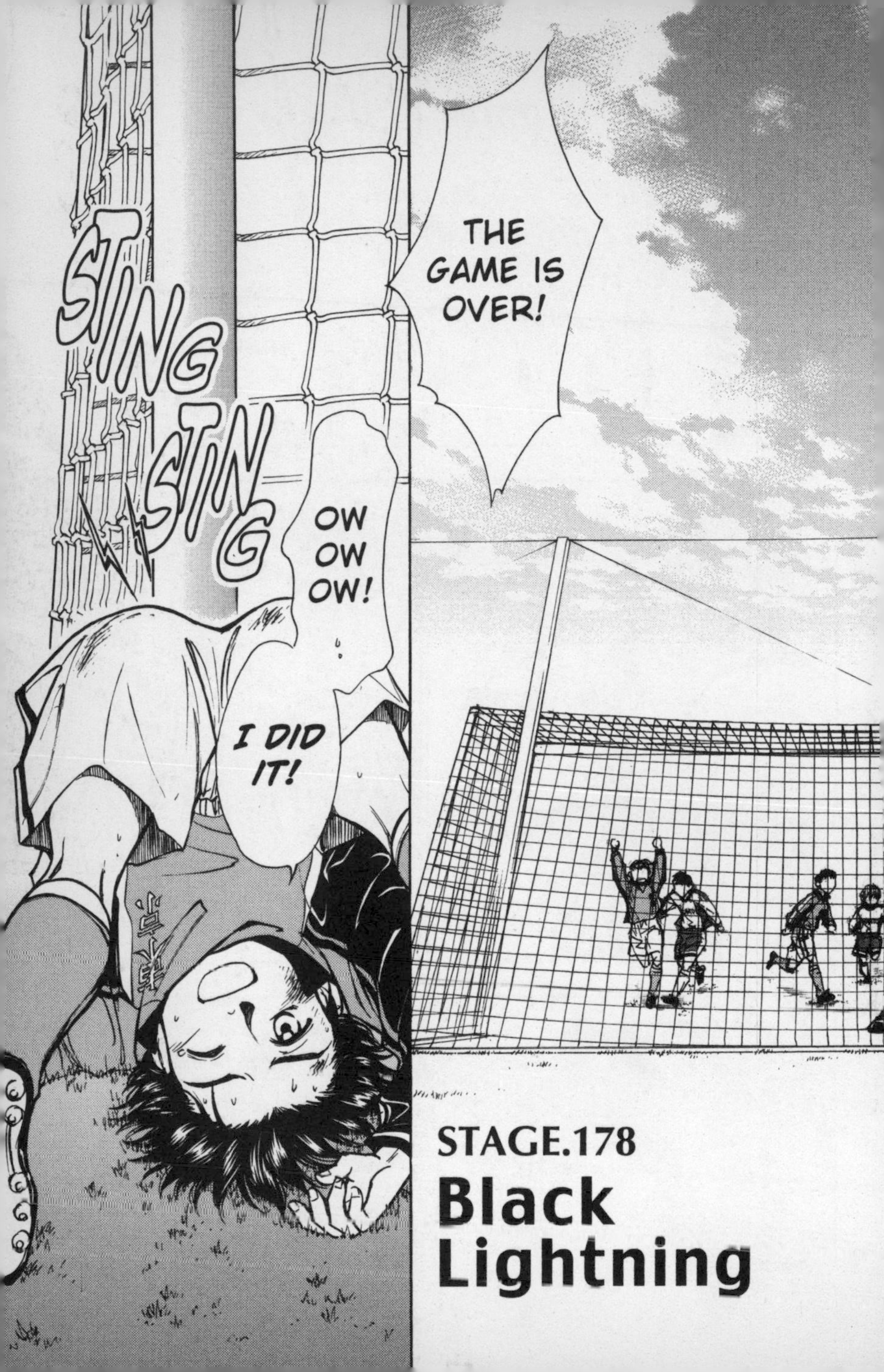
THE GAME IS OVER!
STING
STING
OW OW OW!
I DID IT!

STAGE.178
Black Lightning

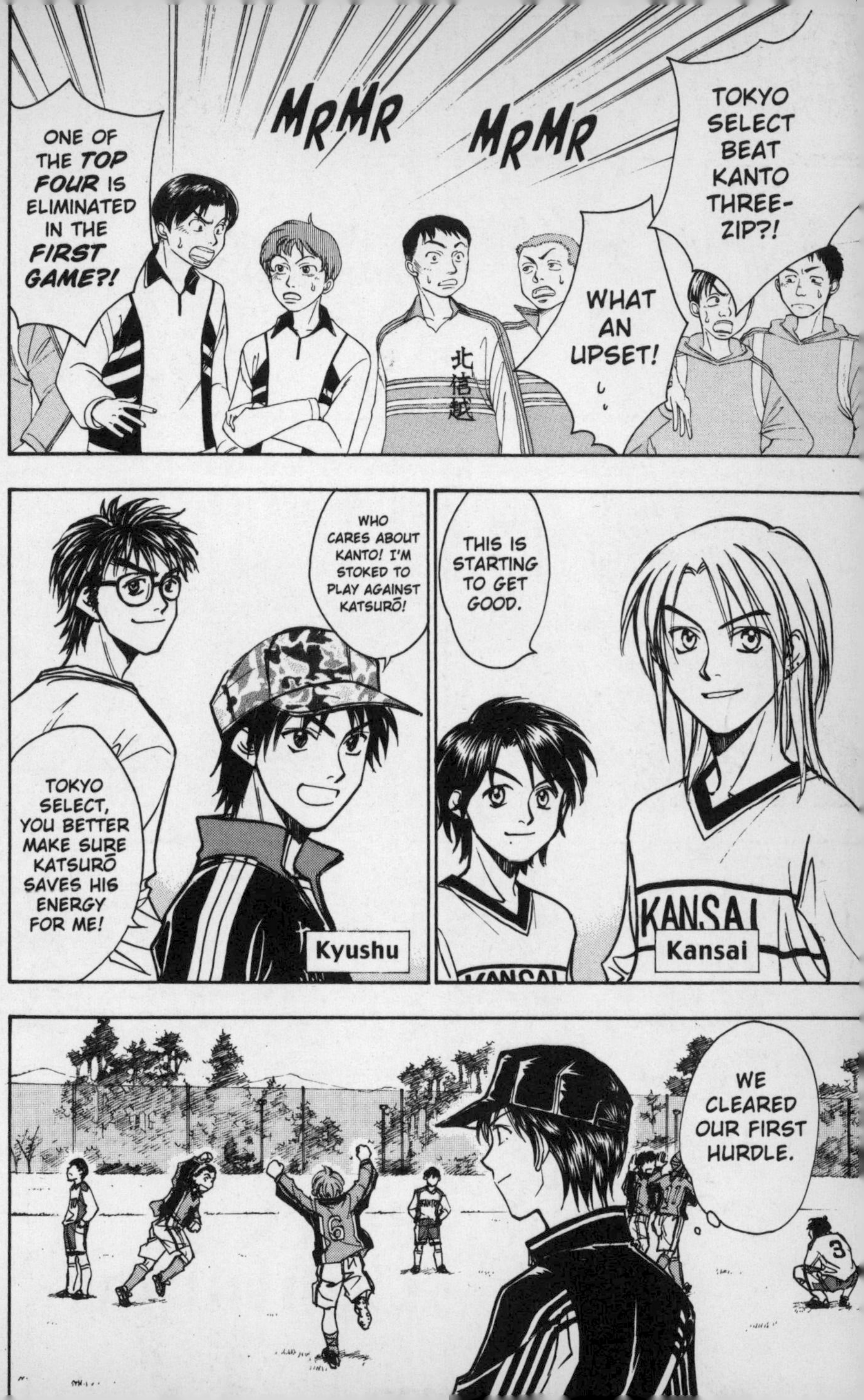
TOKYO SELECT BEAT KANTO THREE-ZIP?!
WHAT AN UPSET!
MRMR
MRMR
北信越
ONE OF THE TOP FOUR IS ELIMINATED IN THE FIRST GAME?!
THIS IS STARTING TO GET GOOD.
Kansai
KANSAI
WHO CARES ABOUT KANTO! I'M STOKED TO PLAY AGAINST KATSURŌ!
TOKYO SELECT, YOU BETTER MAKE SURE KATSURŌ SAVES HIS ENERGY FOR ME!
Kyushu
WE CLEARED OUR FIRST HURDLE.

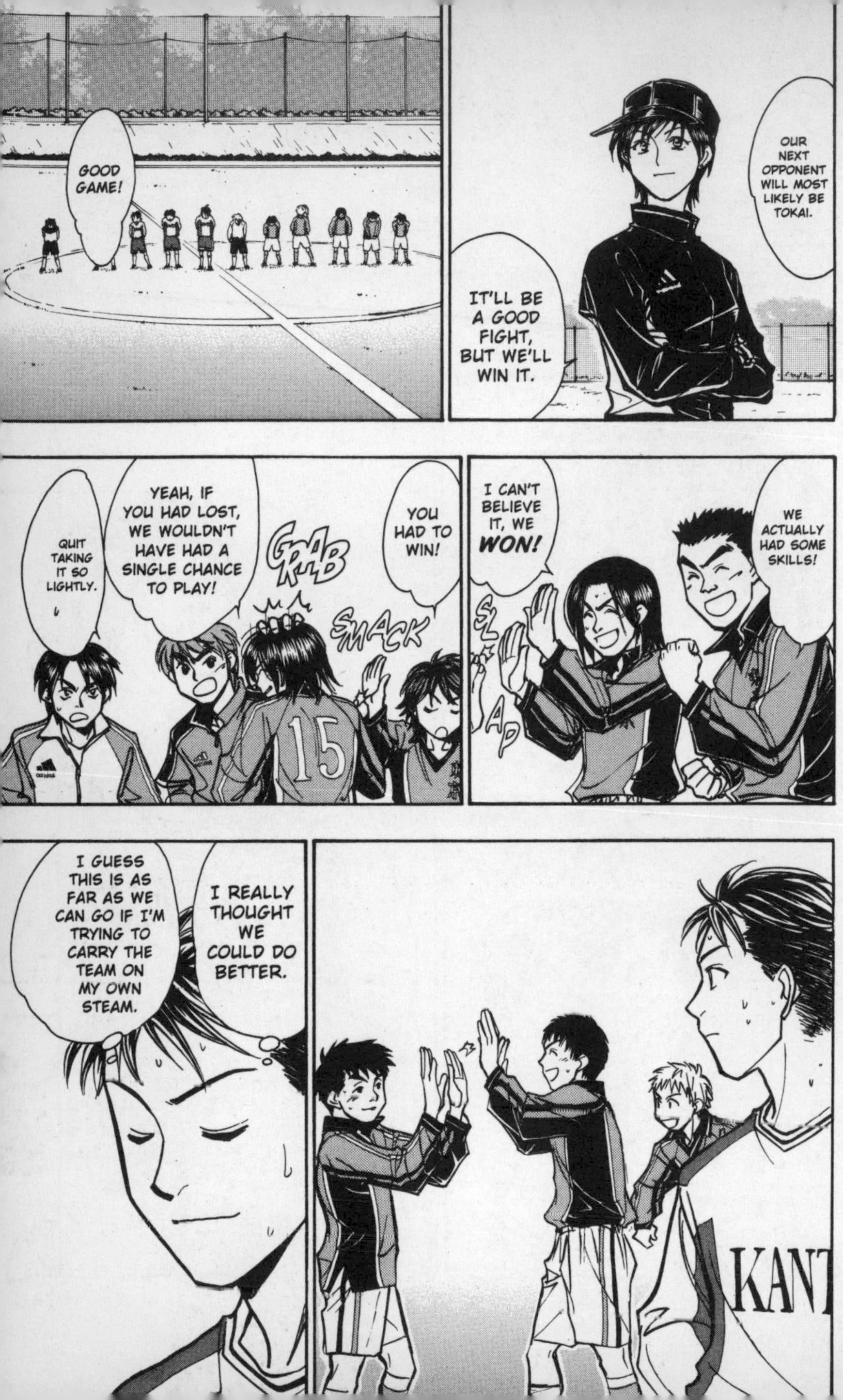
OUR NEXT OPPONENT WILL MOST LIKELY BE TOKAI.
IT'LL BE A GOOD FIGHT, BUT WE'LL WIN IT.
GOOD GAME!
WE ACTUALLY HAD SOME SKILLS!
I CAN'T BELIEVE IT, WE WON!
SLAP
YOU HAD TO WIN!
SMACK
GRAB
YEAH, IF YOU HAD LOST, WE WOULDN'T HAVE HAD A SINGLE CHANCE TO PLAY!
QUIT TAKING IT SO LIGHTLY.
KANT
I REALLY THOUGHT WE COULD DO BETTER.
I GUESS THIS IS AS FAR AS WE CAN GO IF I'M TRYING TO CARRY THE TEAM ON MY OWN STEAM.

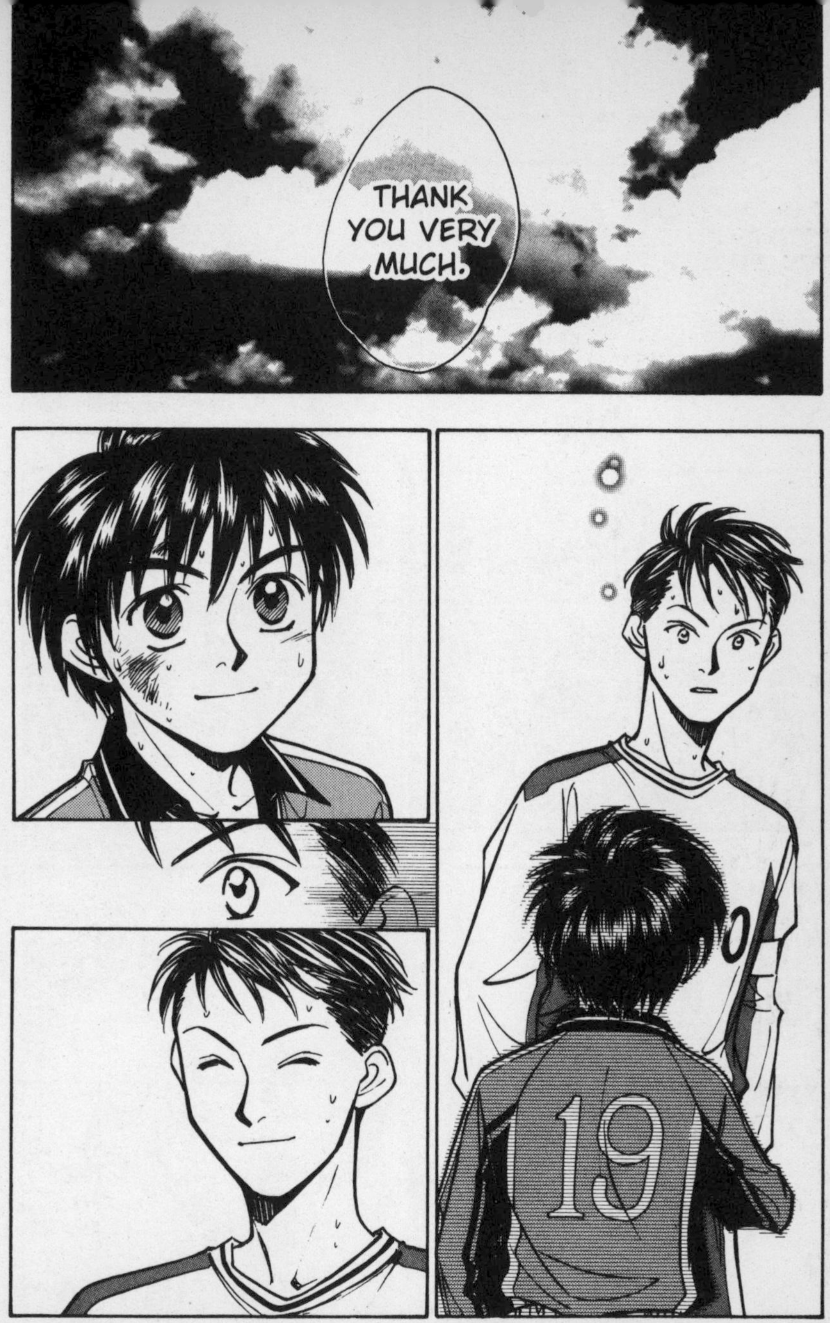
THANK YOU VERY MUCH.

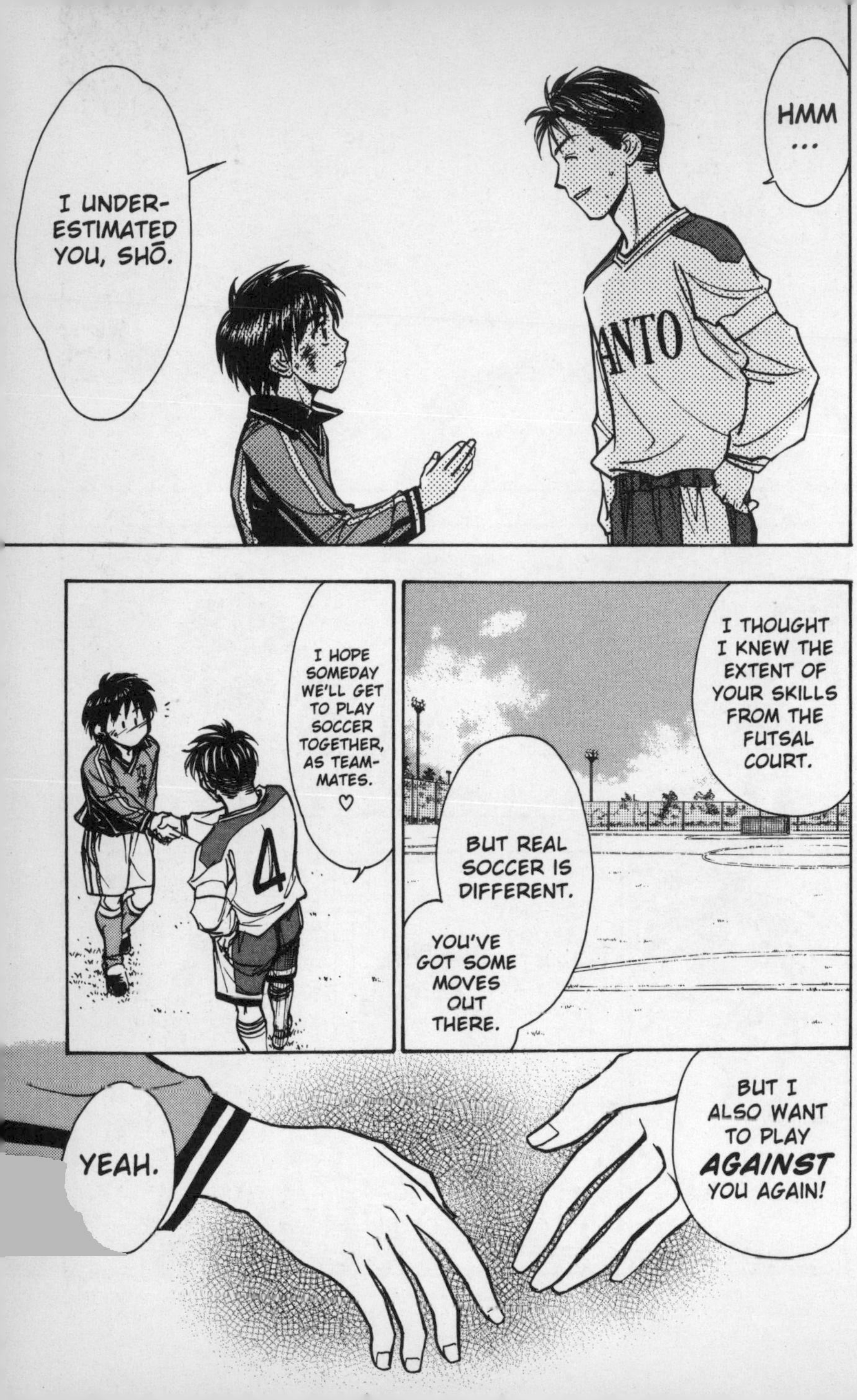
HMM ...
I UNDER-ESTIMATED YOU, SHŌ.
I THOUGHT I KNEW THE EXTENT OF YOUR SKILLS FROM THE FUTSAL COURT.
BUT REAL SOCCER IS DIFFERENT.
YOU'VE GOT SOME MOVES OUT THERE.
I HOPE SOMEDAY WE'LL GET TO PLAY SOCCER TOGETHER, AS TEAM-MATES. ♡
BUT I ALSO WANT TO PLAY *AGAINST* YOU AGAIN!
YEAH.

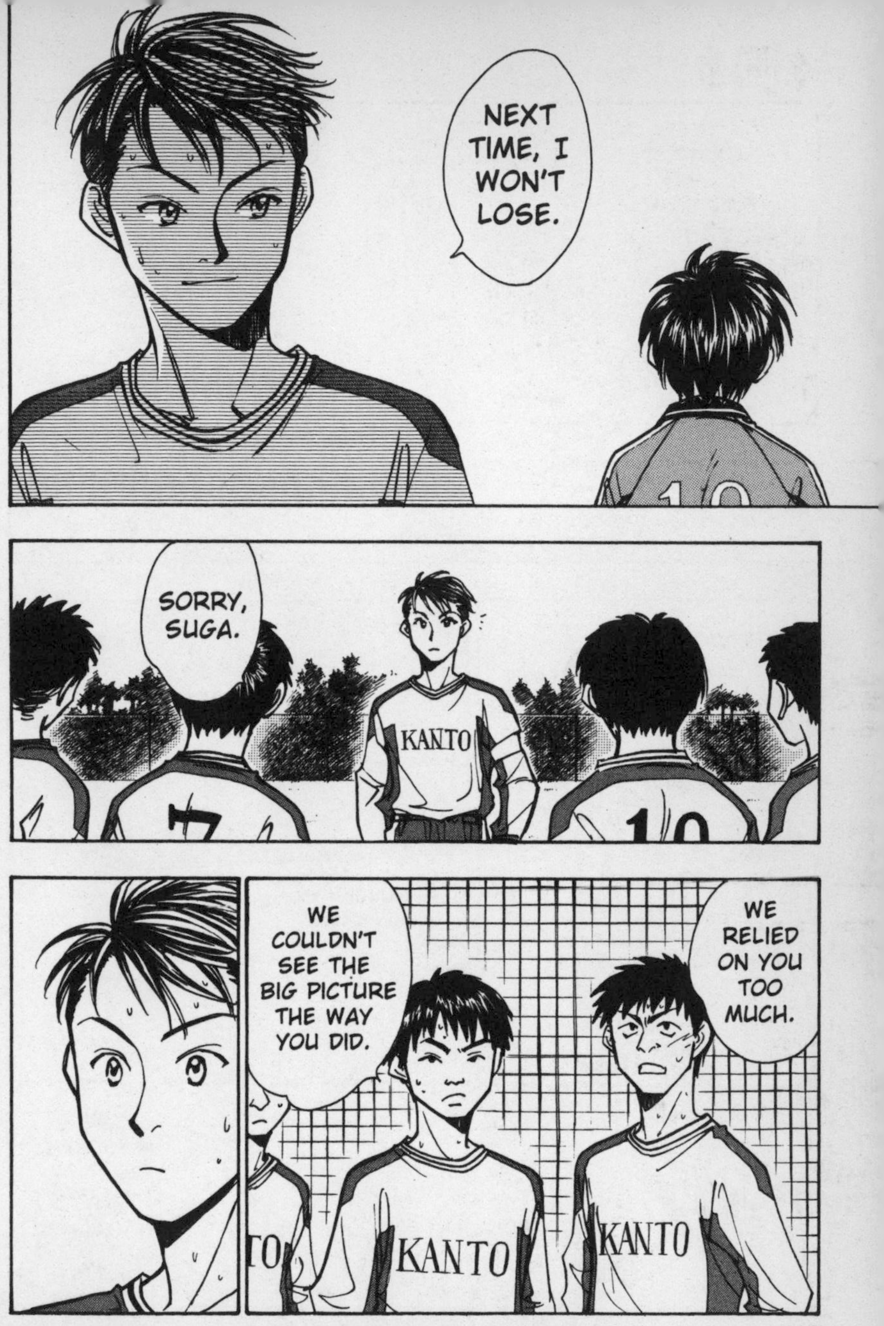
NEXT TIME, I WON'T LOSE.
SORRY, SUGA.
KANTO
WE RELIED ON YOU TOO MUCH.
WE COULDN'T SEE THE BIG PICTURE THE WAY YOU DID.
KANTO
KANTO

READ THIS WAY

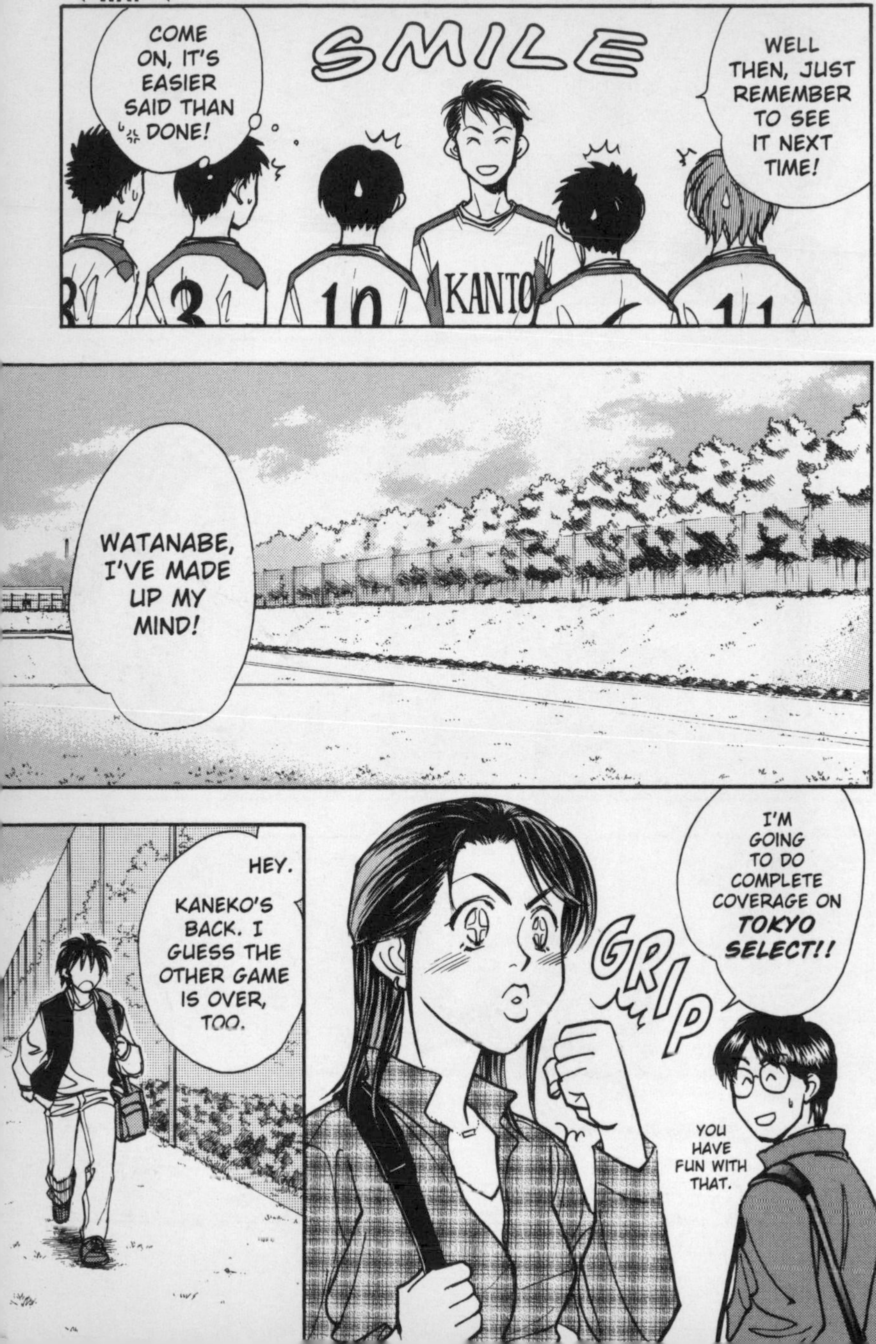
WELL THEN, JUST REMEMBER TO SEE IT NEXT TIME!
SMILE
COME ON, IT'S EASIER SAID THAN DONE!
KANTO
WATANABE, I'VE MADE UP MY MIND!
I'M GOING TO DO COMPLETE COVERAGE ON TOKYO SELECT!!
GRIP
YOU HAVE FUN WITH THAT.
HEY.
KANEKO'S BACK. I GUESS THE OTHER GAME IS OVER, TOO.

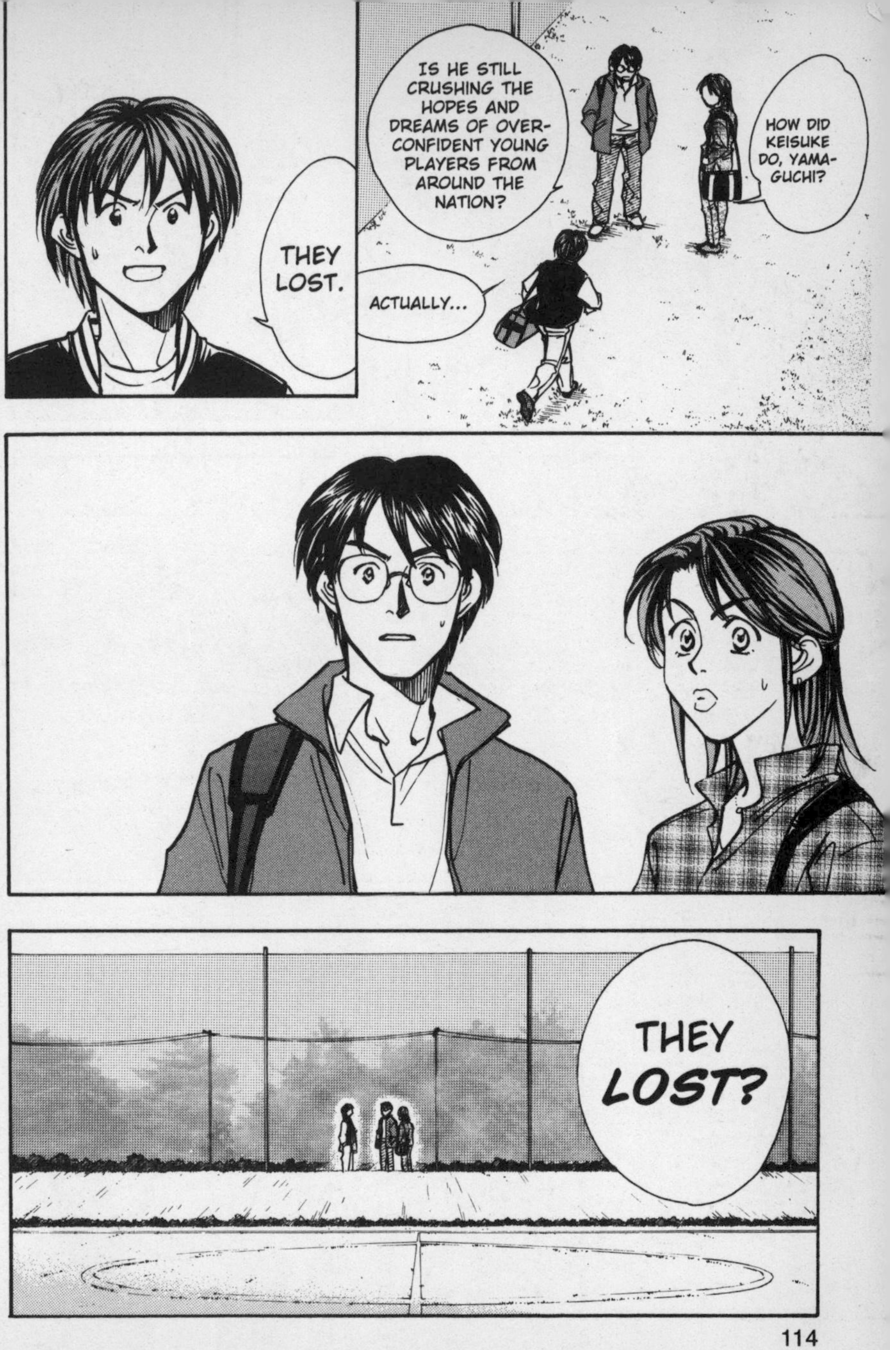
HOW DID KEISUKE DO, YAMAGUCHI?
IS HE STILL CRUSHING THE HOPES AND DREAMS OF OVER-CONFIDENT YOUNG PLAYERS FROM AROUND THE NATION?
ACTUALLY...
THEY LOST.
THEY LOST?

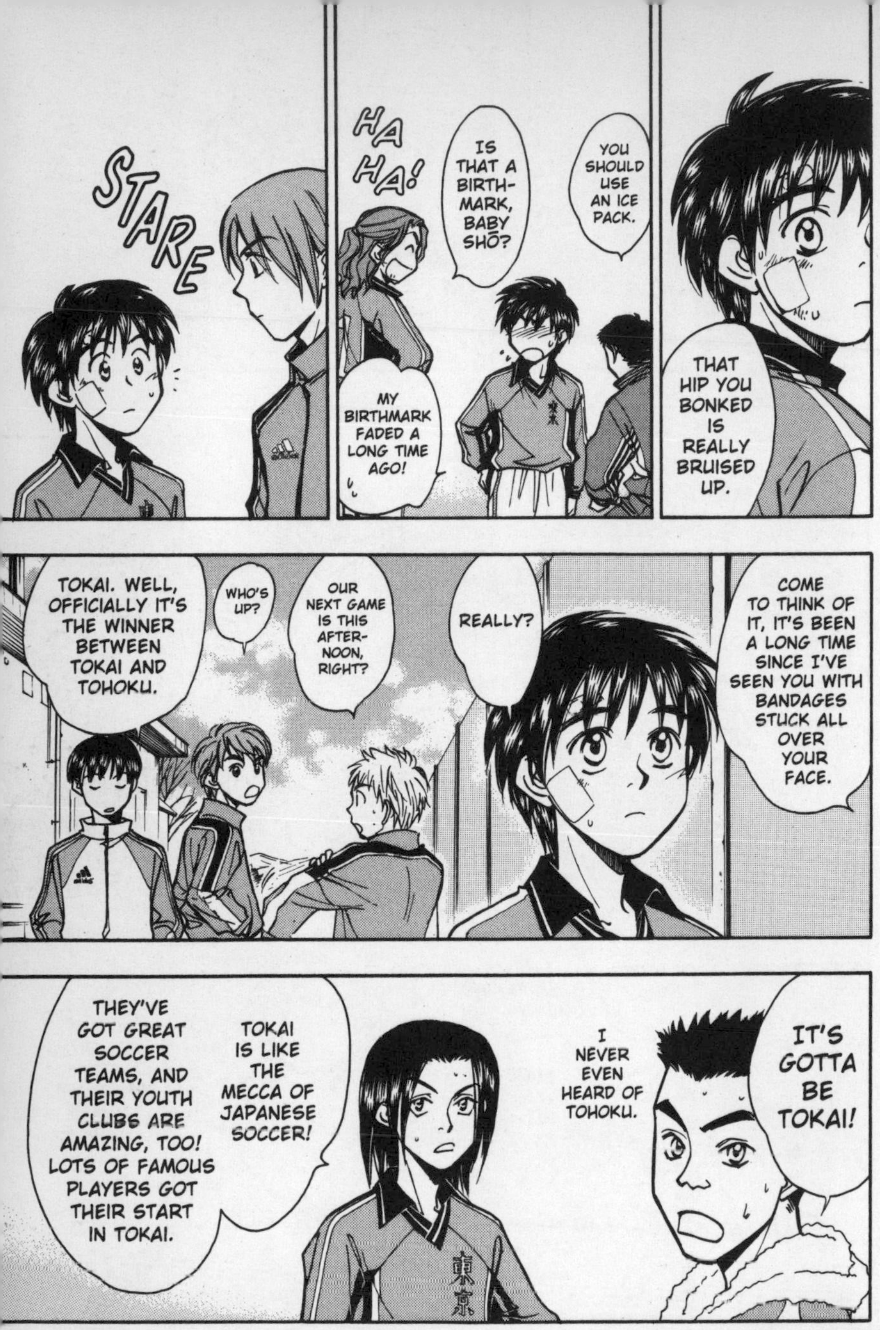
THAT HIP YOU BONKED IS REALLY BRUISED UP.
YOU SHOULD USE AN ICE PACK.
IS THAT A BIRTHMARK, BABY SHŌ?
HA HA!
MY BIRTHMARK FADED A LONG TIME AGO!
STARE
COME TO THINK OF IT, IT'S BEEN A LONG TIME SINCE I'VE SEEN YOU WITH BANDAGES STUCK ALL OVER YOUR FACE.
REALLY?
OUR NEXT GAME IS THIS AFTERNOON, RIGHT?
WHO'S UP?
TOKAI. WELL, OFFICIALLY IT'S THE WINNER BETWEEN TOKAI AND TOHOKU.
IT'S GOTTA BE TOKAI!
I NEVER EVEN HEARD OF TOHOKU.
TOKAI IS LIKE THE MECCA OF JAPANESE SOCCER!
THEY'VE GOT GREAT SOCCER TEAMS, AND THEIR YOUTH CLUBS ARE AMAZING, TOO! LOTS OF FAMOUS PLAYERS GOT THEIR START IN TOKAI.

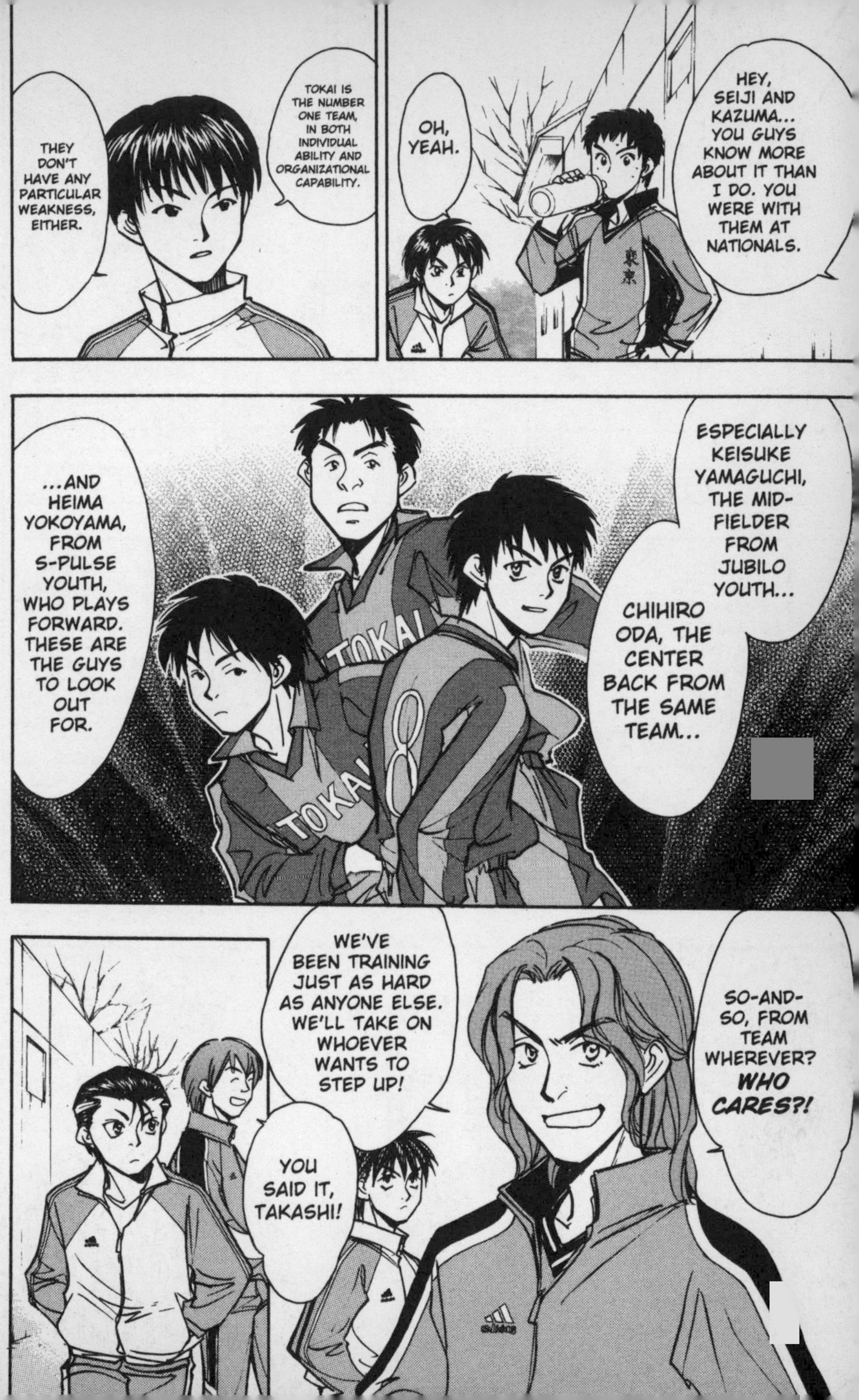
HEY, SEIJI AND KAZUMA... YOU GUYS KNOW MORE ABOUT IT THAN I DO. YOU WERE WITH THEM AT NATIONALS.
OH, YEAH.
TOKAI IS THE NUMBER ONE TEAM, IN BOTH INDIVIDUAL ABILITY AND ORGANIZATIONAL CAPABILITY.
THEY DON'T HAVE ANY PARTICULAR WEAKNESS, EITHER.
ESPECIALLY KEISUKE YAMAGUCHI, THE MID-FIELDER FROM JUBILO YOUTH...
CHIHIRO ODA, THE CENTER BACK FROM THE SAME TEAM...
...AND HEIMA YOKOYAMA, FROM S-PULSE YOUTH, WHO PLAYS FORWARD. THESE ARE THE GUYS TO LOOK OUT FOR.
TOKAI
TOKAI
SO-AND-SO, FROM TEAM WHEREVER? ***WHO CARES?!***
WE'VE BEEN TRAINING JUST AS HARD AS ANYONE ELSE. WE'LL TAKE ON WHOEVER WANTS TO STEP UP!
YOU SAID IT, TAKASHI!

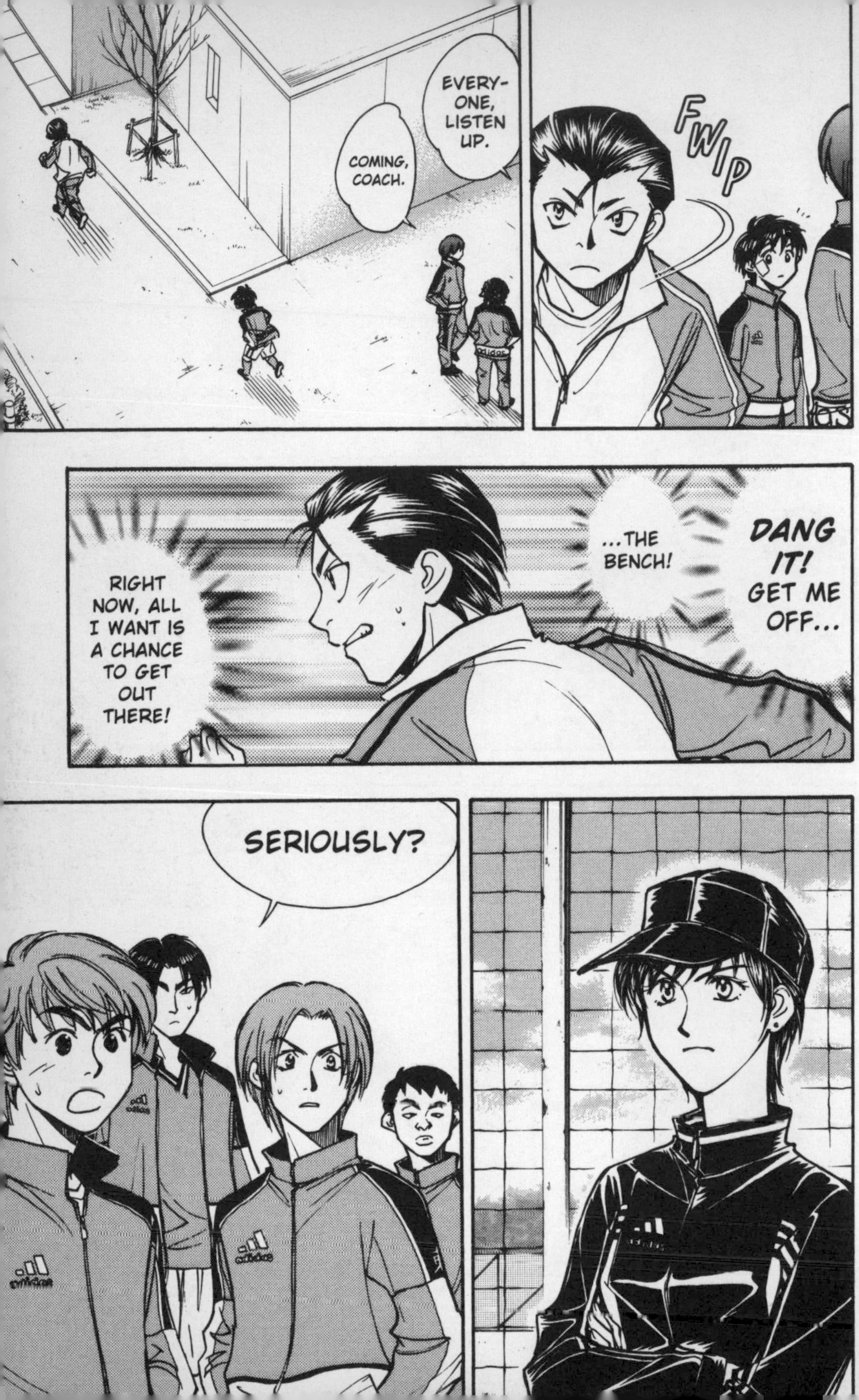
FWIP
EVERY-ONE, LISTEN UP.
COMING, COACH.
DANG IT! GET ME OFF...
...THE BENCH!
RIGHT NOW, ALL I WANT IS A CHANCE TO GET OUT THERE!
SERIOUSLY?

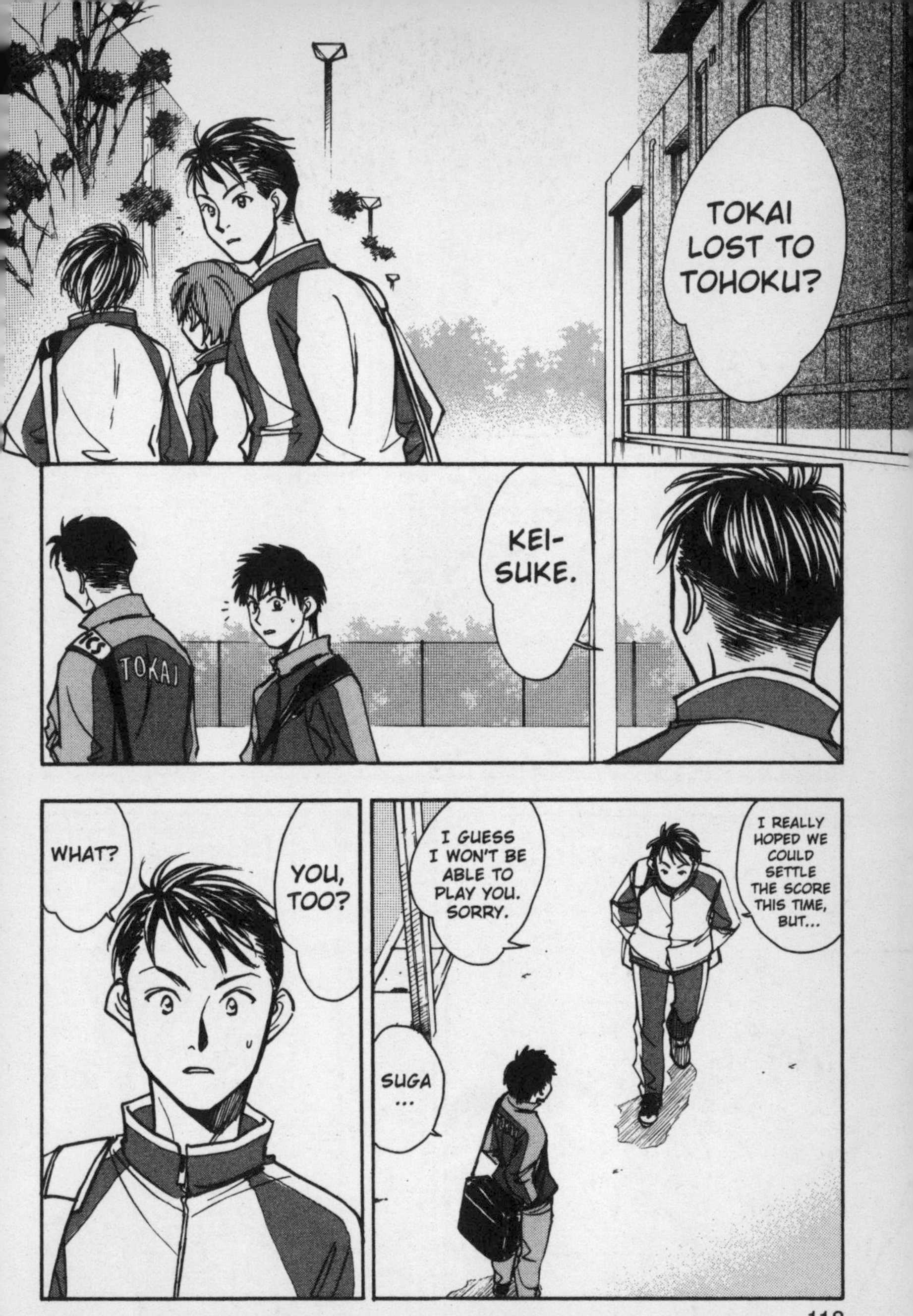
TOKAI LOST TO TOHOKU?
KEI-SUKE.
I REALLY HOPED WE COULD SETTLE THE SCORE THIS TIME, BUT...
I GUESS I WON'T BE ABLE TO PLAY YOU. SORRY.
SUGA...
YOU, TOO?
WHAT?

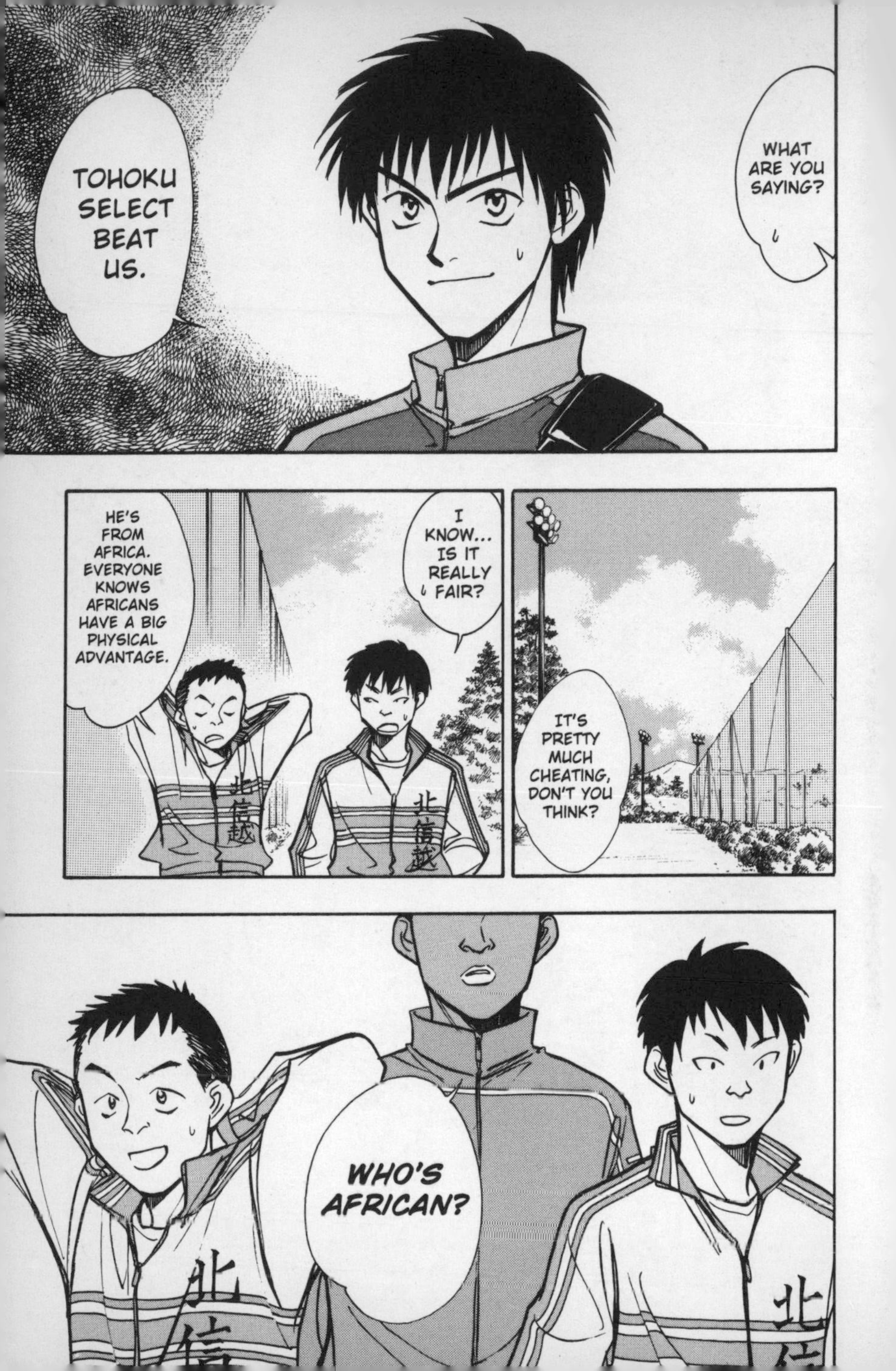
WHAT ARE YOU SAYING?
TOHOKU SELECT BEAT US.
IT'S PRETTY MUCH CHEATING, DON'T YOU THINK?
I KNOW... IS IT REALLY FAIR?
HE'S FROM AFRICA. EVERYONE KNOWS AFRICANS HAVE A BIG PHYSICAL ADVANTAGE.
WHO'S AFRICAN?

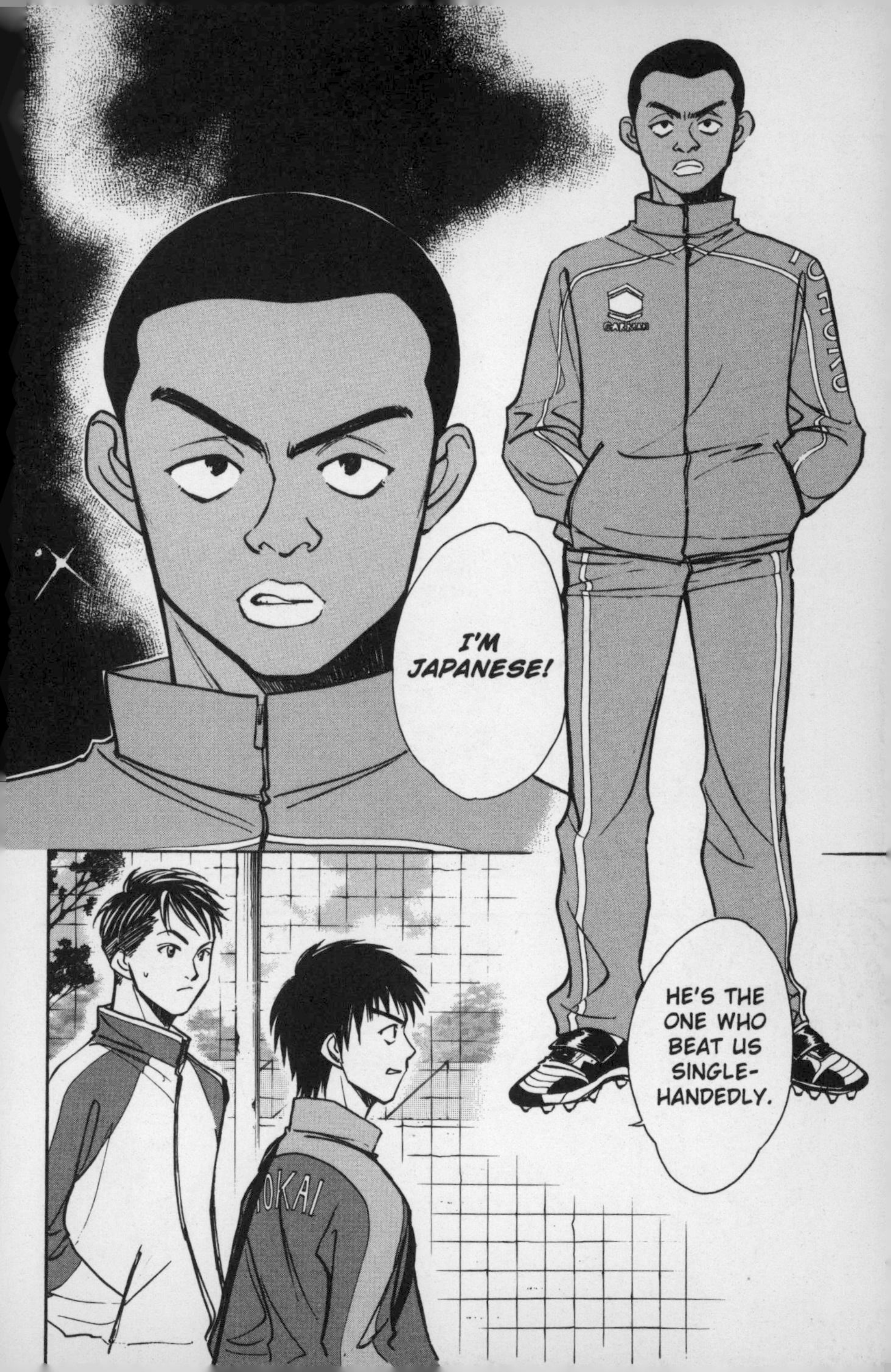
I'M JAPANESE!
HE'S THE ONE WHO BEAT US SINGLE-HANDEDLY.

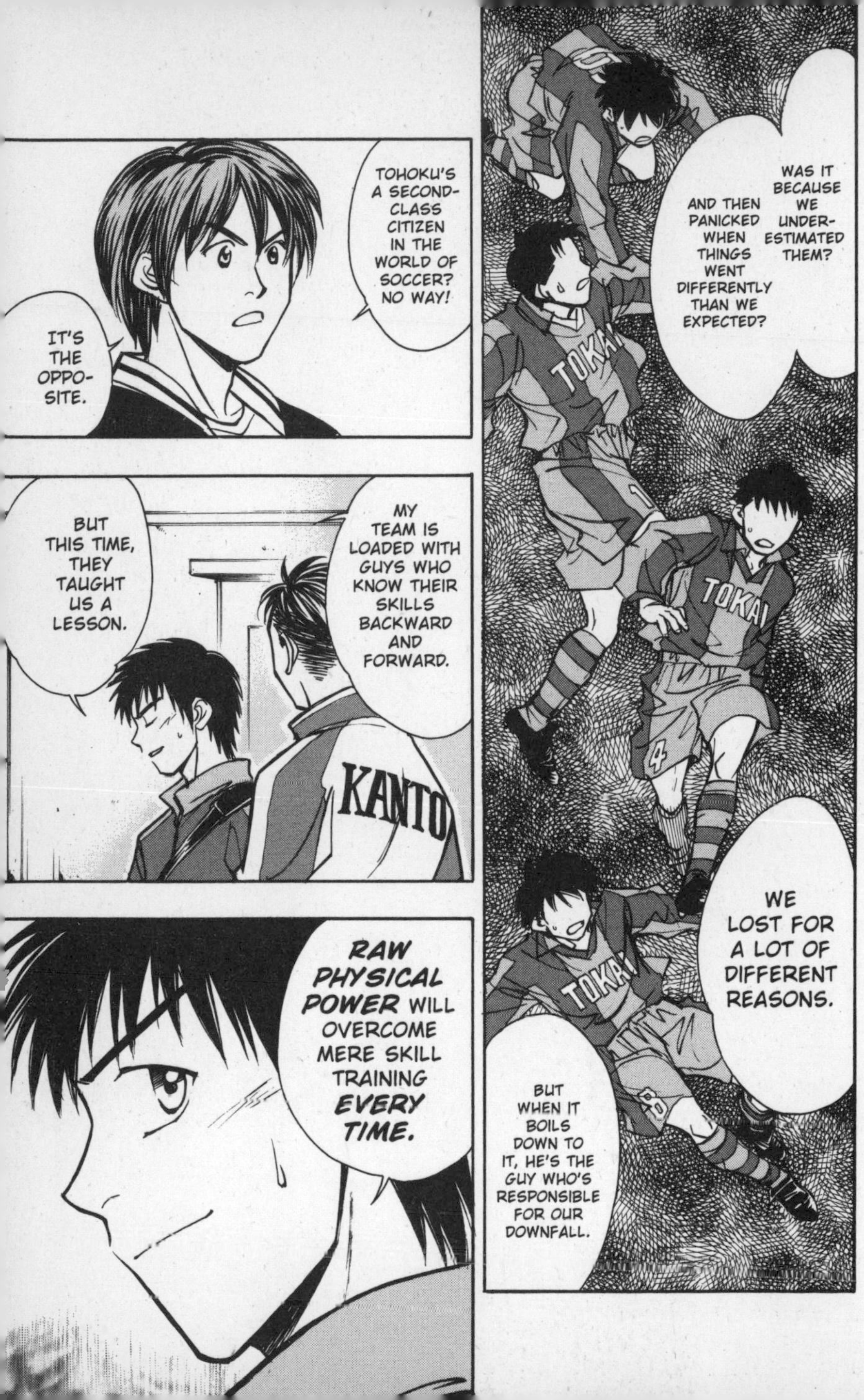
WAS IT BECAUSE WE UNDER-ESTIMATED THEM?
AND THEN PANICKED WHEN THINGS WENT DIFFERENTLY THAN WE EXPECTED?
WE LOST FOR A LOT OF DIFFERENT REASONS.
BUT WHEN IT BOILS DOWN TO IT, HE'S THE GUY WHO'S RESPONSIBLE FOR OUR DOWNFALL.
TOHOKU'S A SECOND-CLASS CITIZEN IN THE WORLD OF SOCCER? NO WAY!
IT'S THE OPPO-SITE.
MY TEAM IS LOADED WITH GUYS WHO KNOW THEIR SKILLS BACKWARD AND FORWARD.
BUT THIS TIME, THEY TAUGHT US A LESSON.
RAW PHYSICAL POWER WILL OVERCOME MERE SKILL TRAINING EVERY TIME.

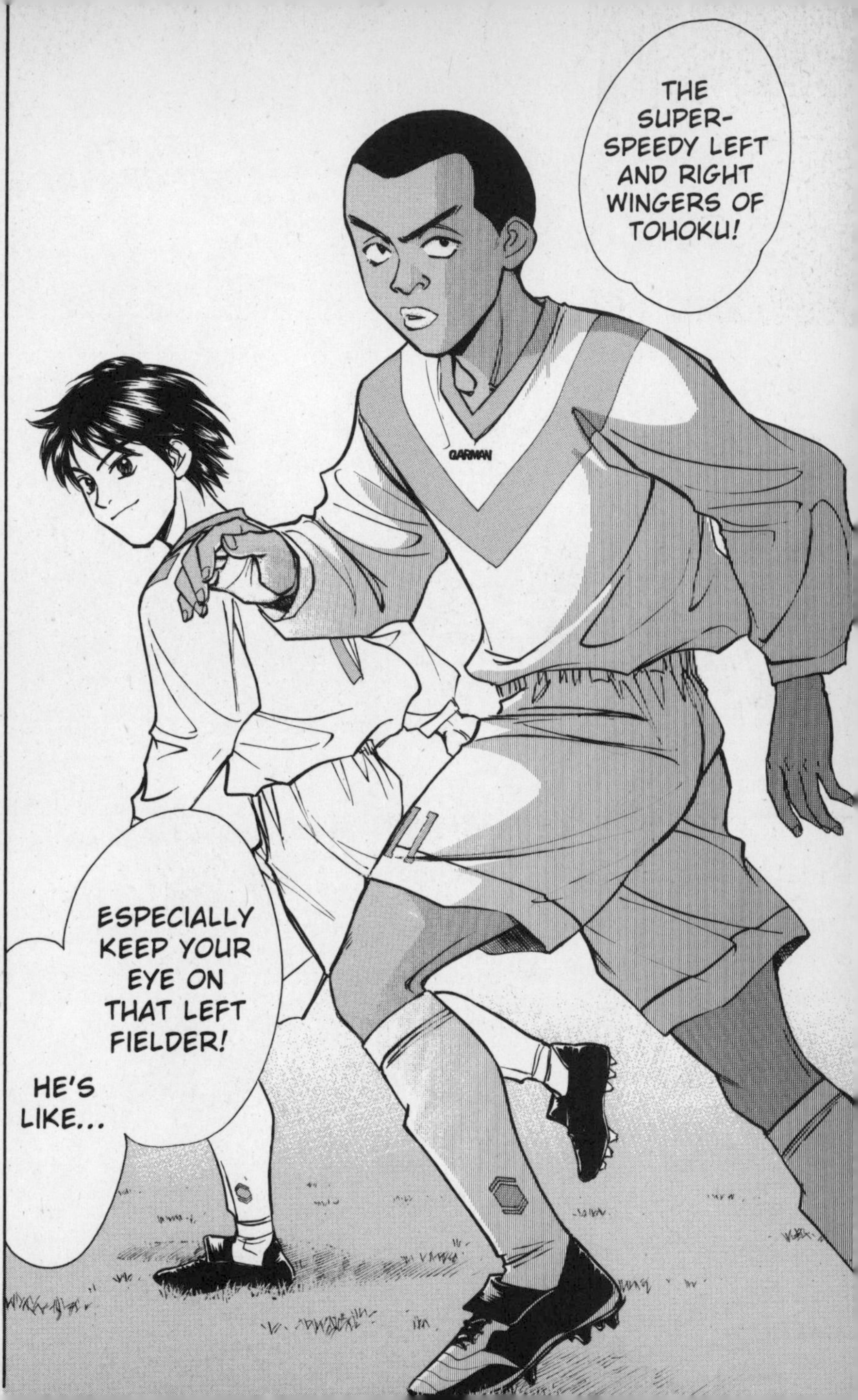
THE SUPER-SPEEDY LEFT AND RIGHT WINGERS OF TOHOKU!
ESPECIALLY KEEP YOUR EYE ON THAT LEFT FIELDER!
HE'S LIKE...

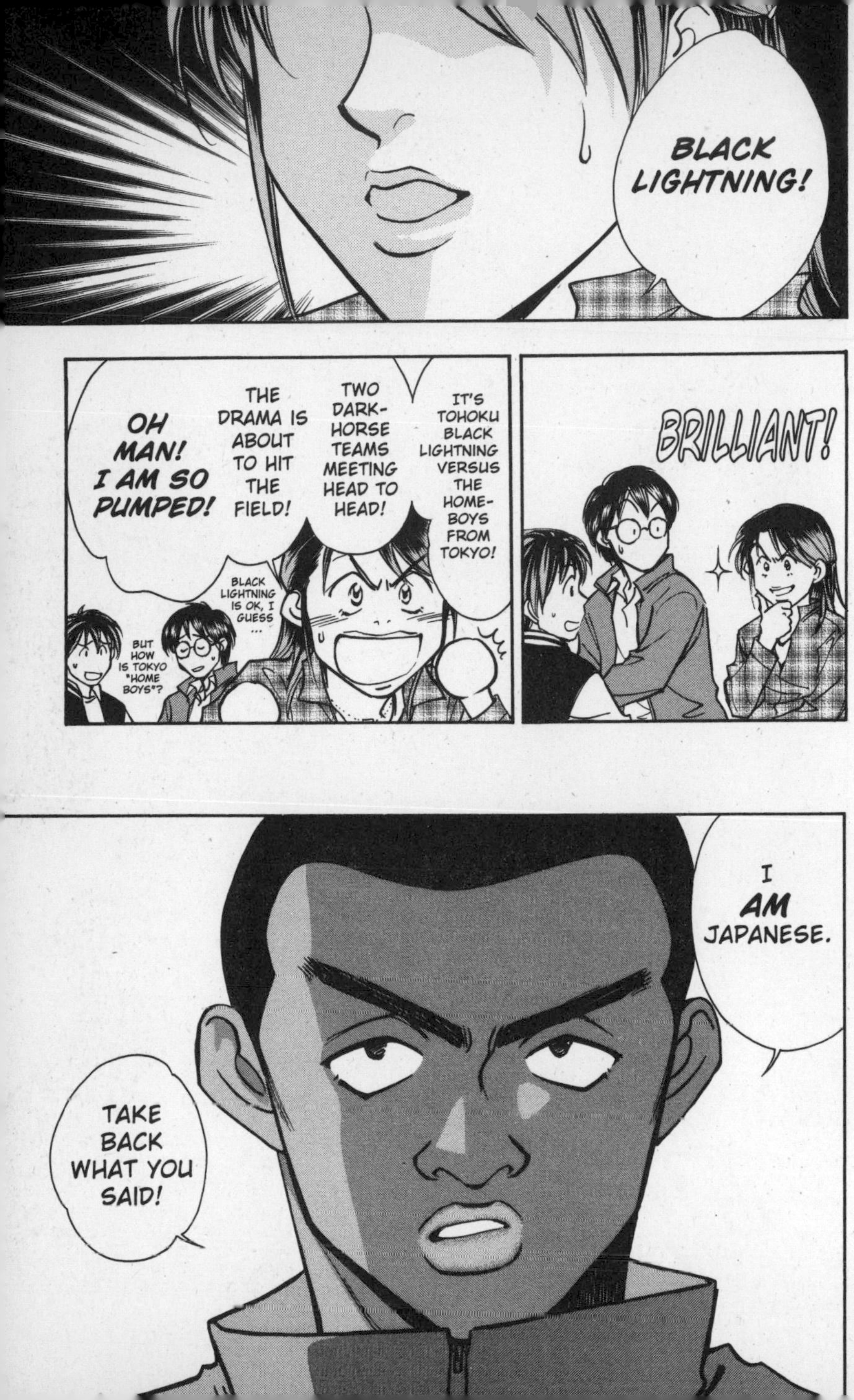
BLACK LIGHTNING!
BRILLIANT!
IT'S TOHOKU BLACK LIGHTNING VERSUS THE HOME-BOYS FROM TOKYO!
TWO DARK-HORSE TEAMS MEETING HEAD TO HEAD!
THE DRAMA IS ABOUT TO HIT THE FIELD!
OH MAN! I AM SO PUMPED!
BLACK LIGHTNING IS OK, I GUESS ...
BUT HOW IS TOKYO "HOME BOYS"?
I AM JAPANESE.
TAKE BACK WHAT YOU SAID!

WHISTLE!

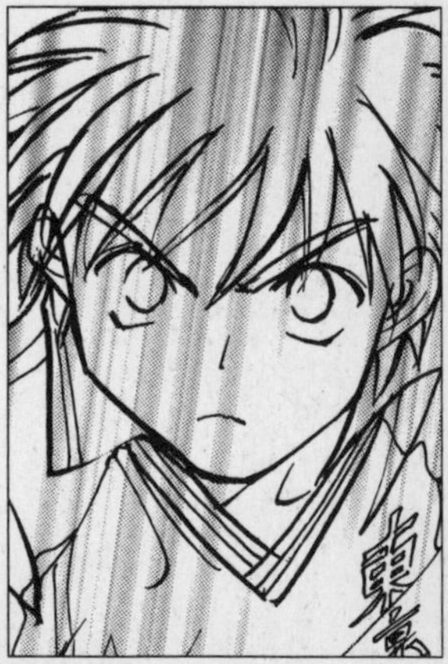

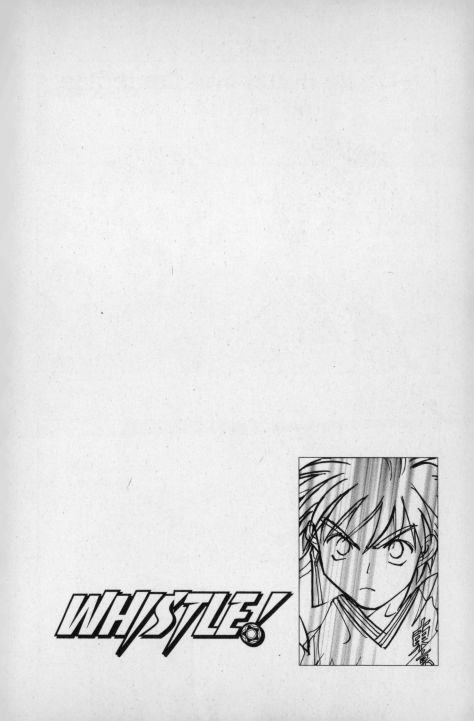

STAGE.179

A Lie He Hopes Will Come True

(GO ON TOGETHER)

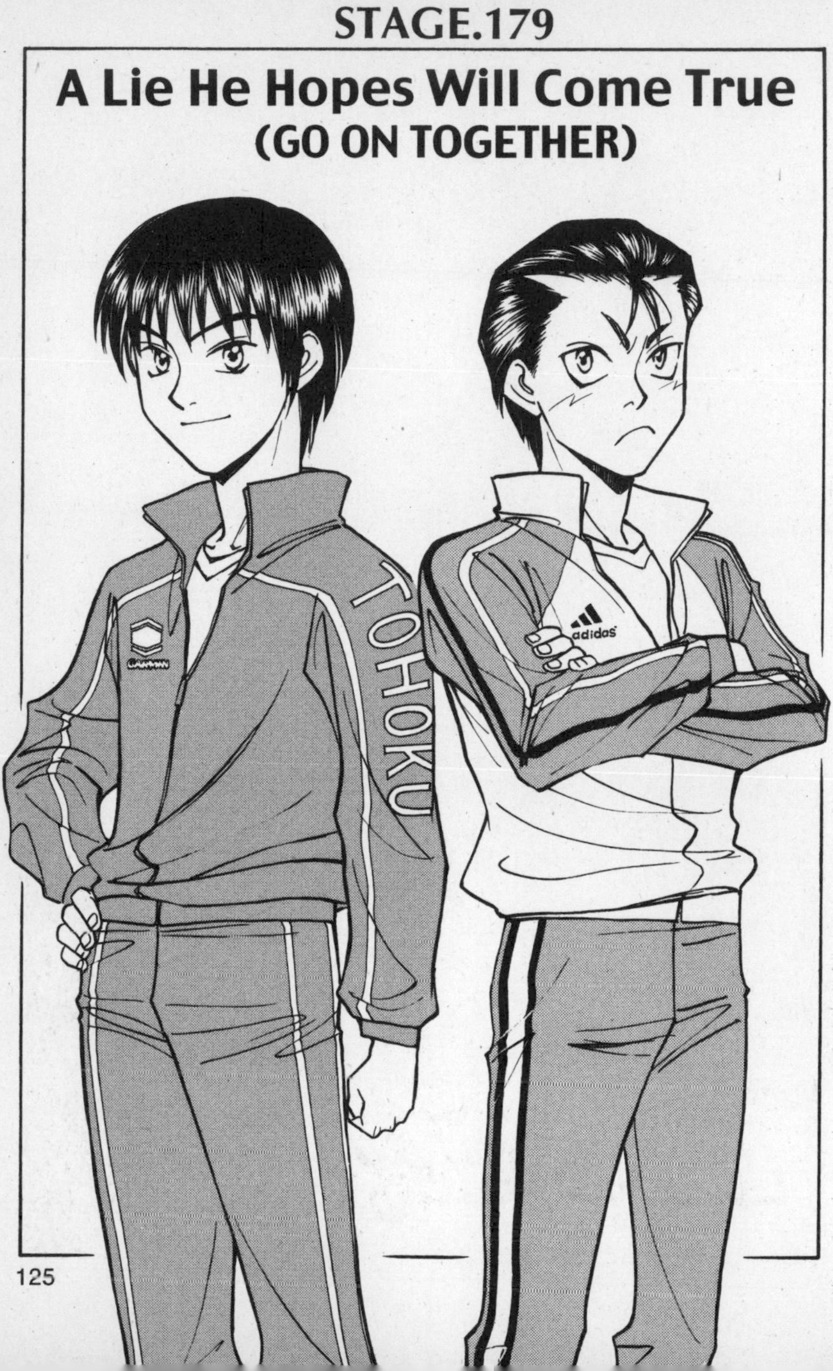
TOHOKU
adidas

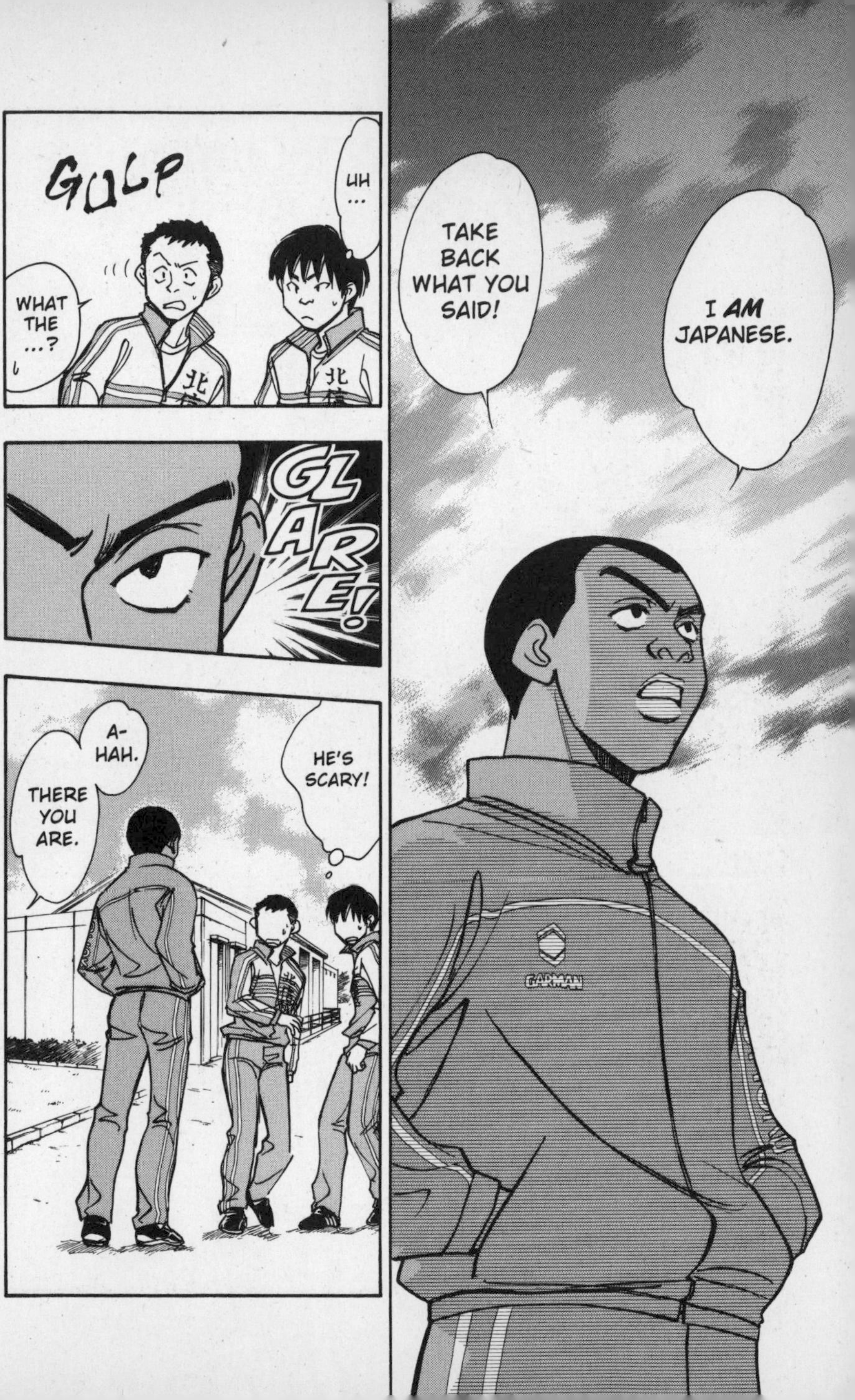
I AM JAPANESE.
TAKE BACK WHAT YOU SAID!
GARMAN
UH ...
GULP
WHAT THE ...?
GLARE!
HE'S SCARY!
A-HAH.
THERE YOU ARE.

READ THIS WAY

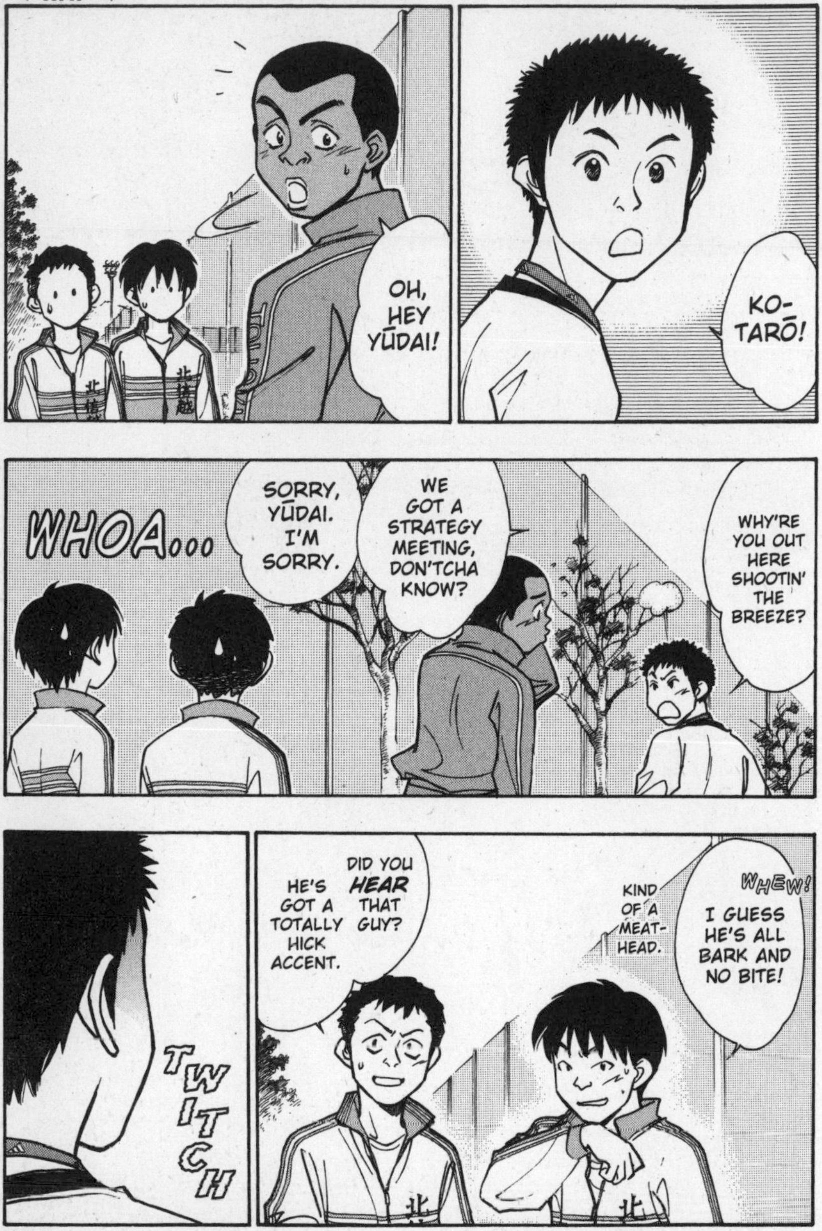
KO-TARŌ!
OH, HEY YŪDAI!
WHY'RE YOU OUT HERE SHOOTIN' THE BREEZE?
WE GOT A STRATEGY MEETING, DON'TCHA KNOW?
SORRY, YŪDAI. I'M SORRY.
WHOA...
WHEW!
I GUESS HE'S ALL BARK AND NO BITE!
KIND OF A MEAT-HEAD.
DID YOU HEAR THAT GUY?
HE'S GOT A TOTALLY HICK ACCENT.
TWITCH

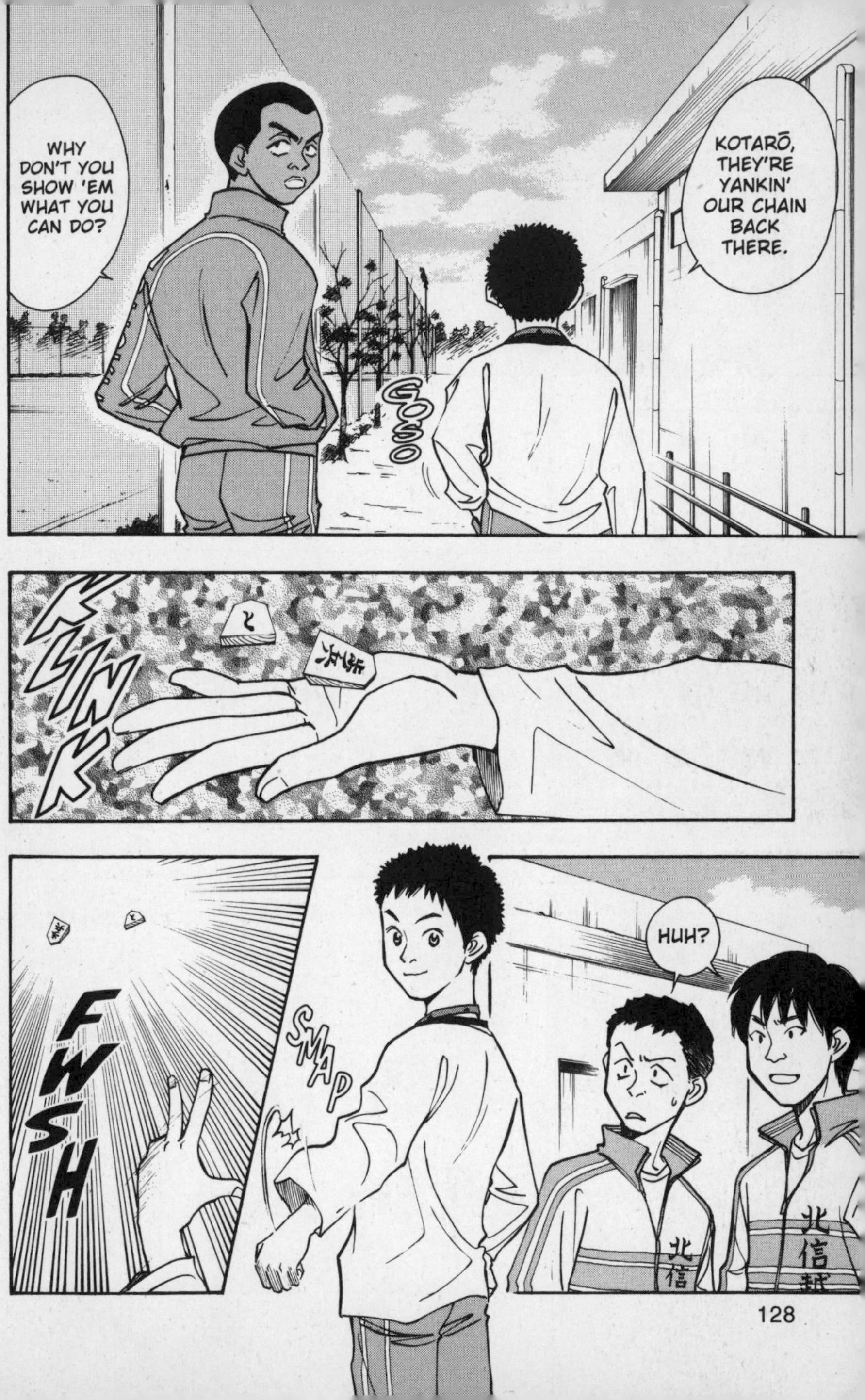
KOTARŌ, THEY'RE YANKIN' OUR CHAIN BACK THERE.
WHY DON'T YOU SHOW 'EM WHAT YOU CAN DO?
GOSO
KLINK
HUH?
SMAP
FWSH

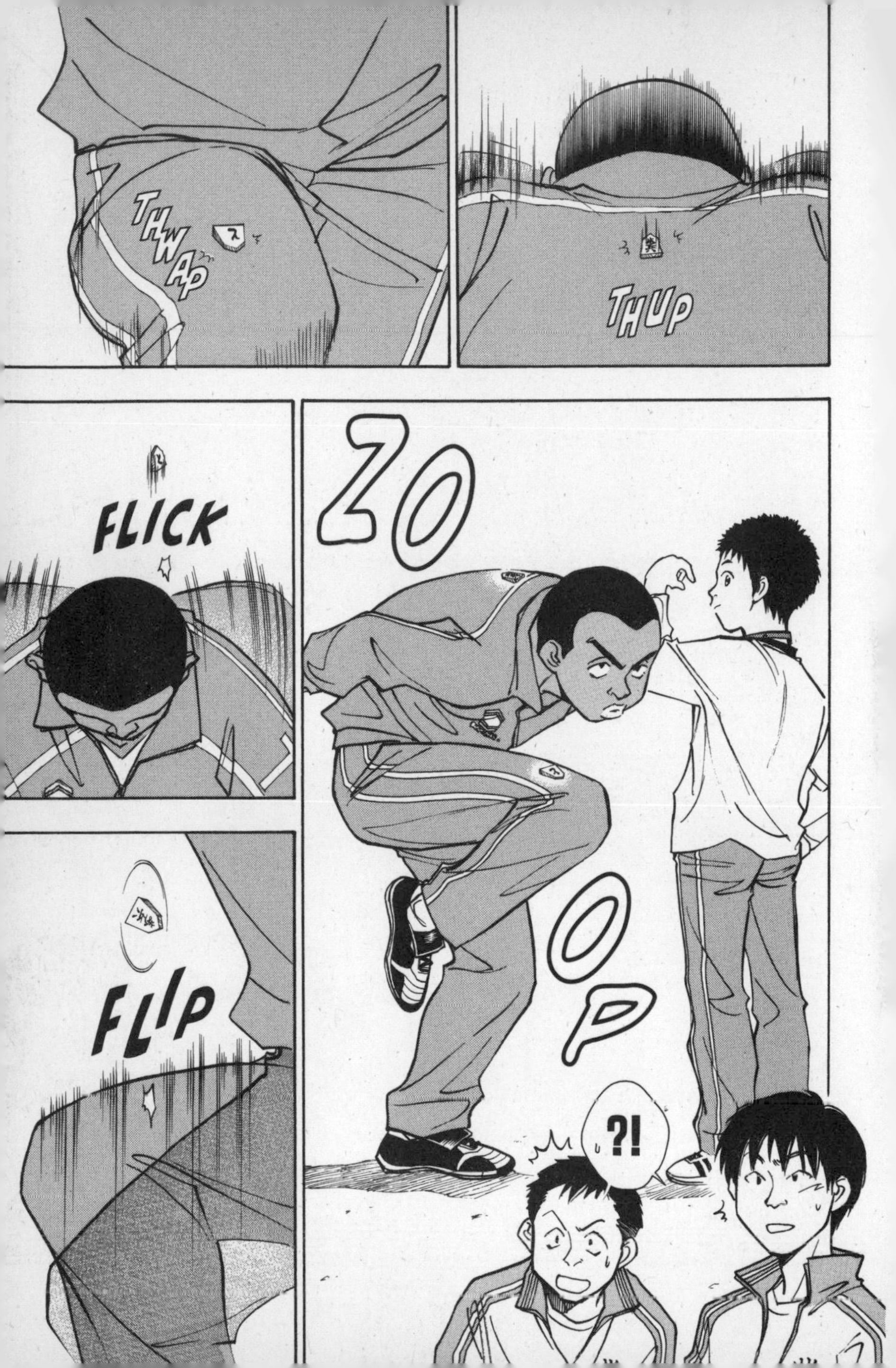
THUP
THWAP
ZOOP
?!
FLICK
FLIP

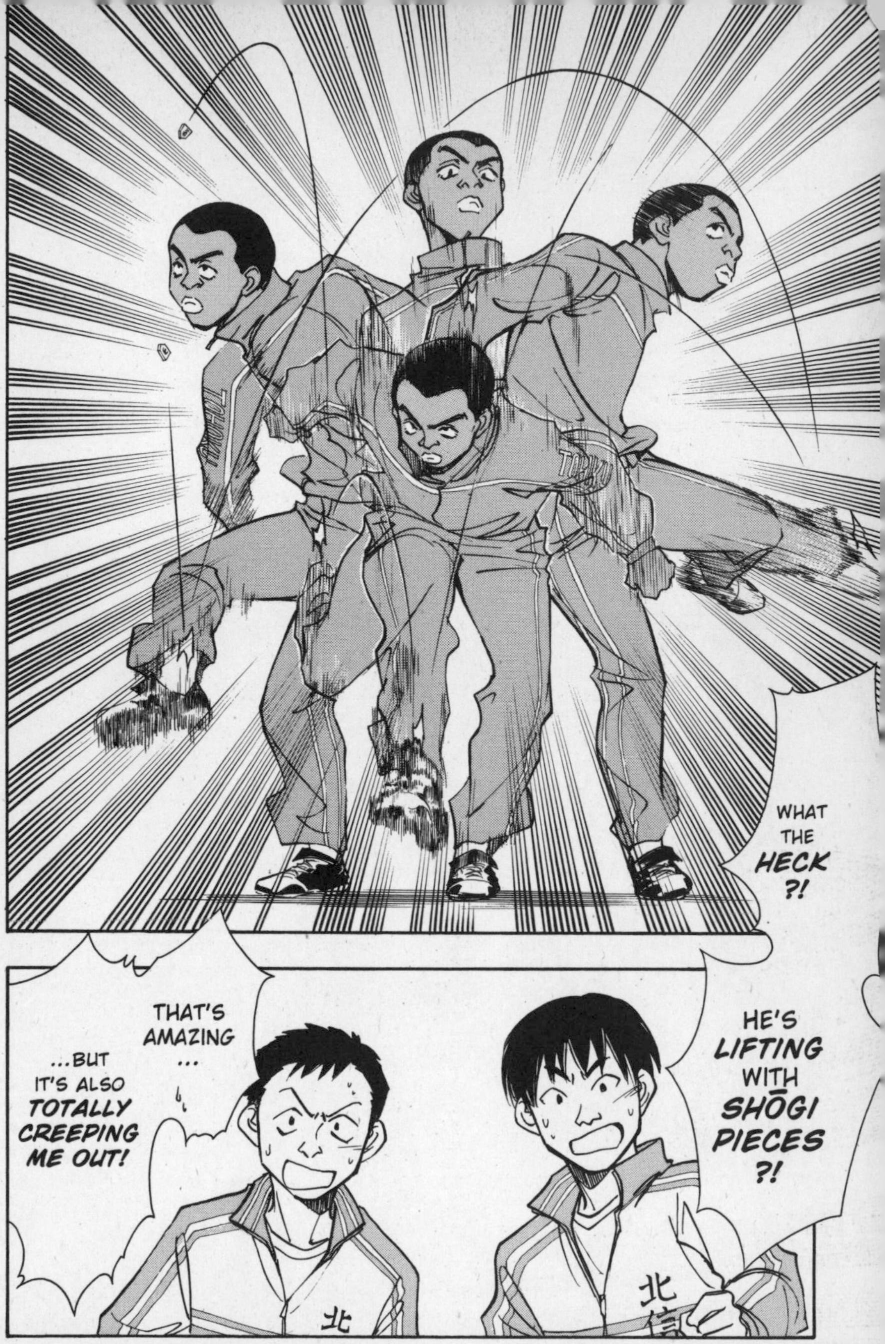
WHAT THE HECK?!
HE'S LIFTING WITH SHŌGI PIECES?!
THAT'S AMAZING...
...BUT IT'S ALSO TOTALLY CREEPING ME OUT!

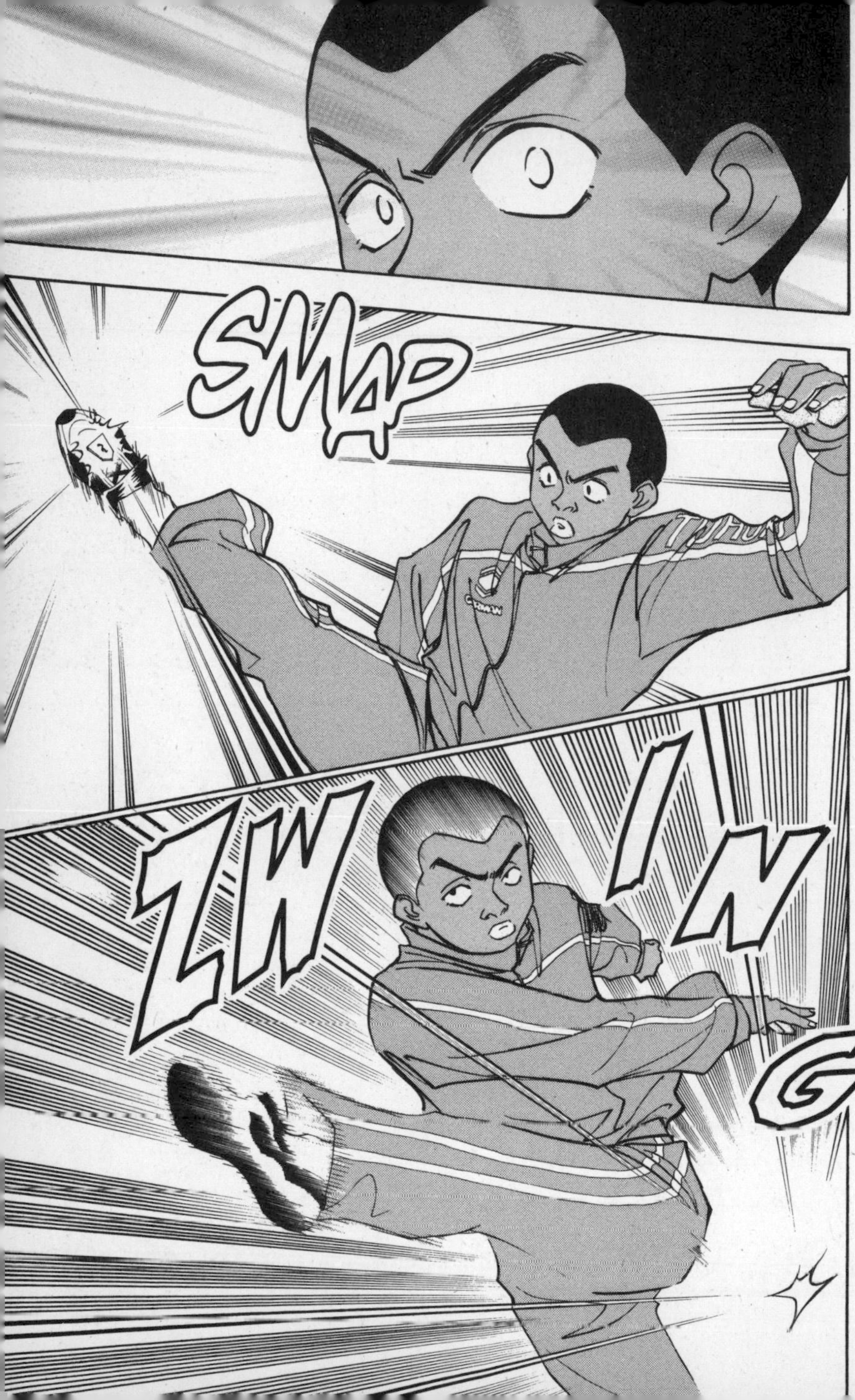
SMAP
ZWING

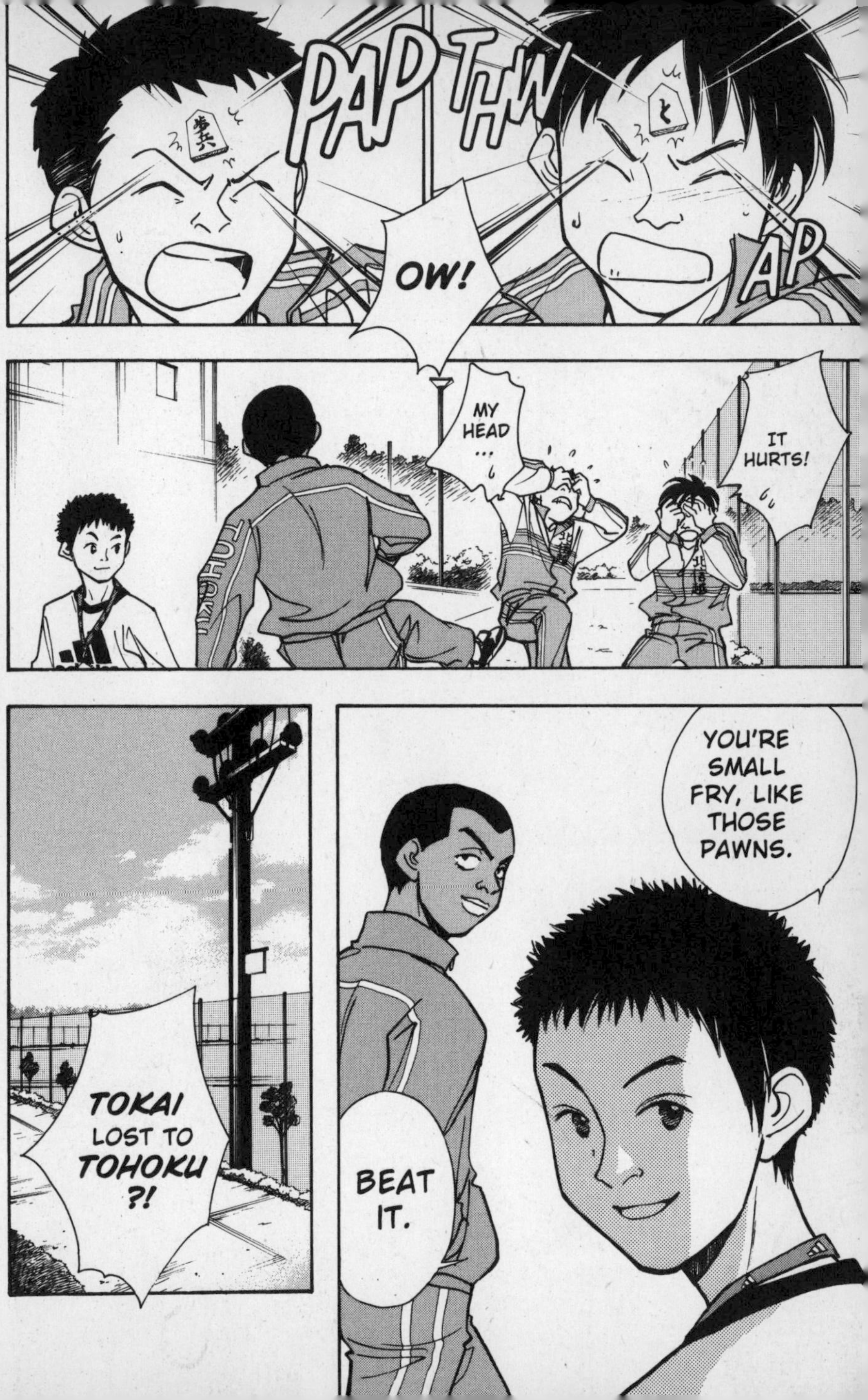
PAP THW
OW!
AP
IT HURTS!
MY HEAD...
YOU'RE SMALL FRY, LIKE THOSE PAWNS.
BEAT IT.
TOKAI LOST TO TOHOKU?!

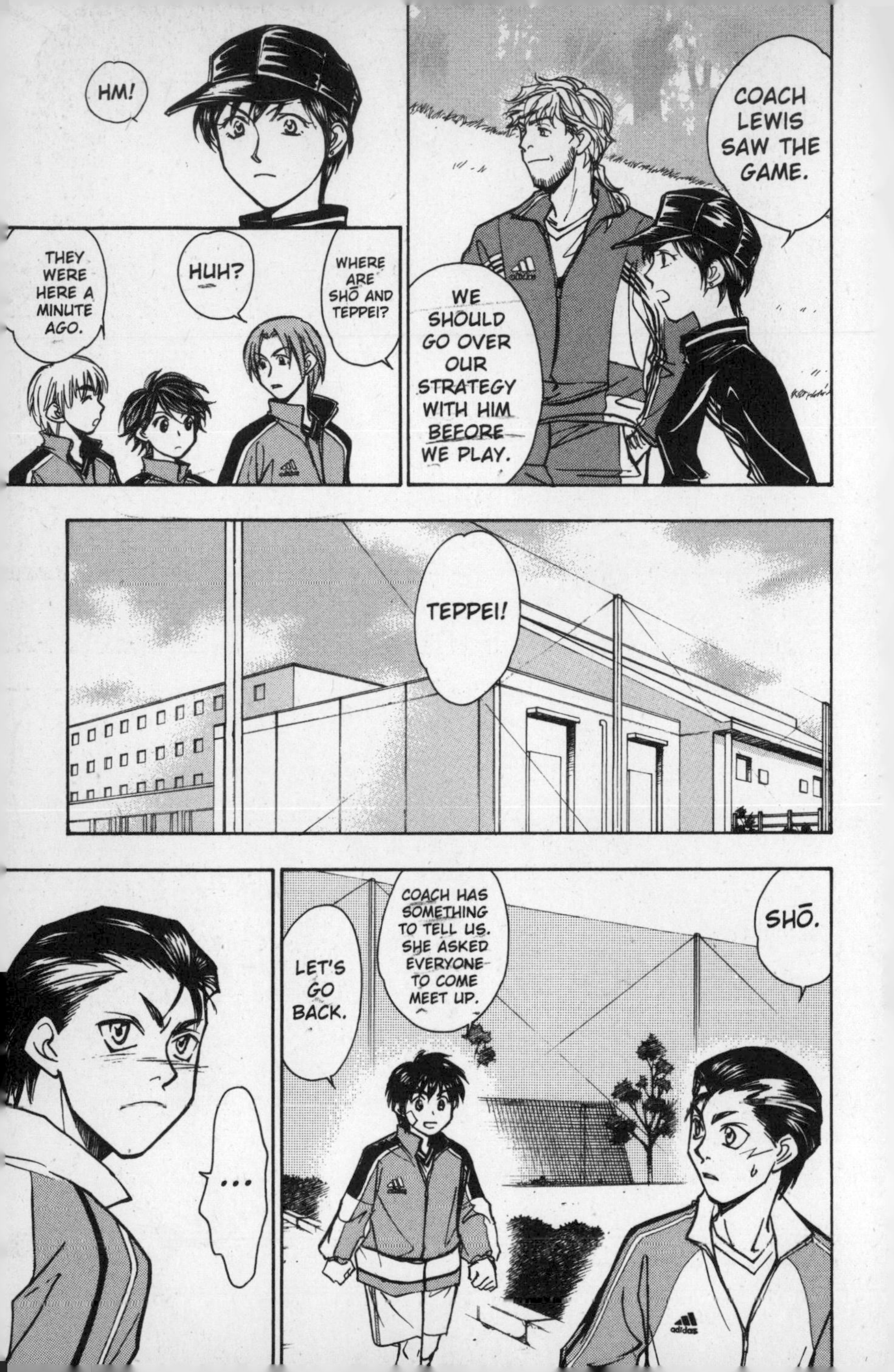
COACH LEWIS SAW THE GAME.
WE SHOULD GO OVER OUR STRATEGY WITH HIM BEFORE WE PLAY.
HM!
WHERE ARE SHŌ AND TEPPEI?
HUH?
THEY WERE HERE A MINUTE AGO.
TEPPEI!
SHŌ.
COACH HAS SOMETHING TO TELL US. SHE ASKED EVERYONE TO COME MEET UP.
LET'S GO BACK.
...

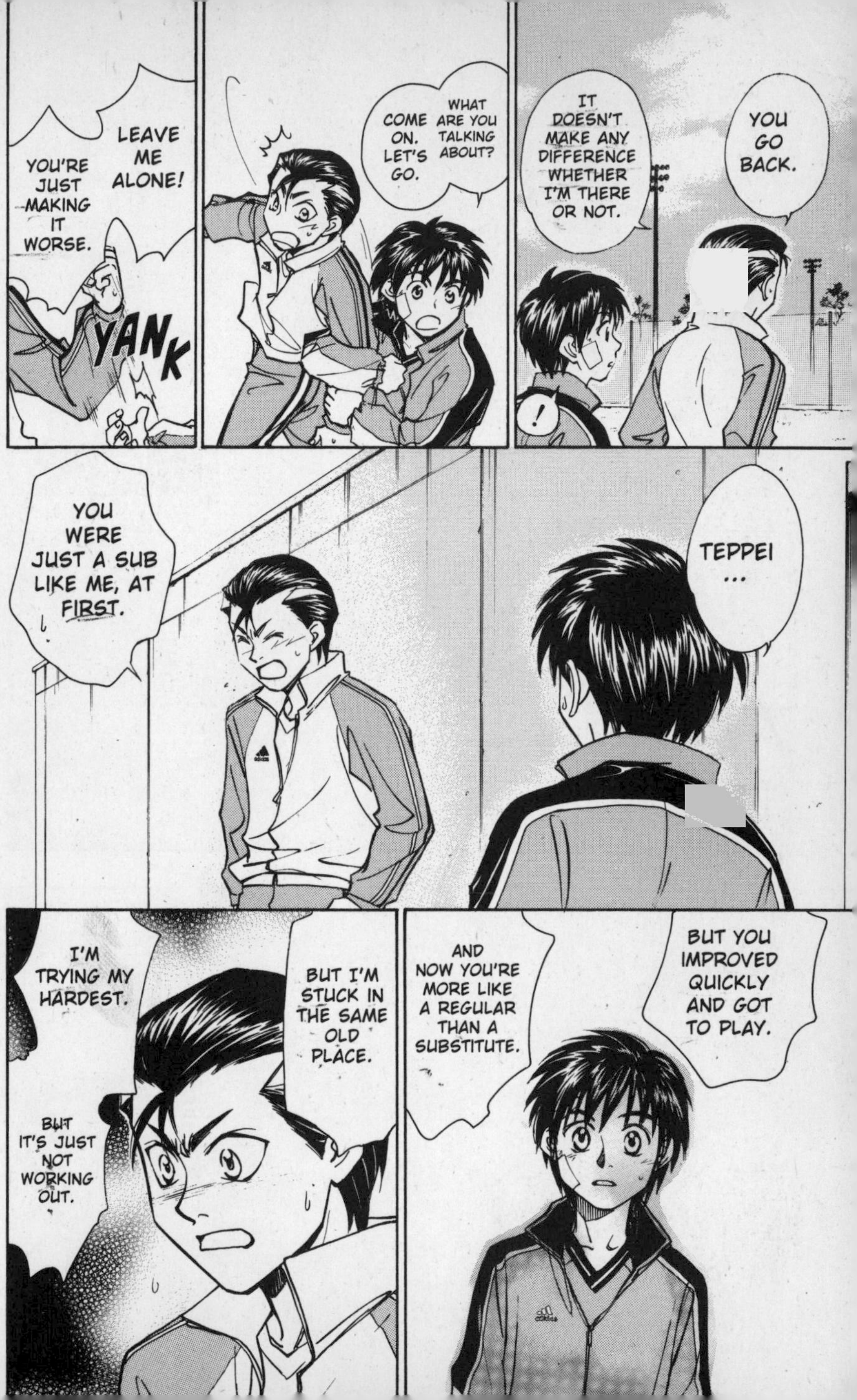
YOU GO BACK.
IT DOESN'T MAKE ANY DIFFERENCE WHETHER I'M THERE OR NOT.
!
WHAT ARE YOU TALKING ABOUT?
COME ON. LET'S GO.
LEAVE ME ALONE!
YOU'RE JUST MAKING IT WORSE.
YANK
TEPPEI ...
YOU WERE JUST A SUB LIKE ME, AT FIRST.
BUT YOU IMPROVED QUICKLY AND GOT TO PLAY.
AND NOW YOU'RE MORE LIKE A REGULAR THAN A SUBSTITUTE.
BUT I'M STUCK IN THE SAME OLD PLACE.
I'M TRYING MY HARDEST.
BUT IT'S JUST NOT WORKING OUT.

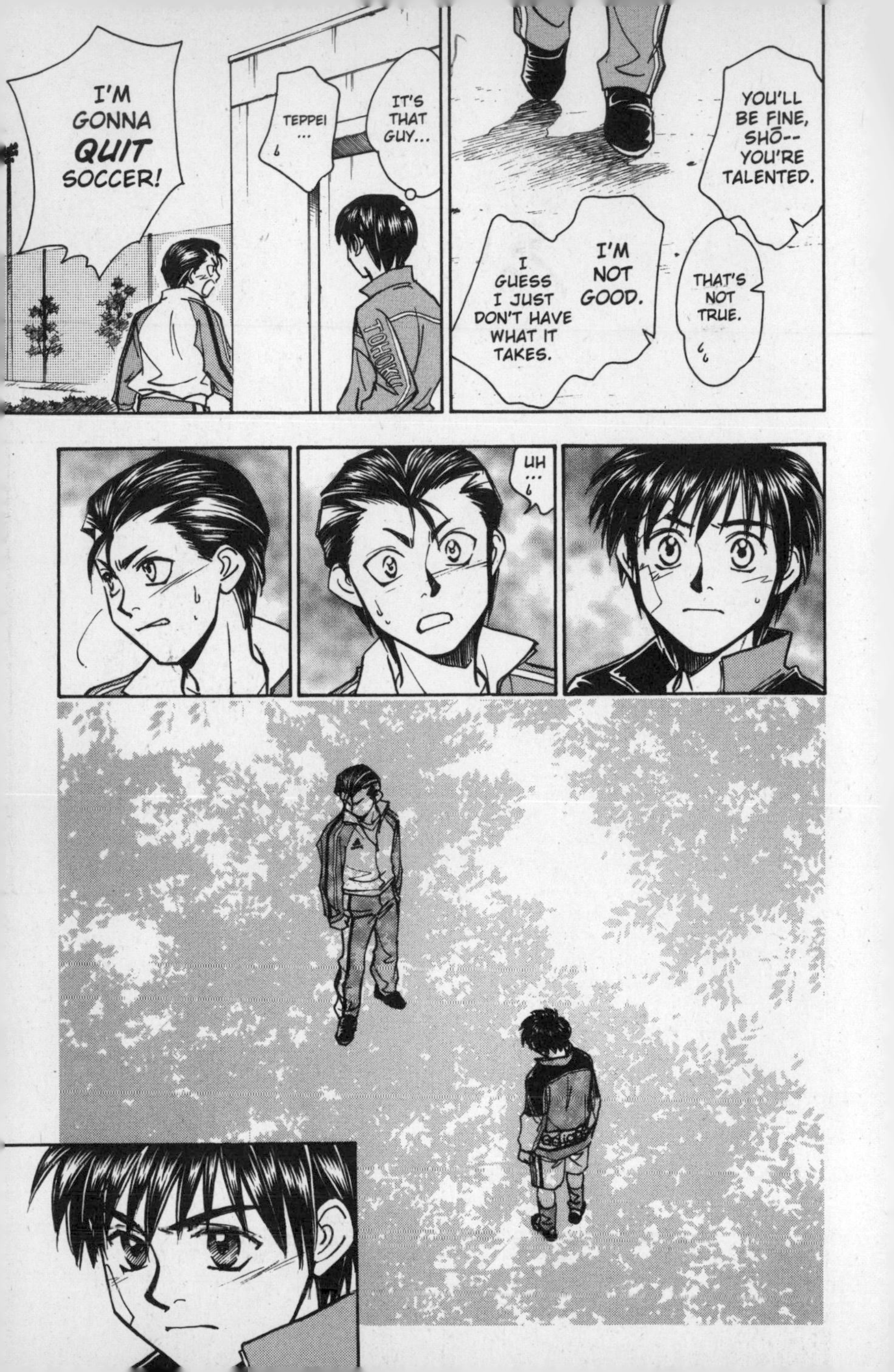
YOU'LL BE FINE, SHŌ-- YOU'RE TALENTED.
THAT'S NOT TRUE.
I'M NOT GOOD.
I GUESS I JUST DON'T HAVE WHAT IT TAKES.
IT'S THAT GUY...
TEPPEI ...
I'M GONNA QUIT SOCCER!
UH ...

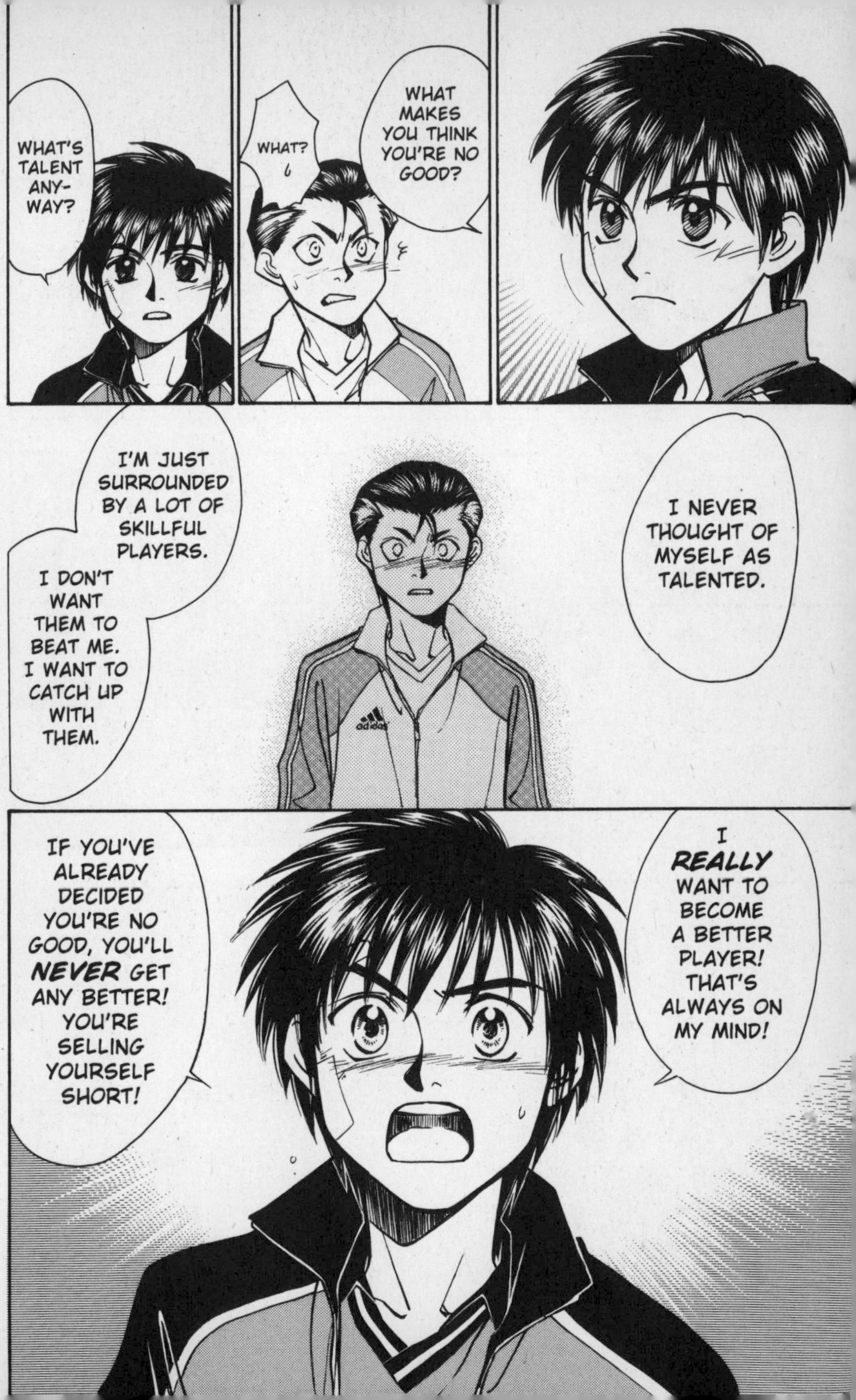
WHAT MAKES YOU THINK YOU'RE NO GOOD?
WHAT?
WHAT'S TALENT ANY-WAY?
I NEVER THOUGHT OF MYSELF AS TALENTED.
I'M JUST SURROUNDED BY A LOT OF SKILLFUL PLAYERS.
I DON'T WANT THEM TO BEAT ME. I WANT TO CATCH UP WITH THEM.
I *REALLY* WANT TO BECOME A BETTER PLAYER! THAT'S ALWAYS ON MY MIND!
IF YOU'VE ALREADY DECIDED YOU'RE NO GOOD, YOU'LL *NEVER* GET ANY BETTER! YOU'RE SELLING YOURSELF SHORT!

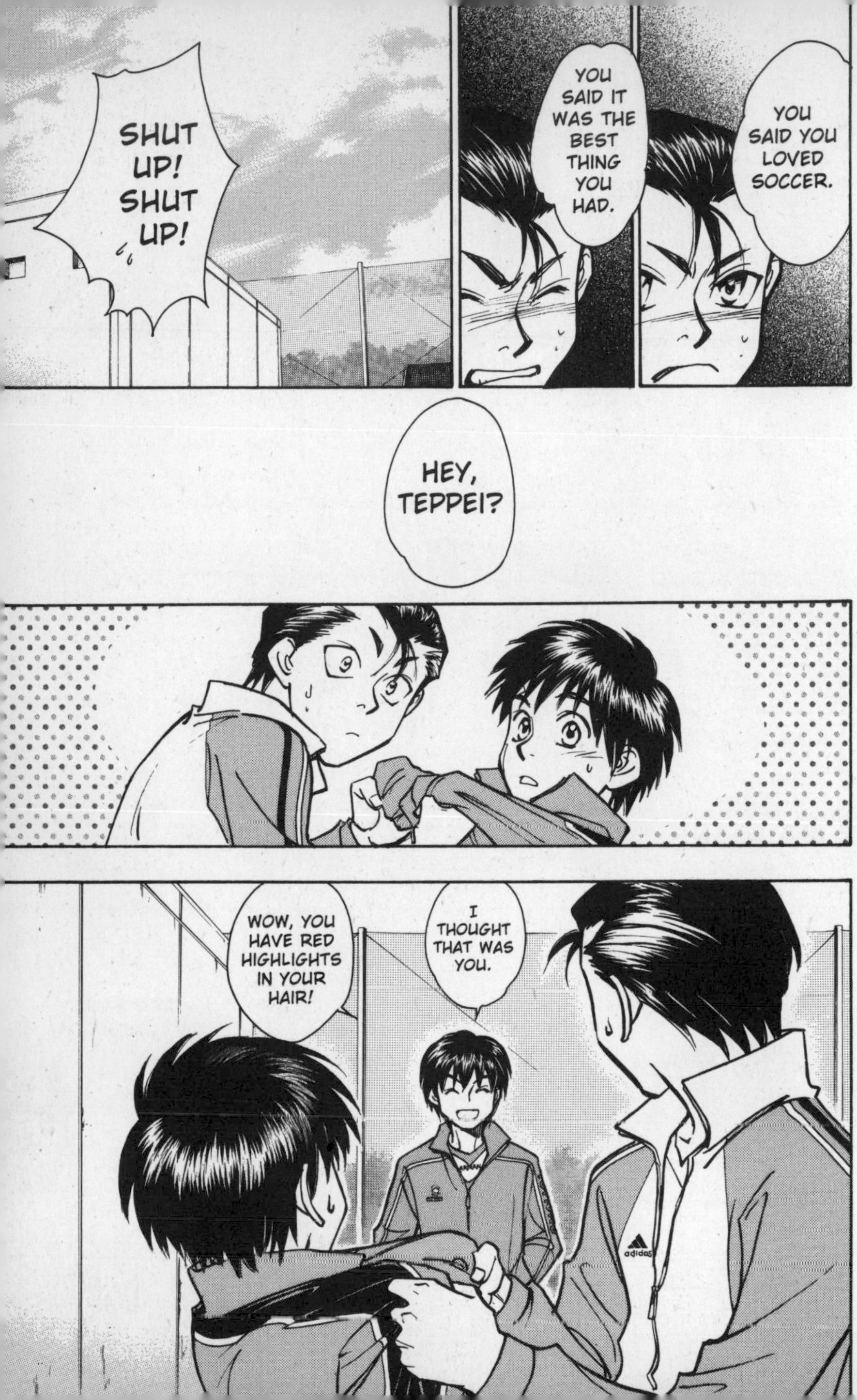
YOU SAID YOU LOVED SOCCER.
YOU SAID IT WAS THE BEST THING YOU HAD.
SHUT UP! SHUT UP!
HEY, TEPPEI?
I THOUGHT THAT WAS YOU.
WOW, YOU HAVE RED HIGHLIGHTS IN YOUR HAIR!

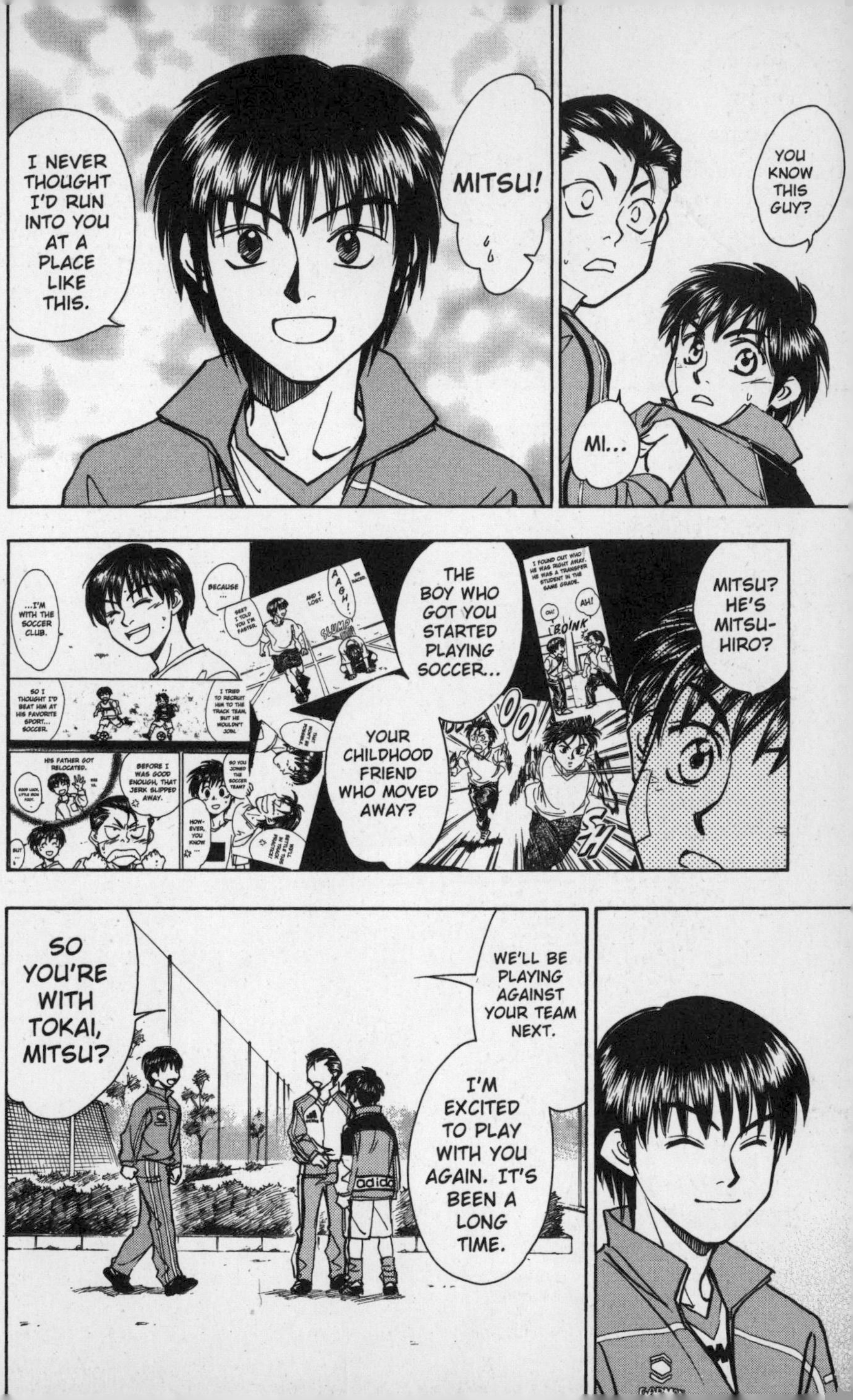
YOU KNOW THIS GUY?
MI...
MITSU!
I NEVER THOUGHT I'D RUN INTO YOU AT A PLACE LIKE THIS.
MITSU? HE'S MITSUHIRO?
I FOUND OUT WHO HE WAS RIGHT AWAY. HE WAS A TRANSFER STUDENT IN THE SAME GRADE.
AH!
OH!
BOINK
THE BOY WHO GOT YOU STARTED PLAYING SOCCER...
YOUR CHILDHOOD FRIEND WHO MOVED AWAY?
AAGH!
AND I LOST.
SLUMP
SEE? I TOLD YOU I'M FASTER.
BECAUSE...
...I'M WITH THE SOCCER CLUB.
I TRIED TO RECRUIT HIM TO THE TRACK TEAM, BUT HE WOULDN'T JOIN.
SO I THOUGHT I'D BEAT HIM AT HIS FAVORITE SPORT... SOCCER.
THAT WON'T BE POSSIBLE.
WE'LL SETTLE THIS IN TRACK PRACTICE!
SO YOU JOINED THE SOCCER TEAM?
HOWEVER, YOU KNOW...
BEFORE I WAS GOOD ENOUGH, THAT JERK SLIPPED AWAY.
HIS FATHER GOT RELOCATED.
BUT...
SO YOU'RE WITH TOKAI, MITSU?
WE'LL BE PLAYING AGAINST YOUR TEAM NEXT.
I'M EXCITED TO PLAY WITH YOU AGAIN. IT'S BEEN A LONG TIME.

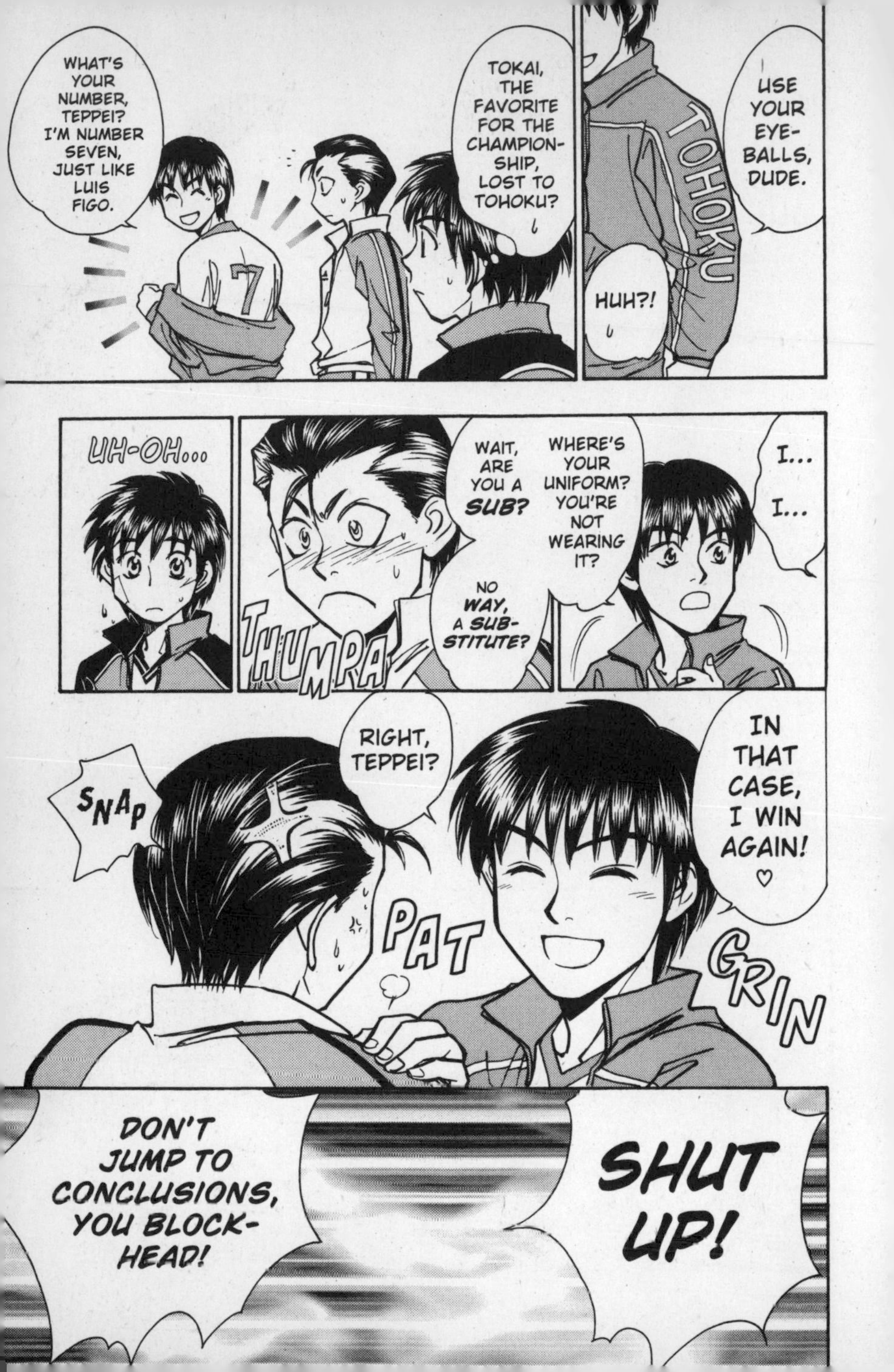
USE YOUR EYE-BALLS, DUDE.
TOHOKU
HUH?!
TOKAI, THE FAVORITE FOR THE CHAMPION-SHIP, LOST TO TOHOKU?
WHAT'S YOUR NUMBER, TEPPEI? I'M NUMBER SEVEN, JUST LIKE LUIS FIGO.
7
I... I...
WHERE'S YOUR UNIFORM? YOU'RE NOT WEARING IT?
WAIT, ARE YOU A *SUB?*
NO *WAY,* A *SUB-STITUTE?*
THUMPA
UH-OH...
IN THAT CASE, I WIN AGAIN! ♡
GRIN
RIGHT, TEPPEI?
SNAP
PAT
SHUT UP!
DON'T JUMP TO CONCLUSIONS, YOU BLOCK-HEAD!

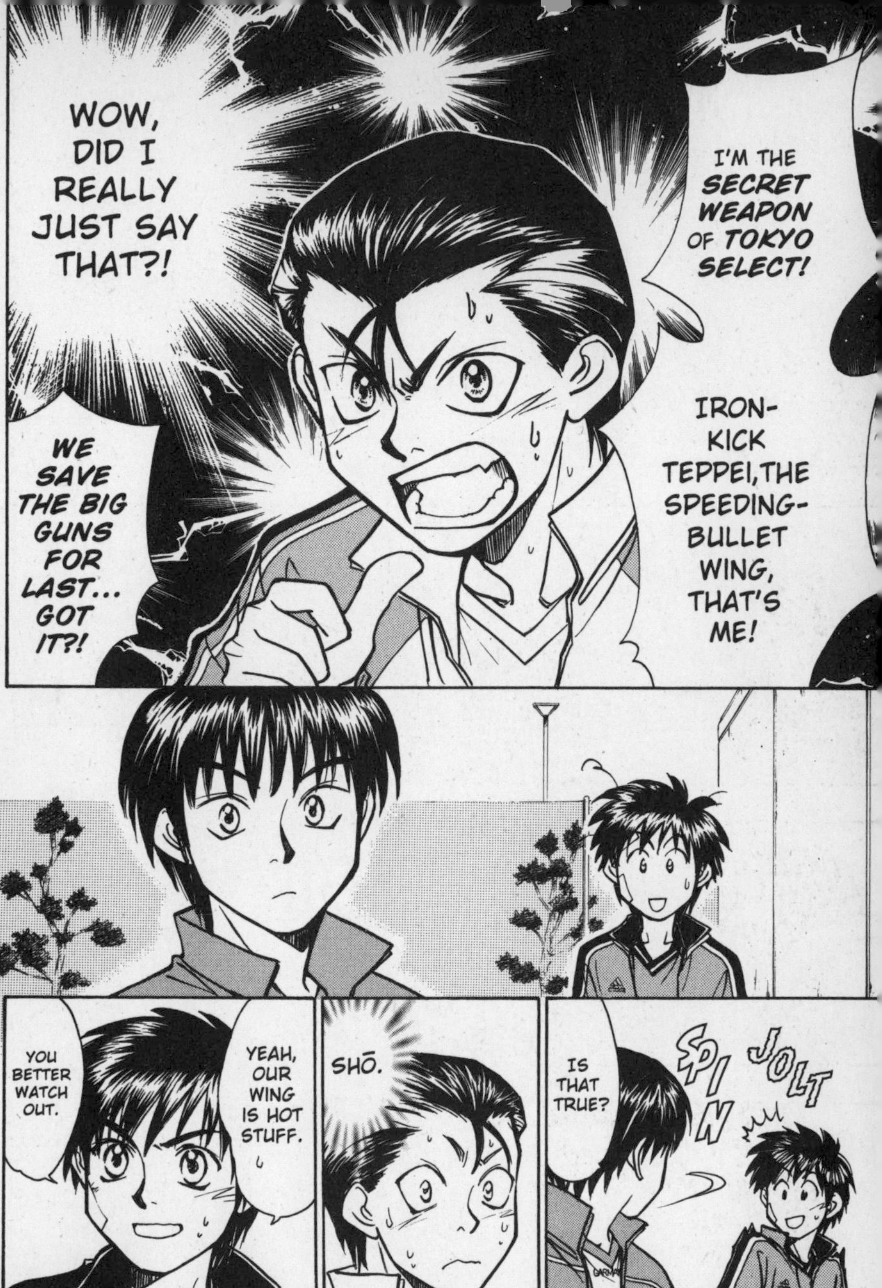

I'M THE SECRET WEAPON OF TOKYO SELECT!
IRON-KICK TEPPEI, THE SPEEDING-BULLET WING, THAT'S ME!
WE SAVE THE BIG GUNS FOR LAST... GOT IT?!
WOW, DID I REALLY JUST SAY THAT?!
JOLT
SPIN
IS THAT TRUE?
SHŌ.
YEAH, OUR WING IS HOT STUFF.
YOU BETTER WATCH OUT.

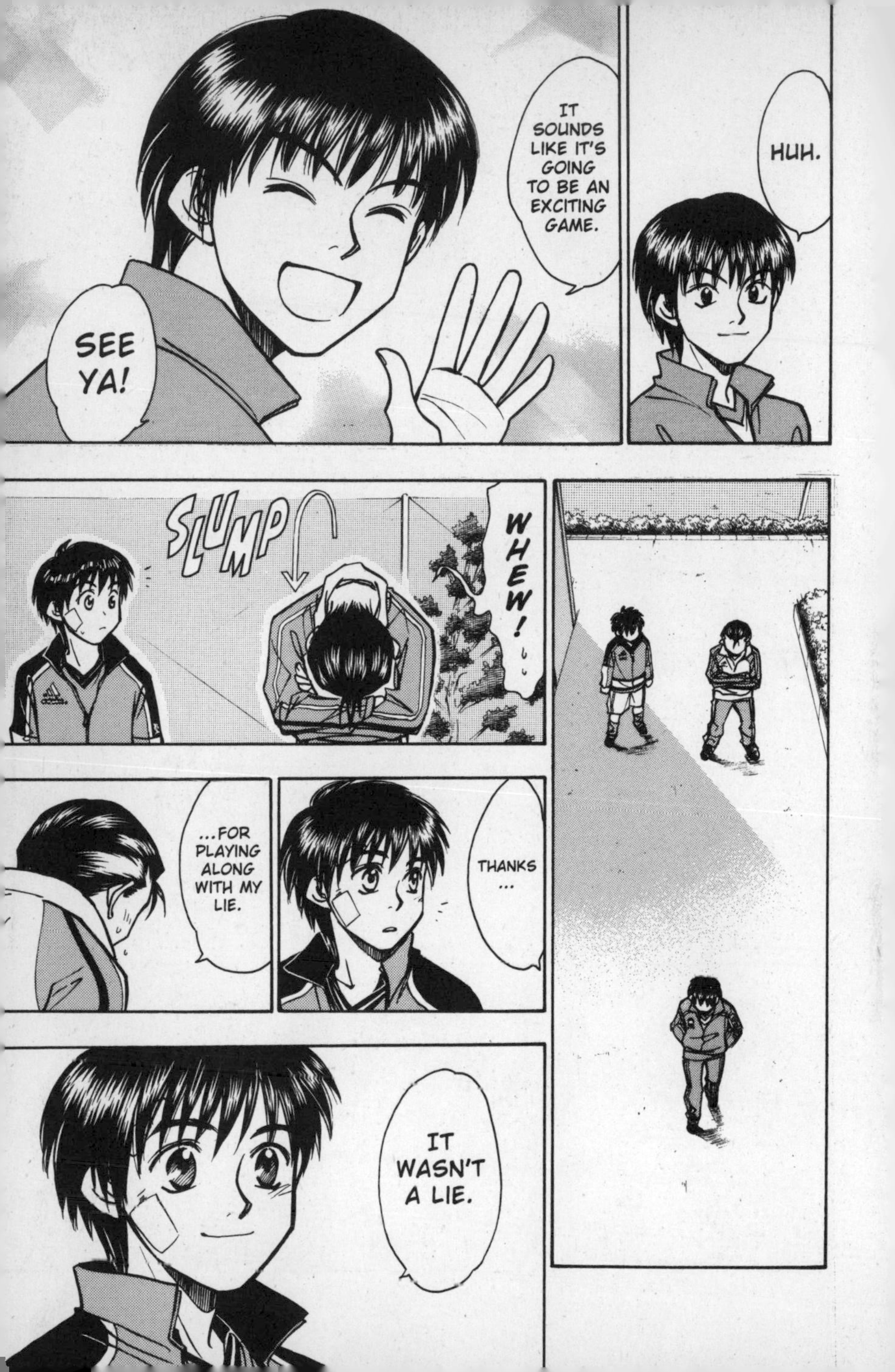
HUH.
IT SOUNDS LIKE IT'S GOING TO BE AN EXCITING GAME.
SEE YA!
WHEW!
SLUMP
THANKS...
...FOR PLAYING ALONG WITH MY LIE.
IT WASN'T A LIE.

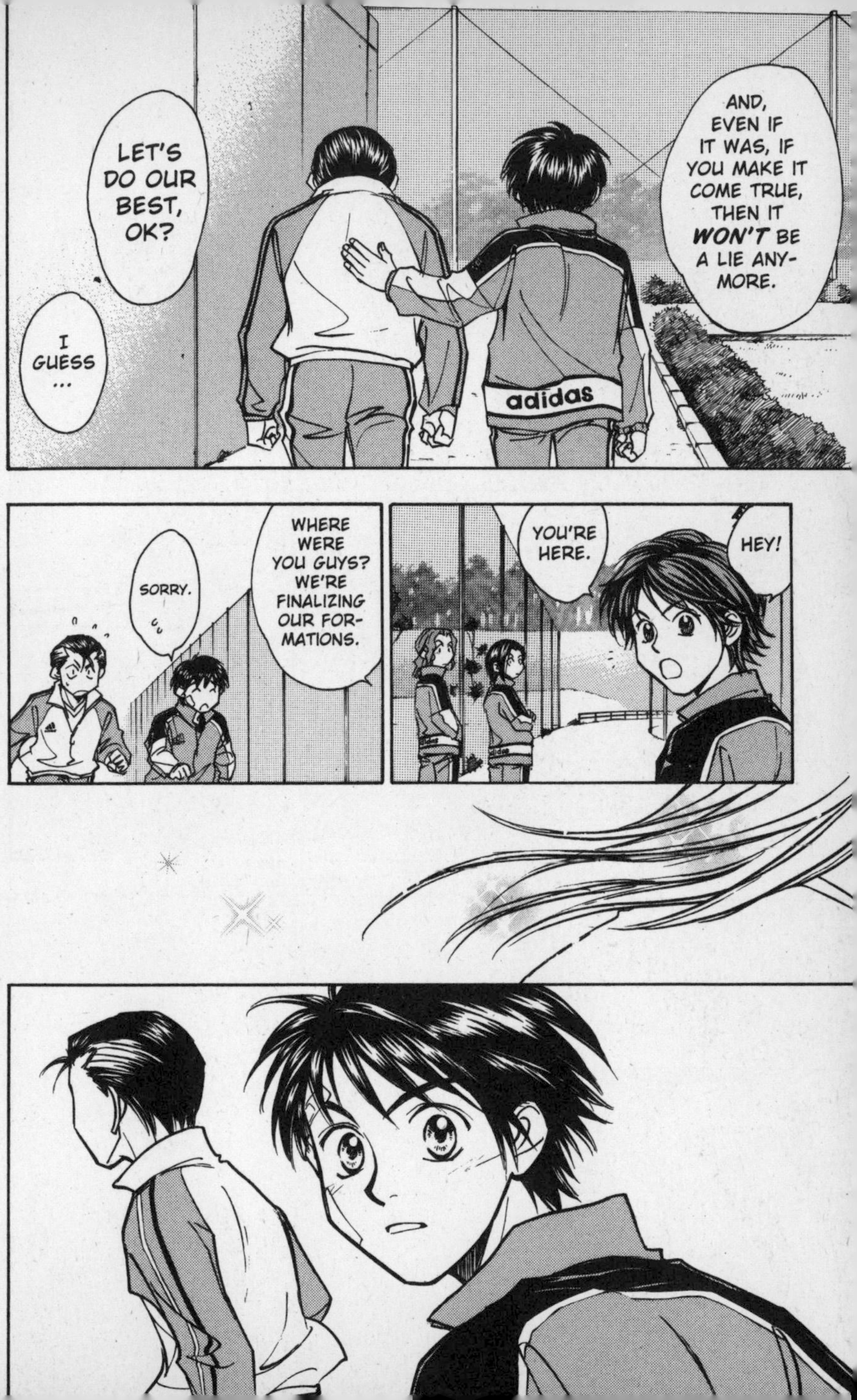
AND, EVEN IF IT WAS, IF YOU MAKE IT COME TRUE, THEN IT **WON'T** BE A LIE ANY-MORE.
LET'S DO OUR BEST, OK?
I GUESS ...
HEY!
YOU'RE HERE.
WHERE WERE YOU GUYS? WE'RE FINALIZING OUR FOR-MATIONS.
SORRY.

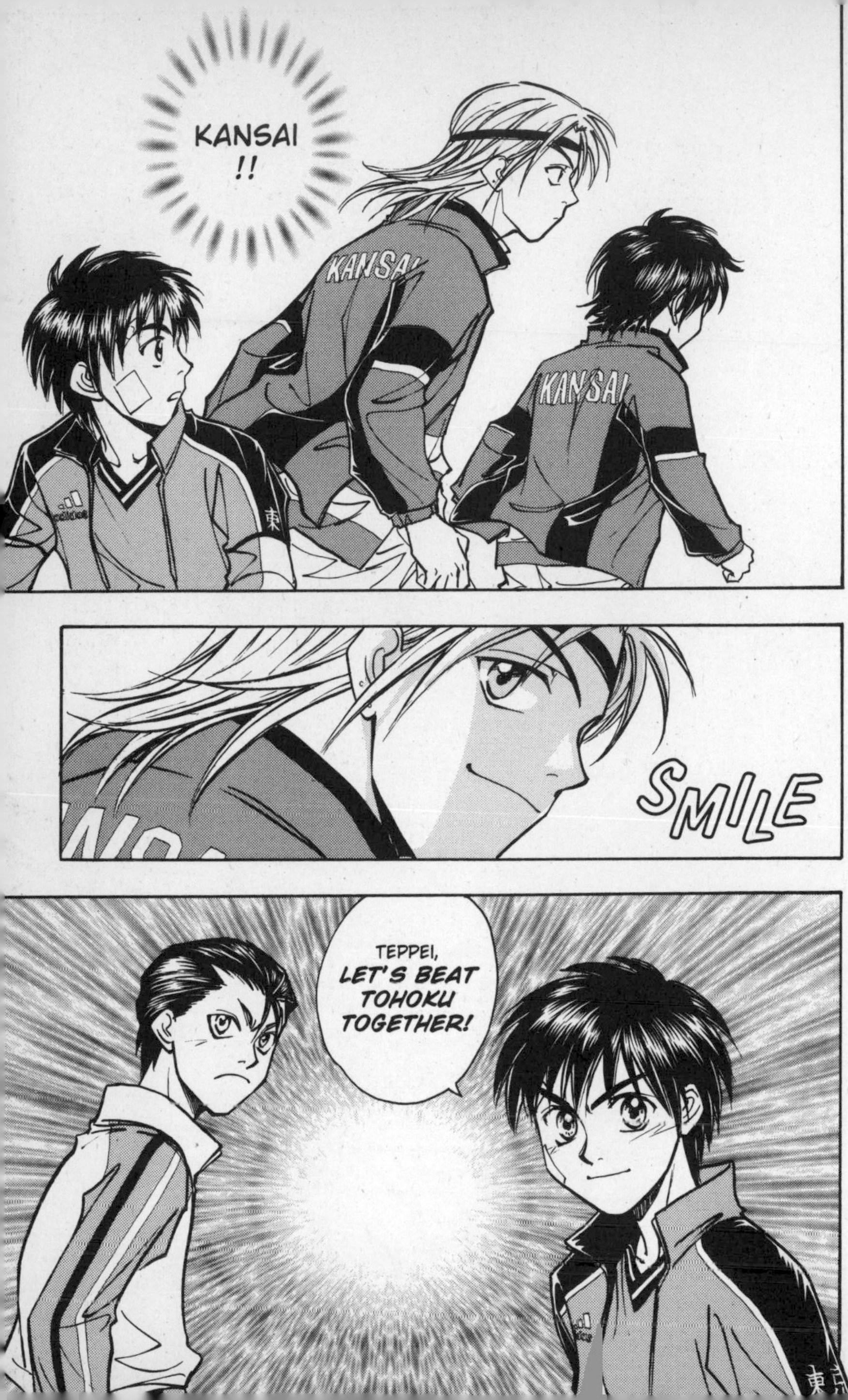
KANSAI !!
KANSAI
KANSAI
SMILE
TEPPEI, LET'S BEAT TOHOKU TOGETHER!

WHISTLE!

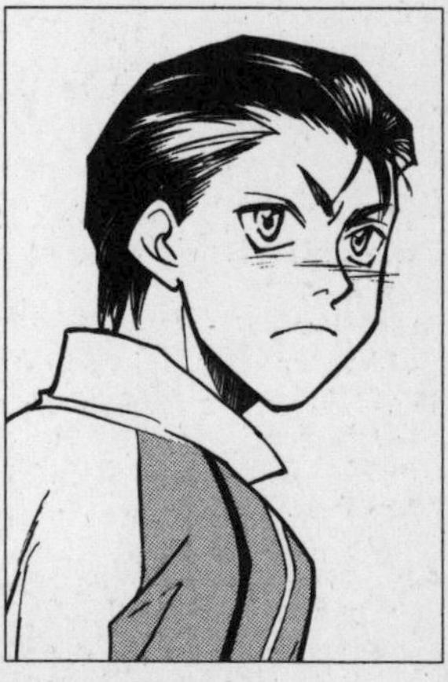

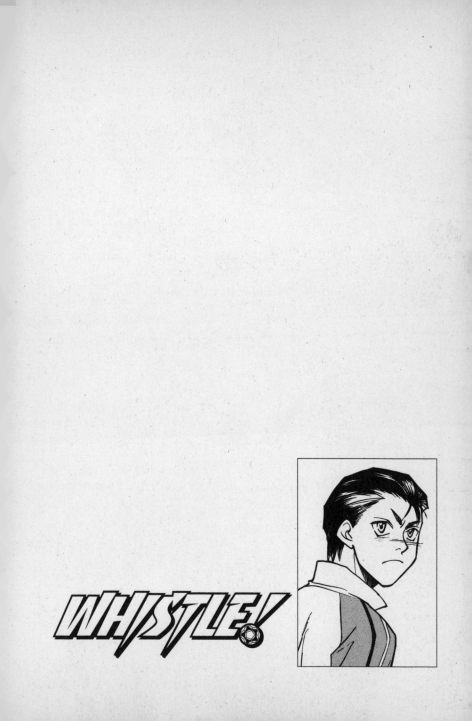

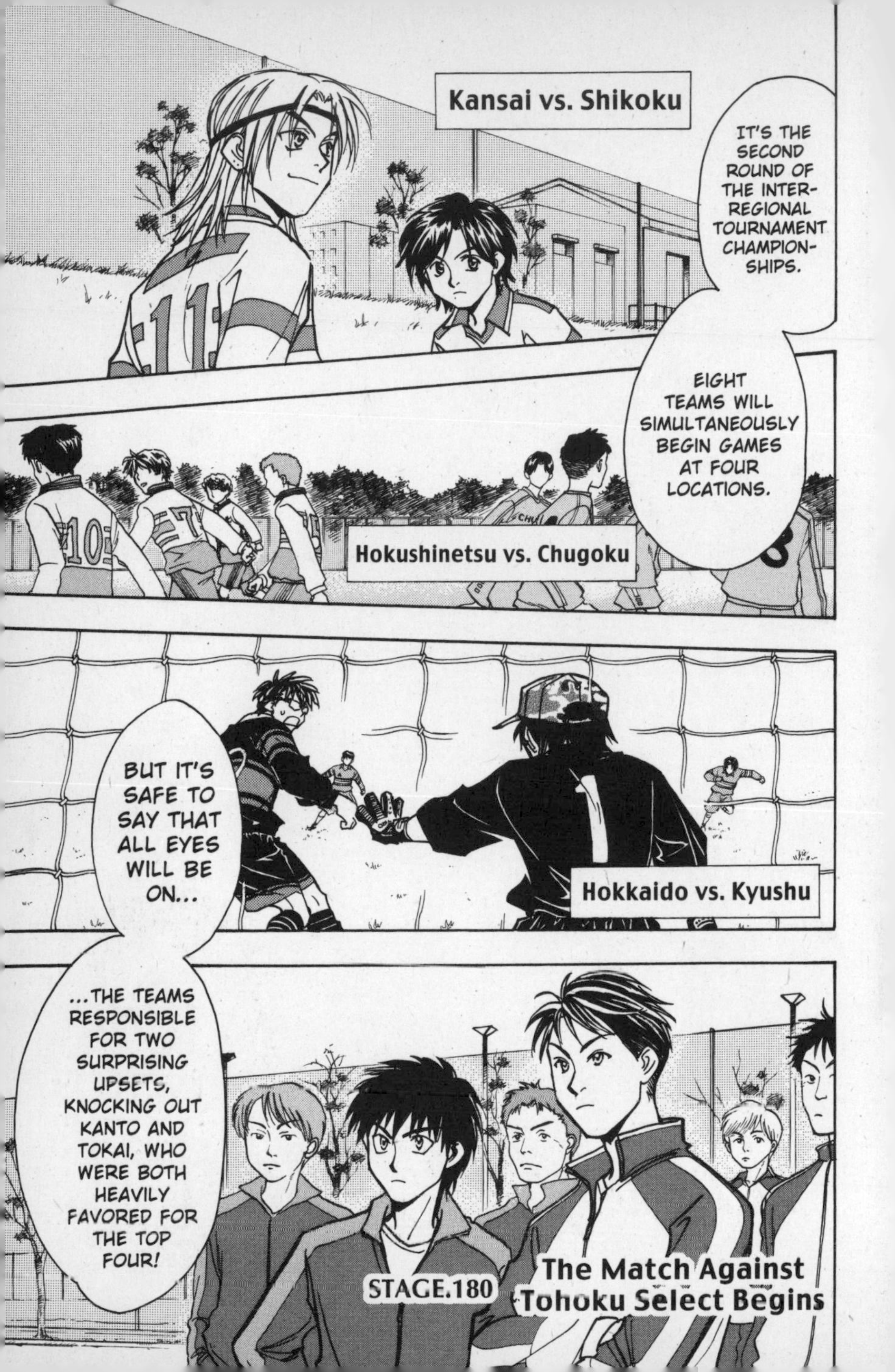
IT'S THE SECOND ROUND OF THE INTER-REGIONAL TOURNAMENT CHAMPIONSHIPS.
Kansai vs. Shikoku
EIGHT TEAMS WILL SIMULTANEOUSLY BEGIN GAMES AT FOUR LOCATIONS.
Hokushinetsu vs. Chugoku
Hokkaido vs. Kyushu
BUT IT'S SAFE TO SAY THAT ALL EYES WILL BE ON...
...THE TEAMS RESPONSIBLE FOR TWO SURPRISING UPSETS, KNOCKING OUT KANTO AND TOKAI, WHO WERE BOTH HEAVILY FAVORED FOR THE TOP FOUR!
STAGE.180
The Match Against Tohoku Select Begins

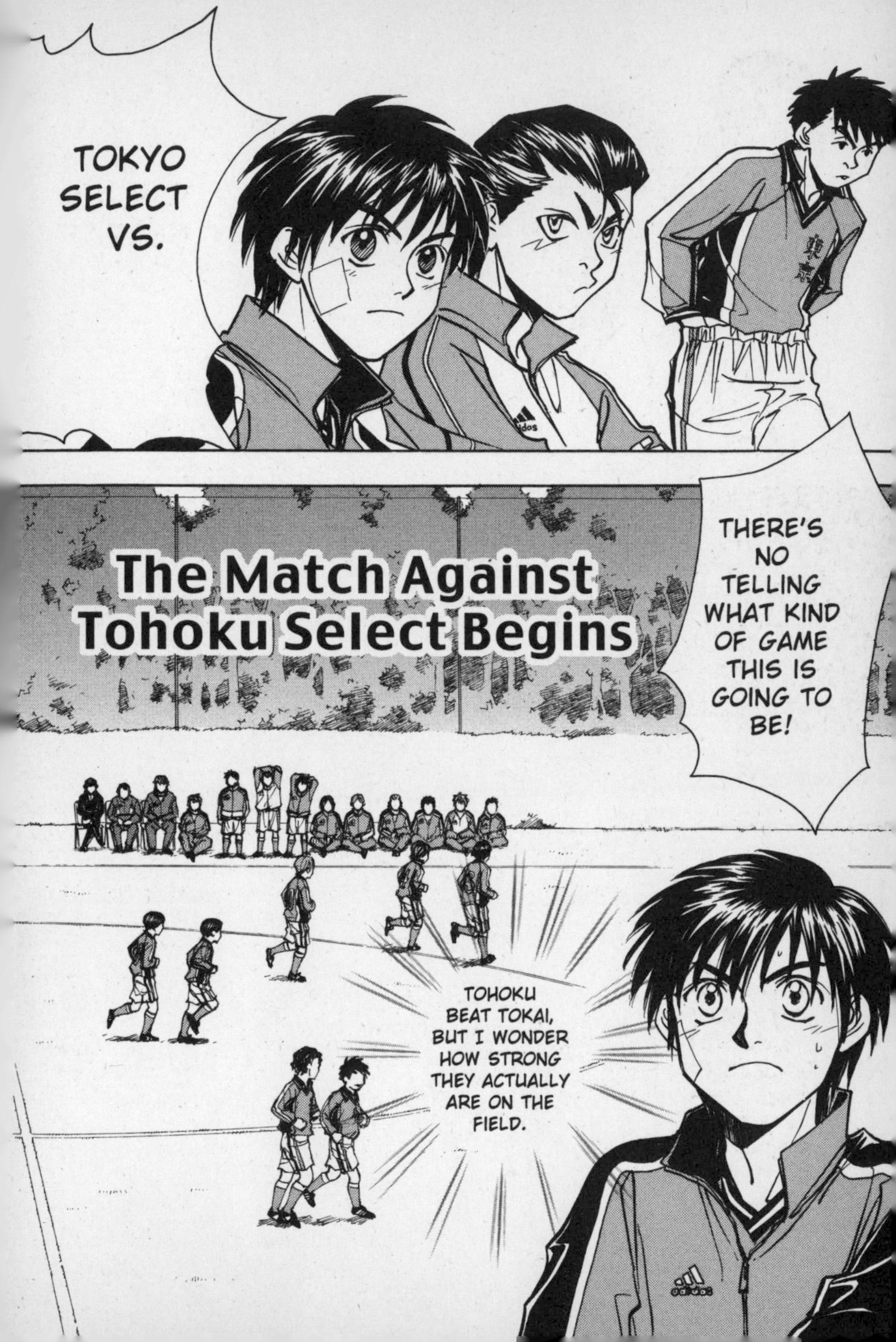
TOKYO SELECT VS.
THERE'S NO TELLING WHAT KIND OF GAME THIS IS GOING TO BE!
The Match Against Tohoku Select Begins
TOHOKU BEAT TOKAI, BUT I WONDER HOW STRONG THEY ACTUALLY ARE ON THE FIELD.

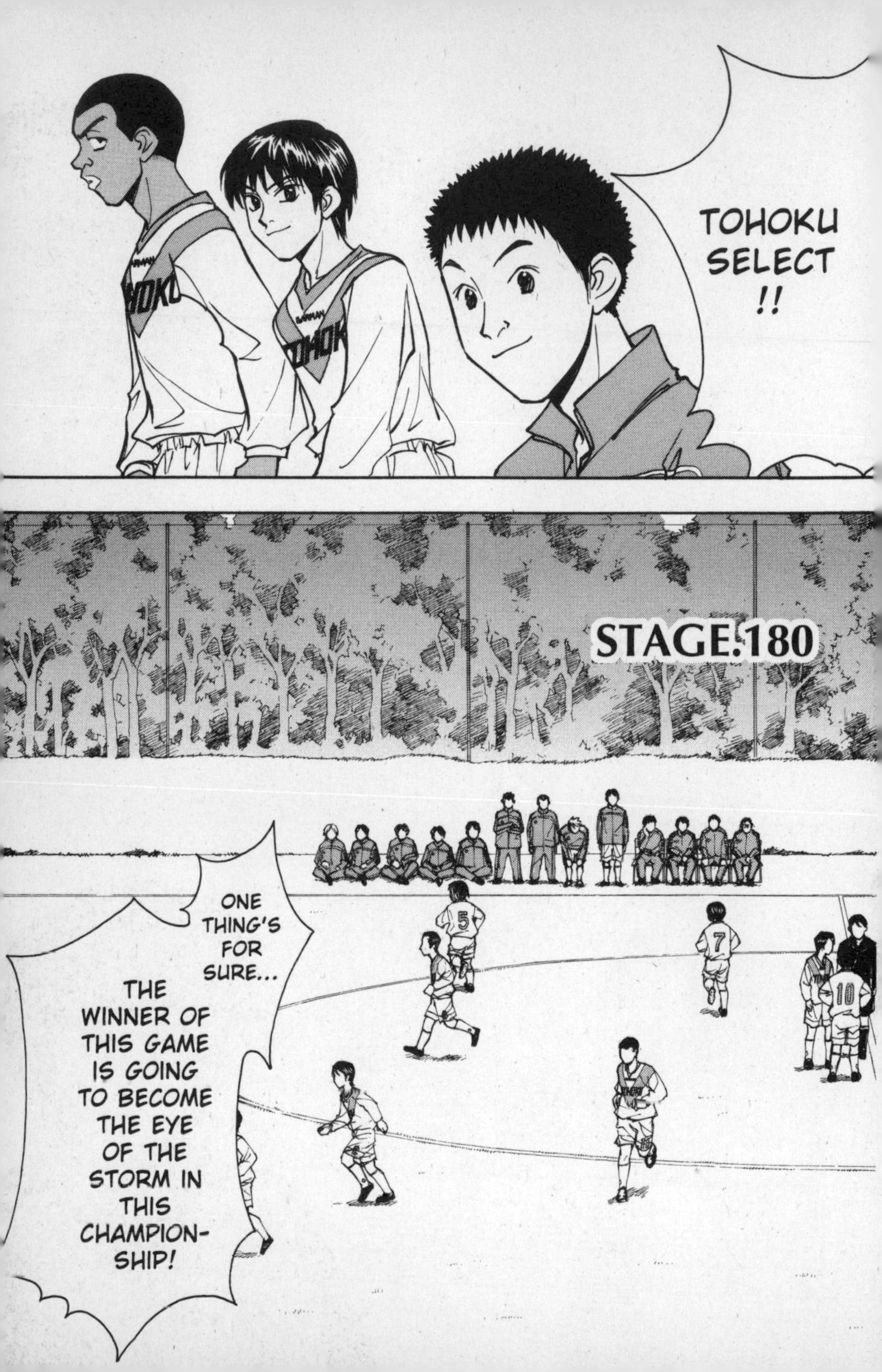
TOHOKU SELECT !!
STAGE.180
ONE THING'S FOR SURE... THE WINNER OF THIS GAME IS GOING TO BECOME THE EYE OF THE STORM IN THIS CHAMPION-SHIP!

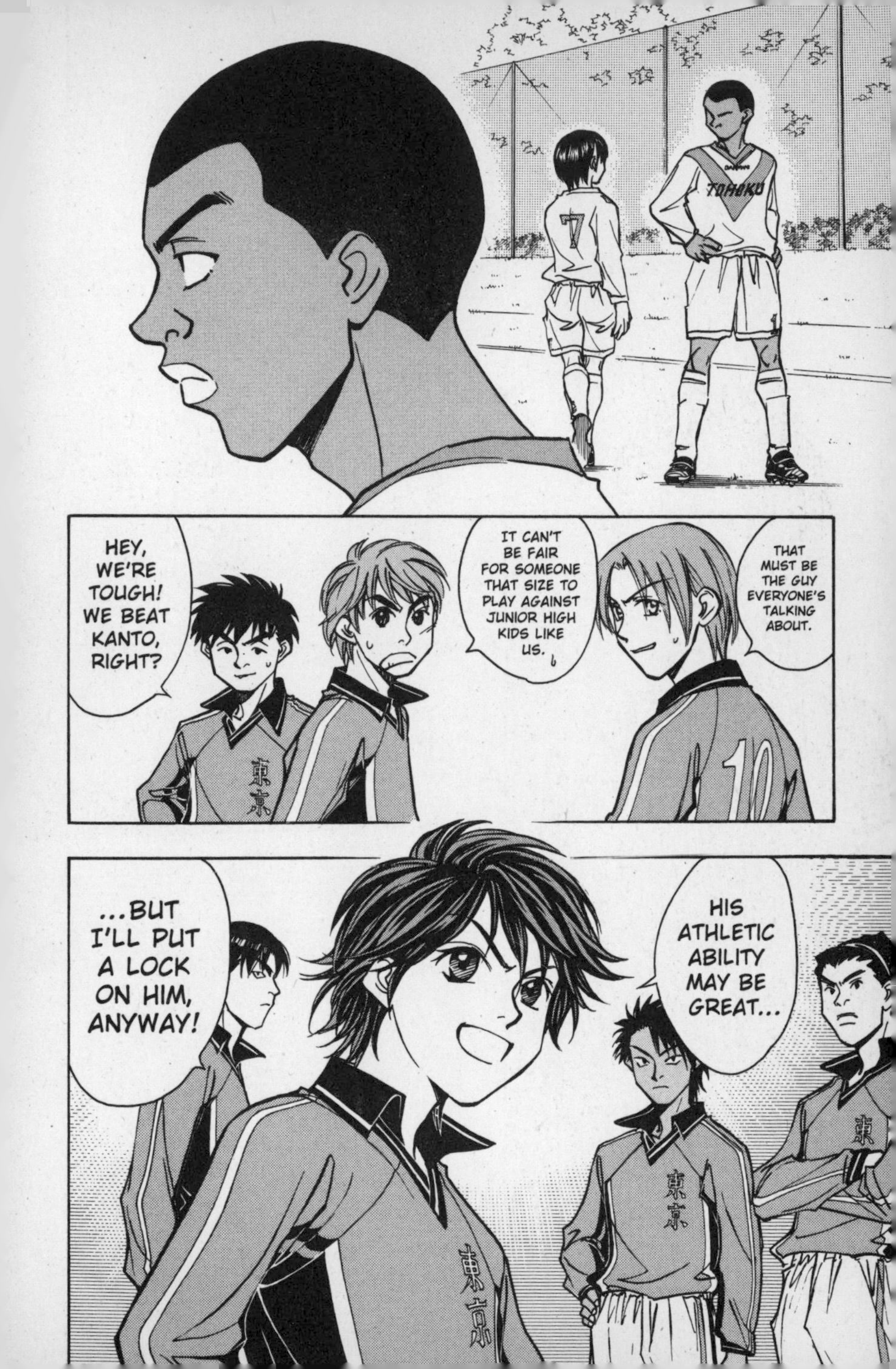
TOHOKU
THAT MUST BE THE GUY EVERYONE'S TALKING ABOUT.
IT CAN'T BE FAIR FOR SOMEONE THAT SIZE TO PLAY AGAINST JUNIOR HIGH KIDS LIKE US.
HEY, WE'RE TOUGH! WE BEAT KANTO, RIGHT?
HIS ATHLETIC ABILITY MAY BE GREAT...
...BUT I'LL PUT A LOCK ON HIM, ANYWAY!

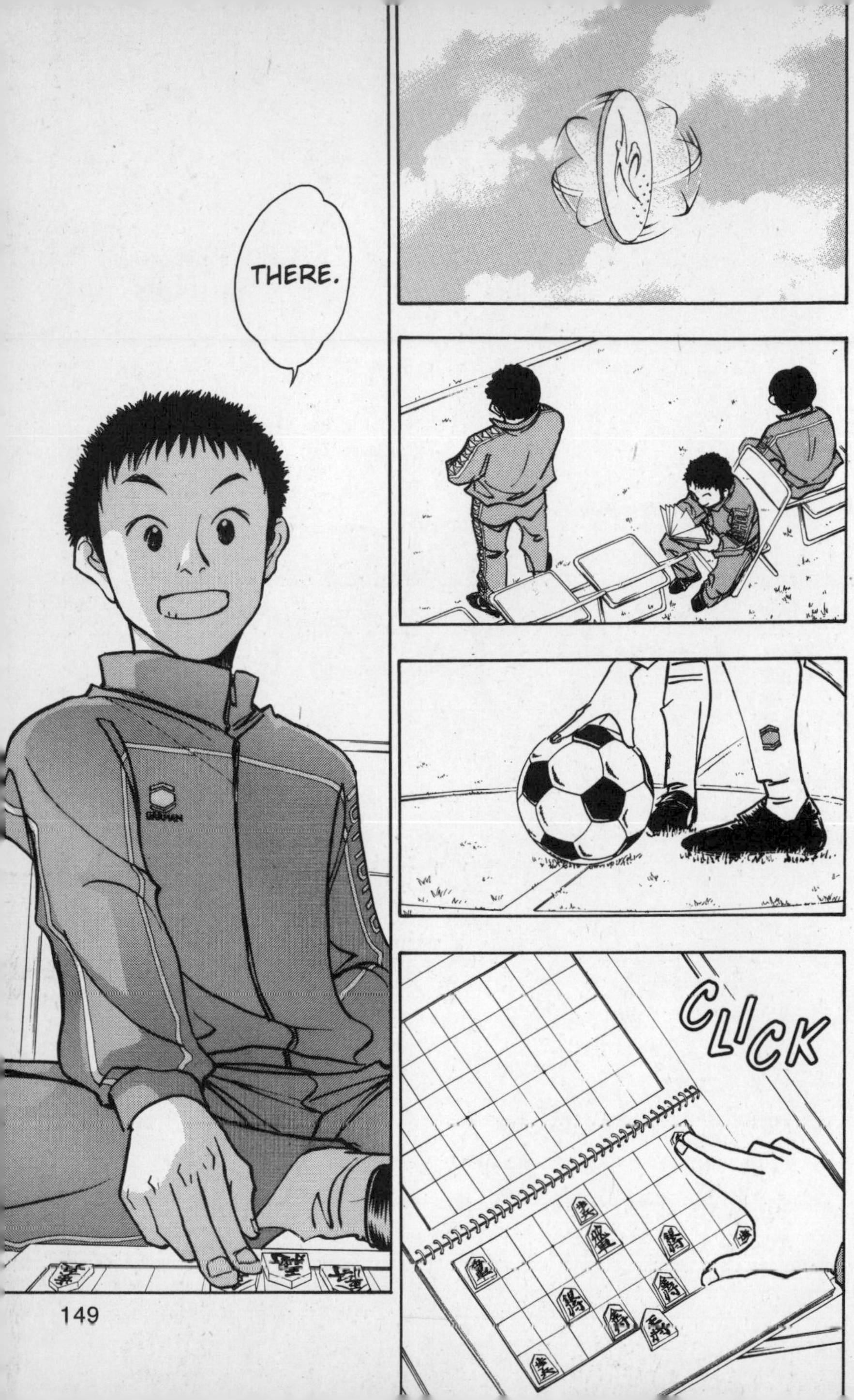
CLICK
THERE.

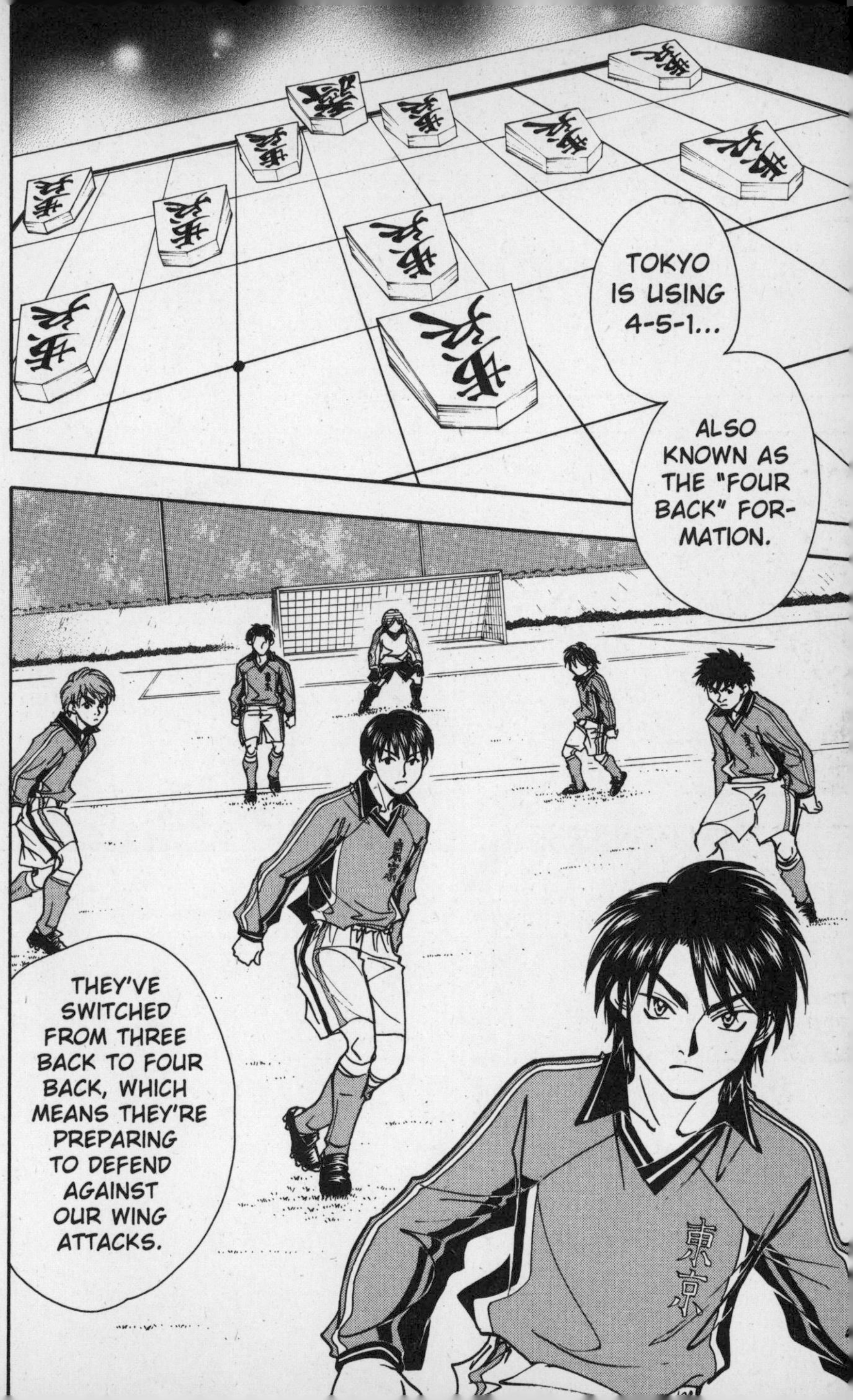
TOKYO IS USING 4-5-1...
ALSO KNOWN AS THE "FOUR BACK" FOR-MATION.
THEY'VE SWITCHED FROM THREE BACK TO FOUR BACK, WHICH MEANS THEY'RE PREPARING TO DEFEND AGAINST OUR WING ATTACKS.

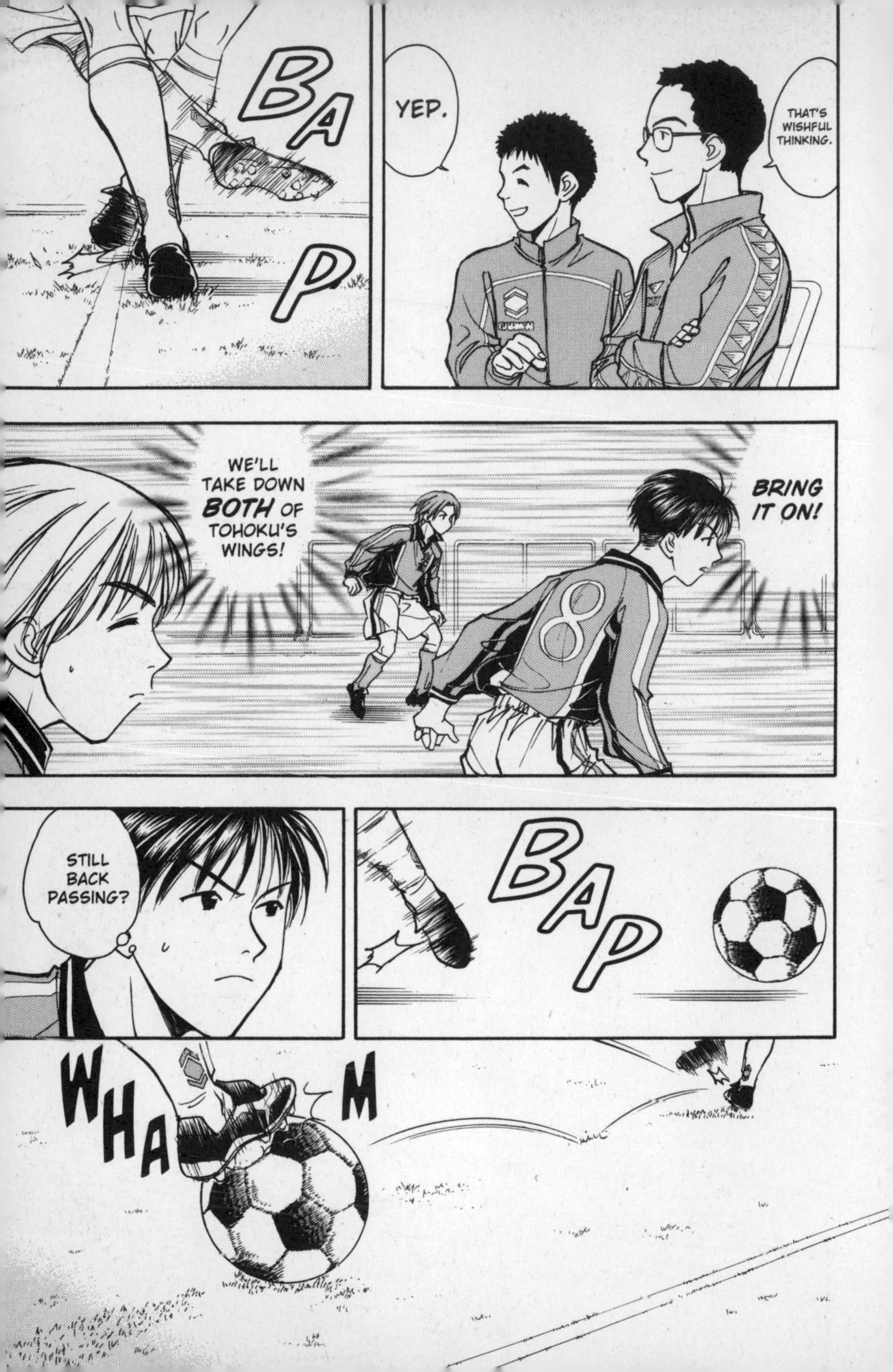
THAT'S WISHFUL THINKING.
YEP.
BAP
BRING IT ON!
WE'LL TAKE DOWN BOTH OF TOHOKU'S WINGS!
BAP
STILL BACK PASSING?
WHAM

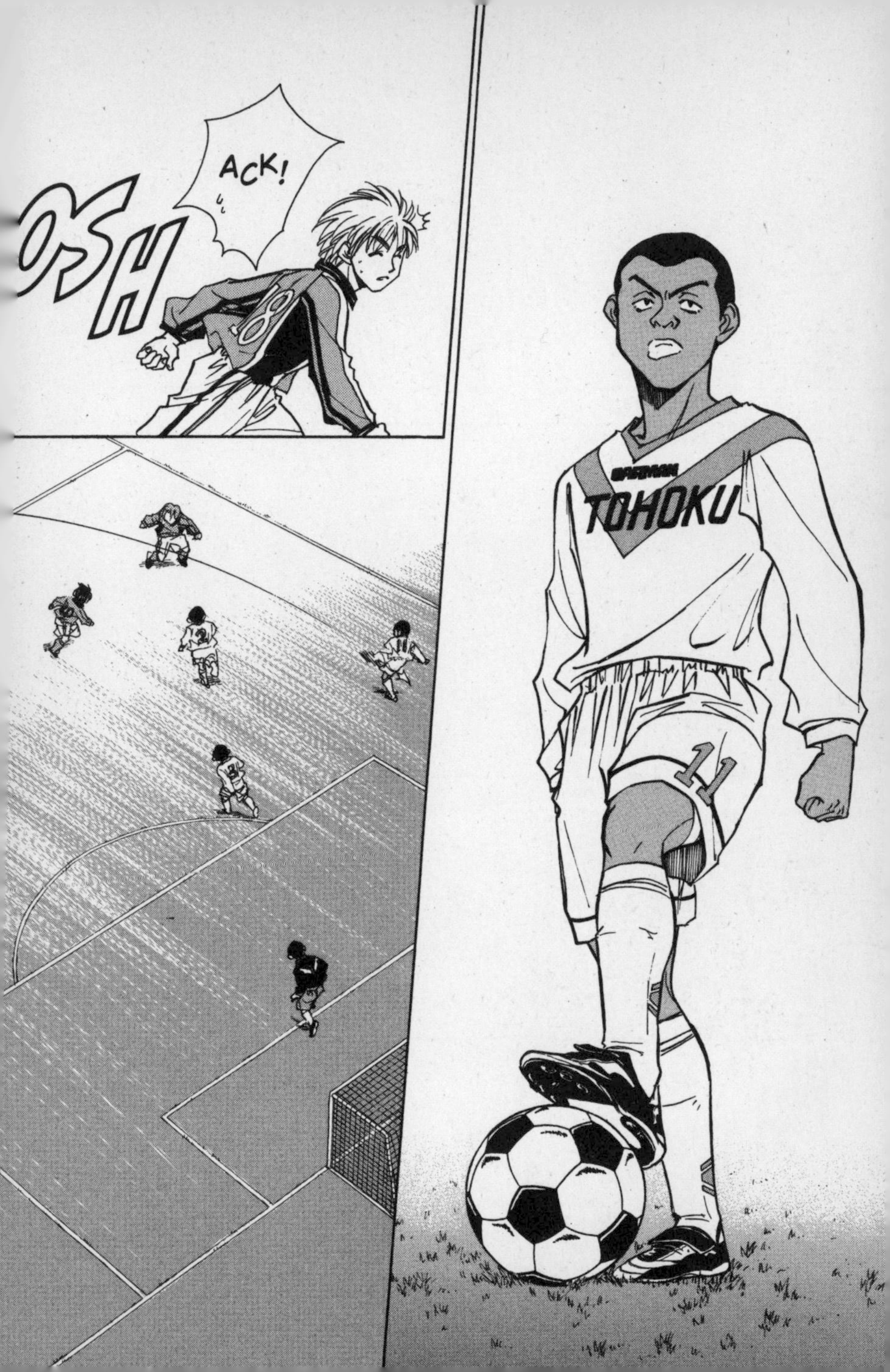
TOHOKU
OSH
ACK!

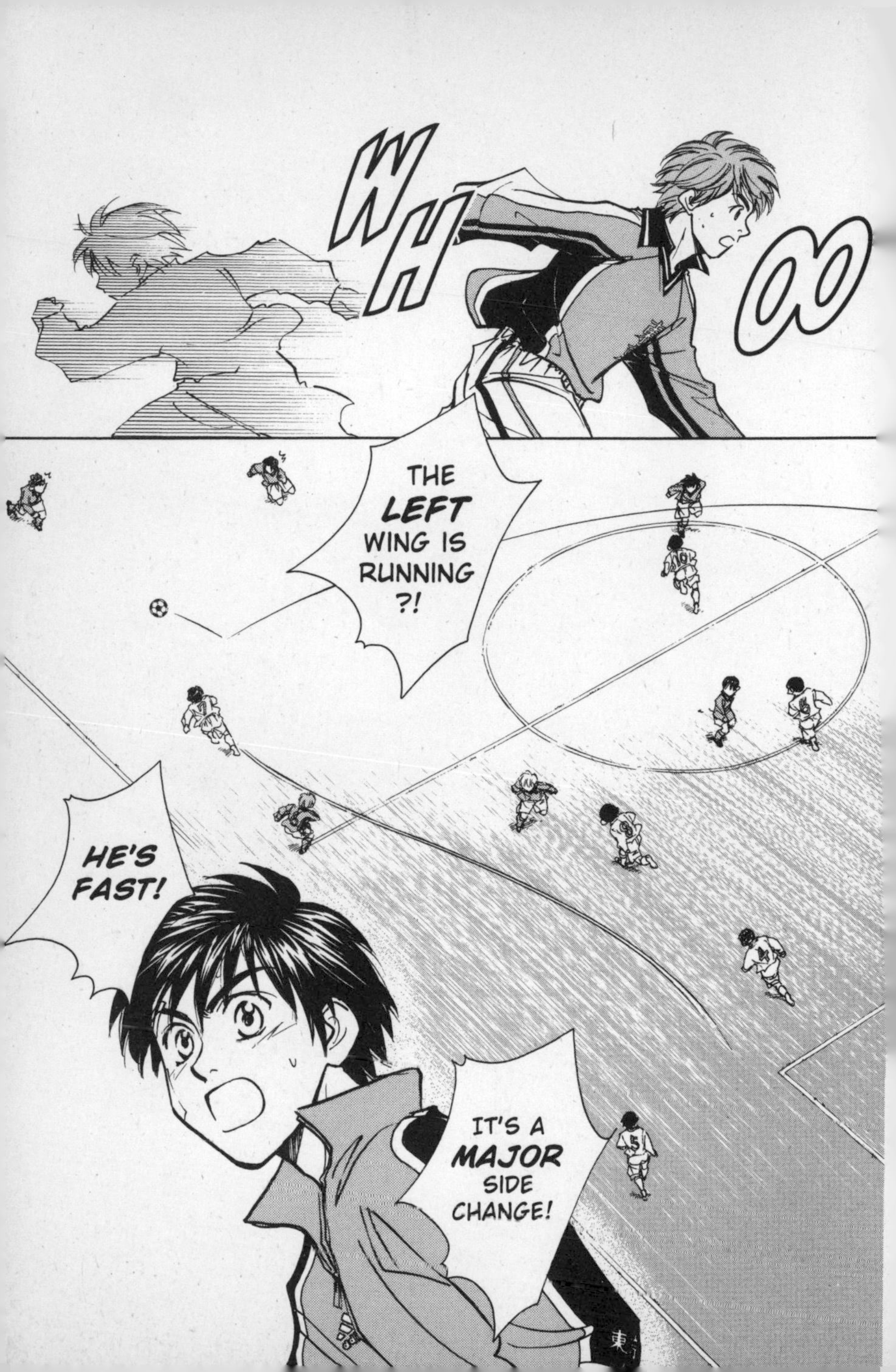
WHOO
THE LEFT WING IS RUNNING ?!
HE'S FAST!
IT'S A MAJOR SIDE CHANGE!

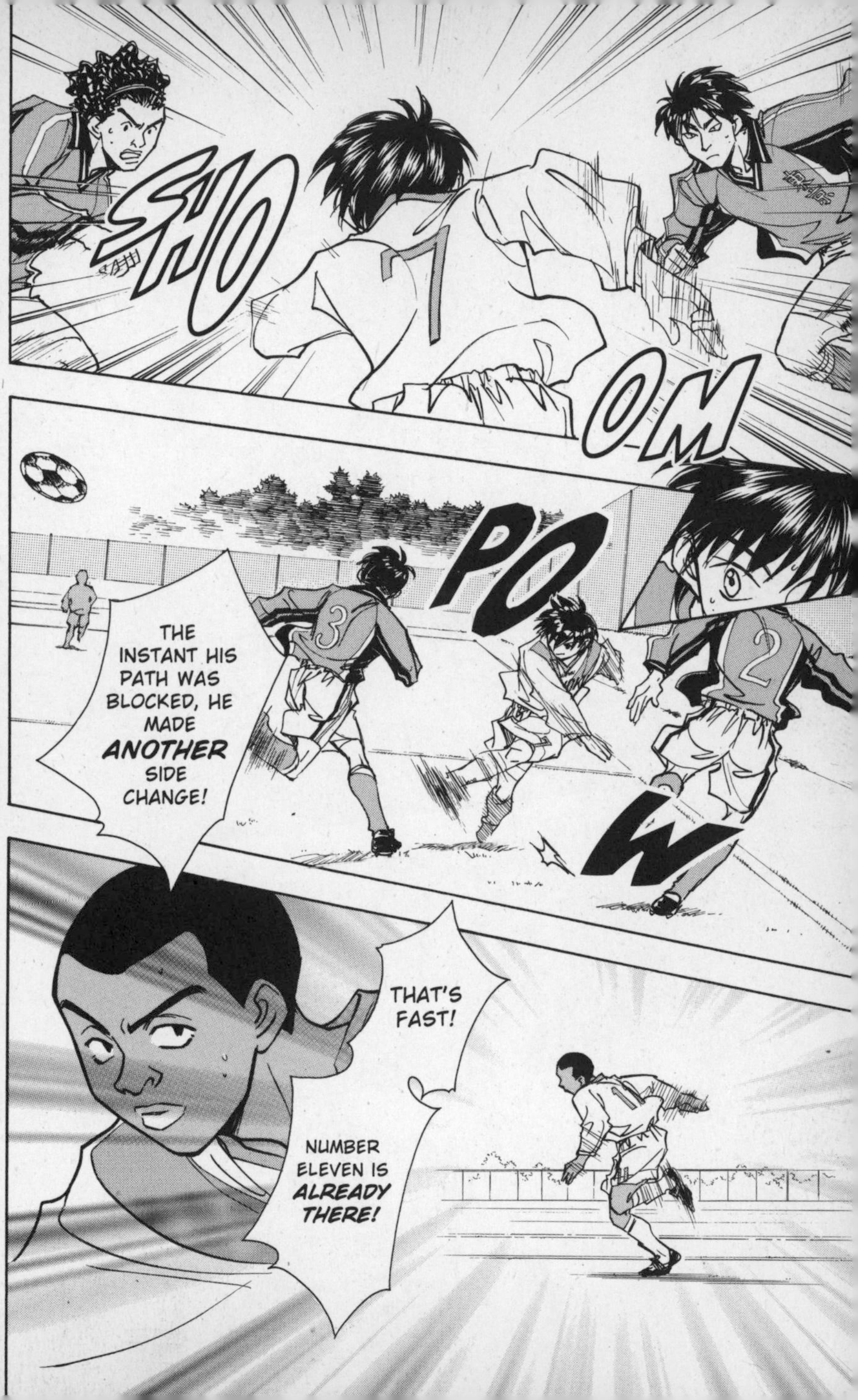
SHOOM
POW
THE INSTANT HIS PATH WAS BLOCKED, HE MADE **ANOTHER** SIDE CHANGE!
THAT'S FAST!
NUMBER ELEVEN IS ***ALREADY THERE!***

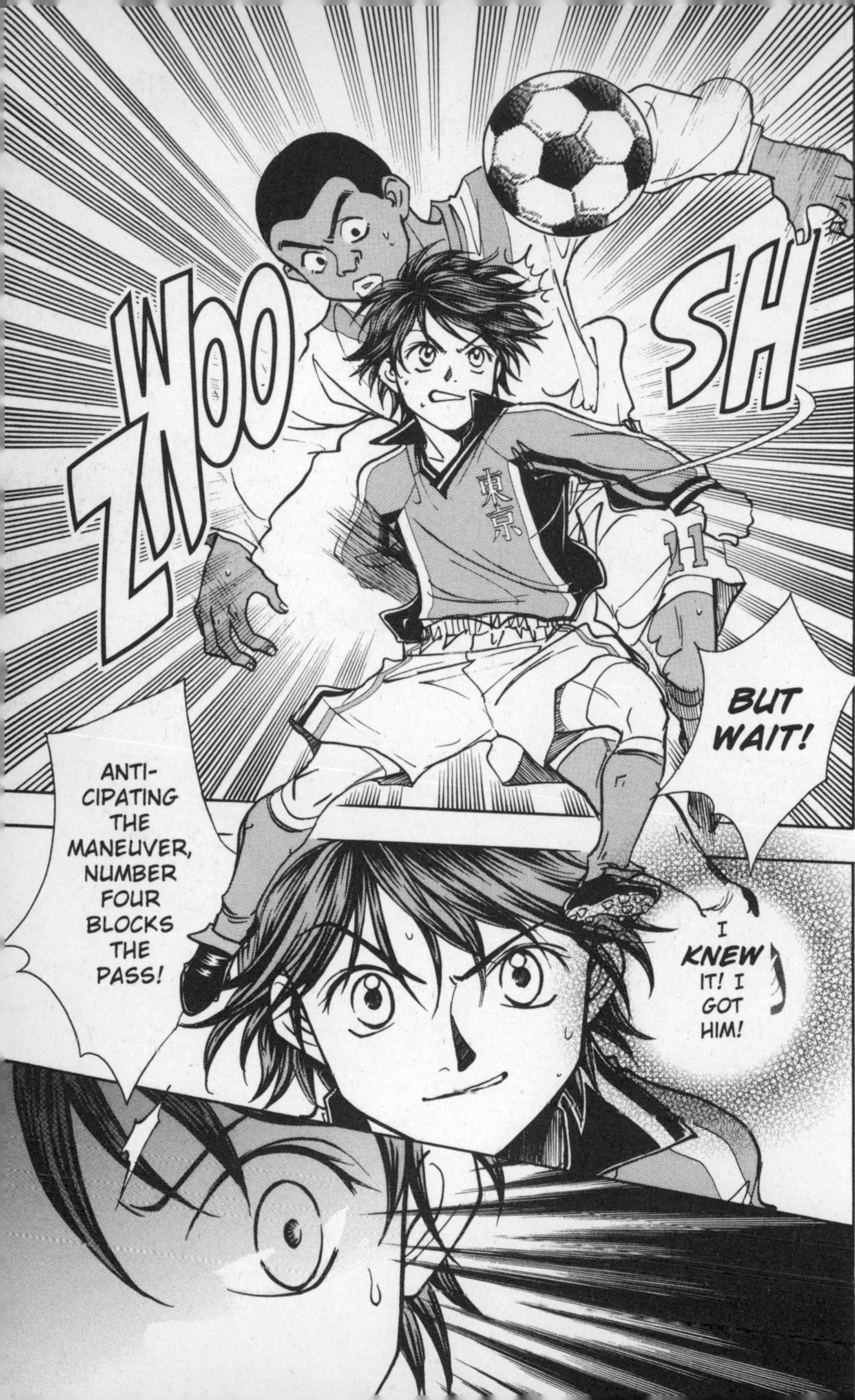
ZWOOSH
BUT WAIT!
ANTI-CIPATING THE MANEUVER, NUMBER FOUR BLOCKS THE PASS!
I KNEW IT! I GOT HIM!

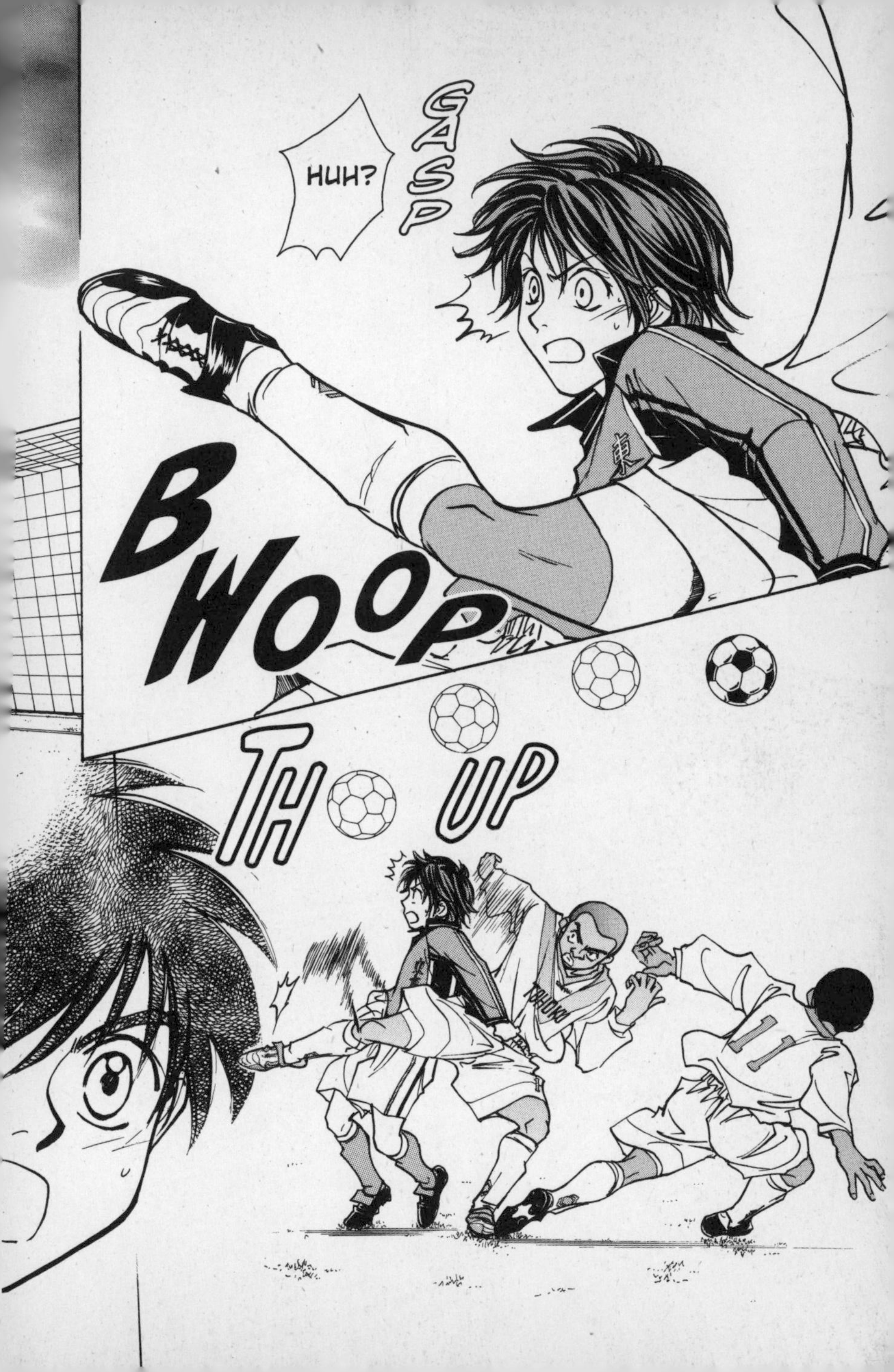
GASP
HUH?
BWOOP
TH UP

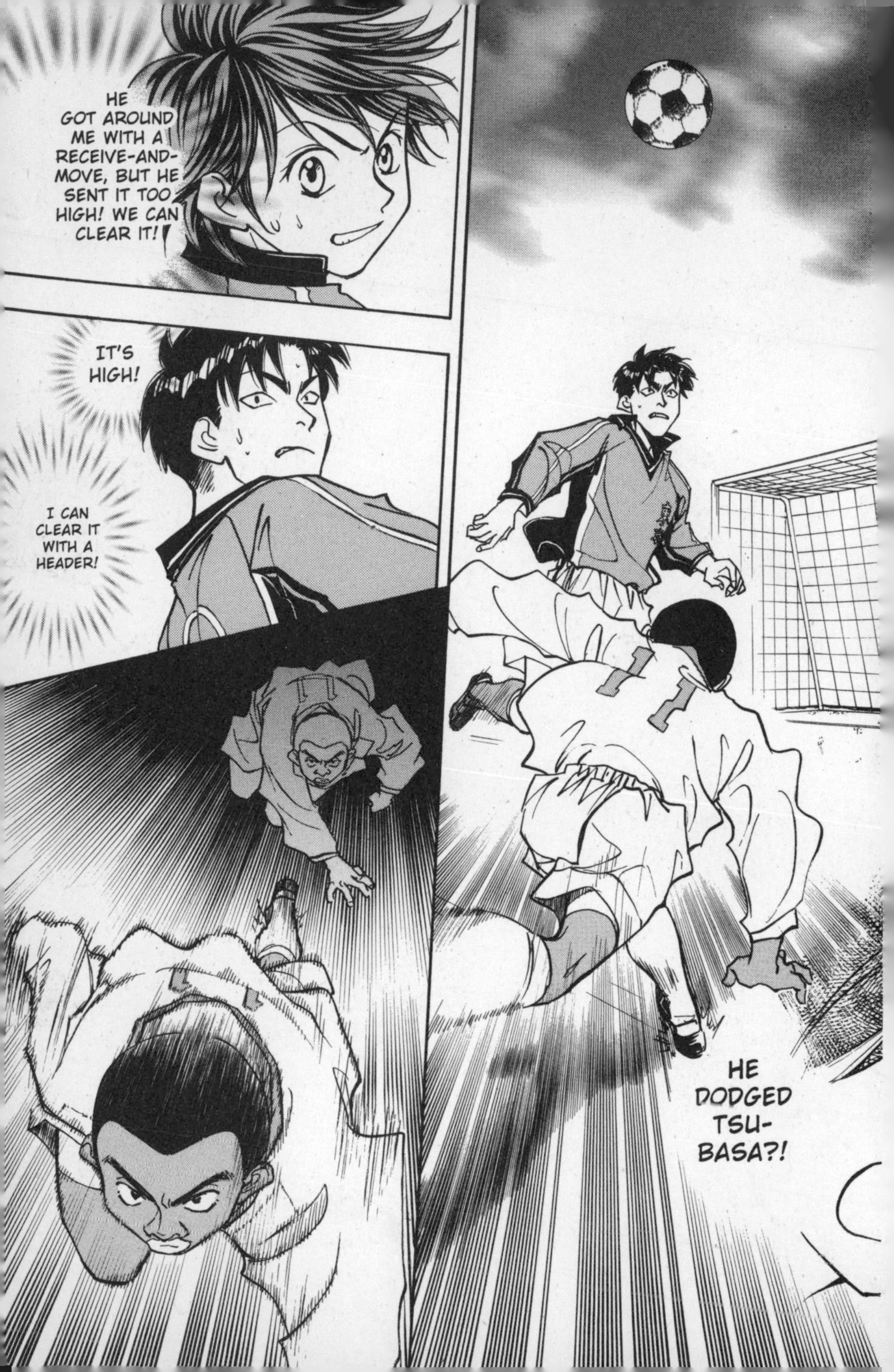
HE DODGED TSU-BASA?!
HE GOT AROUND ME WITH A RECEIVE-AND-MOVE, BUT HE SENT IT TOO HIGH! WE CAN CLEAR IT!
IT'S HIGH!
I CAN CLEAR IT WITH A HEADER!

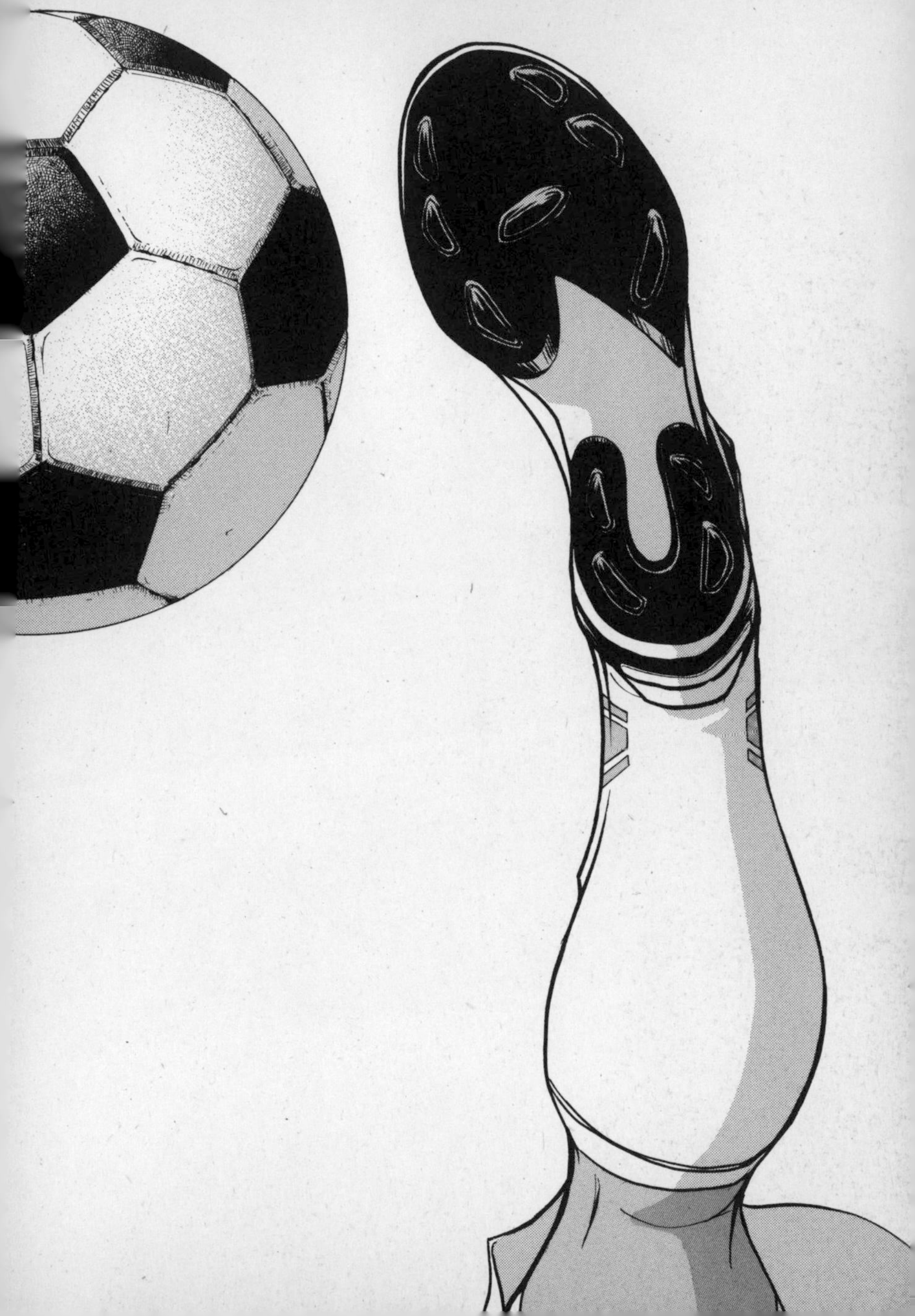

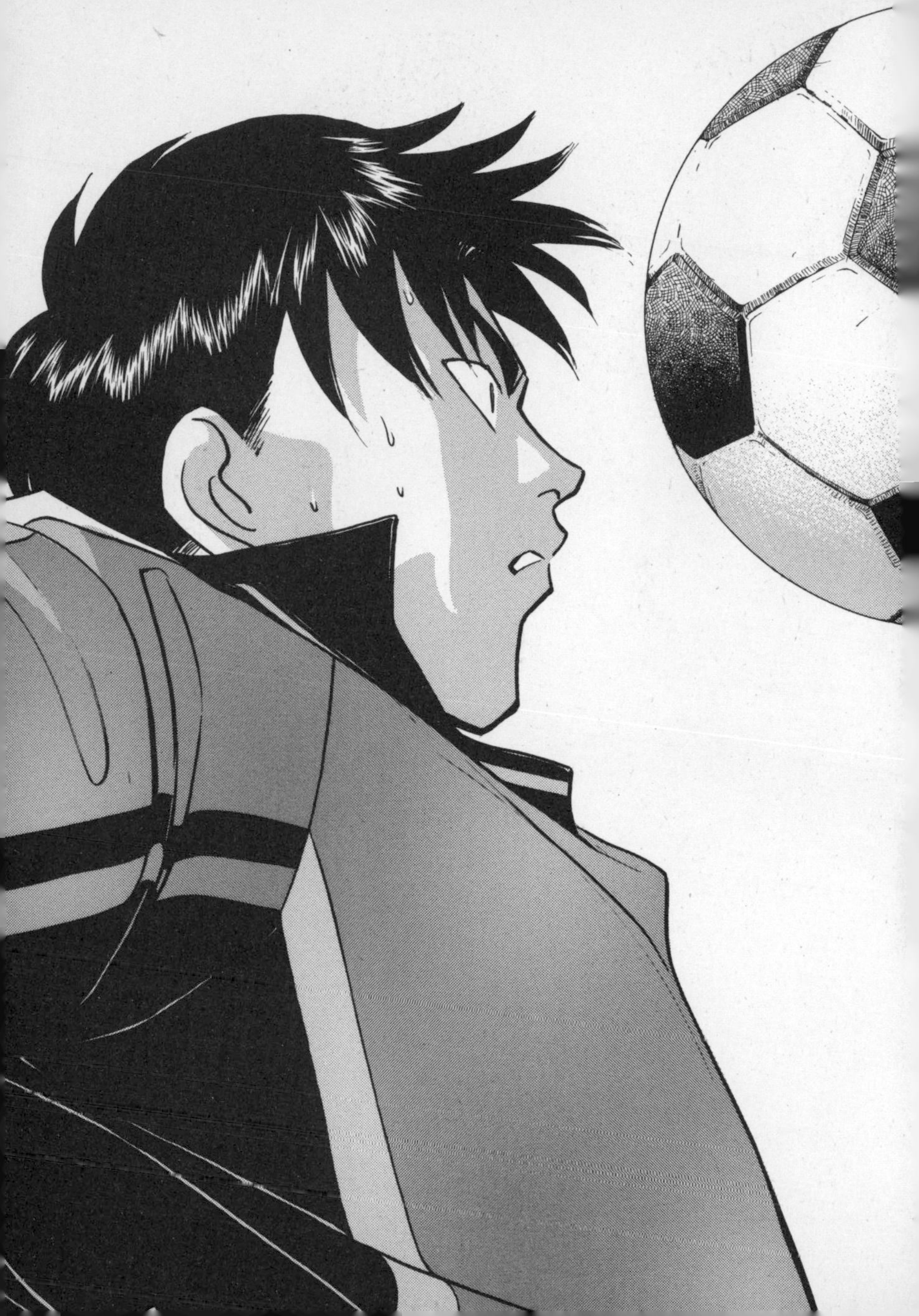

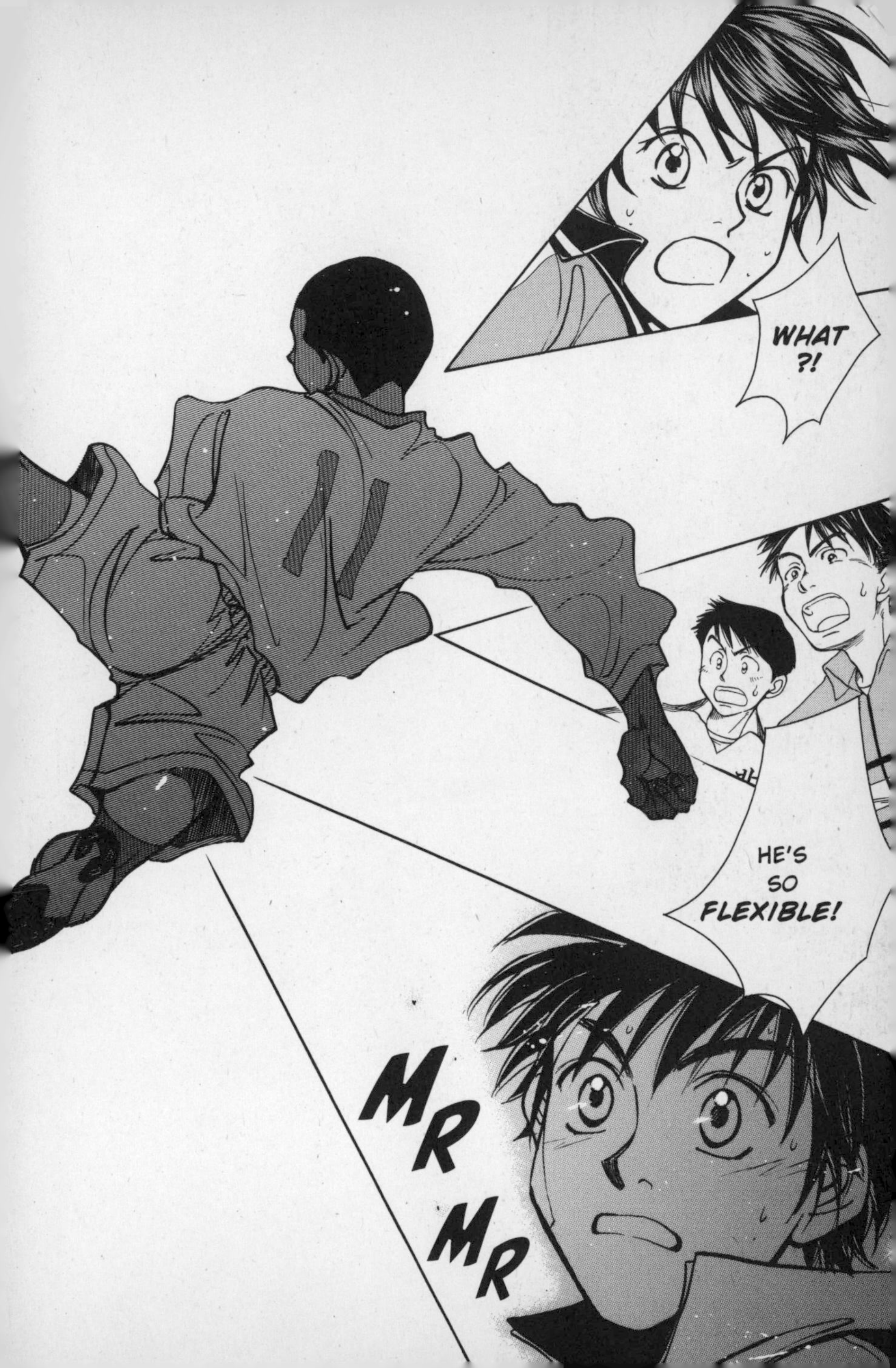
WHAT ?!
HE'S SO FLEXIBLE!
MR MR

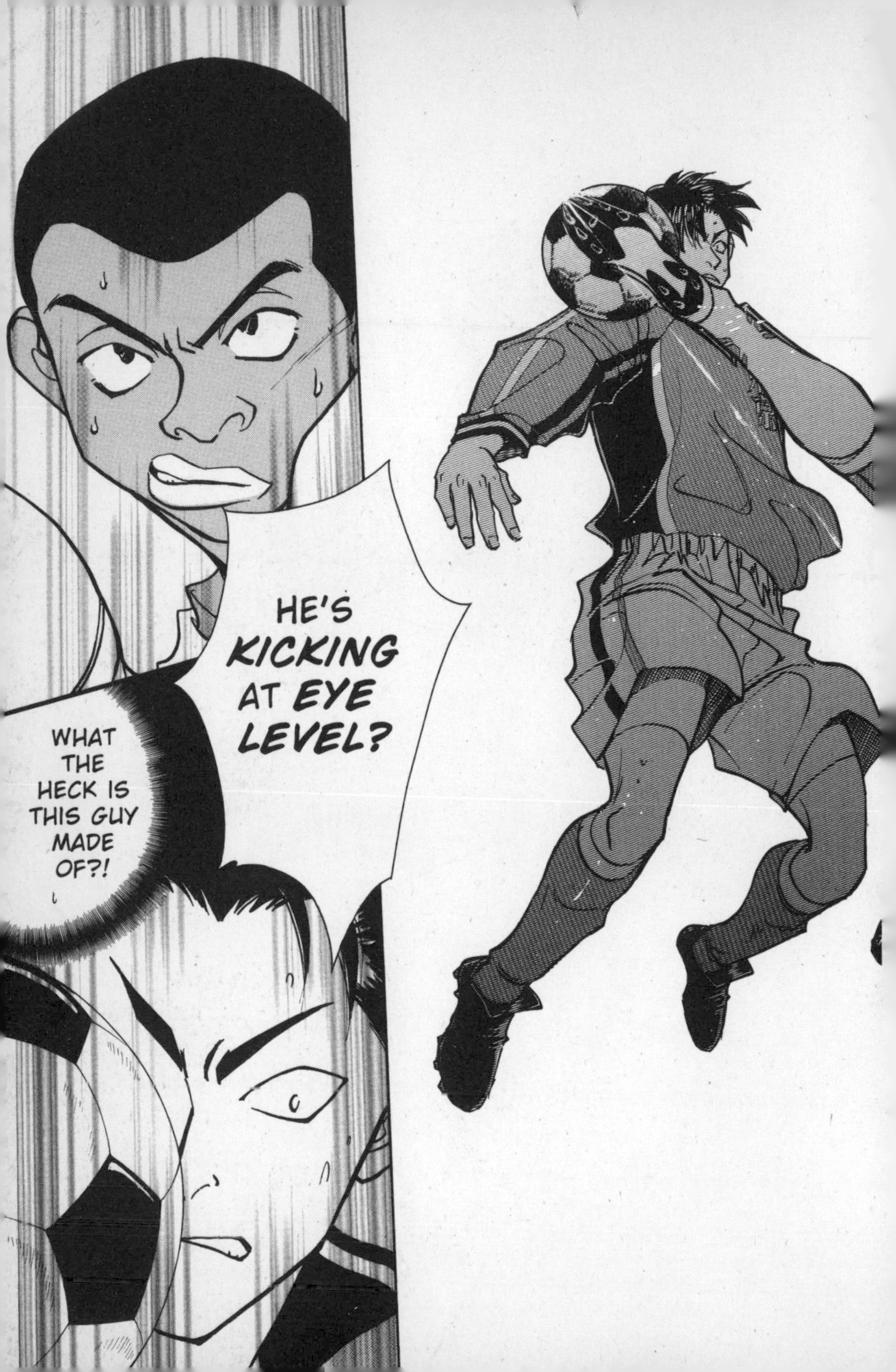
HE'S KICKING AT EYE LEVEL?
WHAT THE HECK IS THIS GUY MADE OF?!

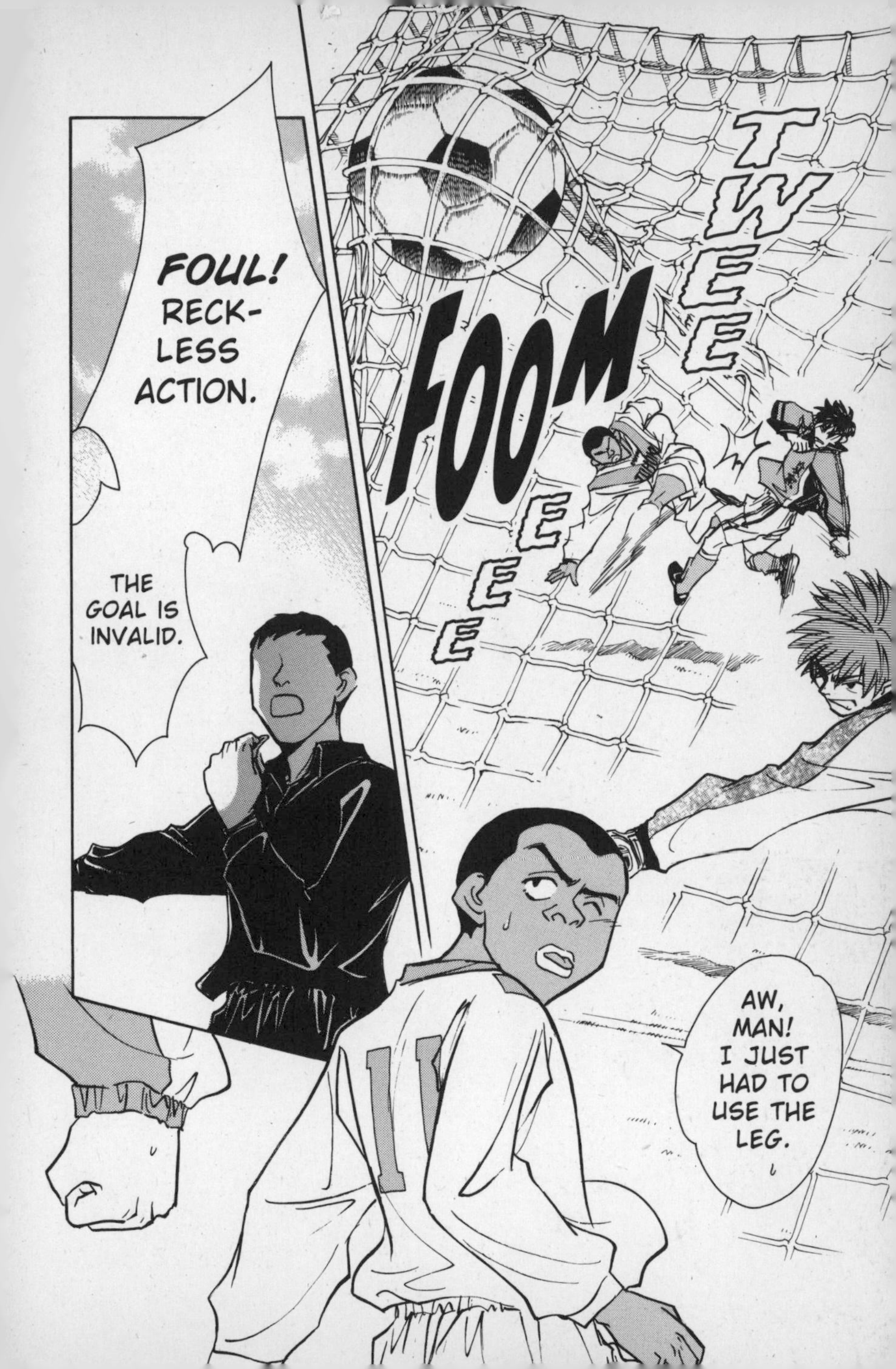
FOOM
TWEEEEEEE
AW, MAN! I JUST HAD TO USE THE LEG.
FOUL! RECK-LESS ACTION.
THE GOAL IS INVALID.

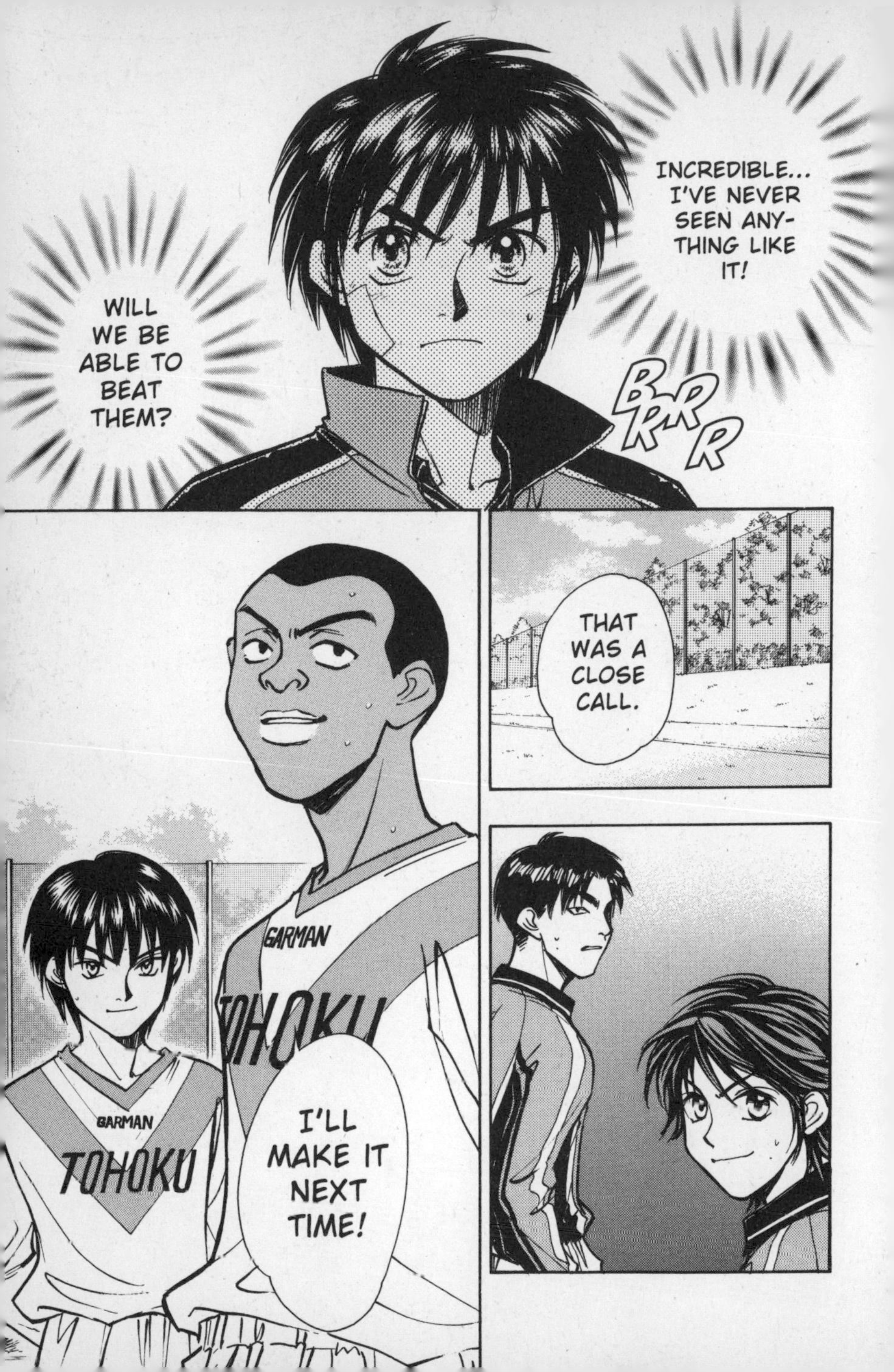
INCREDIBLE... I'VE NEVER SEEN ANYTHING LIKE IT!
BRRR
WILL WE BE ABLE TO BEAT THEM?
THAT WAS A CLOSE CALL.
I'LL MAKE IT NEXT TIME!
GARMAN
TOHOKU

WHISTLE!

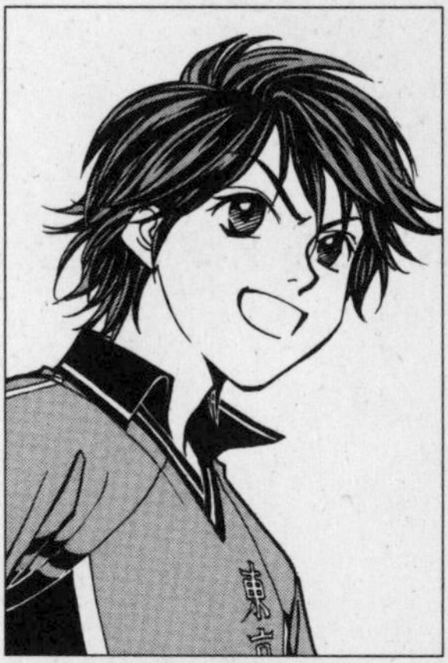

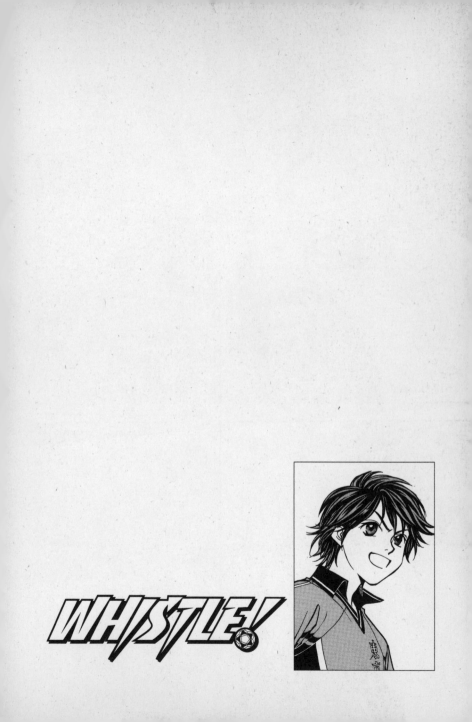

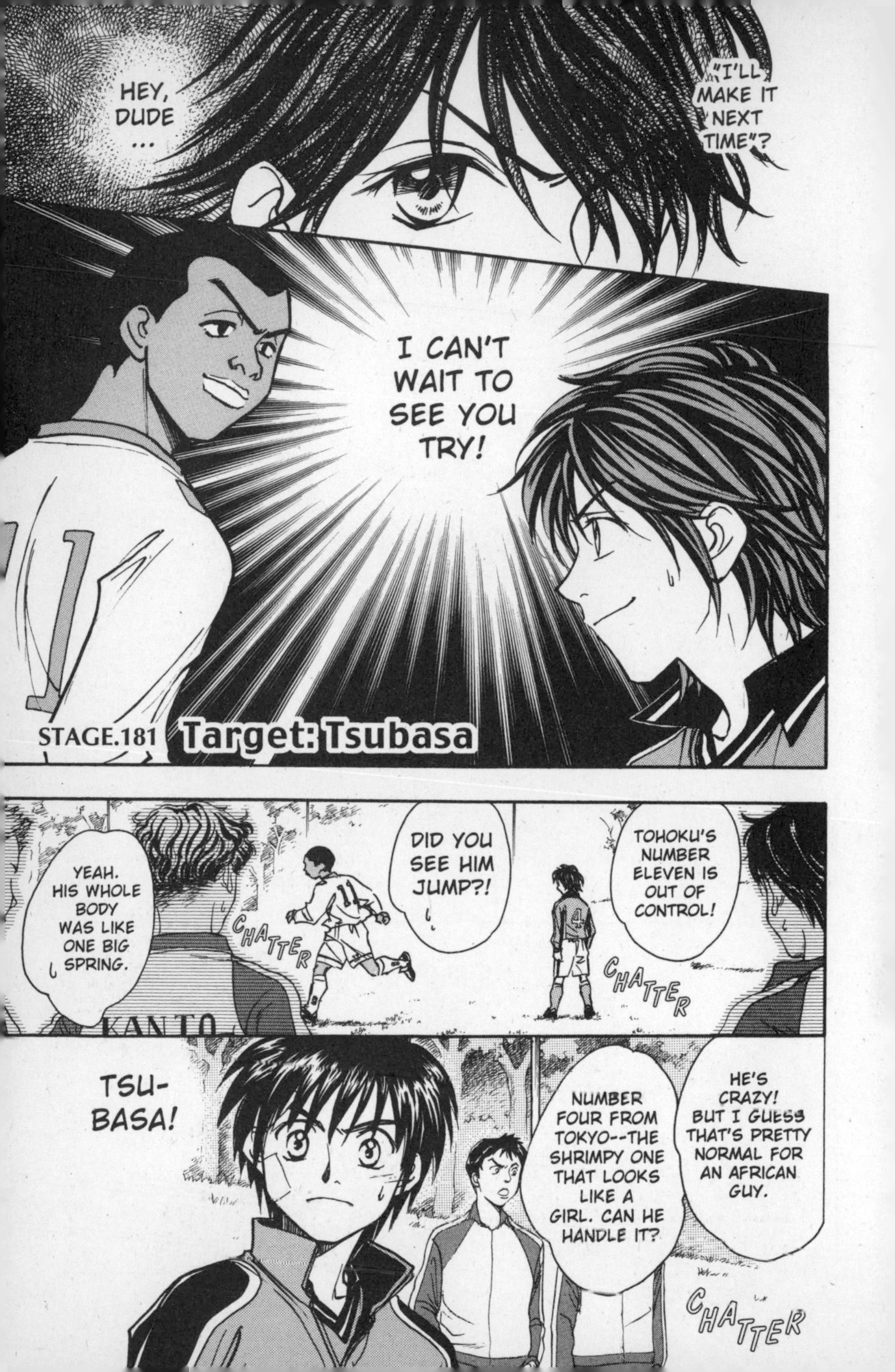
"I'LL MAKE IT NEXT TIME"?
HEY, DUDE ...
I CAN'T WAIT TO SEE YOU TRY!
STAGE.181 Target: Tsubasa
TOHOKU'S NUMBER ELEVEN IS OUT OF CONTROL!
CHATTER
DID YOU SEE HIM JUMP?!
CHATTER
YEAH. HIS WHOLE BODY WAS LIKE ONE BIG SPRING.
KANTO
HE'S CRAZY! BUT I GUESS THAT'S PRETTY NORMAL FOR AN AFRICAN GUY.
NUMBER FOUR FROM TOKYO--THE SHRIMPY ONE THAT LOOKS LIKE A GIRL. CAN HE HANDLE IT?
TSU-BASA!
CHATTER

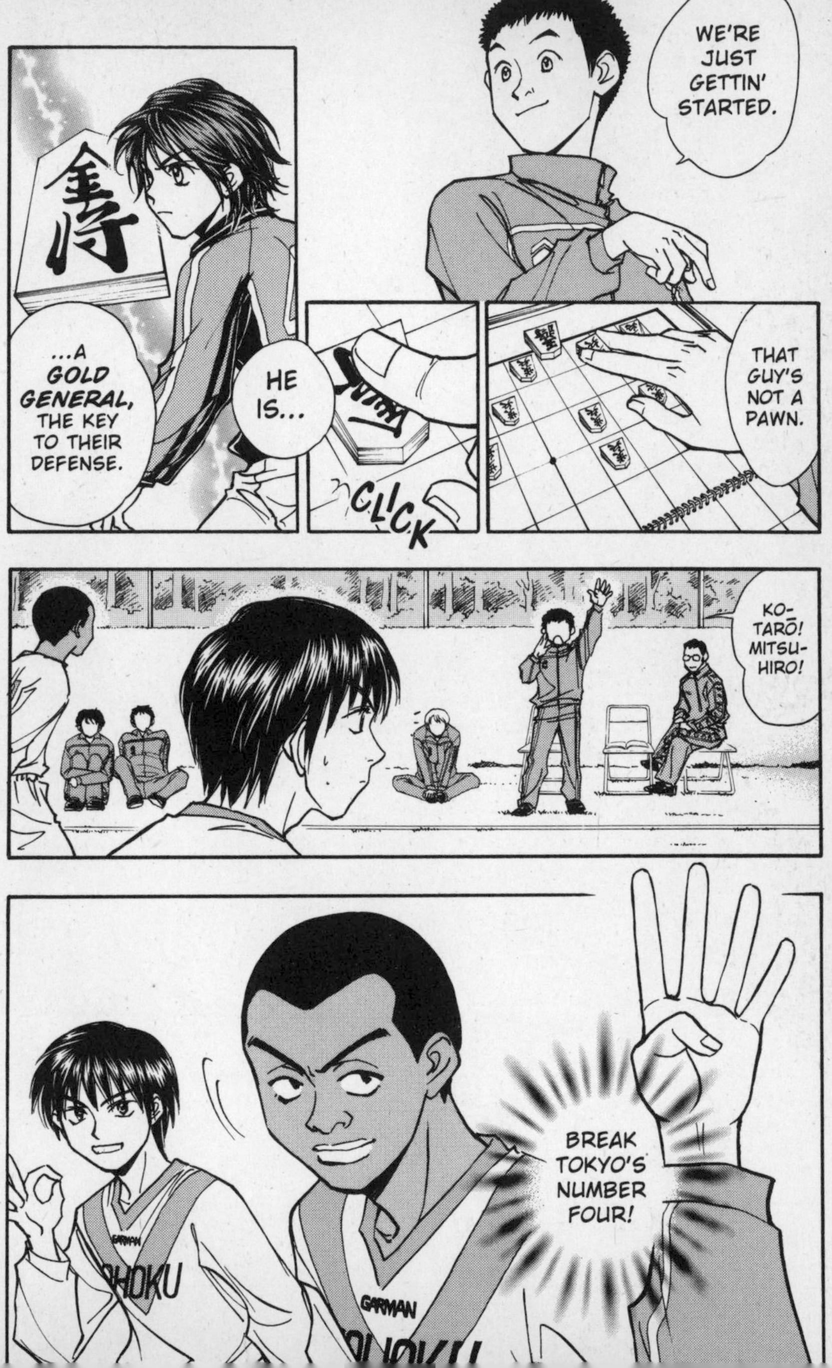
WE'RE JUST GETTIN' STARTED.
THAT GUY'S NOT A PAWN.
HE IS...
CLICK
...A *GOLD GENERAL*, THE KEY TO THEIR DEFENSE.
KO-TARŌ! MITSU-HIRO!
BREAK TOKYO'S NUMBER FOUR!

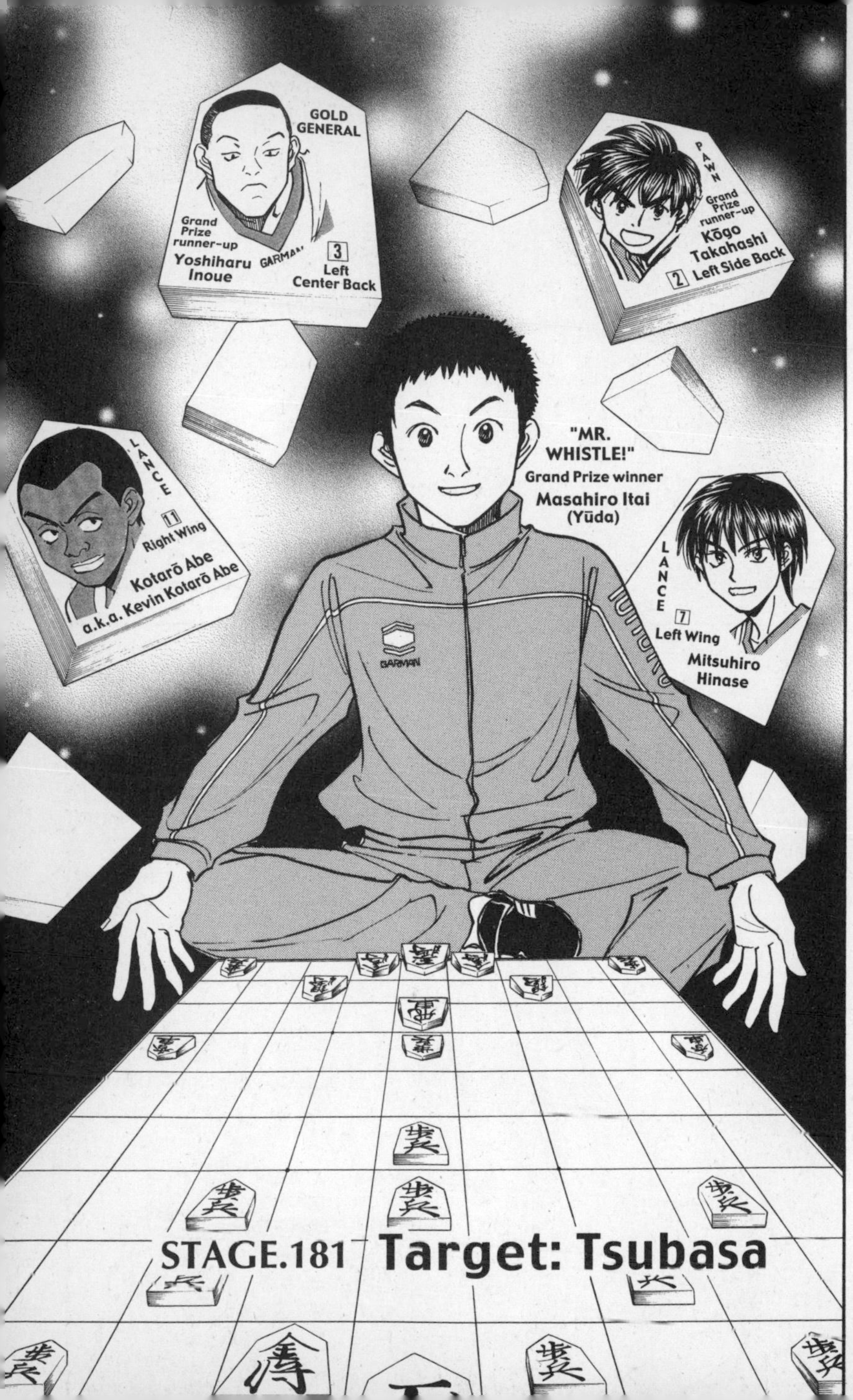
PAWN
Grand Prize runner-up
Kōgo Takahashi
2 Left Side Back
GOLD GENERAL
Grand Prize runner-up
Yoshiharu Inoue
3 Left Center Back
GARMAN
"MR. WHISTLE!"
Grand Prize winner
Masahiro Itai (Yūda)
GARMAN
LANCE
7 Left Wing
Mitsuhiro Hinase
LANCE
11 Right Wing
Kotarō Abe
a.k.a. Kevin Kotarō Abe

STAGE.181 Target: Tsubasa

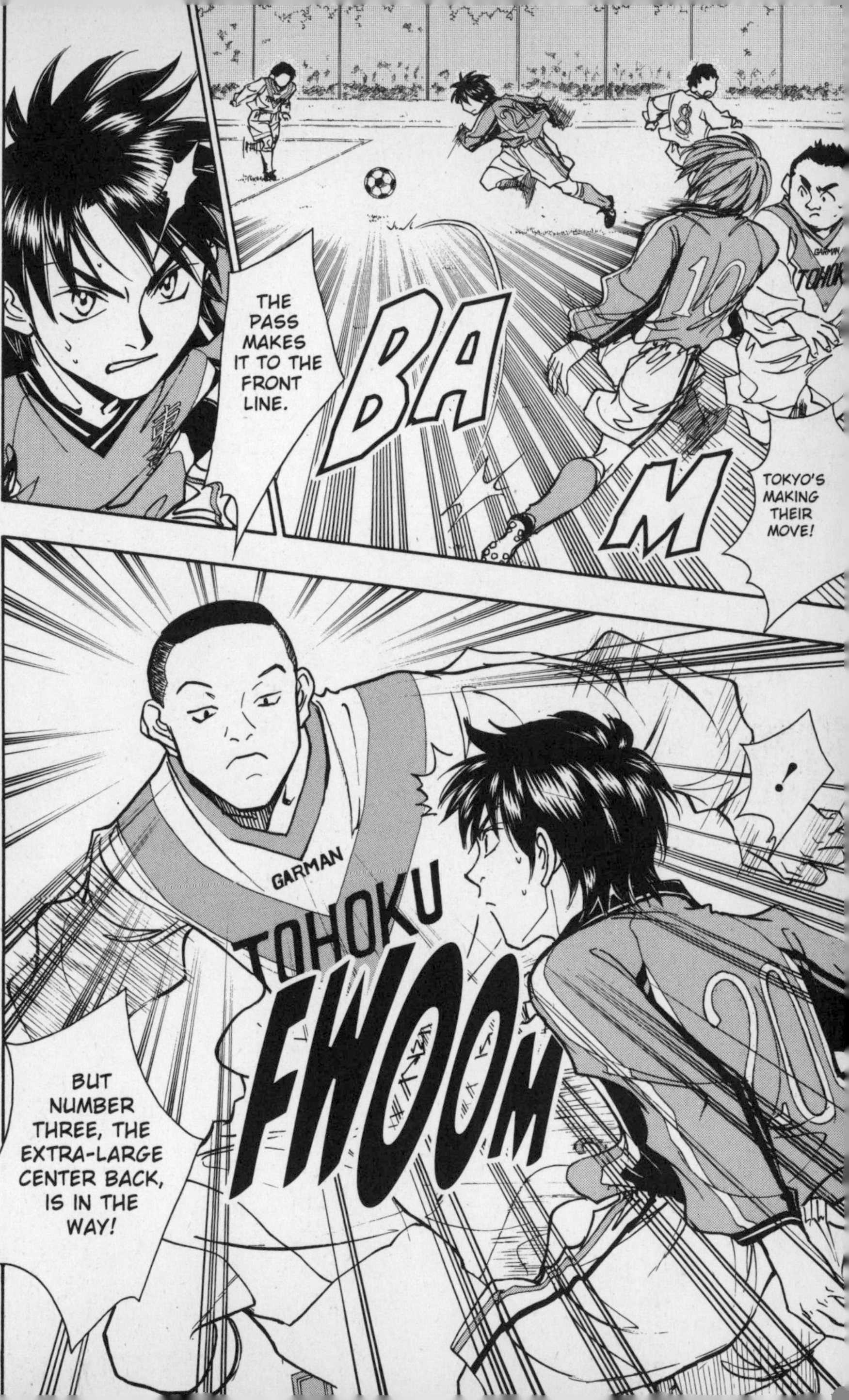
TOKYO'S MAKING THEIR MOVE!
BAM
THE PASS MAKES IT TO THE FRONT LINE.
!
FWOOM
BUT NUMBER THREE, THE EXTRA-LARGE CENTER BACK, IS IN THE WAY!

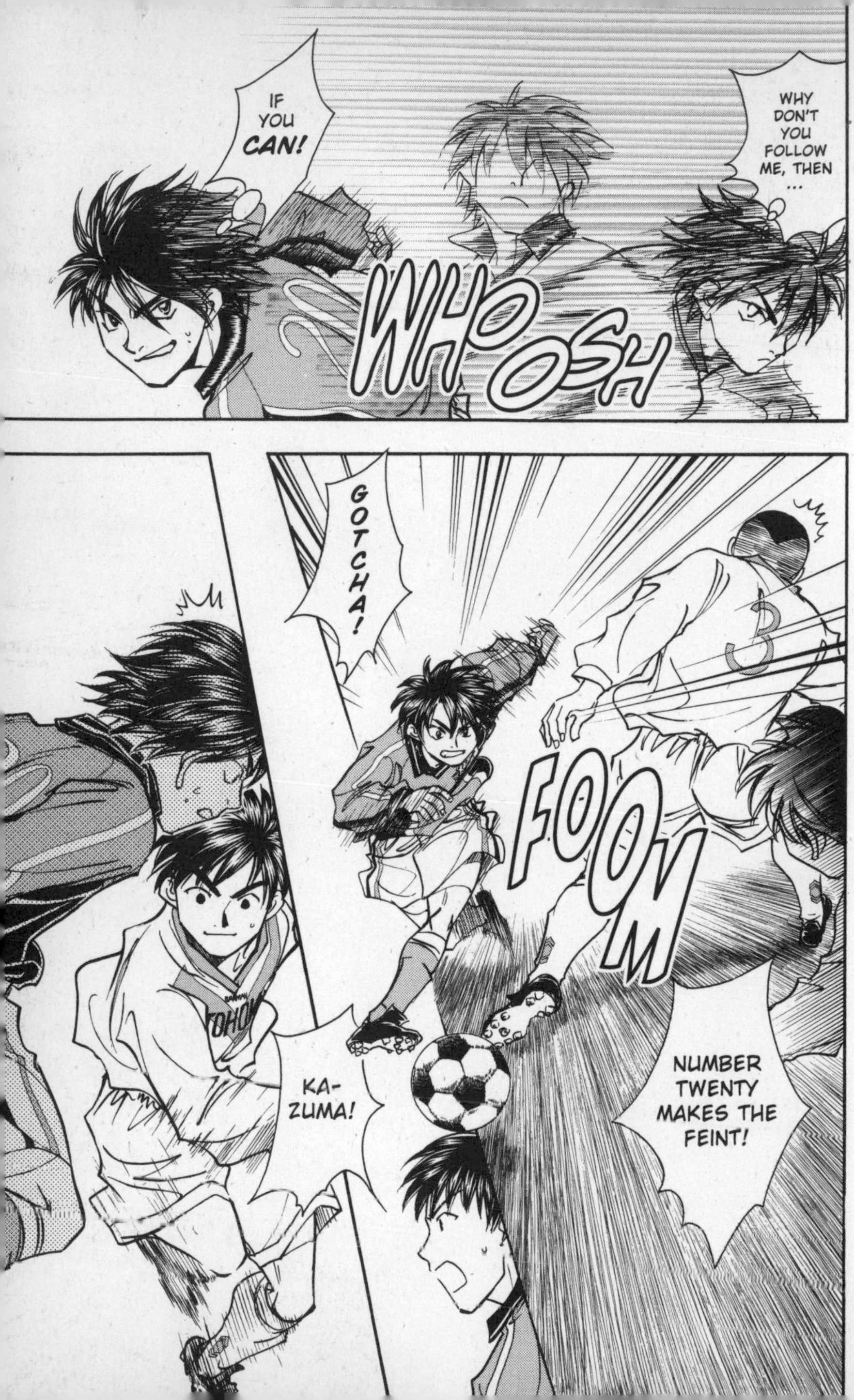
WHY DON'T YOU FOLLOW ME, THEN ...
IF YOU CAN!
WHOOSH
GOTCHA!
FOOM
NUMBER TWENTY MAKES THE FEINT!
KA-ZUMA!

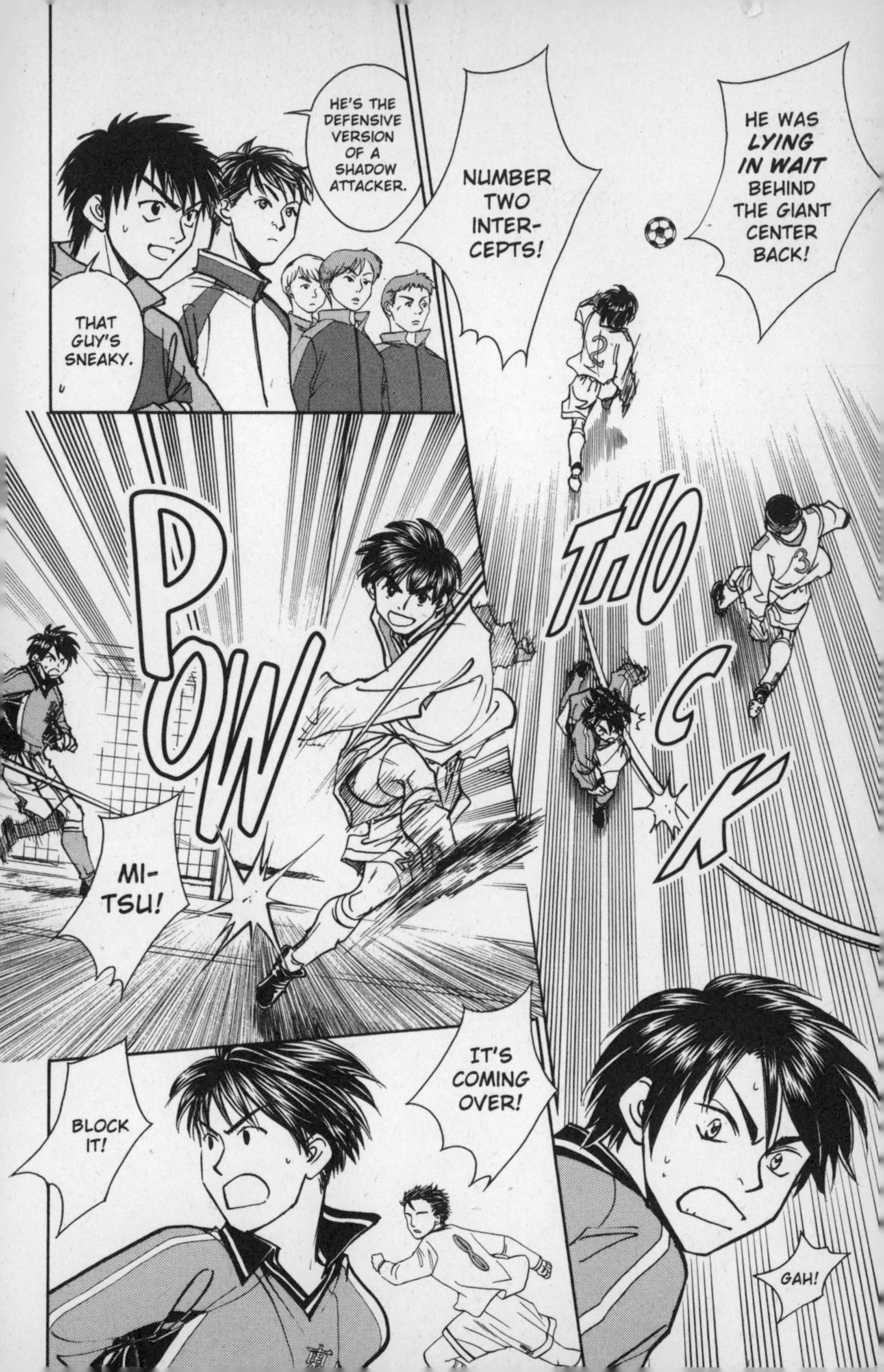
HE WAS *LYING IN WAIT* BEHIND THE GIANT CENTER BACK!
NUMBER TWO INTER-CEPTS!
THOCK
HE'S THE DEFENSIVE VERSION OF A SHADOW ATTACKER.
THAT GUY'S SNEAKY.
POW
MI-TSU!
GAH!
IT'S COMING OVER!
BLOCK IT!

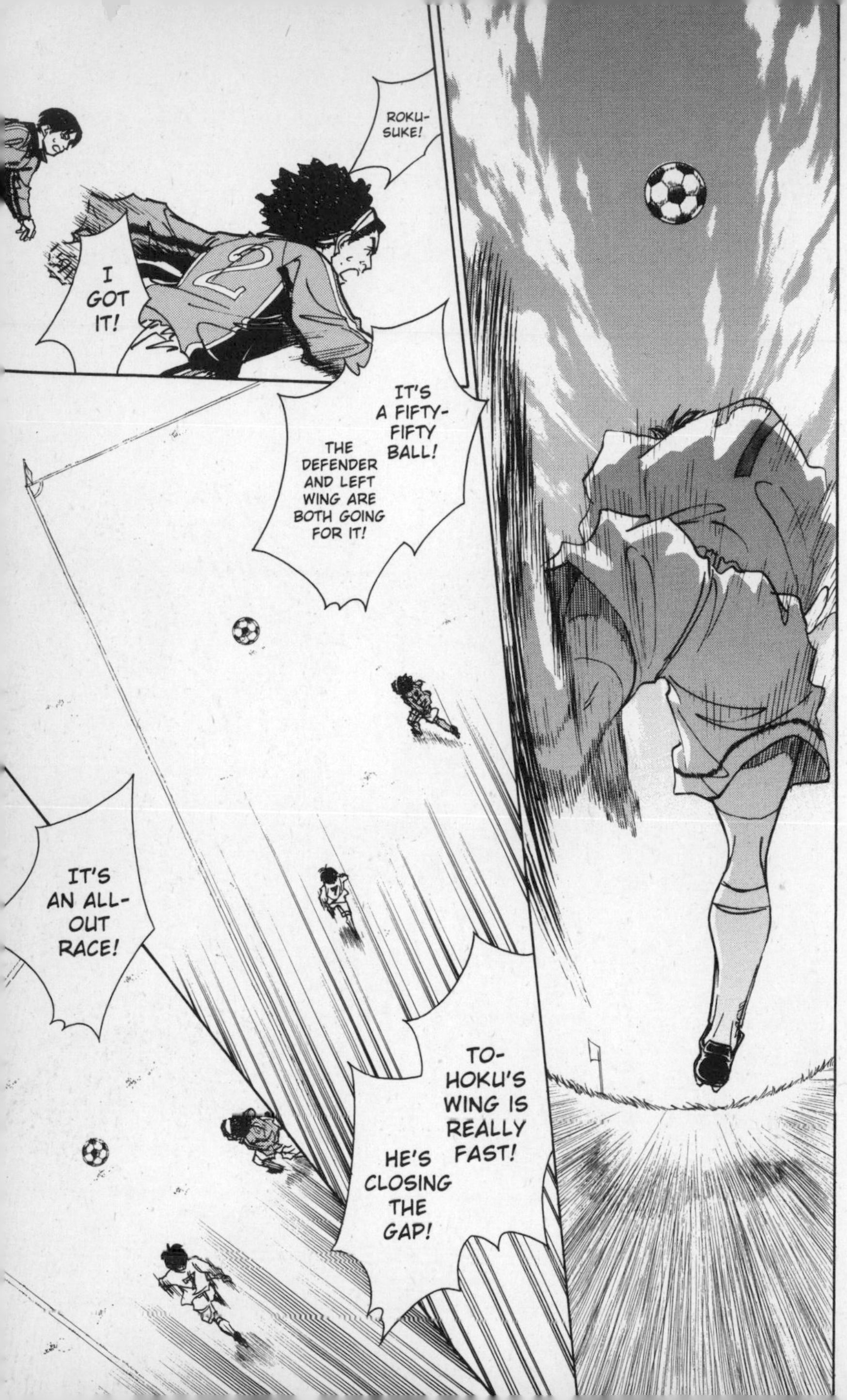
ROKU-SUKE!
I GOT IT!
IT'S A FIFTY-FIFTY BALL!
THE DEFENDER AND LEFT WING ARE BOTH GOING FOR IT!
IT'S AN ALL-OUT RACE!
TO-HOKU'S WING IS REALLY FAST!
HE'S CLOSING THE GAP!

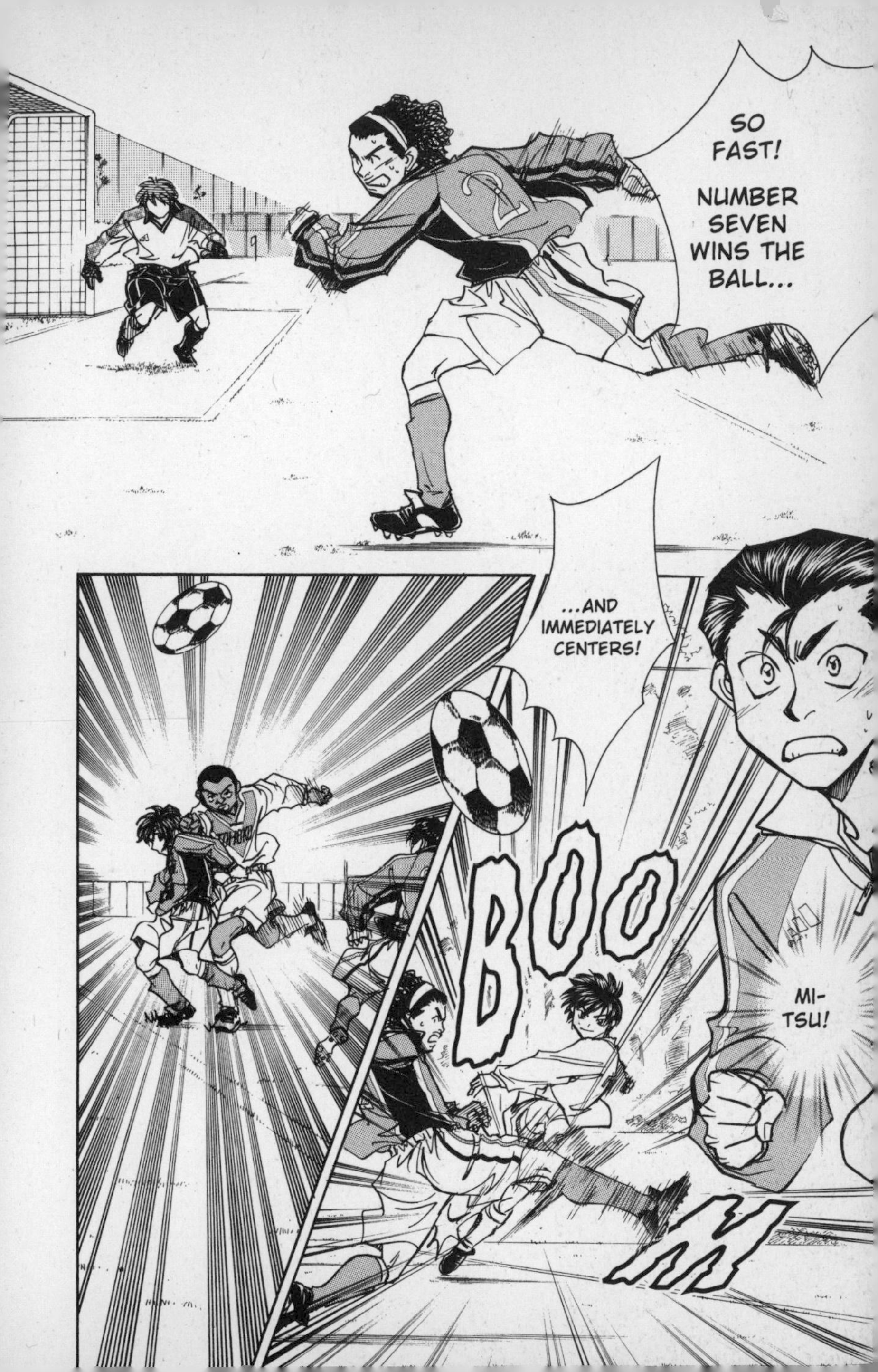
SO FAST!
NUMBER SEVEN WINS THE BALL...
...AND IMMEDIATELY CENTERS!
MI-TSU!
BOOOM

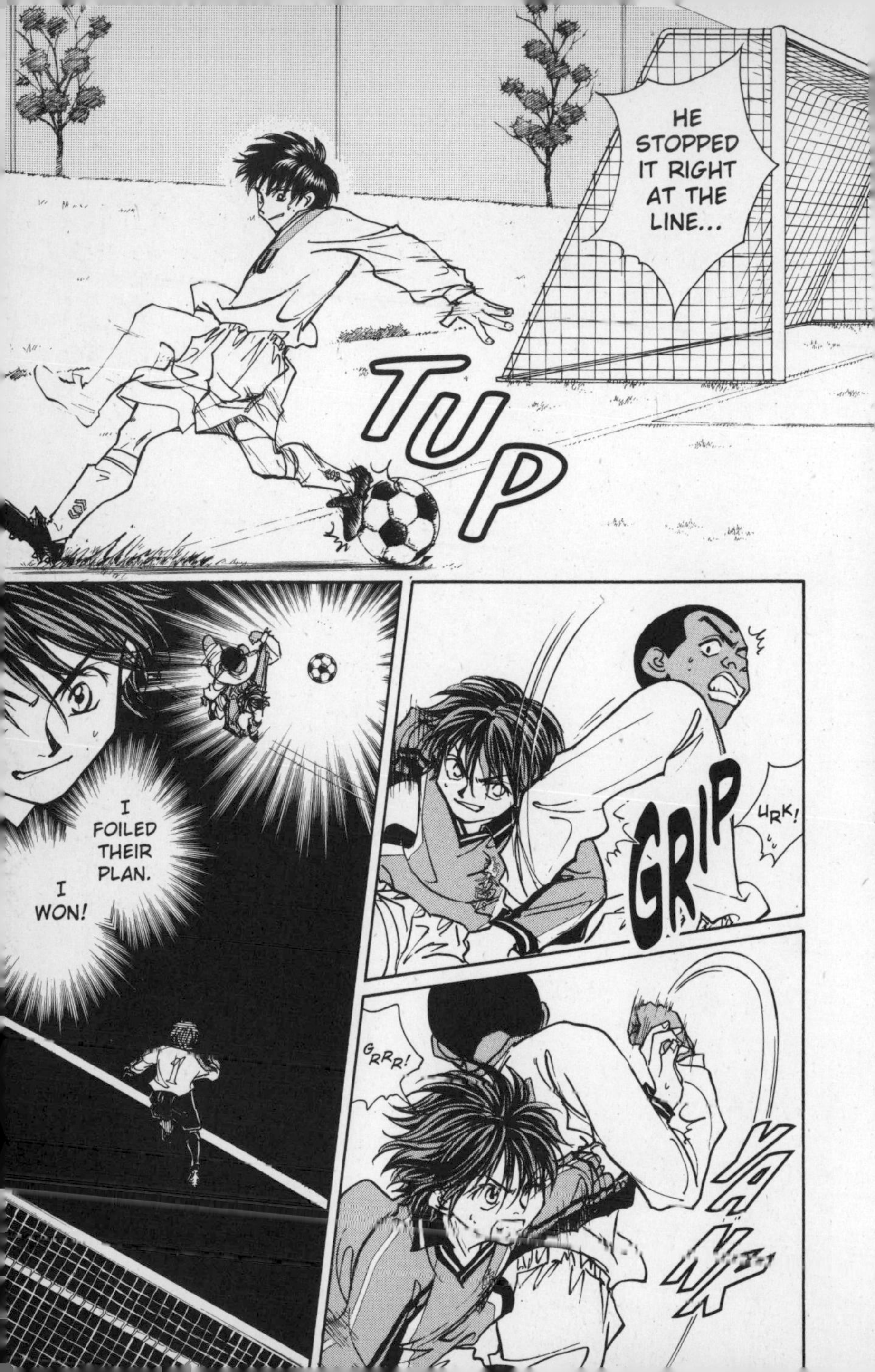
HE STOPPED IT RIGHT AT THE LINE...
TUP
GRIP
URK!
GRRR!
I FOILED THEIR PLAN.
I WON!

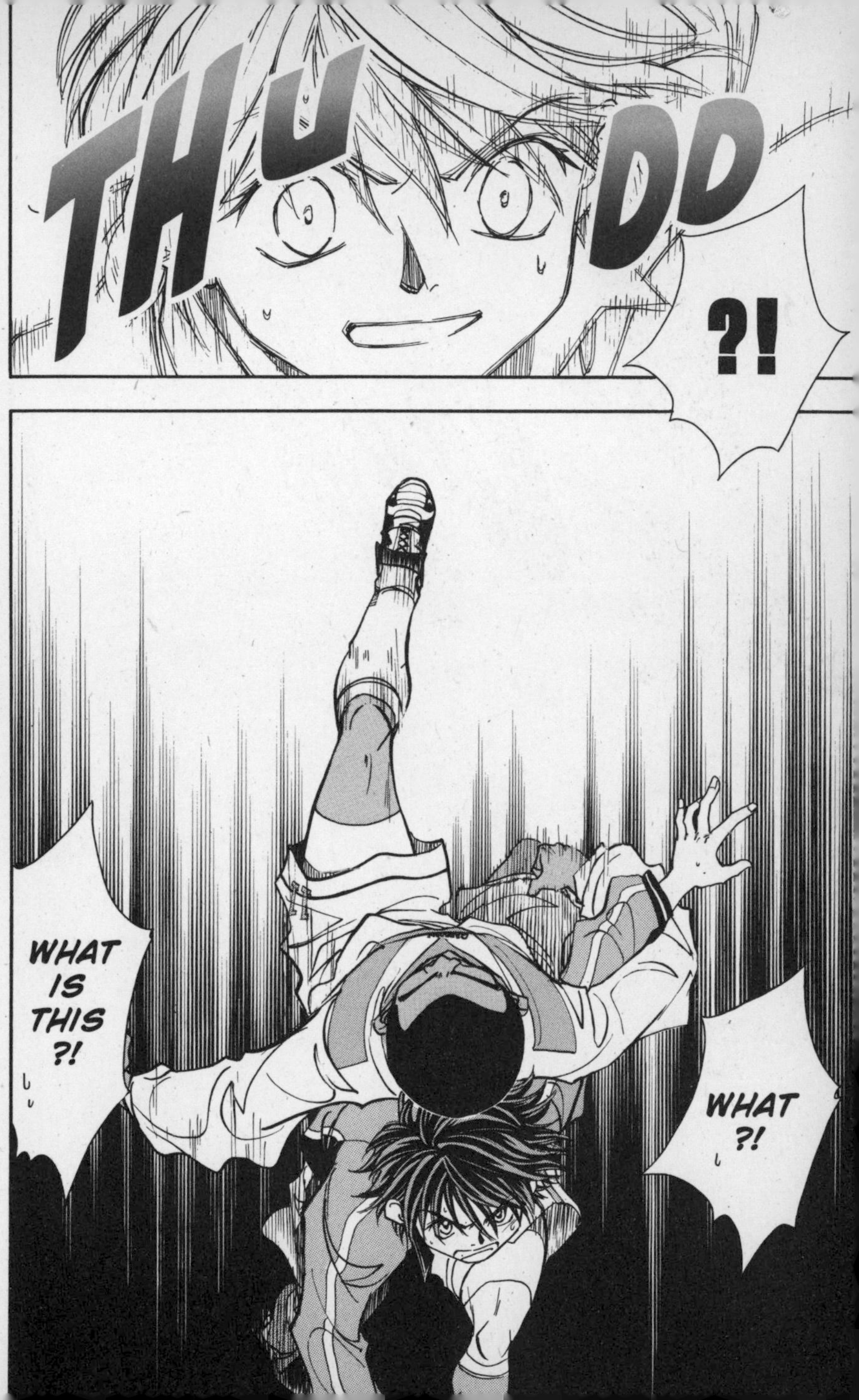
THUDD
?!
WHAT ?!
WHAT IS THIS ?!

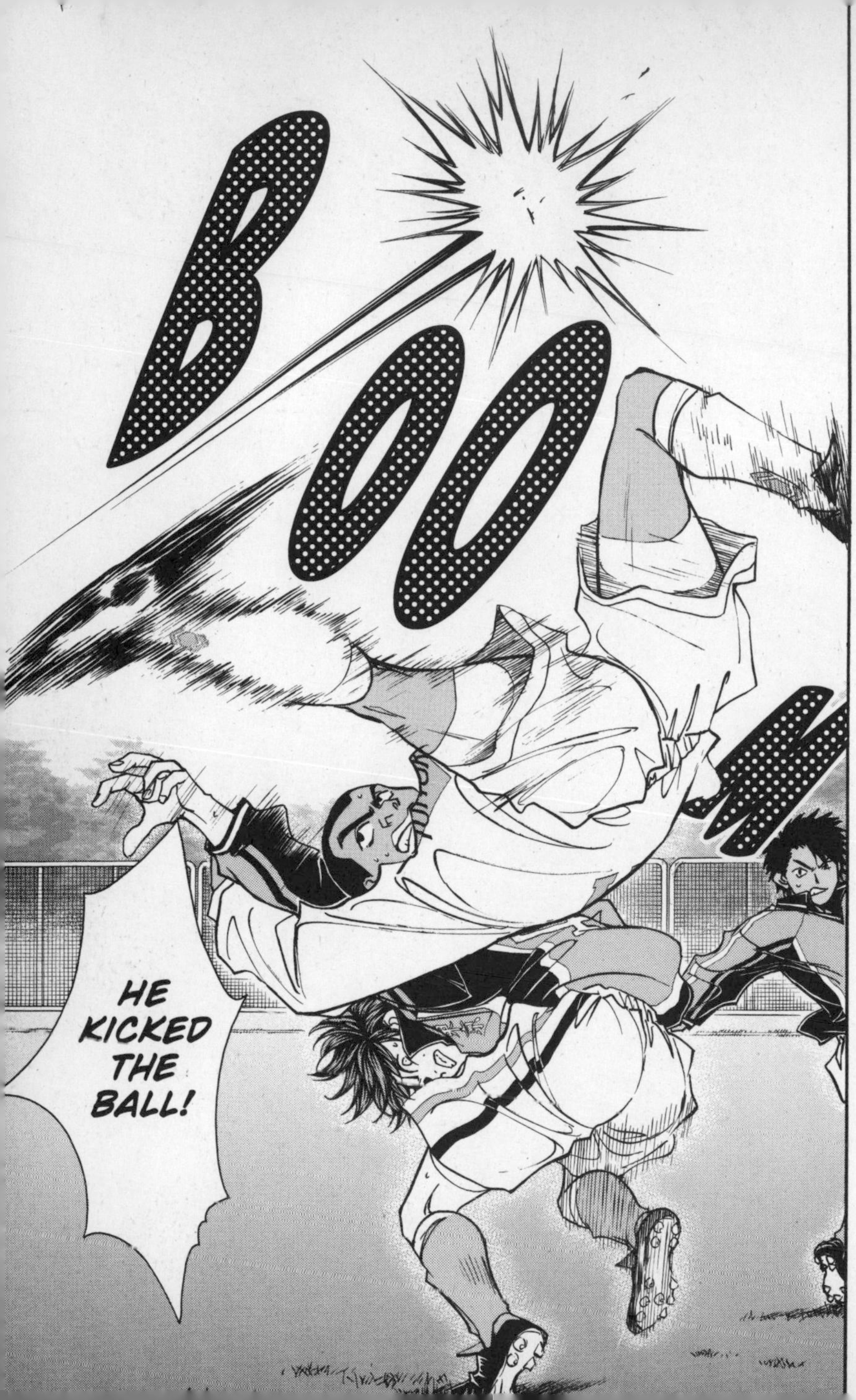
BOOOM
HE KICKED THE BALL!

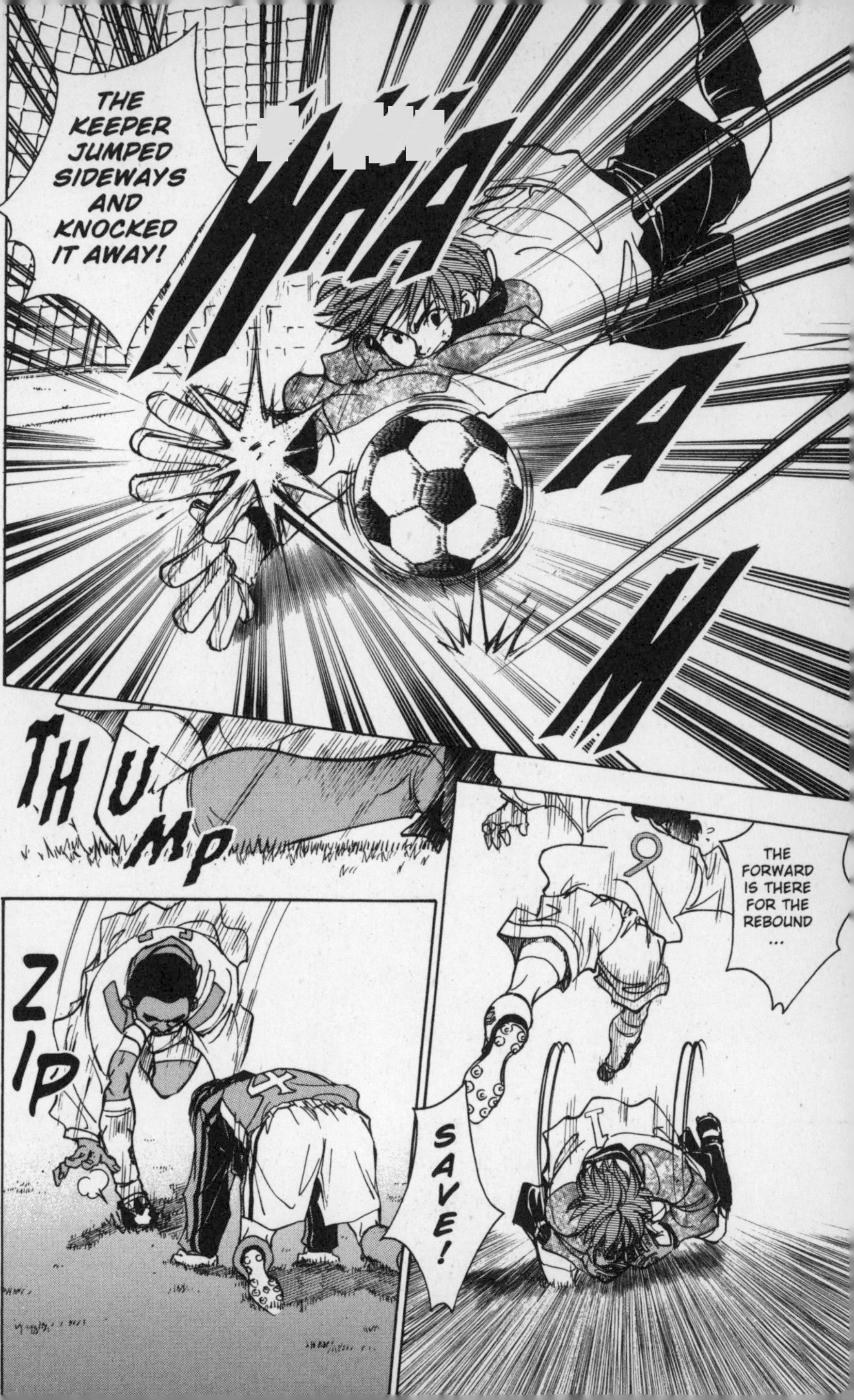
THE KEEPER JUMPED SIDEWAYS AND KNOCKED IT AWAY!
WHAAM
THUMP
THE FORWARD IS THERE FOR THE REBOUND ...
SAVE!
ZIP

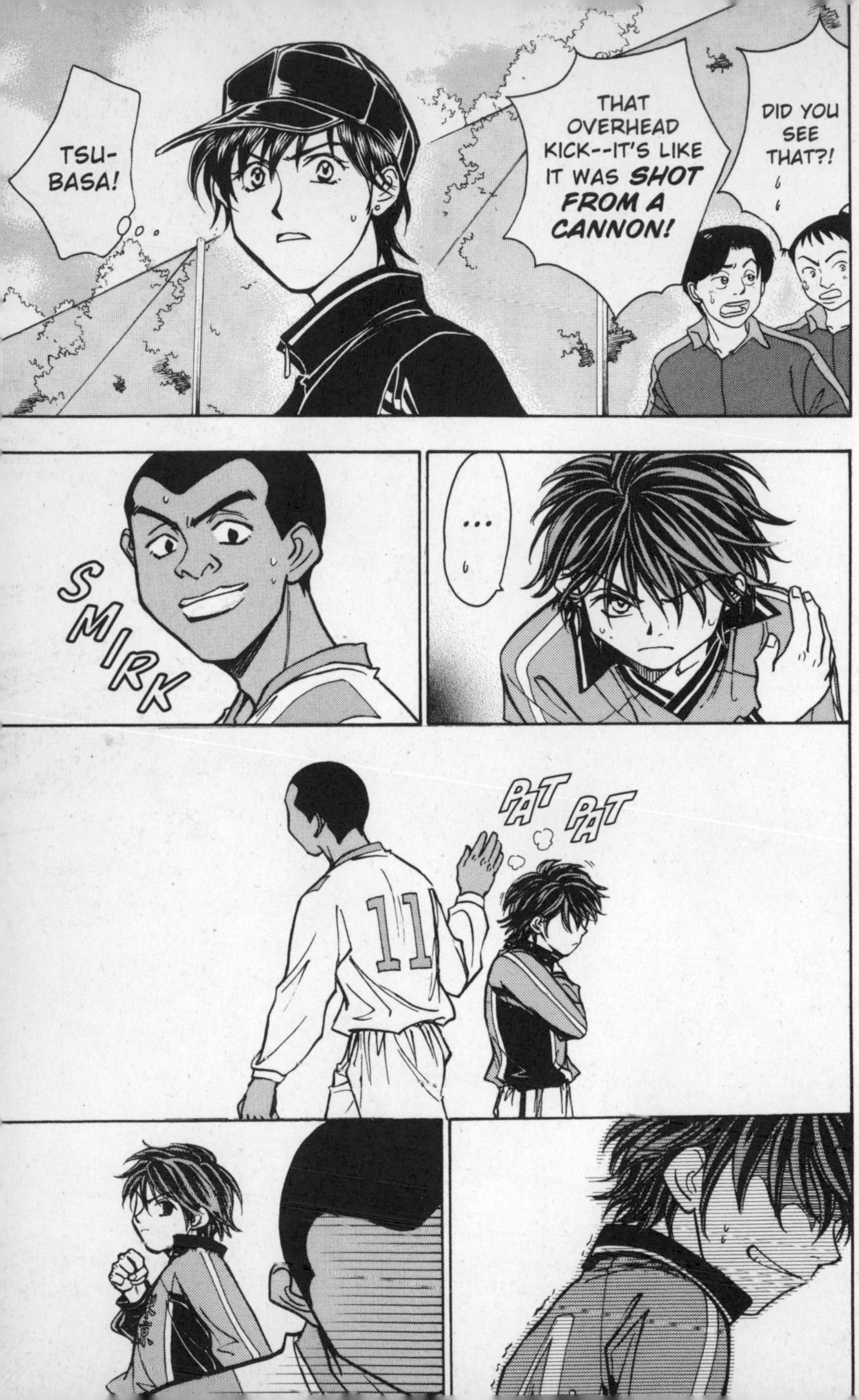
DID YOU SEE THAT?!
THAT OVERHEAD KICK--IT'S LIKE IT WAS SHOT FROM A CANNON!
TSU-BASA!
...
SMIRK
PAT PAT

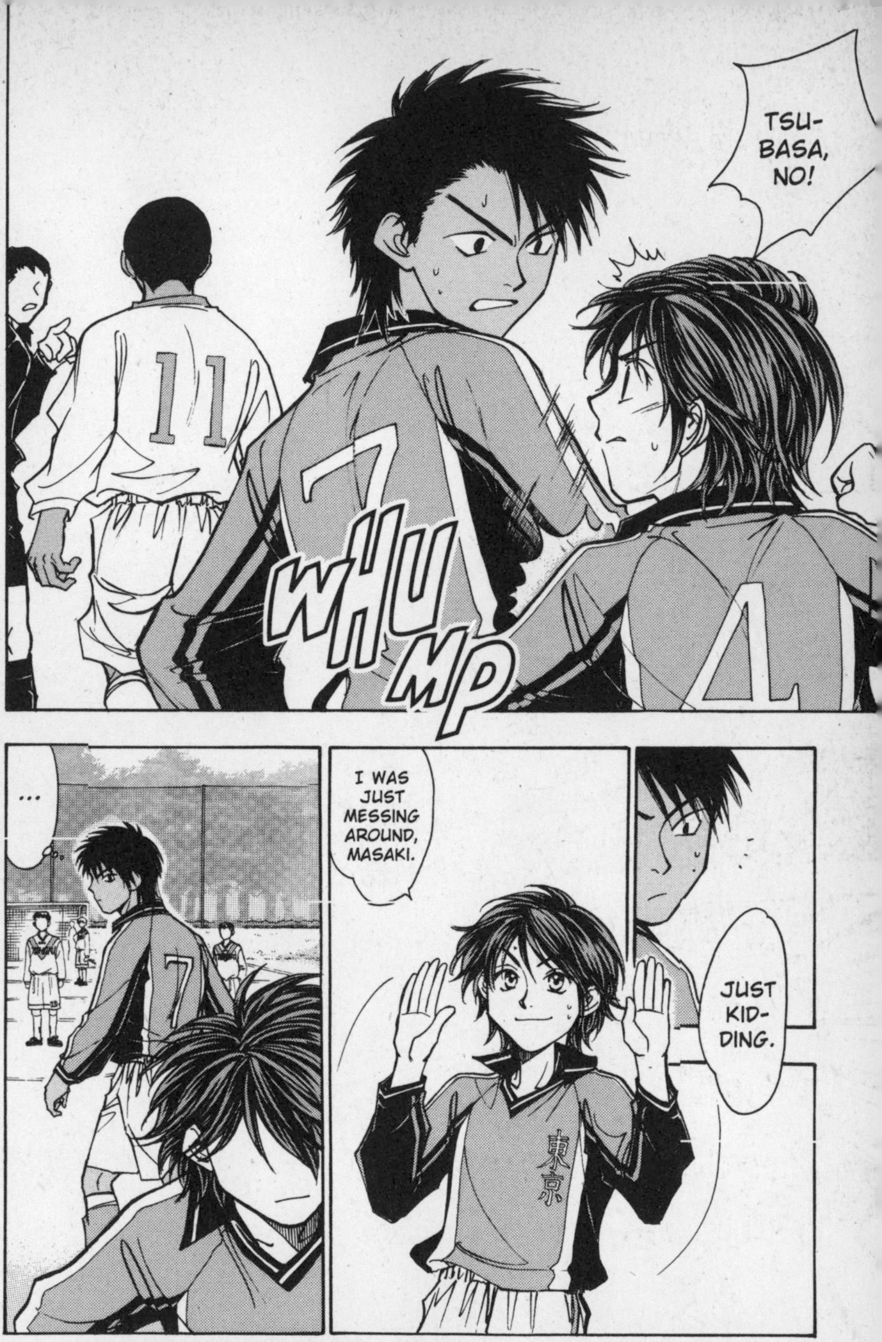
TSU-BASA, NO!
WHUMP
I WAS JUST MESSING AROUND, MASAKI.
JUST KID-DING.
...

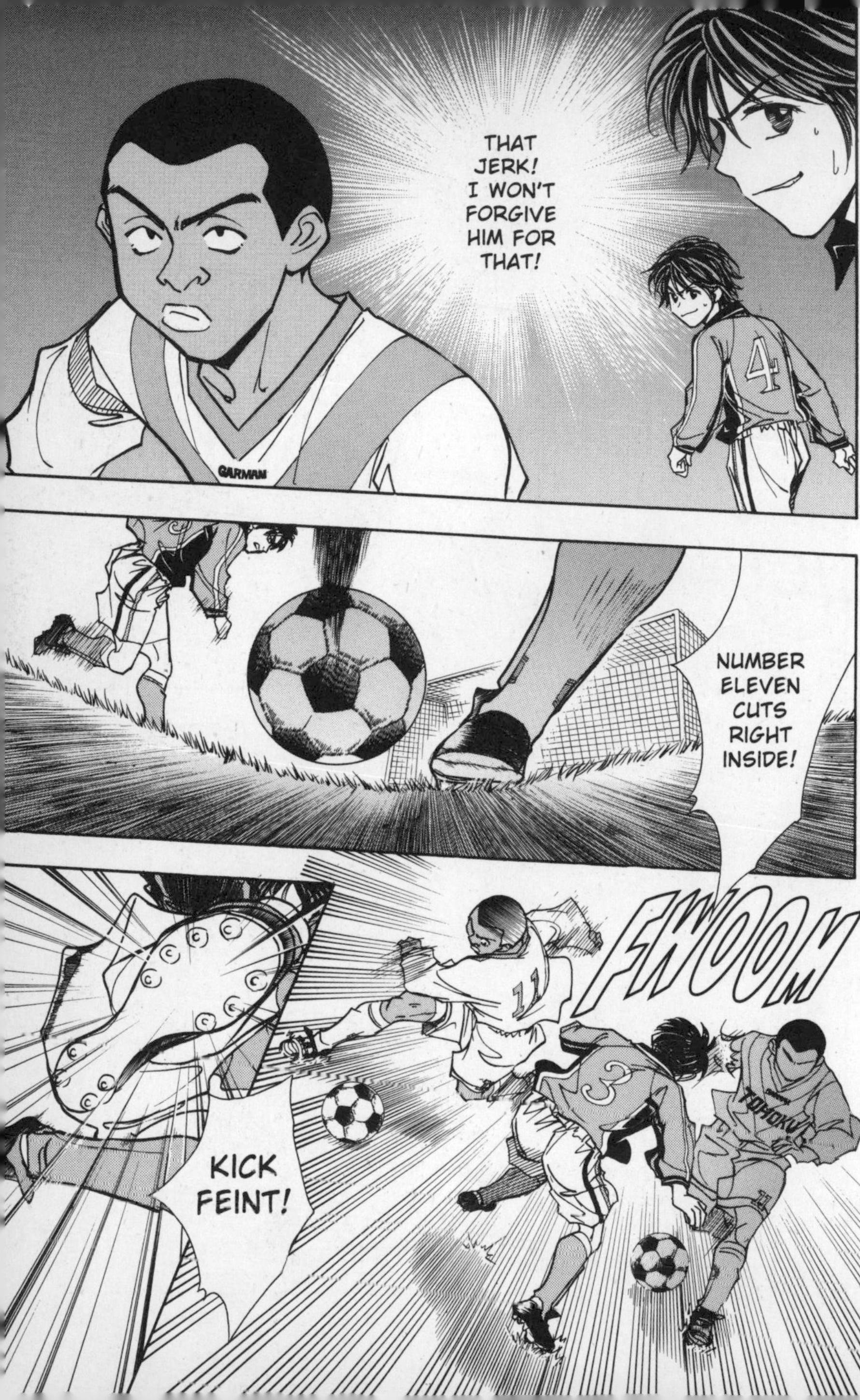
THAT JERK! I WON'T FORGIVE HIM FOR THAT!
GARMAN
NUMBER ELEVEN CUTS RIGHT INSIDE!
FWOOM
TOHOKU
KICK FEINT!

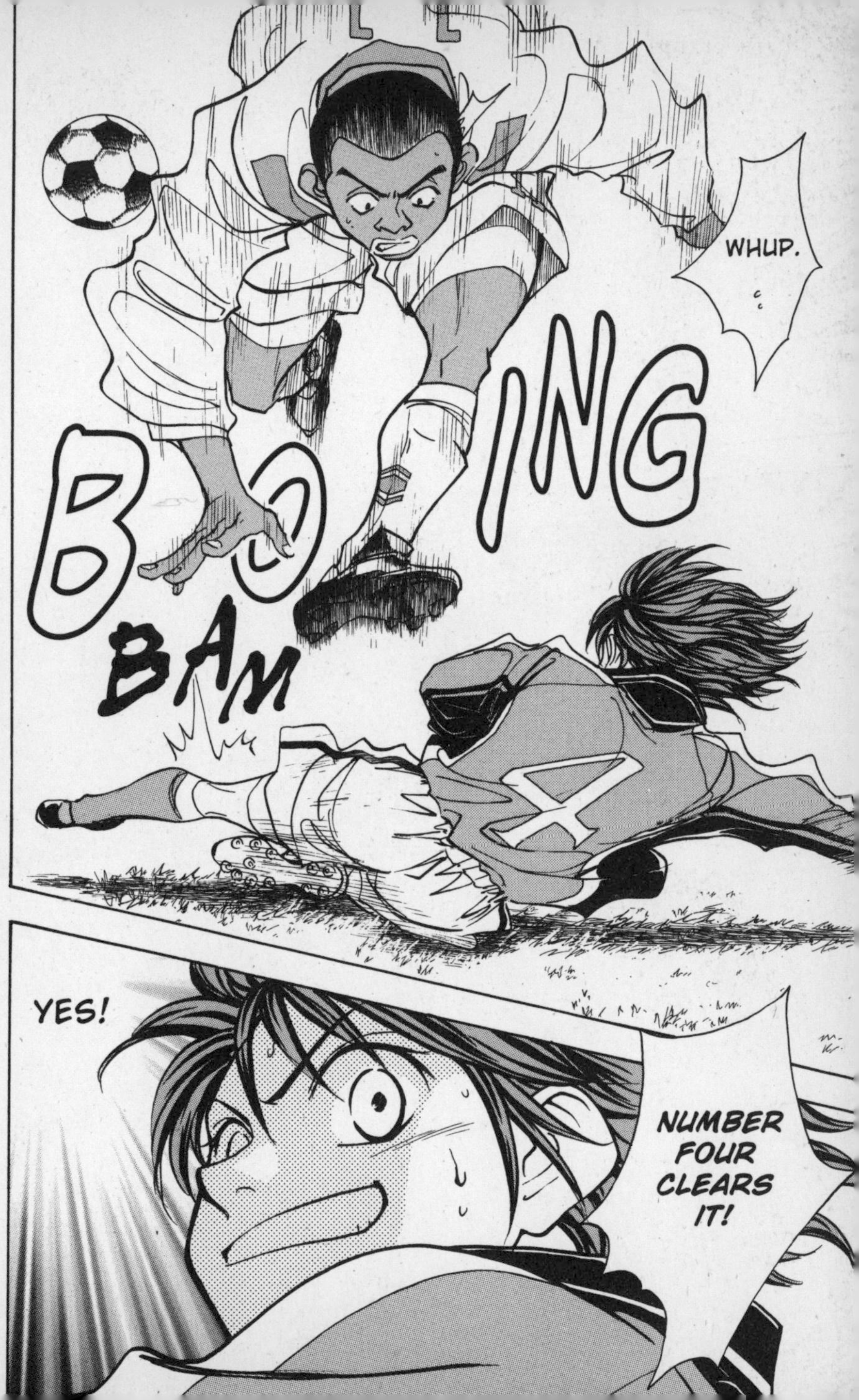
WHUP.
BOOING
BAM
NUMBER FOUR CLEARS IT!
YES!

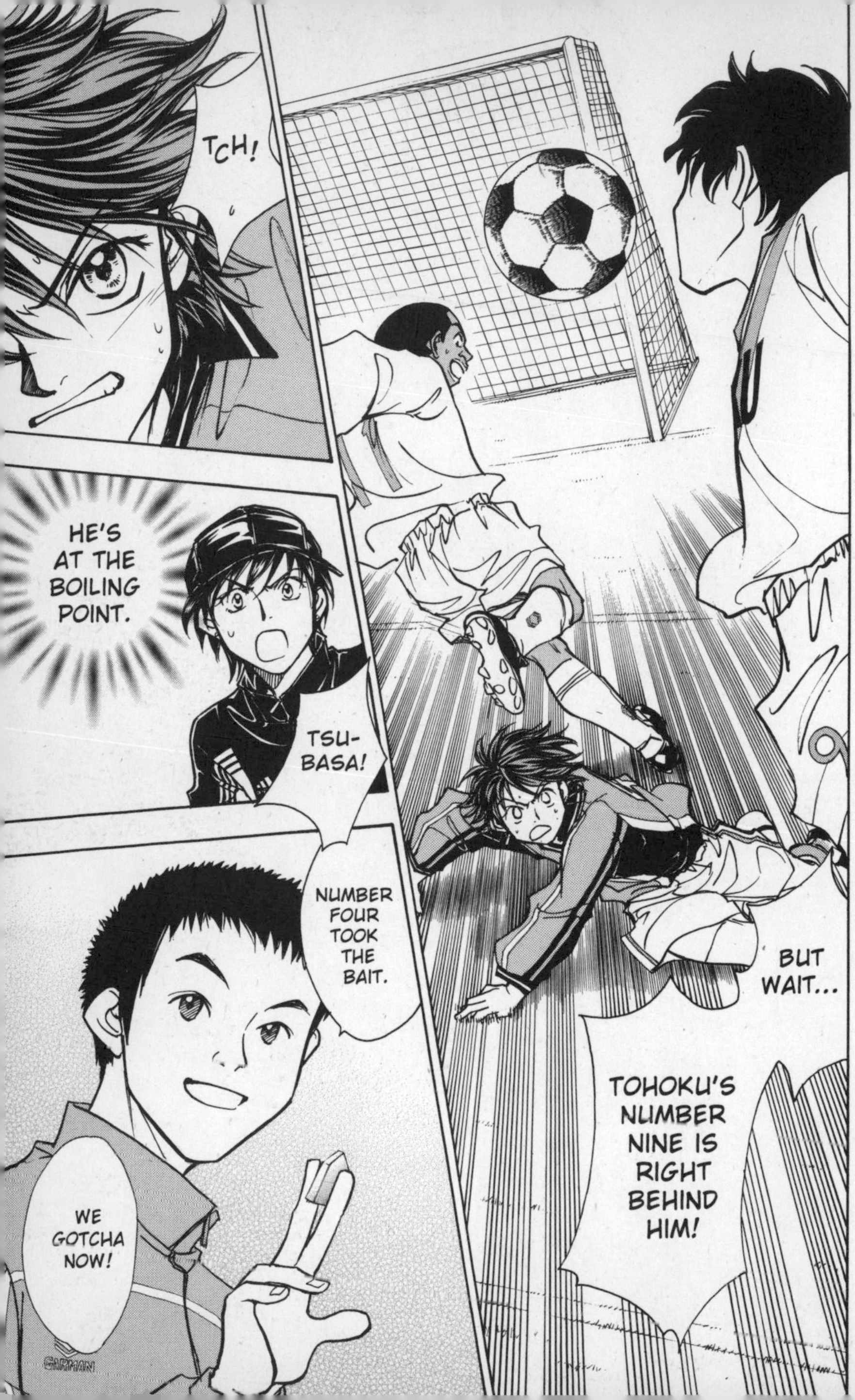
BUT WAIT...
TOHOKU'S NUMBER NINE IS RIGHT BEHIND HIM!
TCH!
HE'S AT THE BOILING POINT.
TSU-BASA!
NUMBER FOUR TOOK THE BAIT.
WE GOTCHA NOW!
GARMAN

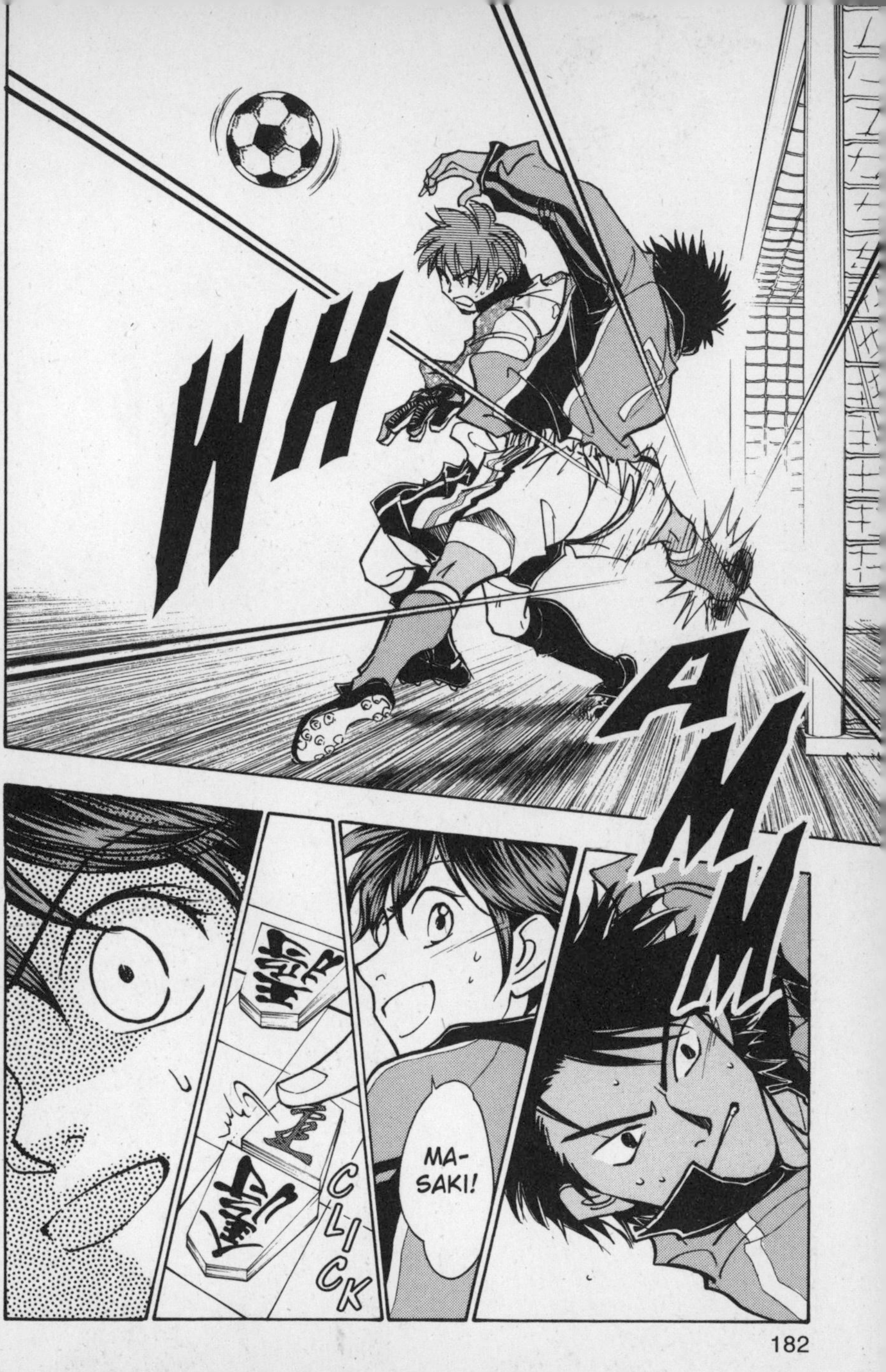
WHAMM
MA-SAKI!
CLICK

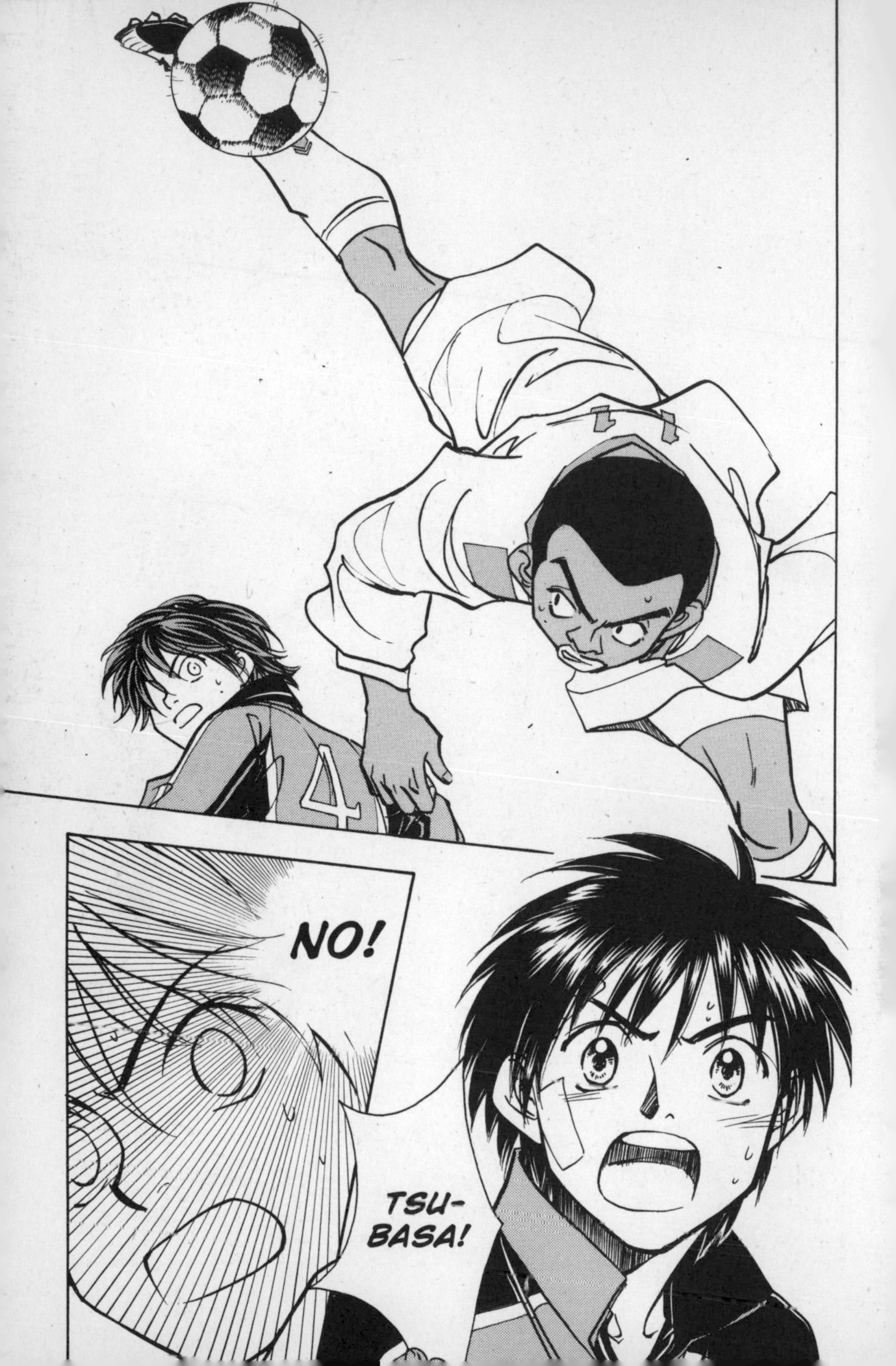
TSU-
BASA!
NO!

WHISTLE!

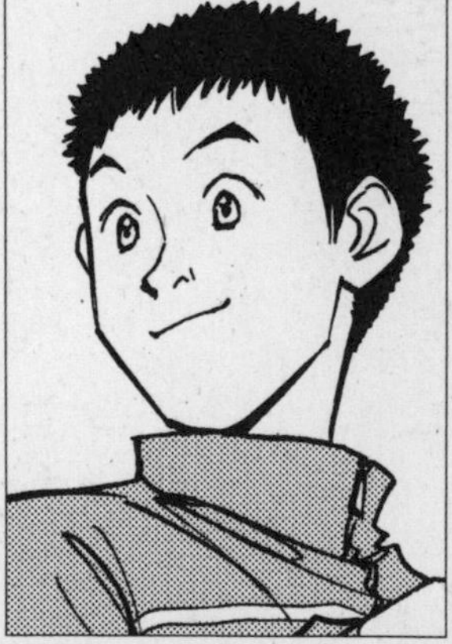

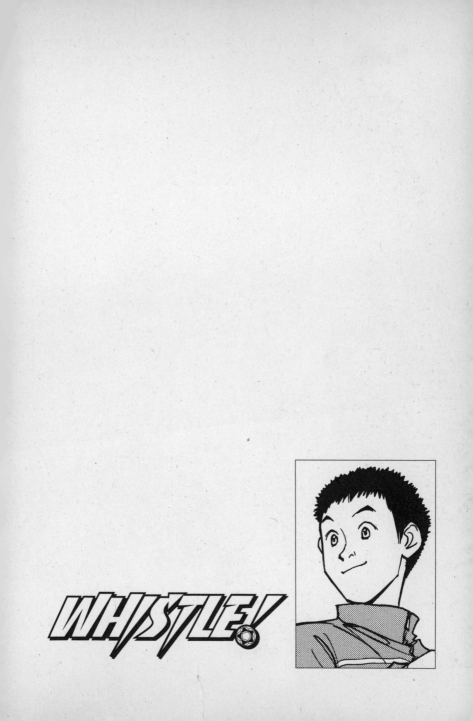

STAGE.182 Tsubasa Shot Down in the Dark

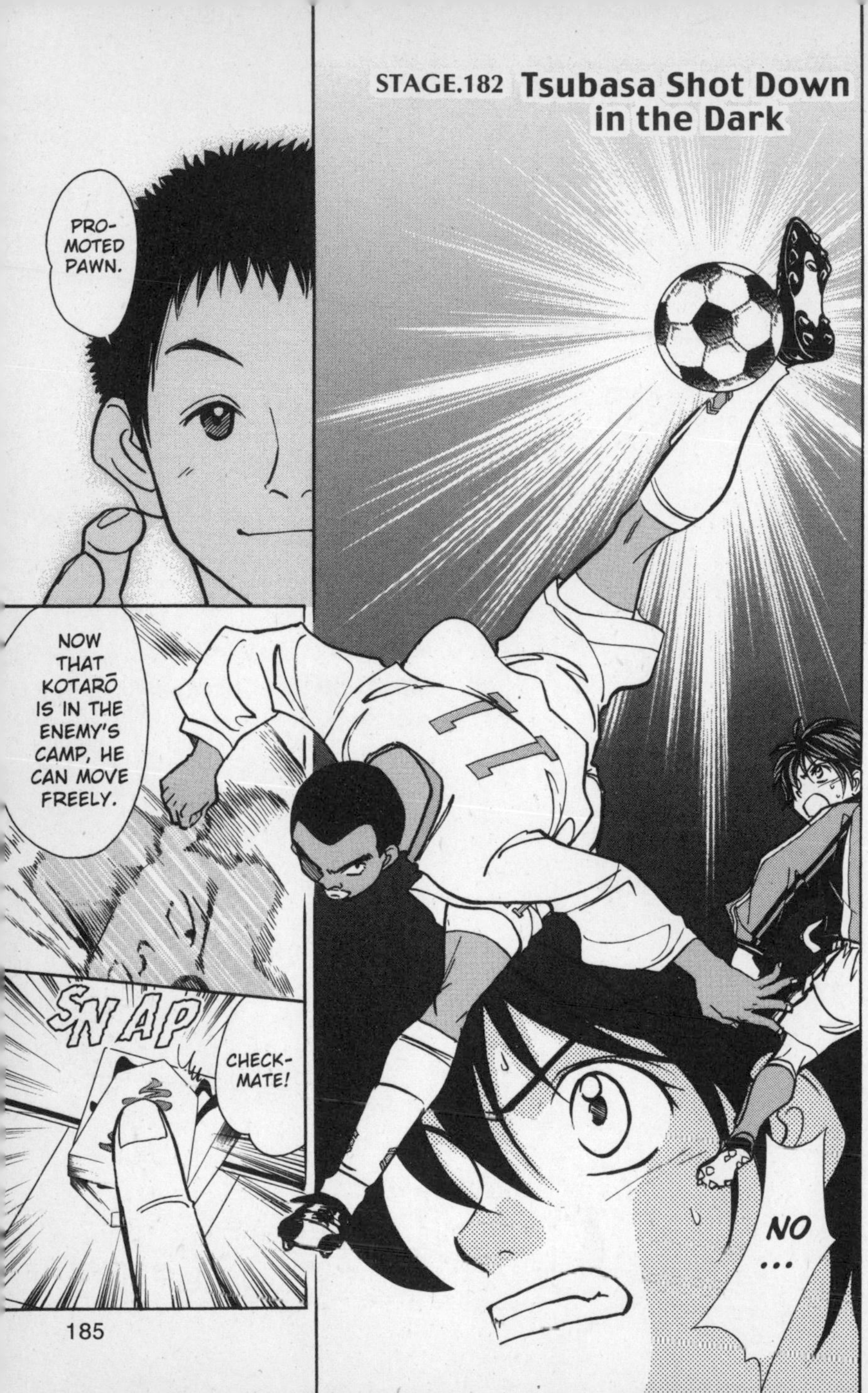
NO ...
PRO-MOTED PAWN.
NOW THAT KOTARŌ IS IN THE ENEMY'S CAMP, HE CAN MOVE FREELY.
SNAP
CHECK-MATE!

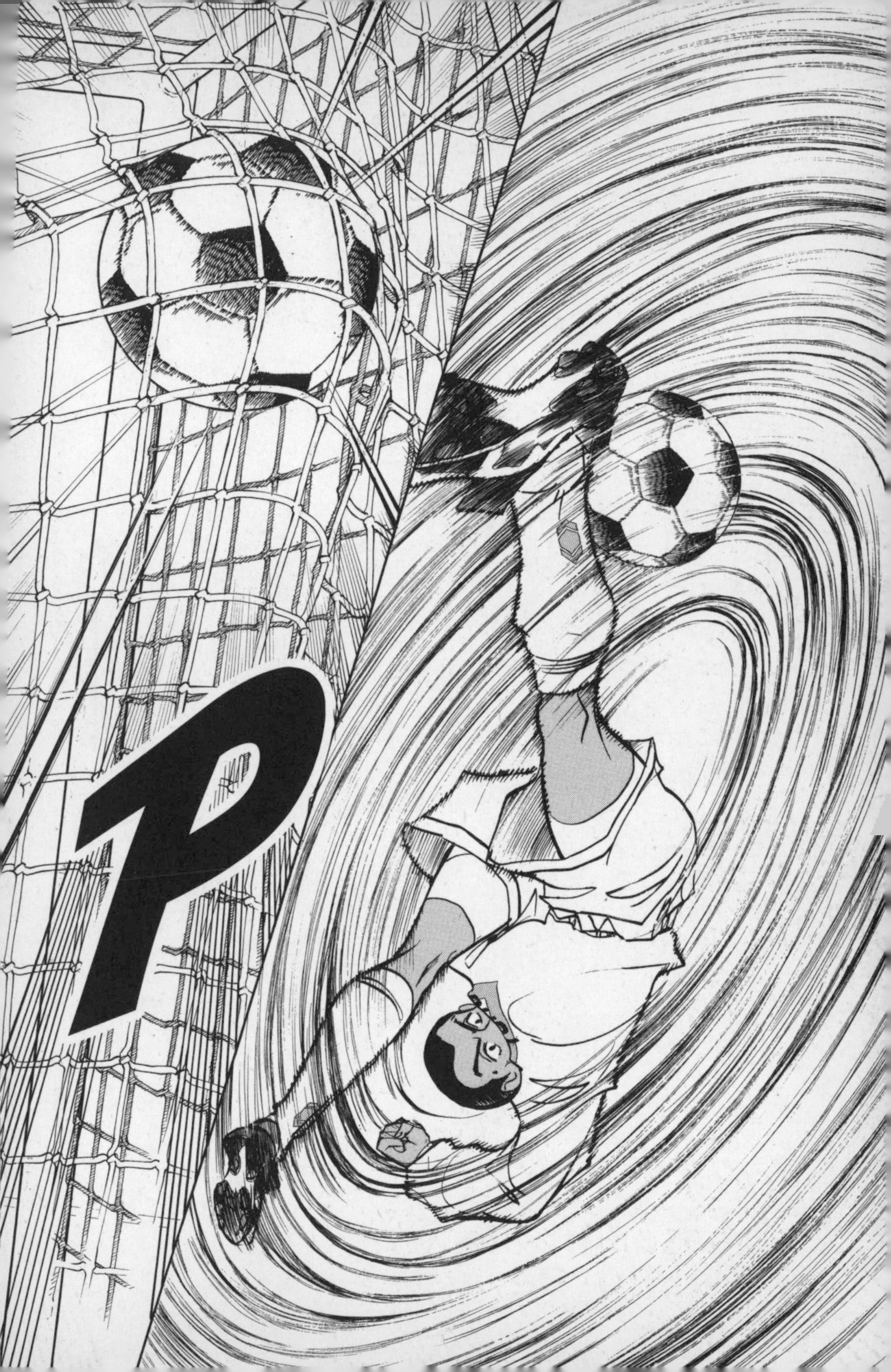
P

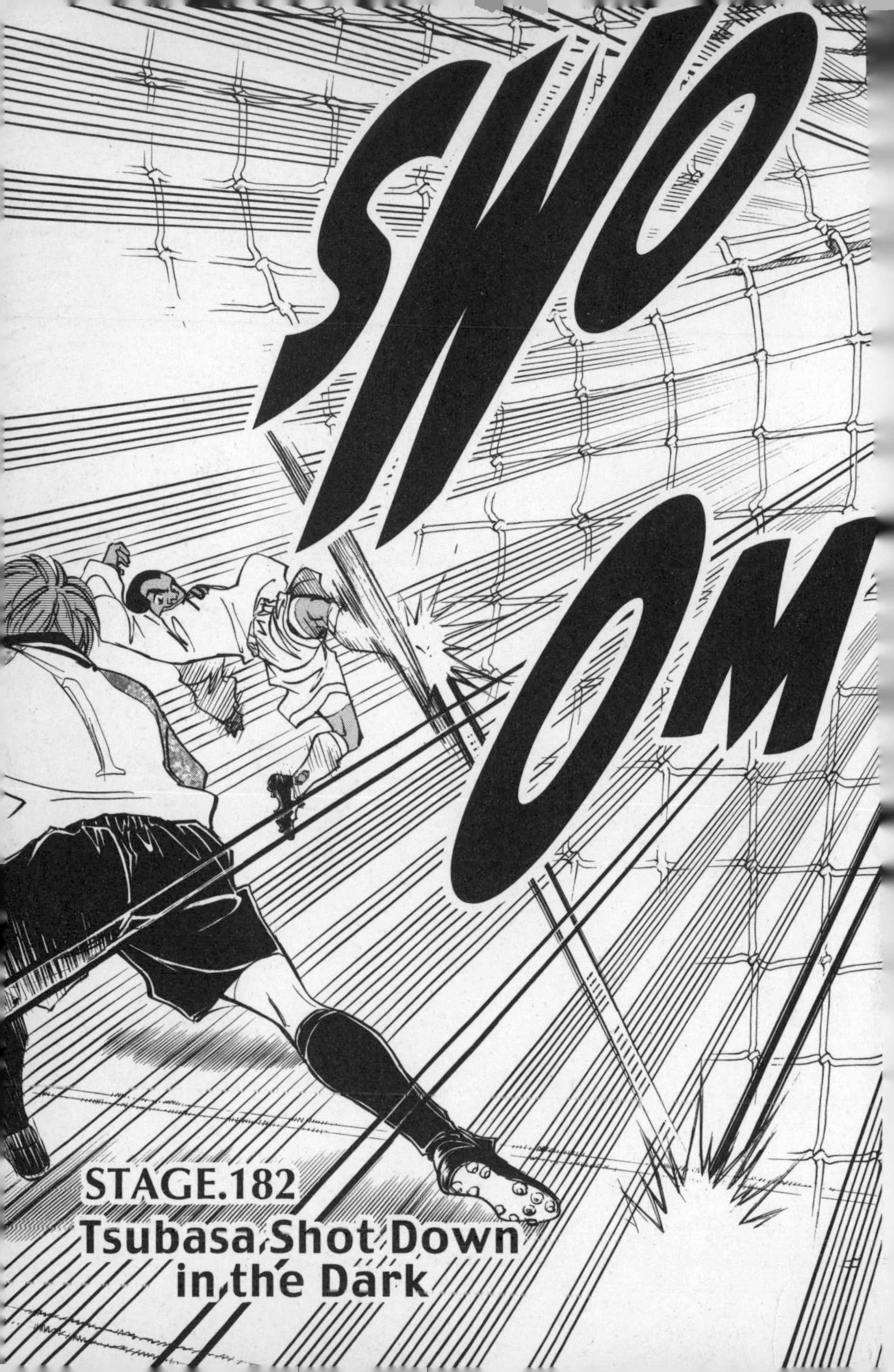
SWOOM
STAGE.182
Tsubasa Shot Down in the Dark

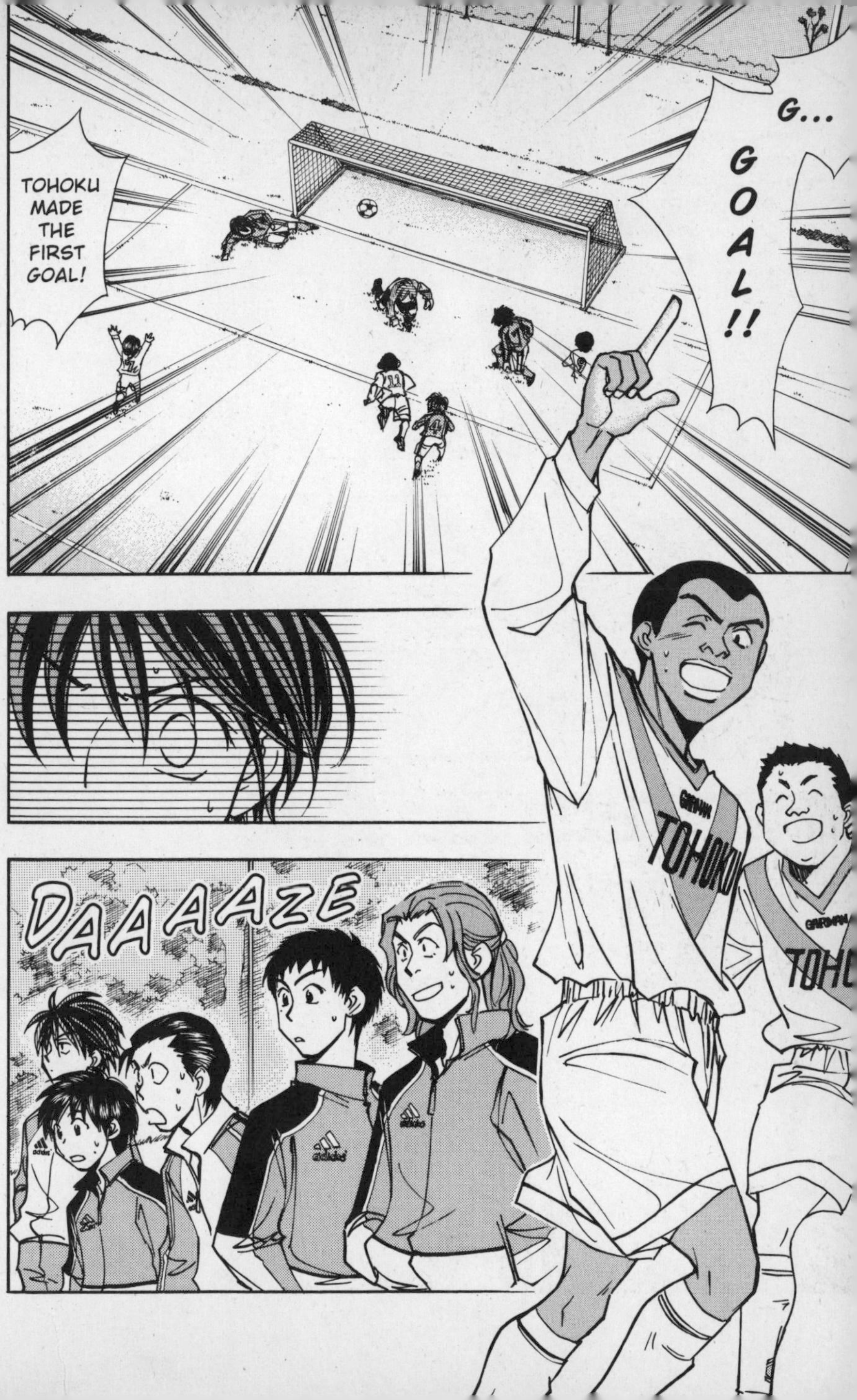
G... GOAL!!
TOHOKU MADE THE FIRST GOAL!
DAAAAZE

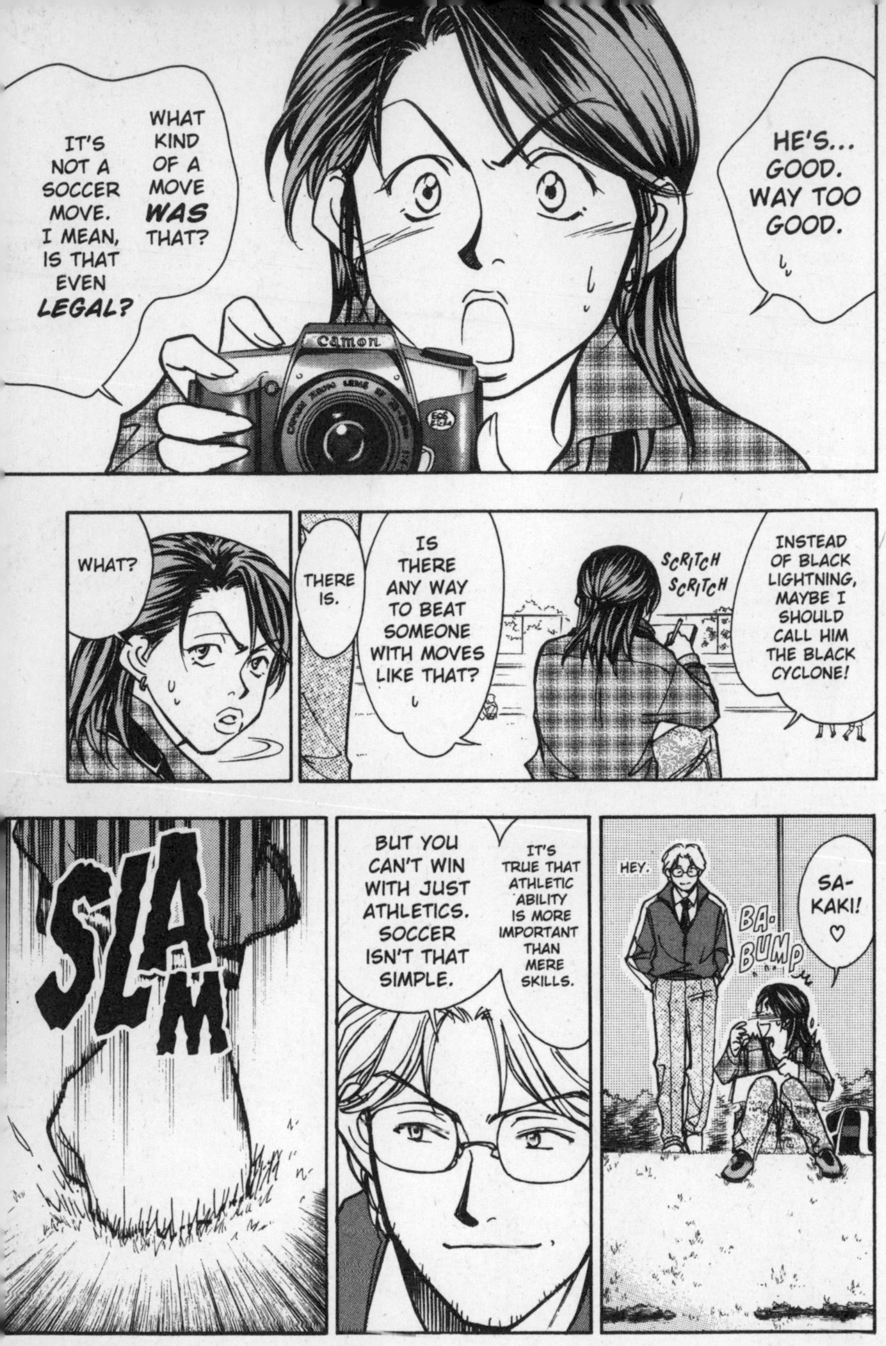
HE'S... GOOD. WAY TOO GOOD.
WHAT KIND OF A MOVE WAS THAT?
IT'S NOT A SOCCER MOVE. I MEAN, IS THAT EVEN LEGAL?
INSTEAD OF BLACK LIGHTNING, MAYBE I SHOULD CALL HIM THE BLACK CYCLONE!
SCRITCH SCRITCH
IS THERE ANY WAY TO BEAT SOMEONE WITH MOVES LIKE THAT?
THERE IS.
WHAT?
SA-KAKI! ♡
BA-BUMP
HEY.
IT'S TRUE THAT ATHLETIC ABILITY IS MORE IMPORTANT THAN MERE SKILLS.
BUT YOU CAN'T WIN WITH JUST ATHLETICS. SOCCER ISN'T THAT SIMPLE.
SLAM

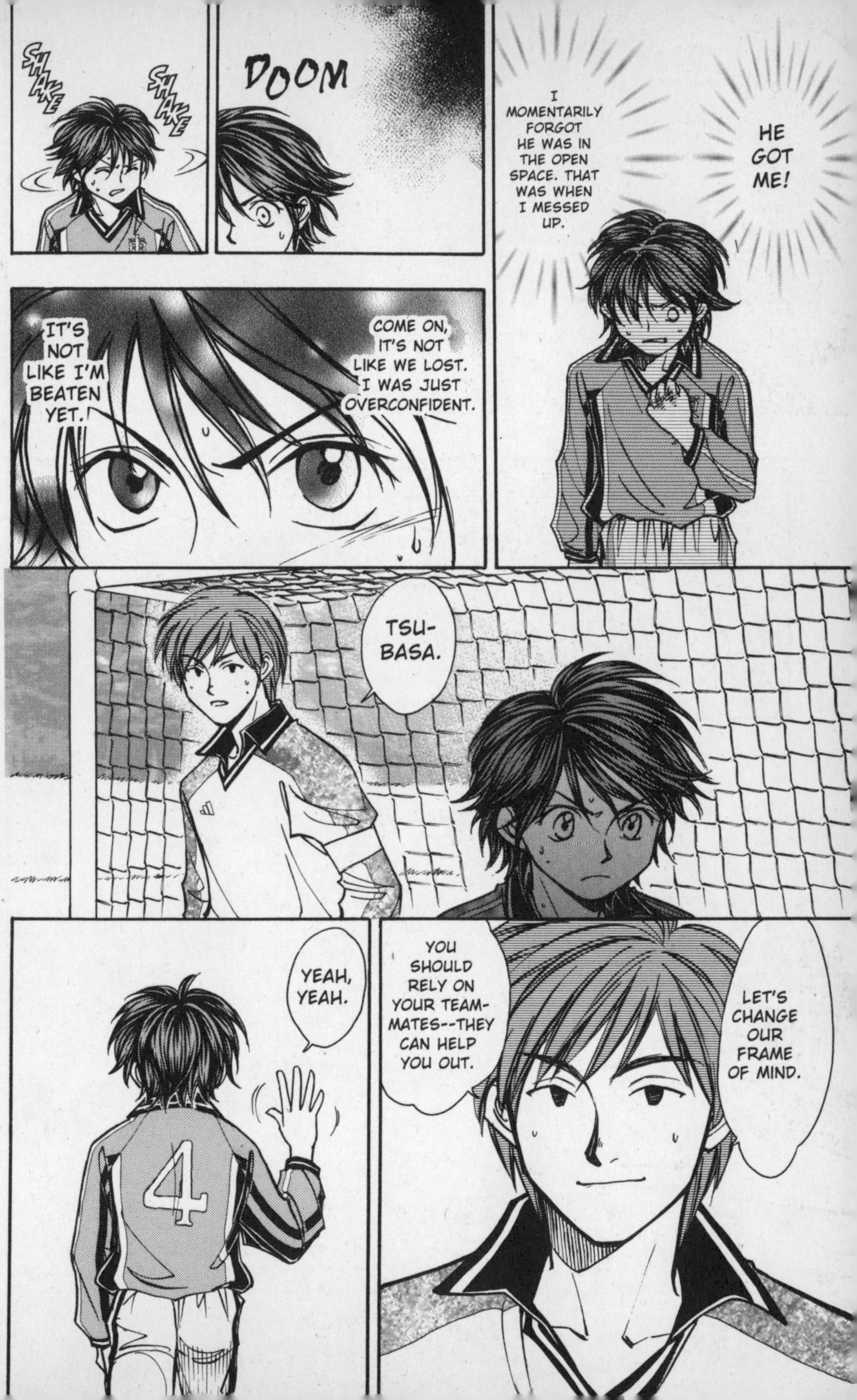
HE GOT ME!
I MOMENTARILY FORGOT HE WAS IN THE OPEN SPACE. THAT WAS WHEN I MESSED UP.
DOOM
SHAKE
SHAKE
COME ON, IT'S NOT LIKE WE LOST. I WAS JUST OVERCONFIDENT.
IT'S NOT LIKE I'M BEATEN YET.
TSU-BASA.
LET'S CHANGE OUR FRAME OF MIND.
YOU SHOULD RELY ON YOUR TEAM-MATES--THEY CAN HELP YOU OUT.
YEAH, YEAH.

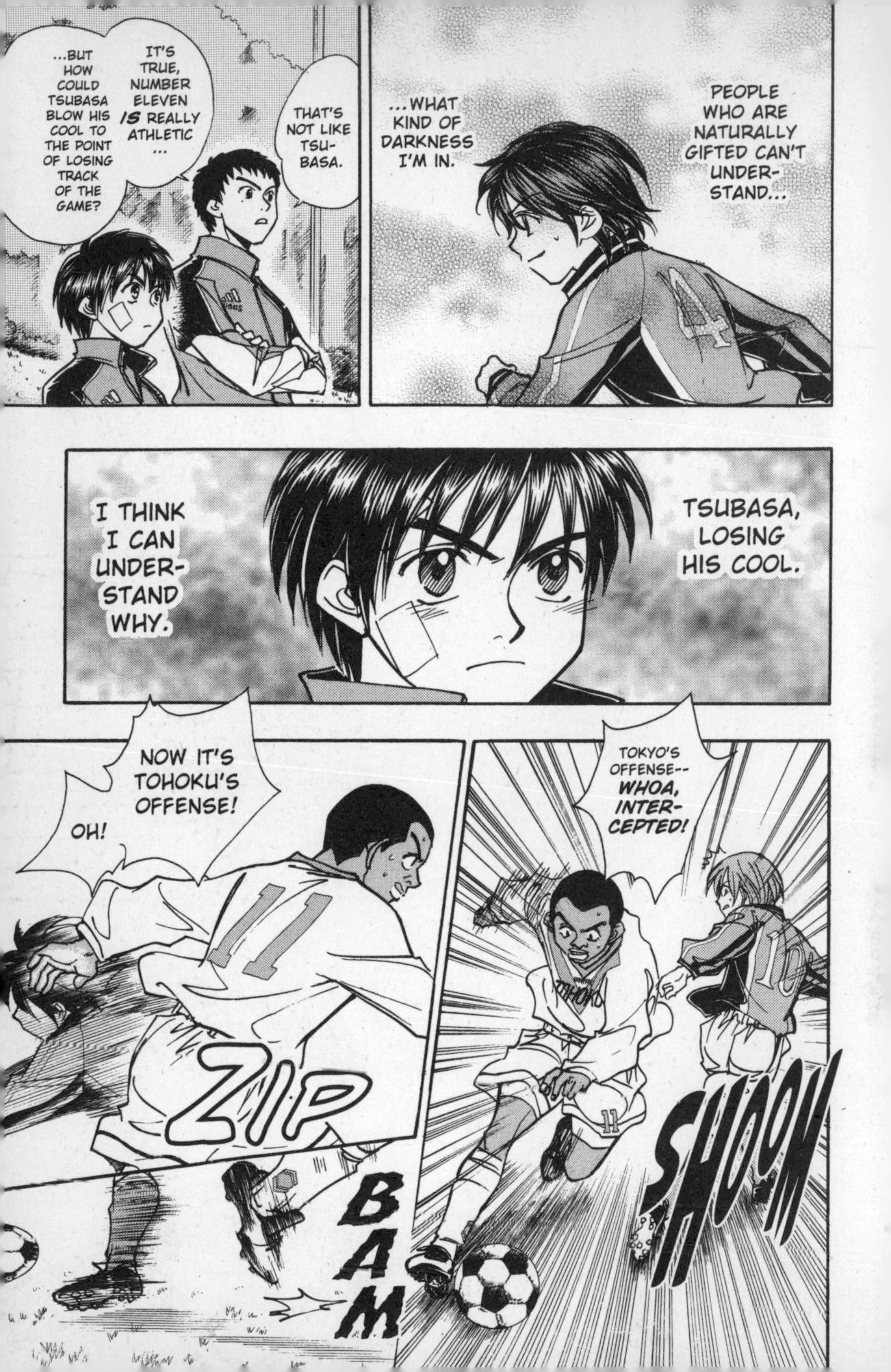
PEOPLE WHO ARE NATURALLY GIFTED CAN'T UNDER-STAND...
...WHAT KIND OF DARKNESS I'M IN.
THAT'S NOT LIKE TSU-BASA.
IT'S TRUE, NUMBER ELEVEN IS REALLY ATHLETIC ...
...BUT HOW COULD TSUBASA BLOW HIS COOL TO THE POINT OF LOSING TRACK OF THE GAME?
TSUBASA, LOSING HIS COOL.
I THINK I CAN UNDER-STAND WHY.
TOKYO'S OFFENSE-- WHOA, INTER-CEPTED!
SHOOM
BAM
NOW IT'S TOHOKU'S OFFENSE!
OH!
ZIP

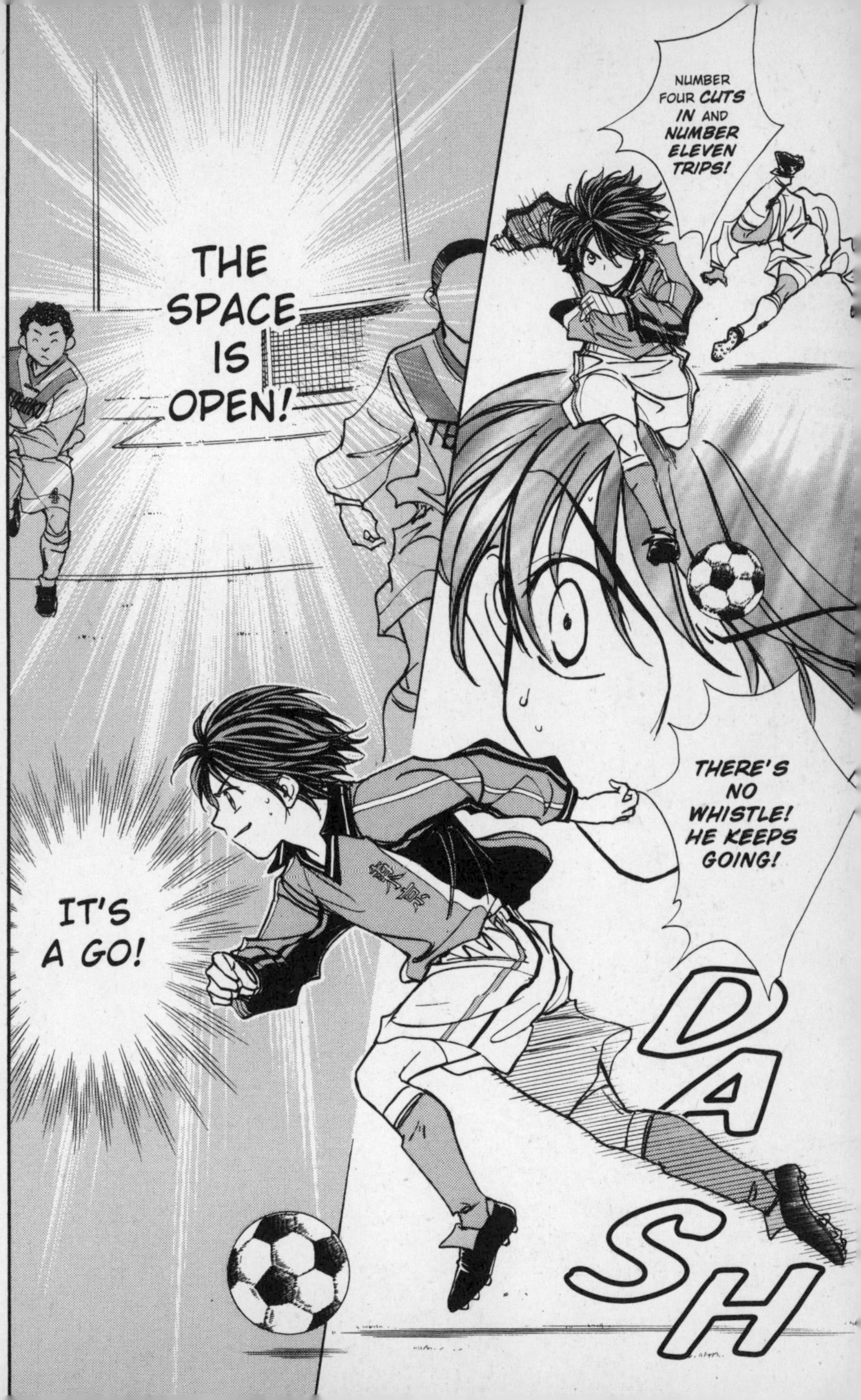
NUMBER FOUR CUTS IN AND NUMBER ELEVEN TRIPS!
THERE'S NO WHISTLE! HE KEEPS GOING!
DASH
THE SPACE IS OPEN!
IT'S A GO!

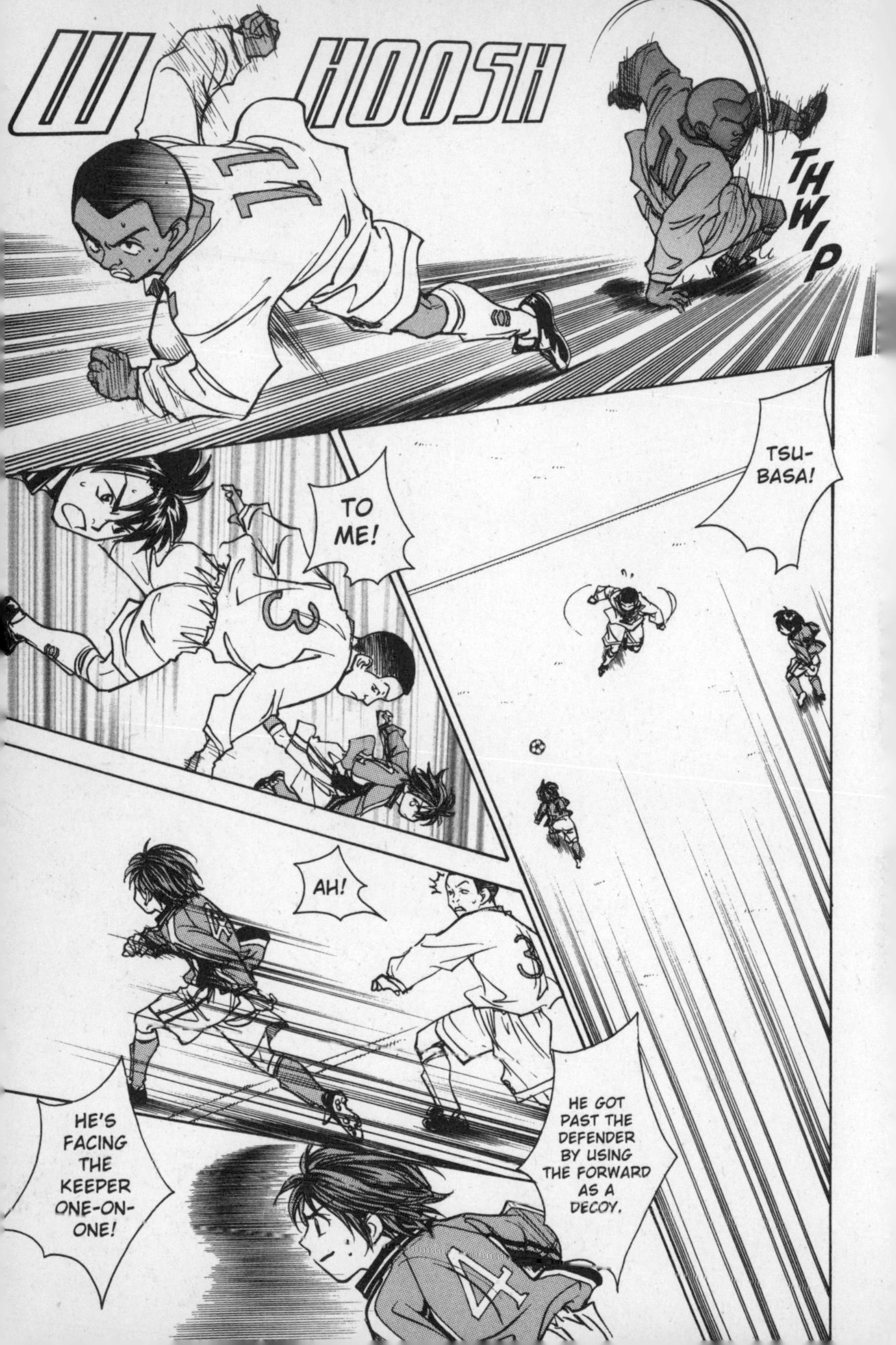
WHOOSH
THWIP
TSU-BASA!
TO ME!
AH!
HE GOT PAST THE DEFENDER BY USING THE FORWARD AS A DECOY.
HE'S FACING THE KEEPER ONE-ON-ONE!

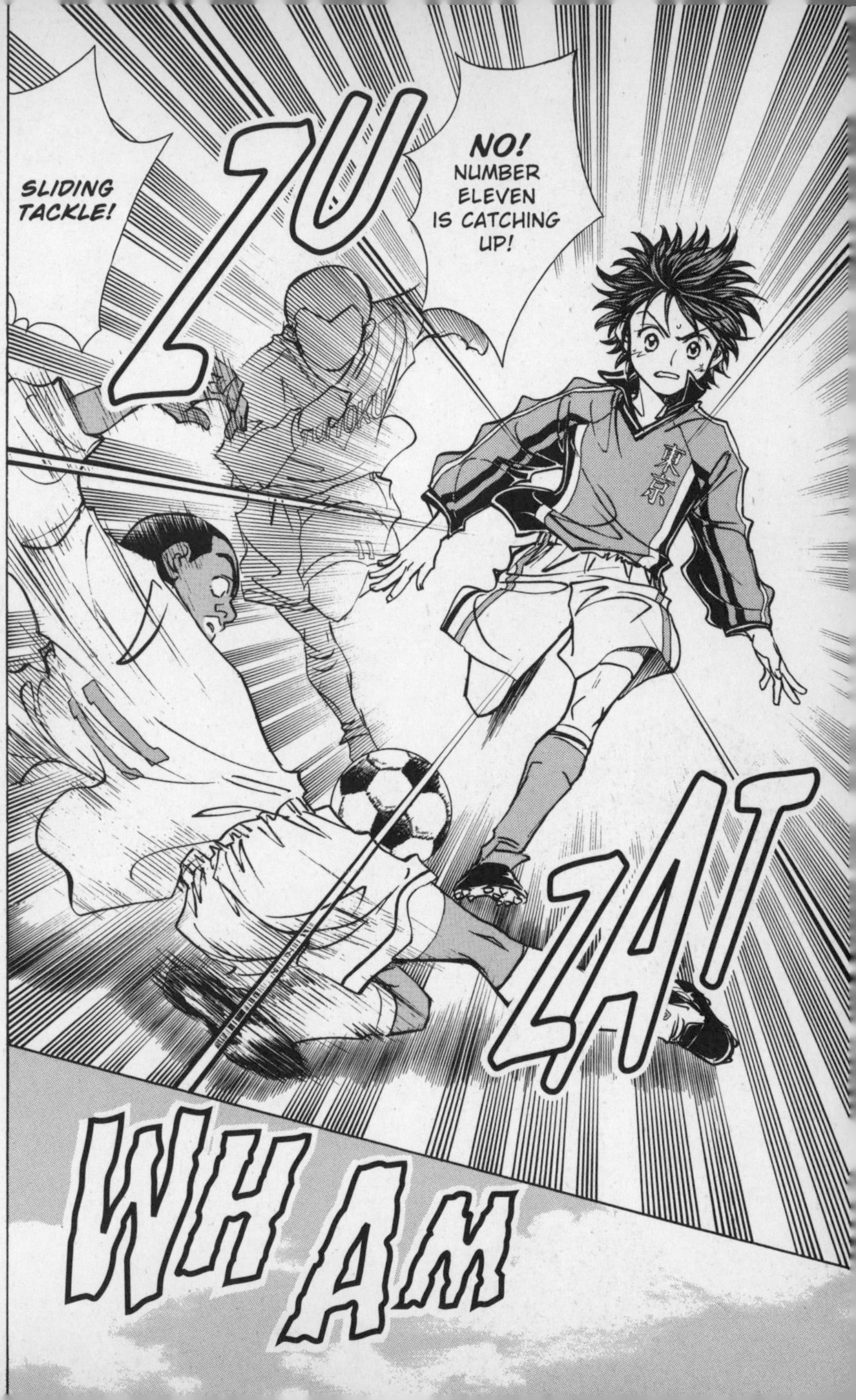
NO! NUMBER ELEVEN IS CATCHING UP!
ZU
SLIDING TACKLE!
ZA!
WHAM

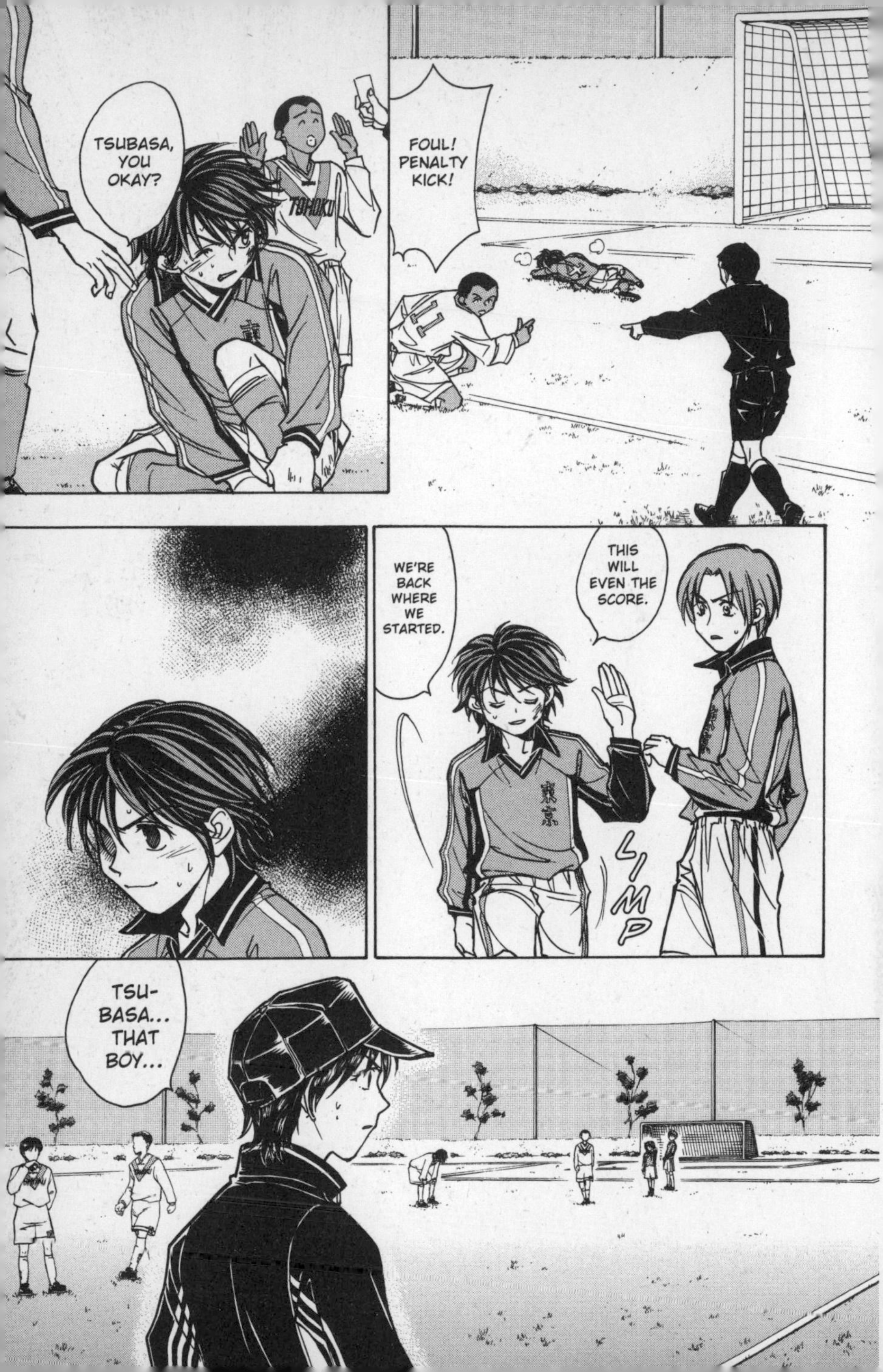
FOUL! PENALTY KICK!
TSUBASA, YOU OKAY?
THIS WILL EVEN THE SCORE.
WE'RE BACK WHERE WE STARTED.
LIMP
TSU-BASA... THAT BOY...

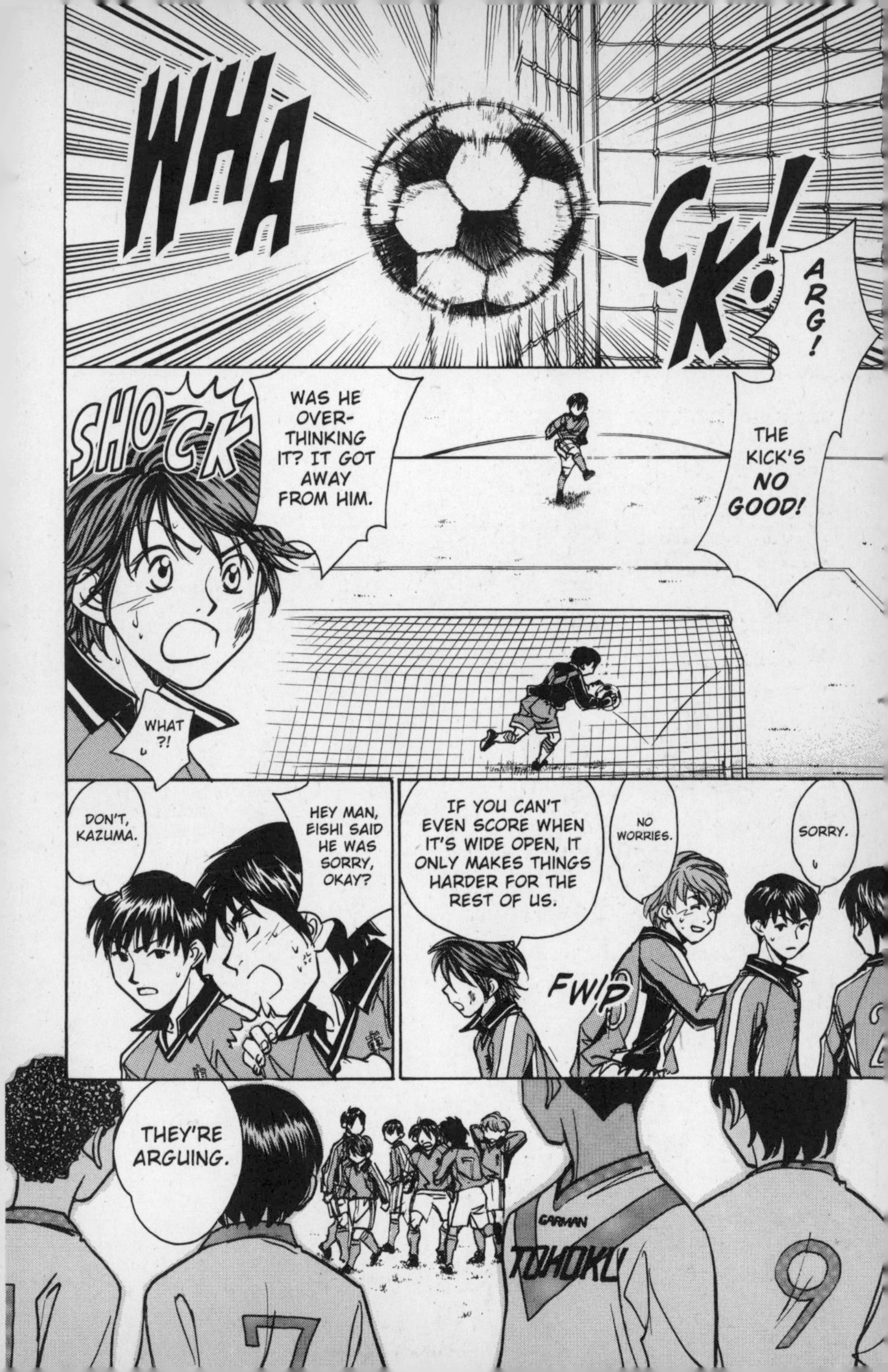
WHACK!
ARG!
THE KICK'S NO GOOD!
WAS HE OVER-THINKING IT? IT GOT AWAY FROM HIM.
SHOCK
WHAT?!
SORRY.
NO WORRIES.
IF YOU CAN'T EVEN SCORE WHEN IT'S WIDE OPEN, IT ONLY MAKES THINGS HARDER FOR THE REST OF US.
FWIP
HEY MAN, EISHI SAID HE WAS SORRY, OKAY?
DON'T, KAZUMA.
THEY'RE ARGUING.

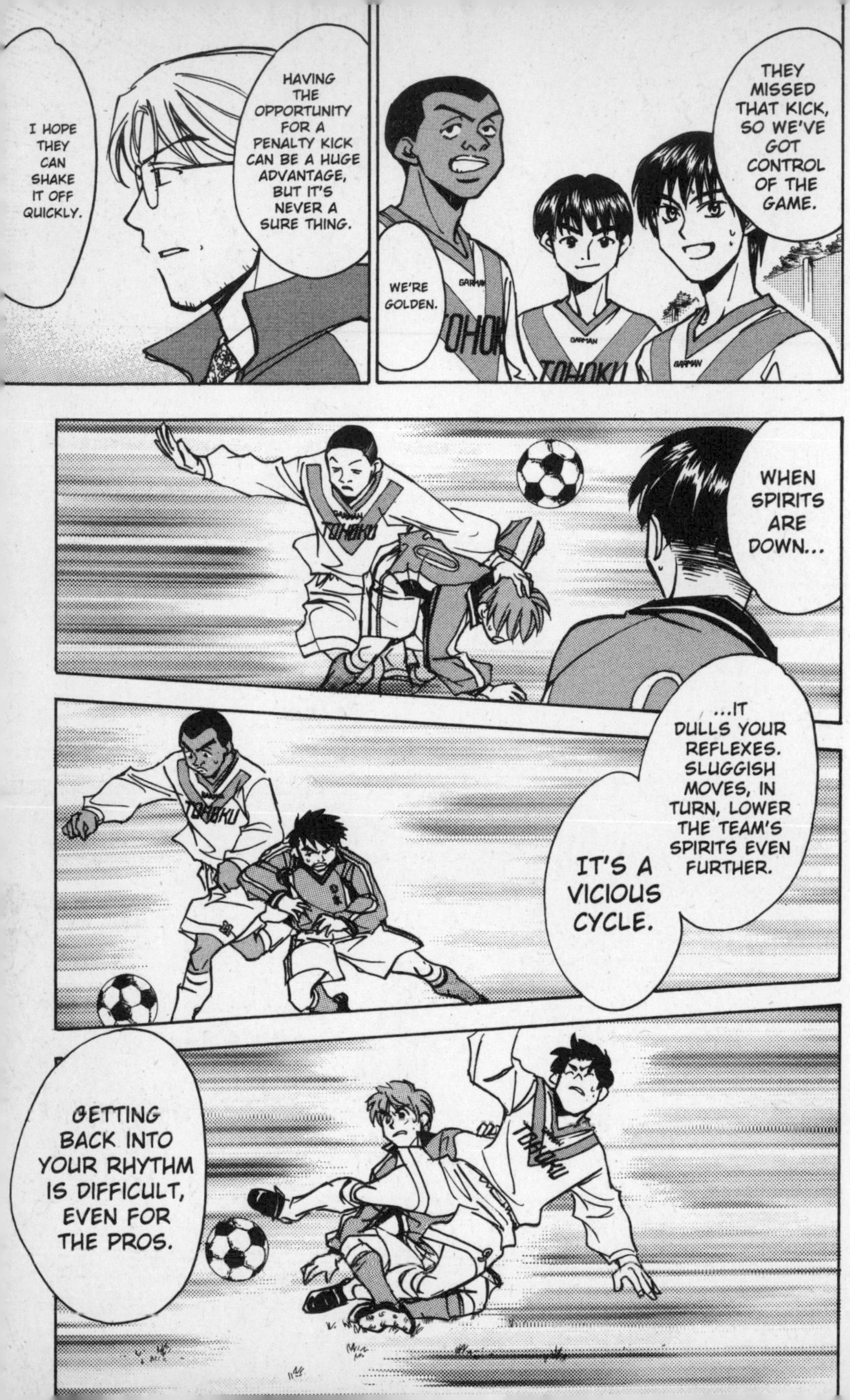
THEY MISSED THAT KICK, SO WE'VE GOT CONTROL OF THE GAME.
WE'RE GOLDEN.
HAVING THE OPPORTUNITY FOR A PENALTY KICK CAN BE A HUGE ADVANTAGE, BUT IT'S NEVER A SURE THING.
I HOPE THEY CAN SHAKE IT OFF QUICKLY.
WHEN SPIRITS ARE DOWN...
...IT DULLS YOUR REFLEXES. SLUGGISH MOVES, IN TURN, LOWER THE TEAM'S SPIRITS EVEN FURTHER.
IT'S A VICIOUS CYCLE.
GETTING BACK INTO YOUR RHYTHM IS DIFFICULT, EVEN FOR THE PROS.

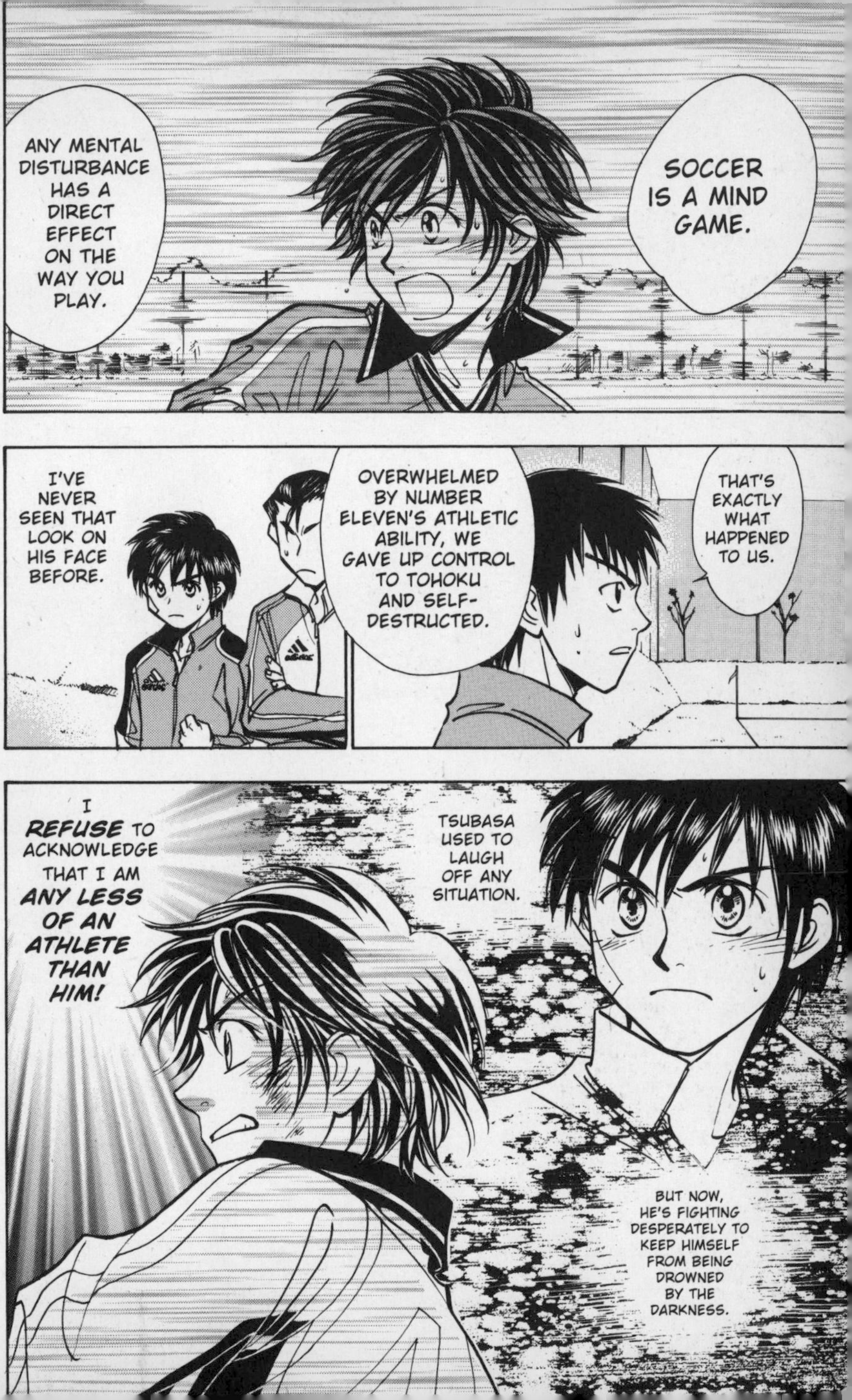
SOCCER IS A MIND GAME.
ANY MENTAL DISTURBANCE HAS A DIRECT EFFECT ON THE WAY YOU PLAY.
THAT'S EXACTLY WHAT HAPPENED TO US.
OVERWHELMED BY NUMBER ELEVEN'S ATHLETIC ABILITY, WE GAVE UP CONTROL TO TOHOKU AND SELF-DESTRUCTED.
I'VE NEVER SEEN THAT LOOK ON HIS FACE BEFORE.
TSUBASA USED TO LAUGH OFF ANY SITUATION.
BUT NOW, HE'S FIGHTING DESPERATELY TO KEEP HIMSELF FROM BEING DROWNED BY THE DARKNESS.
I ***REFUSE*** TO ACKNOWLEDGE THAT I AM ***ANY LESS OF AN ATHLETE THAN HIM!***

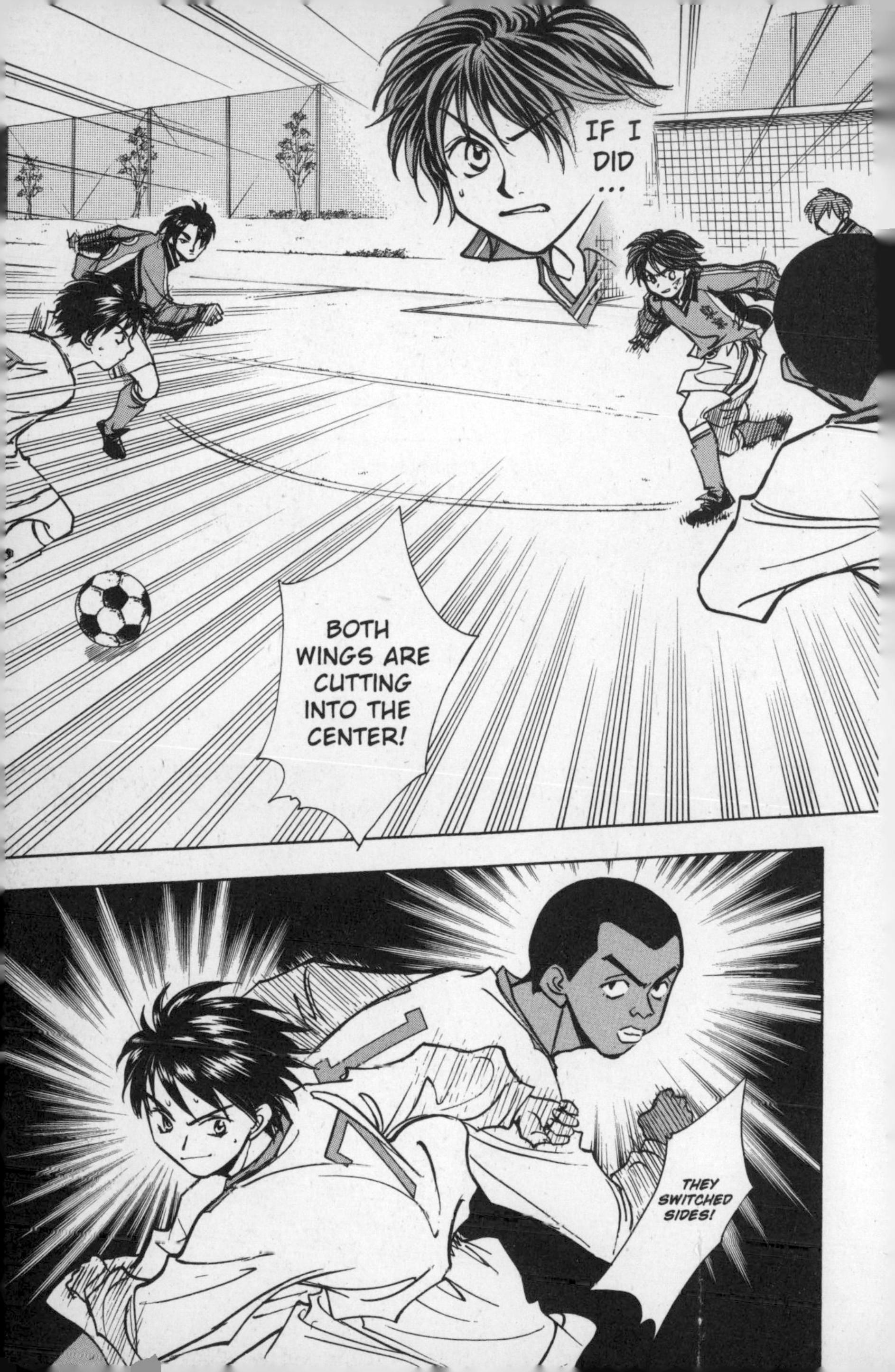
IF I DID ...
BOTH WINGS ARE CUTTING INTO THE CENTER!
THEY SWITCHED SIDES!

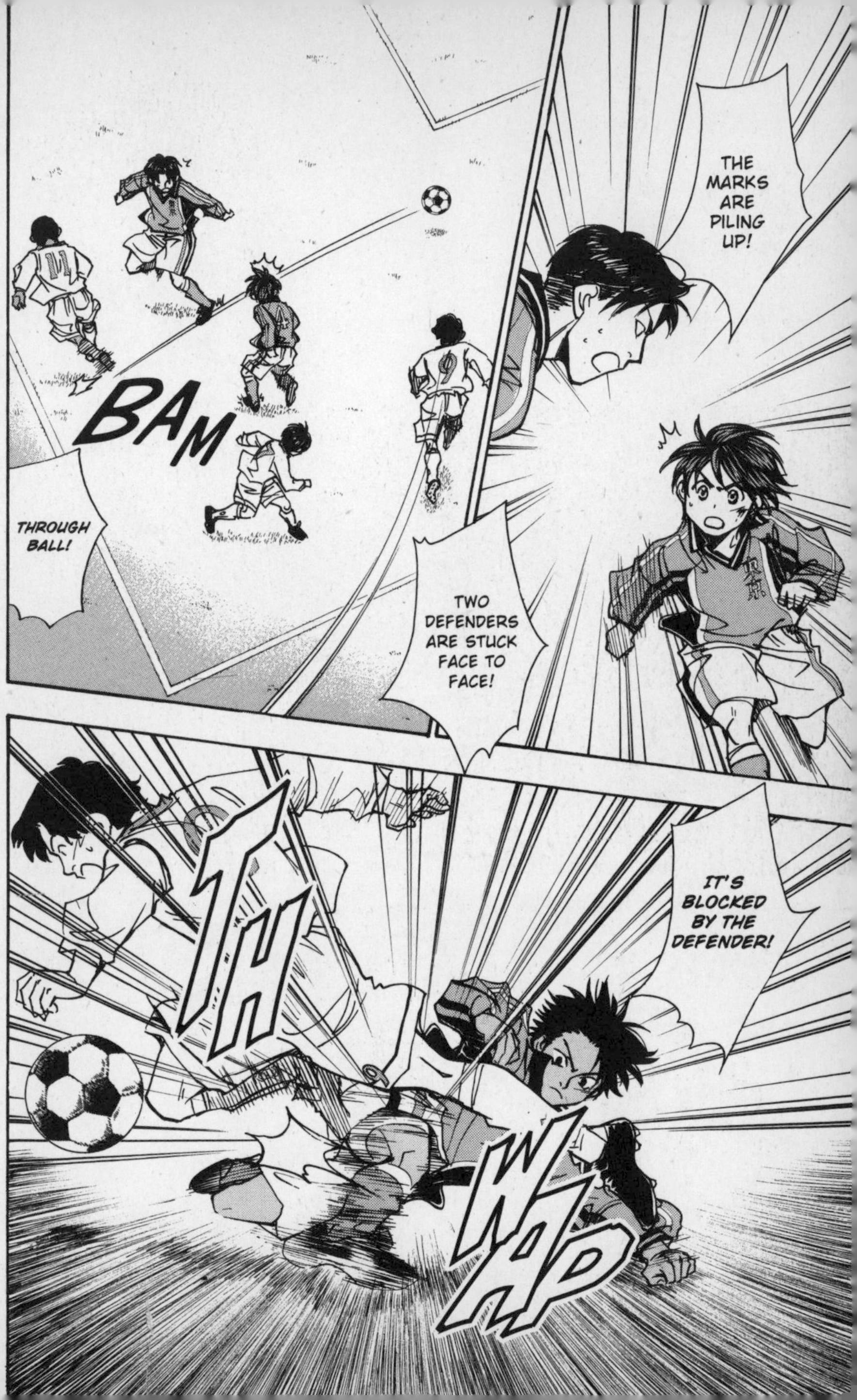

THE MARKS ARE PILING UP!
TWO DEFENDERS ARE STUCK FACE TO FACE!
BAM
THROUGH BALL!
IT'S BLOCKED BY THE DEFENDER!
THWAP

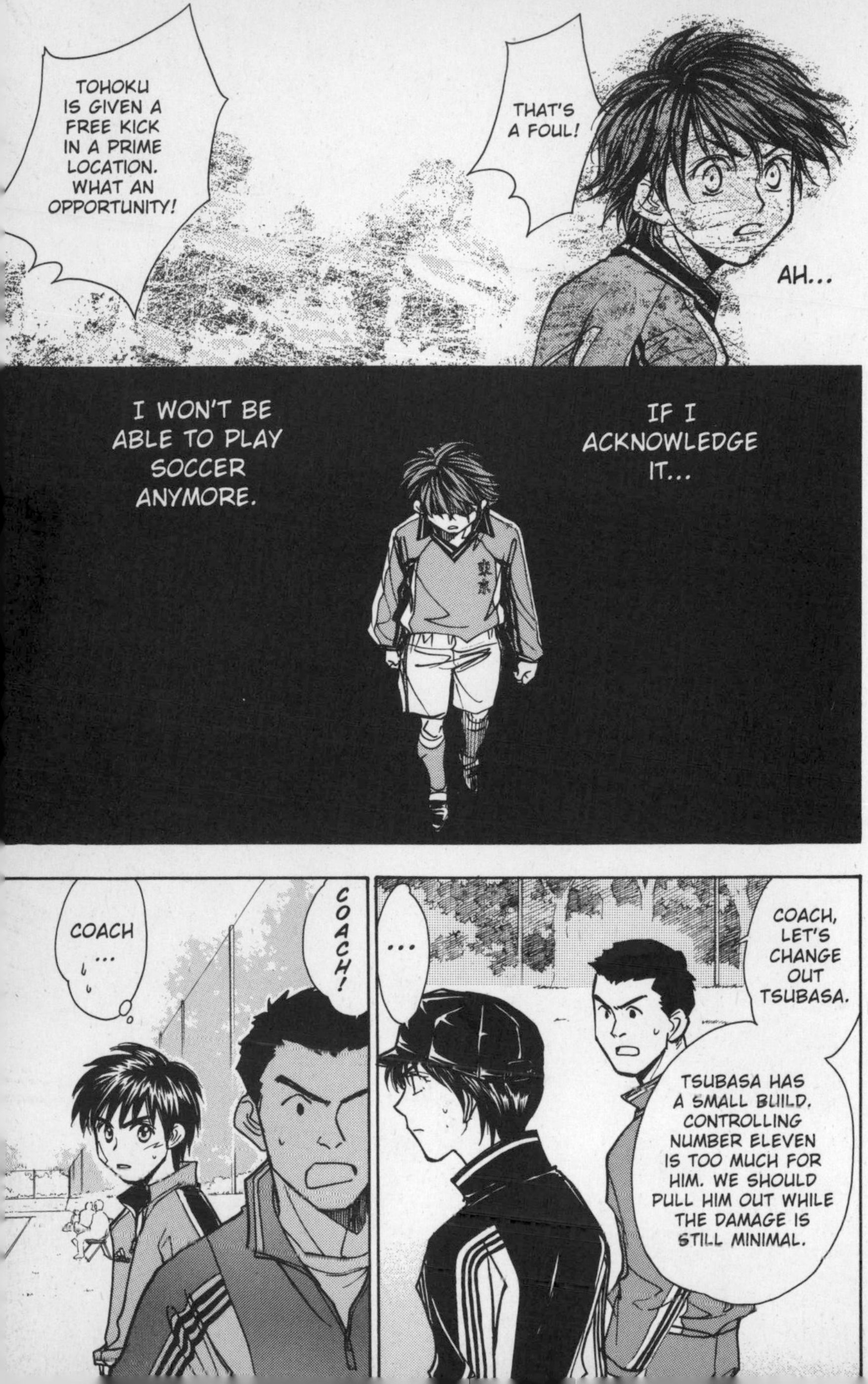
THAT'S A FOUL!
AH...
TOHOKU IS GIVEN A FREE KICK IN A PRIME LOCATION. WHAT AN OPPORTUNITY!
IF I ACKNOWLEDGE IT...
I WON'T BE ABLE TO PLAY SOCCER ANYMORE.
COACH, LET'S CHANGE OUT TSUBASA.
...
TSUBASA HAS A SMALL BUILD. CONTROLLING NUMBER ELEVEN IS TOO MUCH FOR HIM. WE SHOULD PULL HIM OUT WHILE THE DAMAGE IS STILL MINIMAL.
COACH!
COACH ...

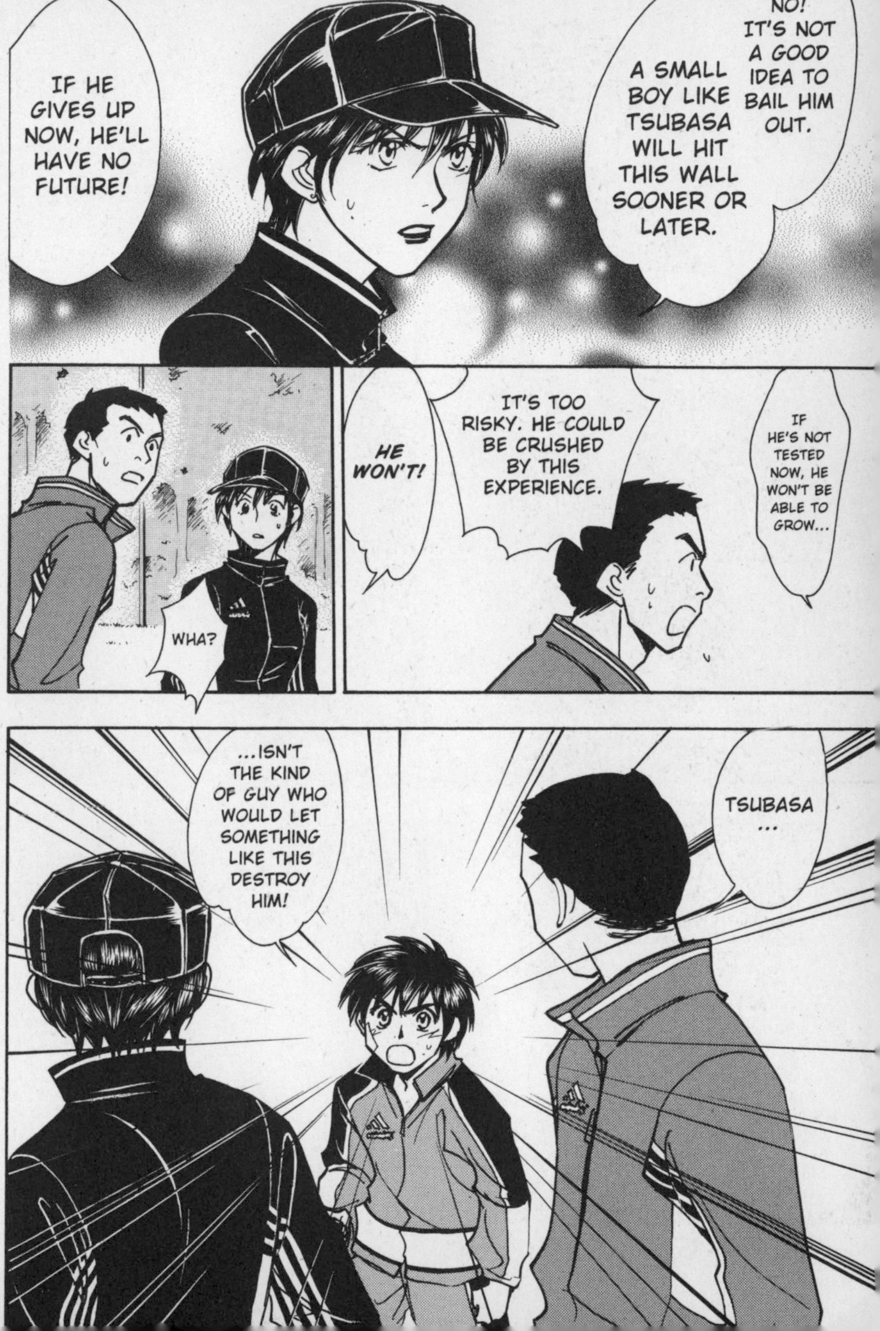
NO! IT'S NOT A GOOD IDEA TO BAIL HIM OUT.
A SMALL BOY LIKE TSUBASA WILL HIT THIS WALL SOONER OR LATER.
IF HE GIVES UP NOW, HE'LL HAVE NO FUTURE!
IF HE'S NOT TESTED NOW, HE WON'T BE ABLE TO GROW...
IT'S TOO RISKY. HE COULD BE CRUSHED BY THIS EXPERIENCE.
HE WON'T!
WHA?
TSUBASA ...
...ISN'T THE KIND OF GUY WHO WOULD LET SOMETHING LIKE THIS DESTROY HIM!

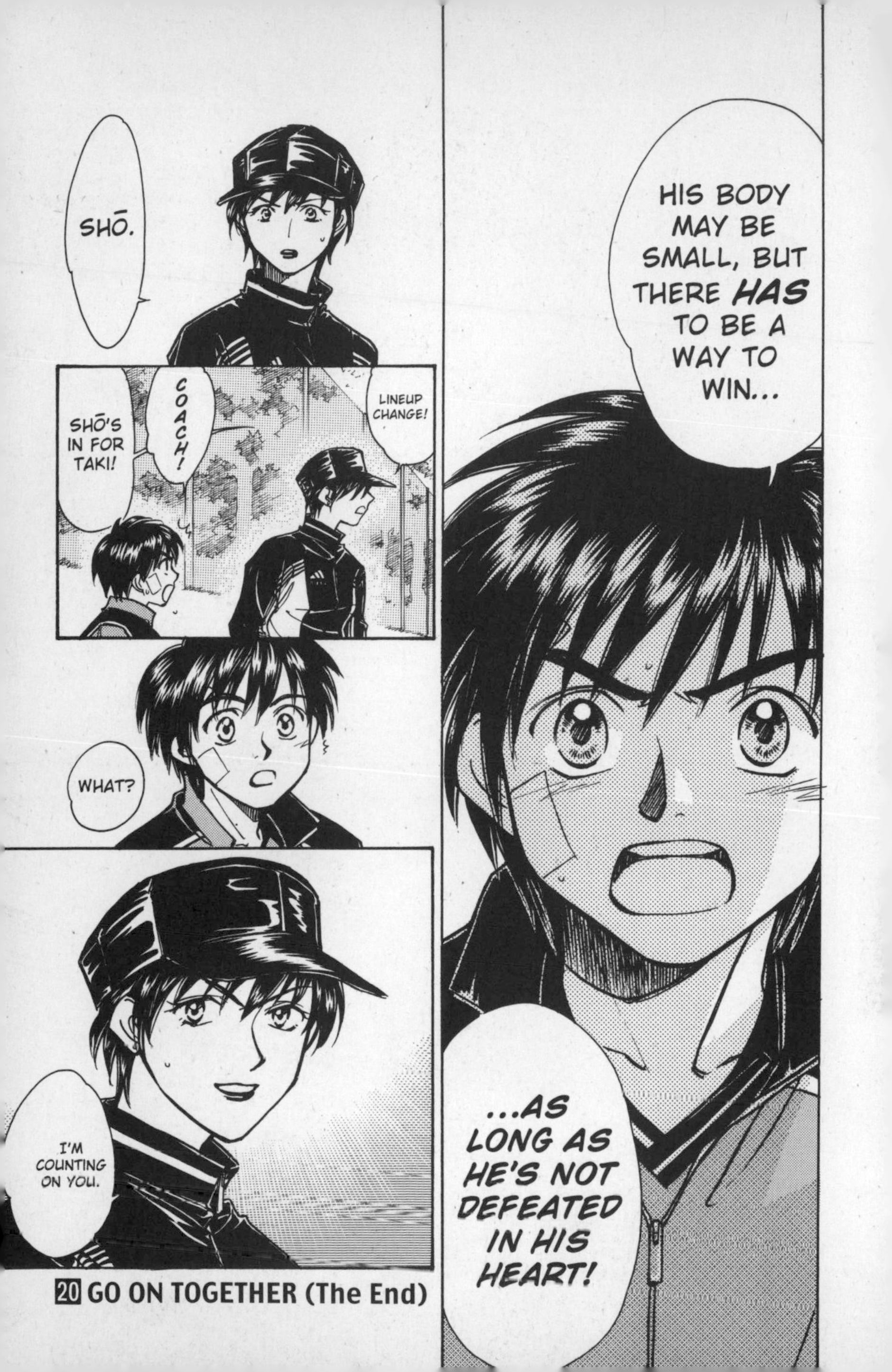
HIS BODY MAY BE SMALL, BUT THERE HAS TO BE A WAY TO WIN...
...AS LONG AS HE'S NOT DEFEATED IN HIS HEART!
SHŌ.
LINEUP CHANGE!
COACH!
SHŌ'S IN FOR TAKI!
WHAT?
I'M COUNTING ON YOU.

20 GO ON TOGETHER (The End)

20th Volume Anniversary Address

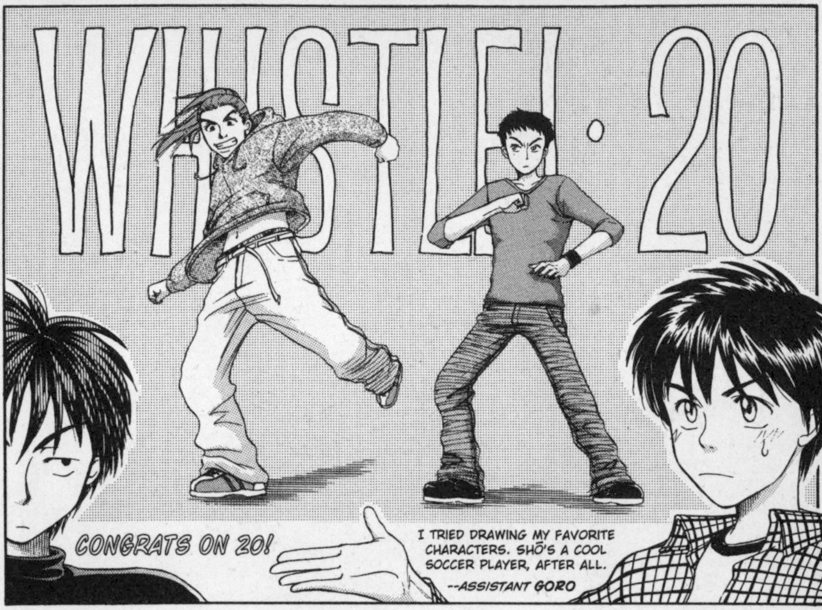

20
I TRIED DRAWING MY FAVORITE CHARACTERS. SHŌ'S A COOL SOCCER PLAYER, AFTER ALL.
--ASSISTANT GORO
CONGRATS ON 20!

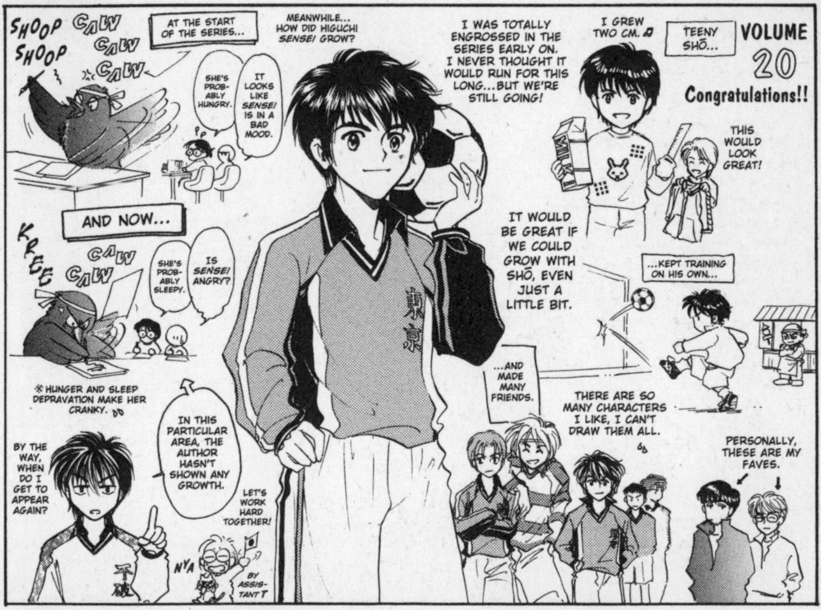

VOLUME 20 Congratulations!!
TEENY SHŌ...
I GREW TWO CM.
THIS WOULD LOOK GREAT!
I WAS TOTALLY ENGROSSED IN THE SERIES EARLY ON. I NEVER THOUGHT IT WOULD RUN FOR THIS LONG...BUT WE'RE STILL GOING!
IT WOULD BE GREAT IF WE COULD GROW WITH SHŌ, EVEN JUST A LITTLE BIT.
...KEPT TRAINING ON HIS OWN...
...AND MADE MANY FRIENDS.
THERE ARE SO MANY CHARACTERS I LIKE, I CAN'T DRAW THEM ALL.
PERSONALLY, THESE ARE MY FAVES.
MEANWHILE... HOW DID HIGUCHI SENSEI GROW?
AT THE START OF THE SERIES...
IT LOOKS LIKE SENSEI IS IN A BAD MOOD.
SHE'S PROBABLY HUNGRY.
SHOOP SHOOP
CAW CAW CAW
AND NOW...
IS SENSEI ANGRY?
SHE'S PROBABLY SLEEPY.
CAW CAW
KREE
※HUNGER AND SLEEP DEPRAVATION MAKE HER CRANKY.
IN THIS PARTICULAR AREA, THE AUTHOR HASN'T SHOWN ANY GROWTH.
LET'S WORK HARD TOGETHER!
BY THE WAY, WHEN DO I GET TO APPEAR AGAIN?
NYA
BY ASSISTANT T

THANKS EVERYONE! ♡ *HIGUCHI*

From ★ Assistants

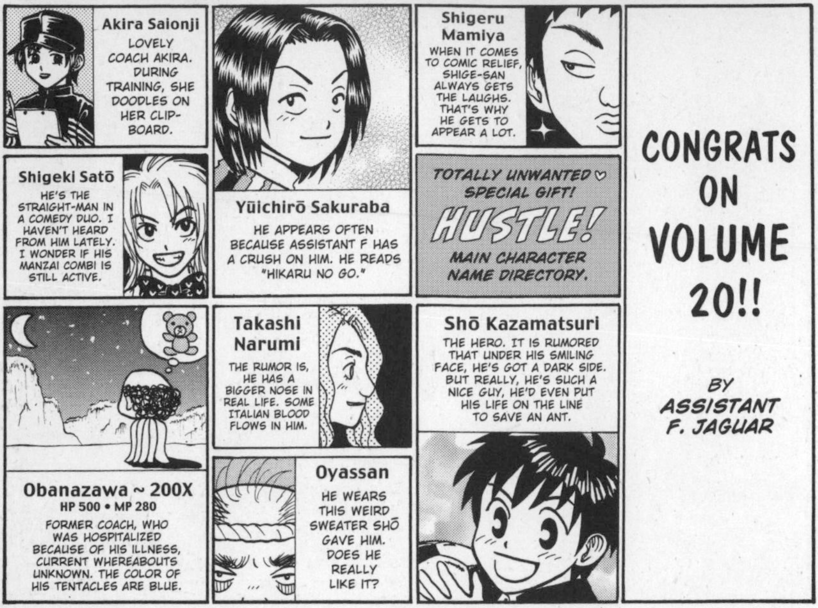
CONGRATS ON VOLUME 20!!
BY ASSISTANT F. JAGUAR
Shigeru Mamiya
WHEN IT COMES TO COMIC RELIEF, SHIGE-SAN ALWAYS GETS THE LAUGHS. THAT'S WHY HE GETS TO APPEAR A LOT.
Yūichirō Sakuraba
HE APPEARS OFTEN BECAUSE ASSISTANT F HAS A CRUSH ON HIM. HE READS "HIKARU NO GO."
Akira Saionji
LOVELY COACH AKIRA. DURING TRAINING, SHE DOODLES ON HER CLIP-BOARD.
TOTALLY UNWANTED♡ SPECIAL GIFT!
HUSTLE!
MAIN CHARACTER NAME DIRECTORY.
Shigeki Satō
HE'S THE STRAIGHT-MAN IN A COMEDY DUO. I HAVEN'T HEARD FROM HIM LATELY. I WONDER IF HIS MANZAI COMBI IS STILL ACTIVE.
Shō Kazamatsuri
THE HERO. IT IS RUMORED THAT UNDER HIS SMILING FACE, HE'S GOT A DARK SIDE. BUT REALLY, HE'S SUCH A NICE GUY, HE'D EVEN PUT HIS LIFE ON THE LINE TO SAVE AN ANT.
Takashi Narumi
THE RUMOR IS, HE HAS A BIGGER NOSE IN REAL LIFE. SOME ITALIAN BLOOD FLOWS IN HIM.
Oyassan
HE WEARS THIS WEIRD SWEATER SHŌ GAVE HIM. DOES HE REALLY LIKE IT?
Obanazawa ~ 200X
HP 500 • MP 280
FORMER COACH, WHO WAS HOSPITALIZED BECAUSE OF HIS ILLNESS, CURRENT WHEREABOUTS UNKNOWN. THE COLOR OF HIS TENTACLES ARE BLUE.

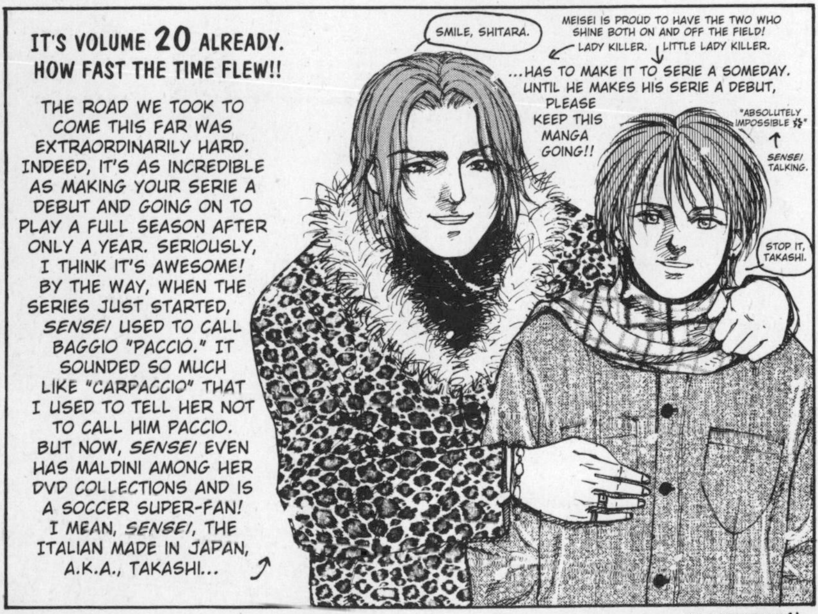
IT'S VOLUME 20 ALREADY. HOW FAST THE TIME FLEW!!
THE ROAD WE TOOK TO COME THIS FAR WAS EXTRAORDINARILY HARD. INDEED, IT'S AS INCREDIBLE AS MAKING YOUR SERIE A DEBUT AND GOING ON TO PLAY A FULL SEASON AFTER ONLY A YEAR. SERIOUSLY, I THINK IT'S AWESOME! BY THE WAY, WHEN THE SERIES JUST STARTED, *SENSEI* USED TO CALL BAGGIO "PACCIO." IT SOUNDED SO MUCH LIKE "CARPACCIO" THAT I USED TO TELL HER NOT TO CALL HIM PACCIO. BUT NOW, *SENSEI* EVEN HAS MALDINI AMONG HER DVD COLLECTIONS AND IS A SOCCER SUPER-FAN! I MEAN, *SENSEI*, THE ITALIAN MADE IN JAPAN, A.K.A., TAKASHI...
MEISEI IS PROUD TO HAVE THE TWO WHO SHINE BOTH ON AND OFF THE FIELD!
LADY KILLER.
LITTLE LADY KILLER.
SMILE, SHITARA.
...HAS TO MAKE IT TO SERIE A SOMEDAY. UNTIL HE MAKES HIS SERIE A DEBUT, PLEASE KEEP THIS MANGA GOING!!
"ABSOLUTELY IMPOSSIBLE"
SENSEI TALKING.
STOP IT, TAKASHI.

BY ASSISTANT N.

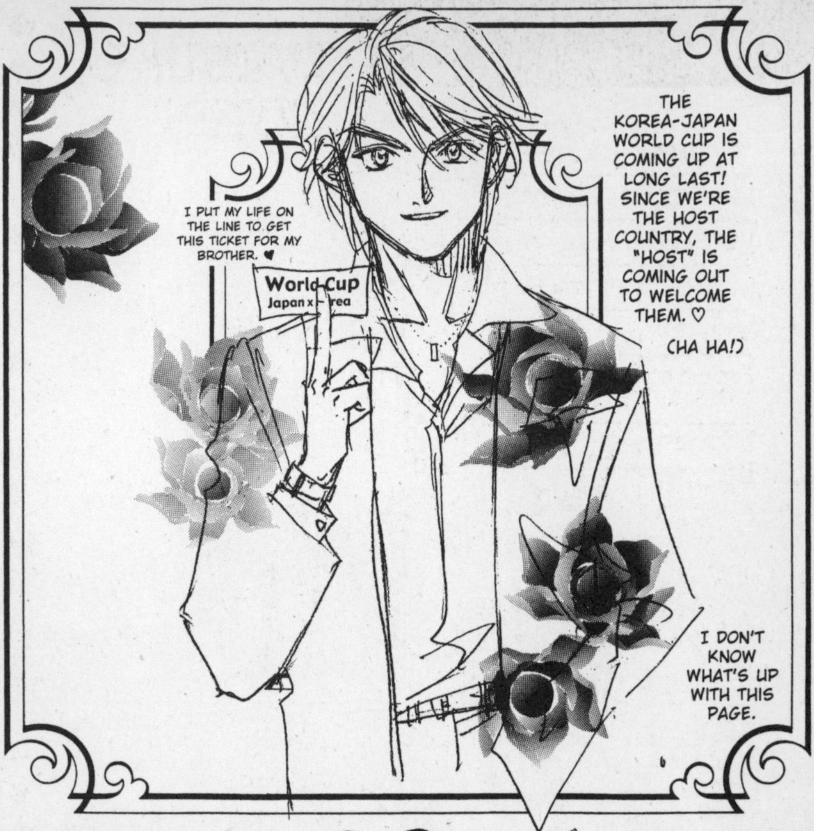
THE KOREA-JAPAN WORLD CUP IS COMING UP AT LONG LAST! SINCE WE'RE THE HOST COUNTRY, THE "HOST" IS COMING OUT TO WELCOME THEM. ♡
(HA HA!)
I PUT MY LIFE ON THE LINE TO GET THIS TICKET FOR MY BROTHER. ♥
World Cup
I DON'T KNOW WHAT'S UP WITH THIS PAGE.

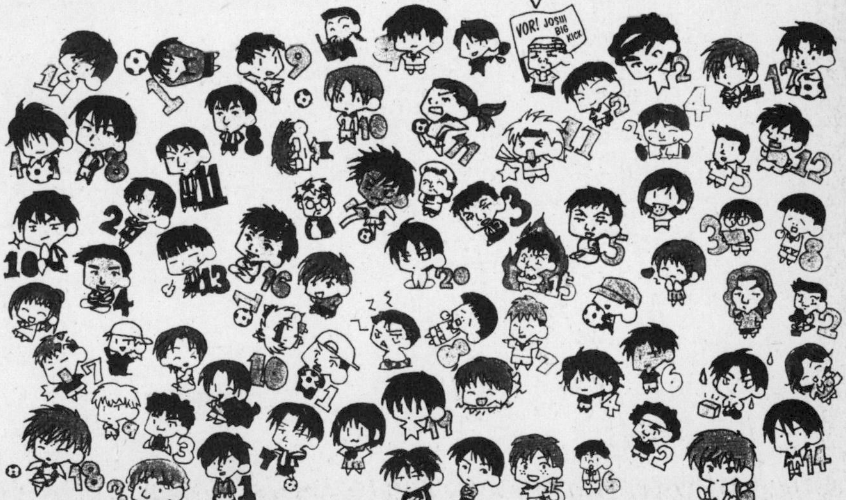
VOR!
BIG KICK

ILLUSTRATION / LIN SAKURA

DAISUKE NOTES

TOSHIKI SUGAMA

PERSONAL DATA	
BIRTHDAY	AUG 27, 1983
SIZE	6' 3" 174 lbs
BLOOD TYPE	B
FAVORITE FOOD	STAMINA BOWL
DISLIKES	BOILED QUAIL EGGS
HOBBY AND SPECIAL SKILLS	MAKING HATS AND SEWING

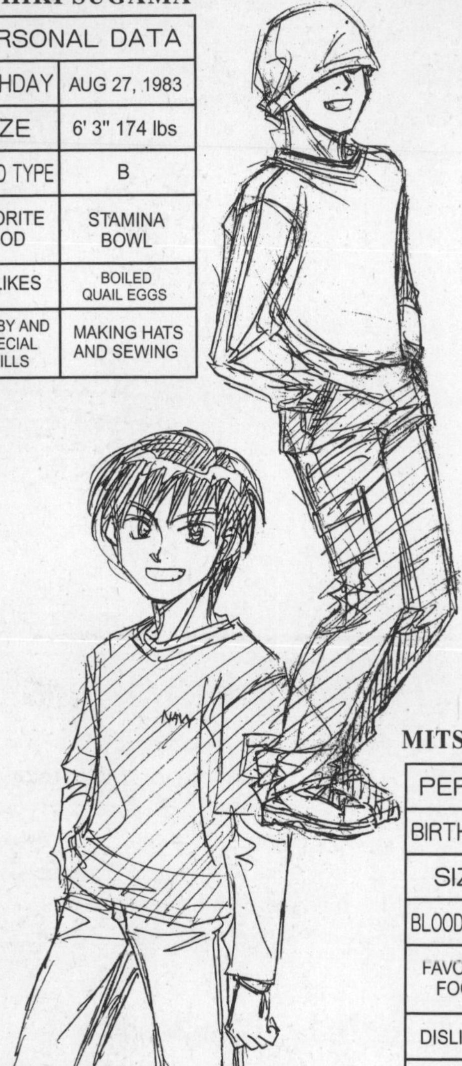

MITSUHIRO HINASE

PERSONAL DATA	
BIRTHDAY	DEC 14, 1984
SIZE	5' 4" 115 lbs
BLOOD TYPE	A
FAVORITE FOOD	UDON NOODLES
DISLIKES	VEGETABLES
HOBBY AND SPECIAL SKILLS	READING BOOKS AND RUNNING

Next in Whistle!

TRY ON MY DREAMS

As the second half starts, Tohoku continues to control the game. But both teams are surprised when Shô's irrepressible force of will starts to sway the game in Tokyo Select's favor. When Shô thwarts Kotarô's efforts, the Tohoku star begins to reveal his weaknesses. But at the same time, Tsubasa begins to lose his cool for being shown up by a mere substitute. With the game on the line, who will crack first—Kotarô, or Tsubasa?

Available January 2009!

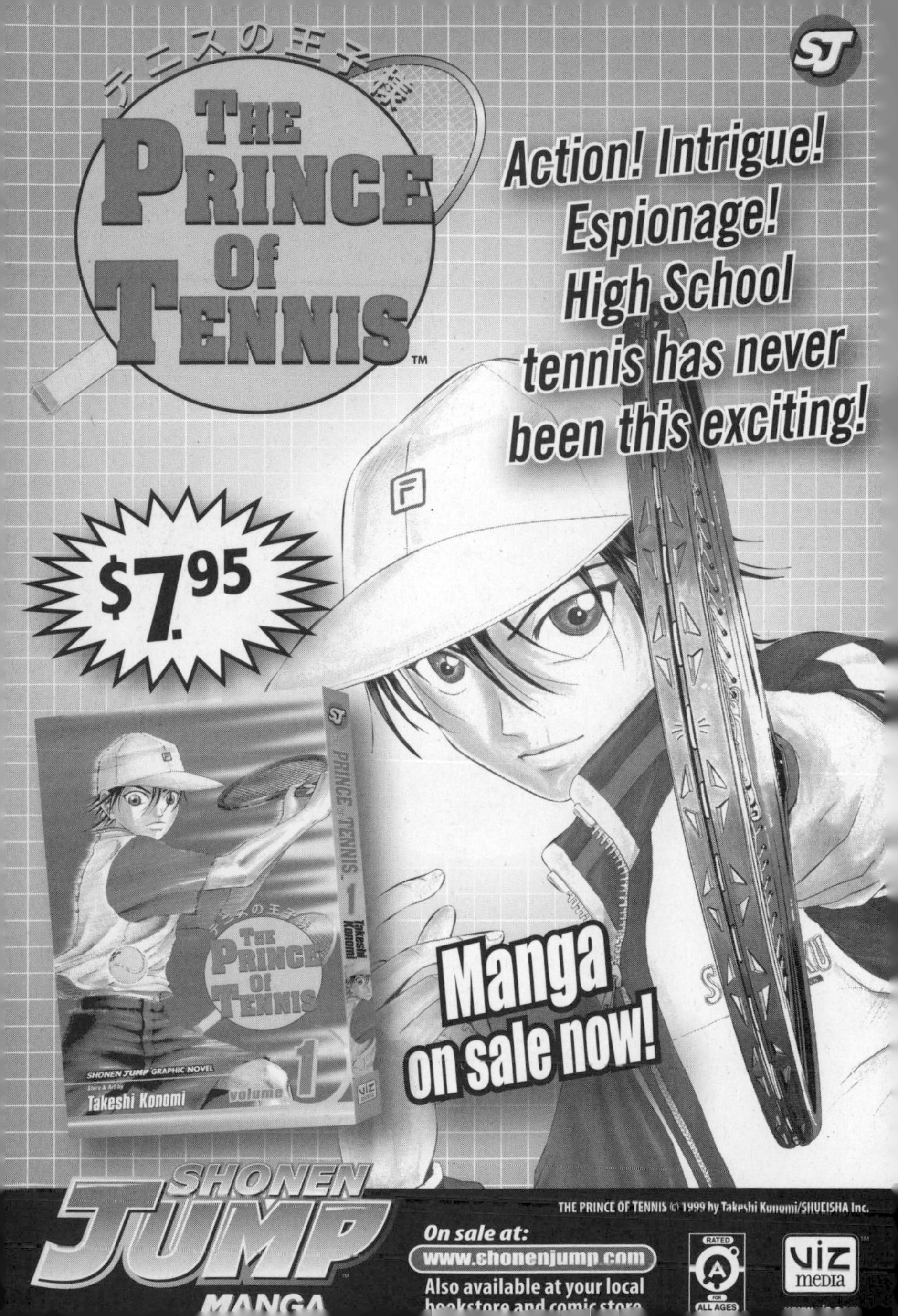
テニスの王子様
THE PRINCE OF TENNIS™
SJ
Action! Intrigue! Espionage! High School tennis has never been this exciting!
$7.95
SJ
THE PRINCE OF TENNIS 1
Takeshi Konomi
テニスの王子様
THE PRINCE OF TENNIS
SHONEN JUMP GRAPHIC NOVEL
Story & Art by
Takeshi Konomi
volume 1
VIZ
Manga on sale now!
SHONEN JUMP™ MANGA
THE PRINCE OF TENNIS © 1999 by Takeshi Konomi/SHUEISHA Inc.
On sale at:
www.shonenjump.com
Also available at your local
RATED A FOR ALL AGES
VIZ media

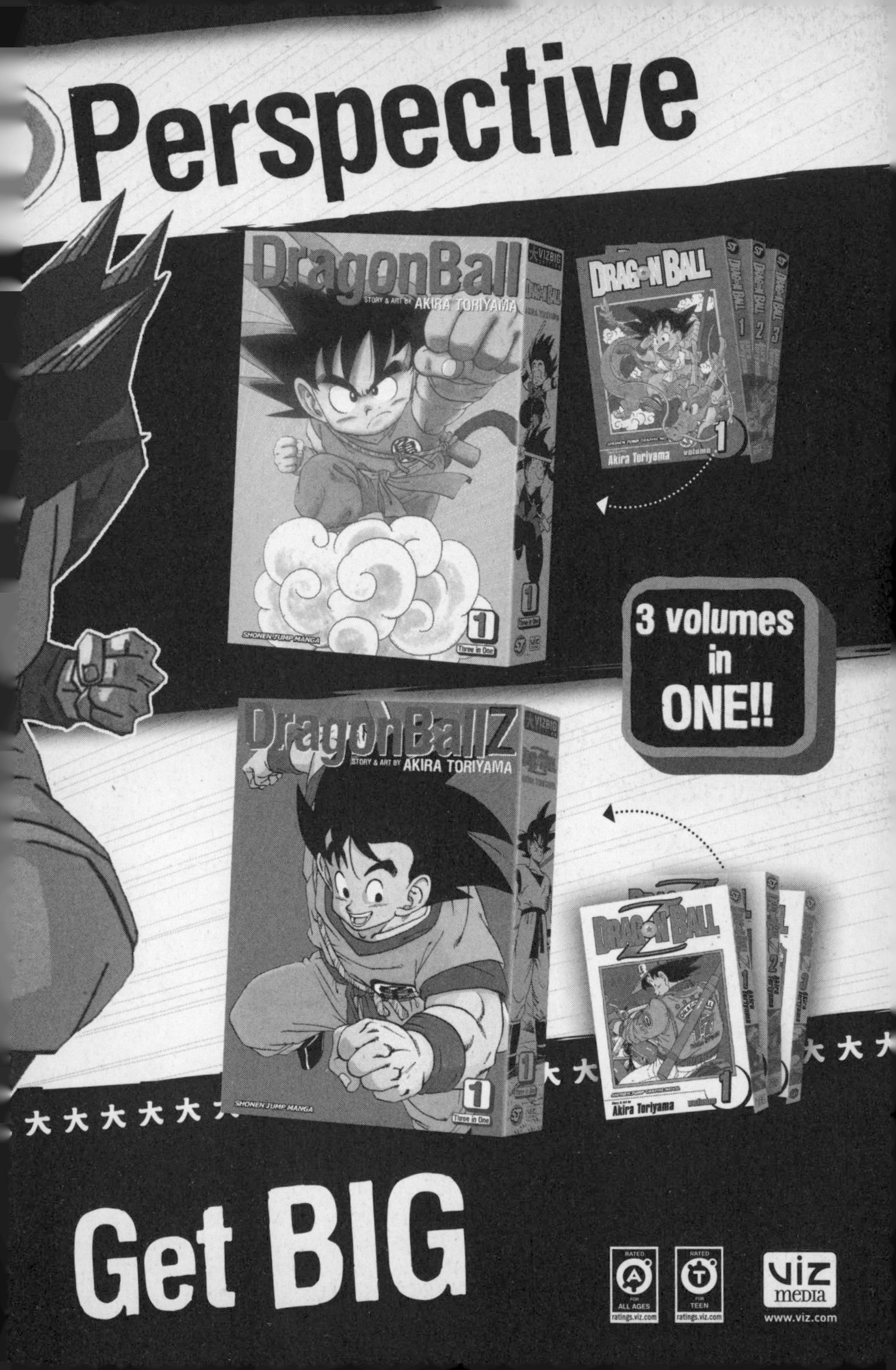
Perspective
DragonBall
STORY & ART BY AKIRA TORIYAMA
SHONEN JUMP MANGA
1
Three in One
DRAGON BALL
Akira Toriyama
volume 1
3 volumes in ONE!!
DragonBallZ
STORY & ART BY AKIRA TORIYAMA
SHONEN JUMP MANGA
1
Three in One
DRAGON BALL Z
Akira Toriyama
1
Get BIG
RATED A FOR ALL AGES ratings.viz.com
RATED T FOR TEEN ratings.viz.com
viz media
www.viz.com

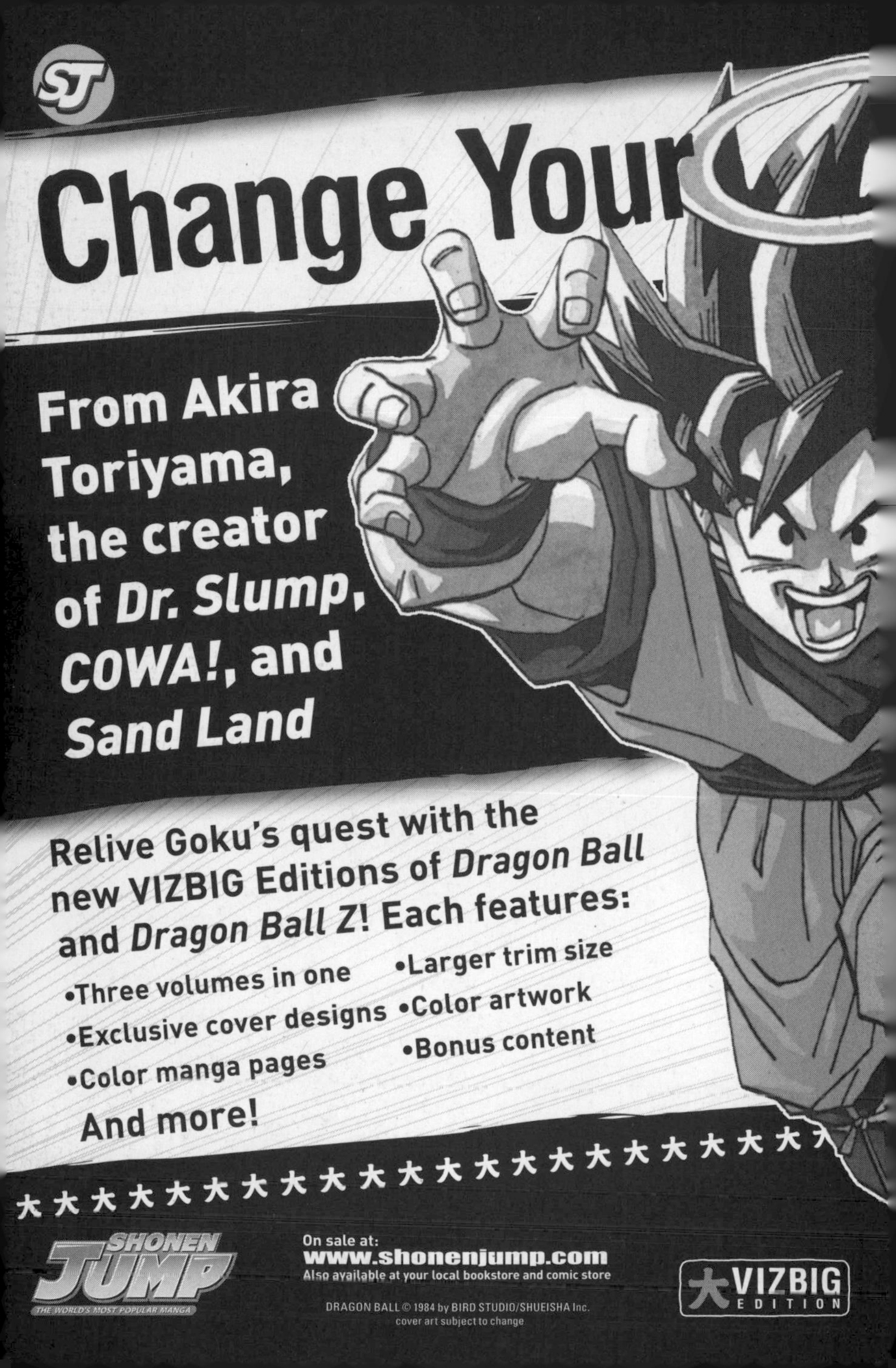
SJ
Change Your
From Akira Toriyama, the creator of *Dr. Slump*, *COWA!*, and *Sand Land*
Relive Goku's quest with the new VIZBIG Editions of *Dragon Ball* and *Dragon Ball Z*! Each features:
•Three volumes in one
•Exclusive cover designs
•Color manga pages
•Larger trim size
•Color artwork
•Bonus content
And more!
SHONEN JUMP
THE WORLD'S MOST POPULAR MANGA
On sale at:
www.shonenjump.com
Also available at your local bookstore and comic store
DRAGON BALL © 1984 by BIRD STUDIO/SHUEISHA Inc.
cover art subject to change
大 VIZBIG EDITION

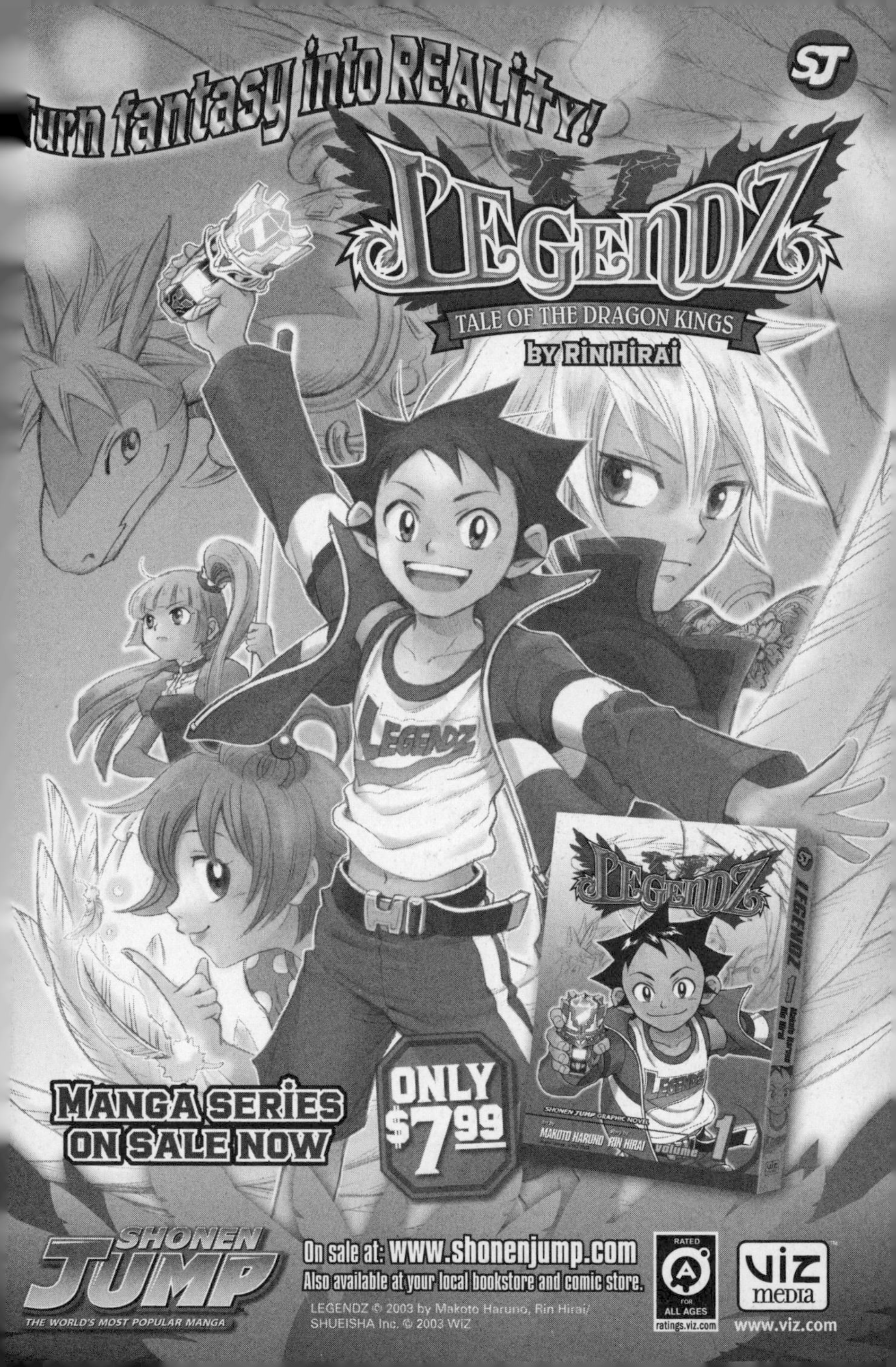

Turn fantasy into REALity!
LEGENDZ
TALE OF THE DRAGON KINGS
BY RIN HIRAI
MANGA SERIES ON SALE NOW
ONLY $7.99
SHONEN JUMP
THE WORLD'S MOST POPULAR MANGA
On sale at: www.shonenjump.com
Also available at your local bookstore and comic store.
LEGENDZ © 2003 by Makoto Haruno, Rin Hirai/ SHUEISHA Inc. © 2003 WIZ
RATED A FOR ALL AGES
ratings.viz.com
VIZ media
www.viz.com

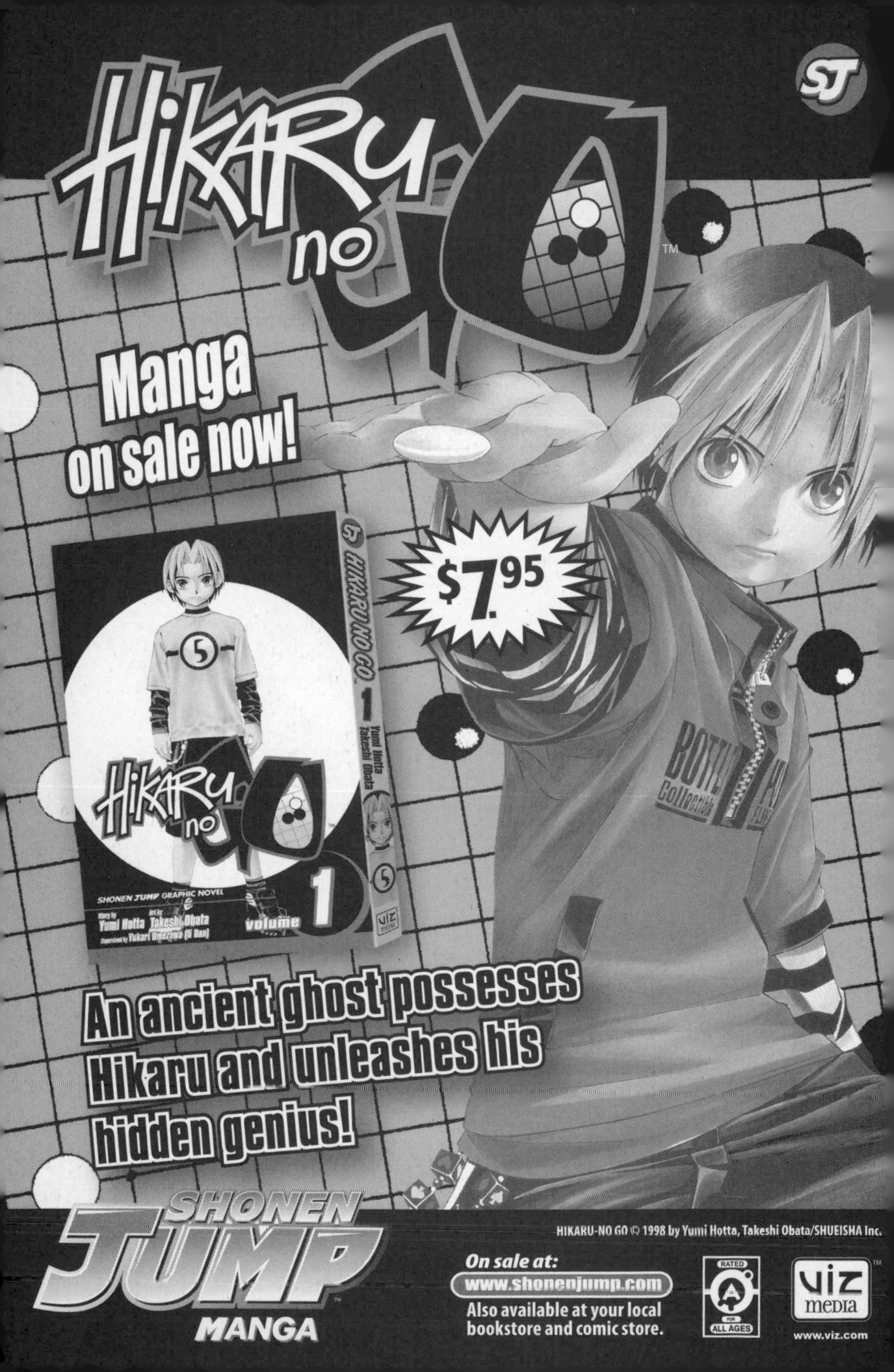

SJ
HIKARU no GO™
Manga on sale now!
$7.95
SJ HIKARU NO GO™ 1 Yumi Hotta Takeshi Obata
SHONEN JUMP GRAPHIC NOVEL
Story by Yumi Hotta Art by Takeshi Obata
Supervised by Yukari Umezawa (5 Dan)
volume 1
An ancient ghost possesses Hikaru and unleashes his hidden genius!
SHONEN JUMP MANGA
HIKARU-NO GO © 1998 by Yumi Hotta, Takeshi Obata/SHUEISHA Inc.
On sale at:
www.shonenjump.com
Also available at your local bookstore and comic store.
RATED A FOR ALL AGES
VIZ media
www.viz.com

Tell us what you think about SHONEN JUMP manga!

Our survey is now available online.
Go to: **www.SHONENJUMP.com/mangasurvey**

Help us make our product offering better!

THE REAL ACTION
STARTS IN...

THE WORLD'S MOST POPULAR MANGA
www.shonenjump.com

ADVANCED

viz media

Save **50% OFF** the cover price!